The Science of Crime Scenes

Please visit the Companion Website to

The Science of Crime Scenes

www.elsevierdirect.com/companions/9780123864642

The Companion Website hosts all the figures
from the volume to assist in understanding volume concepts.

The Science of Crime Scenes

Max M. Houck
Forensic and Intelligence Services, LLC
Arlington, Virginia, USA

Frank Crispino
University of Quebec in Trois-Rivières
Chemistry-Biology Department
Trois-Rivières, Quebec, Canada

Terry McAdam
Tacoma Crime Laboratory
Washington State Patrol
Tacoma, Washington, USA

AMSTERDAM • BOSTON • HEIDELBERG • LONDON
NEW YORK • OXFORD • PARIS • SAN DIEGO
SAN FRANCISCO • SINGAPORE • SYDNEY • TOKYO
Academic Press is an imprint of Elsevier

Academic Press is an imprint of Elsevier
The Boulevard, Langford Lane, Kidlington, Oxford, OX5 1GB, UK
225 Wyman Street, Waltham, MA 02451
525 B Street, Suite 1800, San Diego, CA 92101-4495, USA

Notices
Knowledge and best practice in this field are constantly changing. As new research and experience broaden our understanding, changes in research methods, professional practices, or medical treatment may become necessary.

Practitioners and researchers must always rely on their own experience and knowledge in evaluating and using any information, methods, compounds, or experiments described herein. In using such information or methods they should be mindful of their own safety and the safety of others, including parties for whom they have a professional responsibility.

To the fullest extent of the law, neither the Publisher nor the authors, contributors, or editors, assume any liability for any injury and/or damage to persons or property as a matter of products liability, negligence or otherwise, or from any use or operation of any methods, products, instructions, or ideas contained in the material herein.

Library of Congress Cataloging-in-Publication Data
Houck, Max M.
The science of crime scenes / Max M. Houck, Frank Crispino, Terry McAdam.
    p. cm.
 Includes bibliographical references and index.
 ISBN 978-0-12-386464-2 (alk. paper)
 1. Criminal investigation. 2. Forensic sciences. I. Crispino, Frank. II. McAdam, Terry. III. Title.
 HV8073.H776 2012
 363.25–dc23

                                                                    2012011542

British Library Cataloguing-in-Publication Data
A catalogue record for this book is available from the British Library

For information on all Academic Press publications,
visit our Website: www.store.elsevier.com

Printed in China

12 13 14 15 16   9 8 7 6 5 4 3 2 1

This one is for Liz; she knows why.
–MMH

Contents

Foreword xv
Acknowledgments xvii
Introduction xix

Section 1: The Science of Crime Scene Investigation

Chapter 1.0: The "Forensic Mindset" 3
Forensic Professionals Are Knowledge Workers 3
Hunting as an Origin for Forensic Science. 4
Trifles, Traces, and Clues. 5
From Science to Art to Literature 6
Evidence Is Proxy Data 7
Conclusion 8
References and Bibliography 8

Chapter 1.1: From Scene to Laboratory to Court 11
Access to the Scene. 12
Sensitivity to Initial Conditions 13
Downstream Effects 15
Documentation. 16
Chain of Custody 16
Fruit of the Poisonous Tree. 17
Submitting Evidence for Analysis. 17
Conclusion: Evidence in the Courtroom 18
References and Bibliography 19

Chapter 2.0: What Is a Crime Scene? 21
Introduction. 21
A Definition 23
Staged Crime Scenes 25
Conclusion 26
References and Bibliography 26

**Chapter 2.1: Crime Scene Intelligence: Connecting People,
Places, and Things** 27
Connections through Contact: Transfer and Persistence. 29
Classification and Resolution. 32

Contents

Individualization of Evidence. 35

Relationships and Context 36

Known and Questioned Items. 38

Conclusion 38

References and Bibliography 39

Section 2: Personnel and Procedures

Chapter 3.0: Personnel **43**

Forensic Scientist Focus. 44

Time and Money. 48

Contamination 49

Logistics. 50

Building the Team 50

Conclusion 52

References and Bibliography 52

Chapter 3.1: First Responder on the Scene. 53

Competing Responsibilities 55

Securing the Scene 59

Preserving the Scene 62

Releasing the Scene 63

Conclusion 64

References and Bibliography 64

Chapter 3.2: The Investigator in Charge **65**

Security at the Crime Scene 68

Leadership at the Scene. 69

Conclusion 69

References 69

Chapter 3.3: The Forensic Team: Officers, Scientists, and Specialists . . . 71

A Forensic Team 73

Conclusion 79

Reference 79

**Chapter 3.4: Nonforensic Personnel: Superiors, Officials,
and the Media. 81**

Information: Two Points of View 82

The Public as Reporters 85

Communicating to Superiors. 86

Conclusion 87

Bibliography. 87

Chapter 4.0: General Crime Scene Procedure **89**

Chapter 4.1: "Freezing" the Scene and the Three R's (Recognize, Recover, and Record) **95**

Death Investigations. 96

Preliminary Search. 97

Recognizing Evidence 100

Recovering Evidence. 100

Recording Evidence. 102

Conclusion 103

Chapter 4.2: The Chain of Custody **105**

A Chain of Custody Example 109

Problems with Chains of Custody 111

Conclusion 112

Chapter 4.3: Recording the Scene: Sketching, Photography, and Video **113**

Crime Scene Photography 114

Video. 118

Measurements. 119

Sketching 120

Geographic Information Systems (GISs) and Crime Mapping 124

Conclusion 126

Reference 126

Section 3: Detection and Reconstruction

Chapter 5.0: Searching for Evidence: Recovery. **129**

From Trace to Proof, or Why Only Finding a Trace Is Not Sufficient 130

Which Evidence Is Useful?. 133

The Search for Evidence. 134

Practical Search: Focal and Ancillary Points 135

Optimizing the Search: Applying Locard's Theory. 136

Controlling Contamination 137

Conclusion 138

References and Bibliography. 138

Contents

Chapter 5.1: Detecting **139**

What Is Light and How Do We See an Object? 140

Luminescence 141

From Theory to Practice: The Forensic Light Source .144

General Crime Scene Screening 145

    White Light and Selective Absorption 146

    Reflections 147

    Coaxial Episcopy 148

Photoluminescence. 149

    UV Techniques 150

Specific Crime Scene Screening 151

    Fingerprint Detection. 151

    Earmark Detection 151

    Blood 153

    Semen 153

    Fiber, Hair, Glass 153

    Gunshot Residue 154

    3D Impressions. 154

References and Bibliography 154

Chapter 5.2: Collection **157**

Types of Evidence to Collect 158

Materials and Containers. 160

Available Techniques to Collect Evidence 162

    Whole Substrate Collection 162

    Tweezing. 162

    Tapelifting 164

    Vacuuming. 164

    Microtaping. 164

    Pipetting 165

    Swabbing 166

    Sweeping 166

    Lifting. 166

    Scraping 167

    Casting. 167

    Collection Guidelines 167

References and Bibliography 176

Chapter 5.3: Preserving 177

Threats to Evidence 177

    Damage 177

    Deterioration 178

    Contamination 178

    Infestation 179

    Decomposition 179

    Loss 179

    Tampering 180

Safety at the Scene 180

    Sources and Forms of Dangerous Materials 182

    Universal Precautions 182

    Chemical Safety 183

Conclusion 185

References and Bibliography 185

Chapter 5.4: Submitting Evidence to the Laboratory 187

General Submission Guidelines 188

Biological Evidence 189

Trace Evidence 191

    Hairs 191

    Glass 191

    Clothing and Fibers 192

    Paint 193

Impression Evidence 195

Explosives 197

Physical Match 199

Firearms Evidence 200

Toolmark Evidence 203

Latent Prints Evidence 205

    Lift Cards 205

Chapter 6.0: Evidence Types and Enhancement 207

Chapter 6.1: Chemical Evidence 211

Drugs 211

Arson 213

Explosives 224

GSR 228

Contents

Restoration of Serial Numbers. 233

References and Bibliography 235

Chapter 6.2: Biological Evidence **239**

DNA and Trace DNA 240

Blood 242

Semen 251

Saliva 252

Urine. 253

Feces. 253

Hair 253

Bones 254

Cadaver 254

References and Bibliography 254

Chapter 6.3: Impression Evidence **259**

Human Traces 260

Fingerprints, Palmprints, and Bare Footprints. 260

Earprints 271

Other Human Prints 272

Object Traces 274

Shoeprints and Tireprints 275

Gloveprints. 280

Toolmarks 281

References and Bibliography 281

Chapter 6.4: Other Types of Evidence. **295**

Questioned Documents. 295

Computers, Cellphones, and Other Mass Storages 297

Pollen 299

Bones 299

Insects and Time Since Death 300

Diatoms. 301

Odors 302

Conclusion 303

References and Bibliography 303

Chapter 7.0: Crime Scene Reconstruction. **313**

Conclusion 316

References and Bibiliography 316

Chapter 7.1: An Archaeological Approach **317**

Of Artifacts and Evidence 317

Terminology. 319

Time and Space. 320

Conclusion 320

References and Bibliography 321

Chapter 7.2: Bloodstain Pattern Analysis **323**

Directionality. 327

Grouping Bloodstains. 327

Droplet Size and Force 328

Types of Bloodstains 328

Conclusion 329

Reference 330

Chapter 7.3: Photogrammetry and 3D Reconstruction **331**

Photogrammetry 332

3D Laser Scanners 335

Case Examples of 3D Laser Scanner 338

Conclusion 343

References and Bibliography 345

Section 4: Special Crime Scenes

Chapter 8.0: Special Crime Scenes **349**

Chapter 8.1: Disaster and Mass Fatalities **351**

The Disaster Scene. 353

Human Remains 354

Conclusion 356

Bibliography. 356

Chapter 8.2: Terrorist Crime Scenes **357**

Conclusion 361

References and Bibliography. 361

Chapter 8.3: CBRN Crime Scenes **363**

Preparing for Forensic Collection 366

Collecting Relevant Evidence 366

Entering the Hot Crime Scene. 370

An Operative Flowchart. 370

Contents

Conclusion 371

References and Bibliography 371

Chapter 8.4: Underwater and Underground Crime Scenes 373

Underwater Scenes 373

Locating the Scene 376

Working the Scene. 377

Preservation of Materials in Water 380

Underground Scenes 382

Conclusion 384

References and Bibliography 385

Index 387

Foreword

This book takes a different approach than other crime scene texts, in that the authors assume (1) the reader already has more than a passing knowledge of forensic science and (2) that the reader is already schooled in the ways of science as a method. *The Science of Crime Scenes* is neither encyclopedic in scope nor "cookbook" in practicality; it is intended to touch on the key points in each topic and then delve more deeply in others that have not received as much attention in the literature as they deserve. Certain topics, like photography, are dealt with in greater detail in other books; the interested reader or student is directed to those specific works.

Another aspect of this book is that it has three authors with combined extensive and remarkable crime scene experiences. The authors are also international in origin (United States, France, and Ireland, by order of authorship), with varied approaches based on these global careers. The reader may also hear three distinct voices in this work; while it has been edited for grammar and clarity, the authors' personalities may creep into the writing from time to time. Whether it is considered "authentic" or "uneven," it is nevertheless an accurate, if varied, representation of the authors and their forensic experiences.

Forensic science begins at the crime scene, the *sine qua non* of any future forensic analysis. The processing of a crime scene can take long, arduous hours of difficult work, demanding the most from any forensic professional. Yet, without this hard and uncomfortable work, the public would not be able to rest assured that its public servants were doing their utmost to recognize, recover, and record the best evidence possible in the fight against crime.

—MMH, FC, TM

Disclaimer: The mentioning of commercial products in this textbook is not necessarily an endorsement of the product or its manufacturer. Images from ForensicSource were provided as a courtesy of that company.

Key Terms
Applied research
Basic research
Taphonomy

Acknowledgments

The authors would like to thank the following individuals and entities for their assistance in this project. Allen Miller of ForensicSource is greatly appreciated for allowing the use of certain images throughout this book. The work of two anonymous reviewers who provided commentary and suggestions on a prepublication draft of this book are acknowledged and those reviewers are our heroes. Finally, all of the staff at Elsevier, who helped keep us on track, are also to be thanked; patience is a virtue and we tested theirs.

Max Houck would like to thank Lesley Rockwell for her unfailing support, confidence, and love.

Frank Crispino would like to thank the following officers and petty officers of the French Gendarmerie and experts (also attached to this French police force) for their kind personal support to share their skills and provide illustrations in numerous chapters: Lieutenant-Colonel Jean-François Voillot, former head of the Criminal Intervention National Unit of the Forensic Research Institute of the French Gendarmerie in Rosny sous Bois, France (IRCGN); Commander Laurent Chartier, head of the Signal, Image, Voice Department of the IRCGN; Captain Thierry Lezeau, in charge of crime scene education at the Gendamerie Criminal Education in Fontainebleau, France (CFPJ); First Class Chief Warrant Officer Francis Hebrard and Warrant Officer Pascal Burgueyre, criminalists at the Regional Criminal Investigation Department of the French Gendarmerie in Bordeaux, France (SR33); Chief Warrant Officer Denis Gagnier, (underwater) scene of crime officer of the French Gendarmerie in Pau, France (BDRIJ64); Gendarme Brice Maestracci, (underground) scene of crime officer of the French Gendarmerie at the water brigade in Hendaye, France (GGD64); M. Xavier Gargasi, arson and explosive expert at the Court of Appeal of Bordeaux, France, but also a fresh reserve lieutenant of the French Gendarmerie. Acknowledgments are also sent to Brigadier General Jacques Hebrard and Colonel François Daoust, Head of the Gendarmerie Central Criminal Center (PJGN) and Director of the Forensic Research Institute of the French Gendarmerie (IRCGN), respectively, both in Rosny sous Bois, France, for their kind administrative support. Frank also would like to thank Nathalie, who, as usual, supported this new involvement and give a special thought for his kids, Corentin (and his American future daughter-in-law Megan), Clothilde, and Clement for the time he did not share with them, as he was diving into the writing of this book.

Acknowledgments

Terry McAdam would like to thank all the members, past and present, of the Washington State Patrol Crime Scene Response Team (CSRT). To my former colleagues, Kim Duddy, Matt Noedel, Karen Green, and Chris Hamburg—I began teaching you about crime scenes, but as with all good students, I found that I learned more from you than I taught. I would like to acknowledge the following people: Lynn McIntyre, the Director of the Washington State Patrol Crime Laboratories, for her mentorship and support. I also want to thank my friend and colleague Jim Tarver, who guided the CSRT through murky waters, and made it what it is today. In Chapter 5.4, "Submitting Evidence to the Laboratory," many sections from the Washington State Patrol Crime Laboratory Division Forensic Services Guide were used as source materials, with permission. My daughter and son, Katie and Kieran, who were so understanding when I could not spend time with them. I must give deep thanks to the love of my life, Elizabeth, who kept me focused as I completed this task.

Introduction

…there are collections of artifacts and boneyards of information everywhere. Among these are dissertations that will never be read, codes that will never be deciphered, objects whose particular import will never be understood, and the traces of innumerable human beings lost to history once and for all, without monuments or descendants or living memory, just a name somewhere in an official record consulted rarely if at all.

—*Luc Sante, 1992.* Evidence: NYPD Crime Scene Photographs: 1914–1918,
Farrar Straus Giroux, New York

…history consists of two equal parts; one of these halves is statements of fact, the other half is inference, drawn from the facts. To the experienced student of history there are no difficulties about this; to him the half which is unwritten is as clearly and surely visible, by the help of scientific inference, as if it flashed and flamed in letters of fire before his eyes. When the practiced eye of the simple peasant sees the half of a frog projecting above the water, he unerringly infers the half of the frog which he does not see. To the expert student in our great science, history is a frog; half of it is submerged, but he knows it is there, and he knows the shape of it.
—*Mark Twain, "The Secret History of Eddypus" in* Tales of Wonder

Forensic Science as History

The past is a mystery of necessity. Humans love mysteries and discovery, whether it is about people, places, or things. Because past events cannot be experienced in the present, the past must be interpreted through documents (the *Magna Carta*; Winston Churchill's biography), living participants (World War II veterans), or objects (the *Mona Lisa*); some of these objects also are the (unintentional) remnants of historical acts, like metal shavings from a coin cutter's bench or animal bones with butchering marks. As archaeologist Michael Shiffer notes, humans appreciate the meaning in objects and indications of previous interactions with an almost preternatural ease, citing the children's story of *Goldilocks and the Three Bears*: "'Someone's been sleeping in my bed' said Mama Bear in her middle-sized voice." Shiffer draws the correlation between Mama Bear and an archaeologist's thinking:

Just as Mama Bear concluded that there had been contact between an animate interactor and her bed from the bedspread's visual performance, so too archaeologists infer that a stone tool had been used to butcher an animal on the basis of the artifact's visual performance or that a pot had been employed for cooking rice through chemical performances of food residues. Thus, any past interaction that leaves a trace on—i.e., modifies any property of—an interactor is potentially inferable. (Shiffer, 1999, page 53)

Likewise, forensic science is a historical science, one in which a crime scene investigator (a CSI[1]) or forensic scientist infers past criminal activity through the traces left by those involved (criminal and otherwise) (Houck, 2010). Historians compare themselves to forensic investigators, seeing themselves in the same predicament of a police detective who works to reconstruct a crime he or she has not seen. The historian was no more at the moment in time he or she studies than the crime scene investigator was a witness to the crime committed, and thus both are removed and abstracted from the events they study. The comparison to forensic methods is repeated in other disciplines unrelated to legal matters, including geology, paleontology, art, and physics. If these other sciences (leaving out the argument as to whether history is a science or not) see themselves as "forensic," where does that leave the forensic sciences?

Forensic science and crime scene investigation are a relatively young science. The current popularity of forensic science can be traced to a series of publicized cases in the early 1990s, such as Jeffrey Dahmer, Polly Klaas, the first World Trade Center bombing, the Oklahoma City bombing, JonBenet Ramsey, Orville Lynn Majors, and numerous school shootings in the United States and the United Kingdom. This culminated in the popular imagination with the murders of Nicole Brown Simpson and Ronald Goldman in 1994 and the trials of O.J. Simpson, who was found liable for their wrongful deaths in civil court. The trifecta of Simpson's celebrity, the viciousness of the crimes, and the nonstop worldwide television coverage—even into the courtroom—created a sensational fascination with forensic science and crime scene investigation. Novels followed, schooling the public in semi-fictional forensic particulars they had come to appreciate in real life. Popular nonfiction television shows, such as *Forensic Files*, extended the public's appetite for all things forensic. These factual programs were the genesis for many fictional television dramas, starting with *CSI*, and extending into many other areas of forensic investigation. The discipline and profession have not been the same since (Figure 1).

The popular focus on the wonders of forensic science was quickly followed by interest in some of its problems. Unethical employees, practices, and methodological errors of omission and commission were revealed at certain laboratories; the rest were painted with this same tint of incompetence. Nevertheless, the discipline developed first in science then was co-opted by law enforcement, which stunted its scientific research growth: Police did not

---

[1] The use of the acronym "CSI" began before the eponymous television programs and the following popularity of the term. Agencies previously described the position as "a CSI," otherwise, where would the show have gotten the term? The authors use it throughout this book without irony.

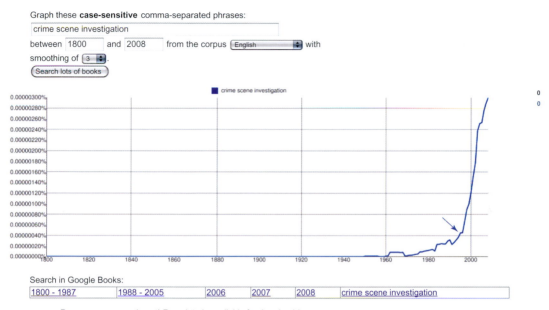

FIGURE 1 An n-gram of the words "crime scene investigation" between 1800 and 2008 based on the more than 15 million books in Google Books. The arrow indicates 1994. For comparison, the television program *CSI* first aired in October 2000. The data are smoothed with a moving average of 3; minimum occurrence for an n-gram is 40 books. An n-gram is a subset of *n* words, syllables, or phonemes from a given sequence. *Source: http://ngrams.googlelabs.com.*

have a scientific appreciation for what the laboratory could do and it was an incomprehensible novelty to the nonscientific police:

> Some of these [law enforcement] agencies which are so eager to have a laboratory have demonstrated to the author's satisfaction that they don't even know what a laboratory is for. Even worse, they have little or no conception of the proper use of a laboratory. (Wilson, 1975, page 100)

The laboratory served the law, not science, and lost some of its scientific foundations, controls, and checks. The patchwork jurisdictional nature of law and law enforcement, particularly in the United States, further fragmented methods, approaches, and training; "There never was nor is there today a uniform system of police organization in cities or towns through this country, each department varying to a slight extent in the method of control and disposition of its force" (Cahalane, 1923, page 7). These systemic issues were recently summed up in the 2009 National Academies of Sciences National Research Council report on the forensic sciences: "Although research has been done in some disciplines, there is a notable dearth of peer-reviewed, published studies establishing the scientific bases and validity of many forensic methods" (NAS/NRC, 2009). It seems contradictory that other sciences see themselves in a forensic light, including history, geology, medicine, and art,[2] but the real forensic methods are not considered "scientific." What is lacking, then, in forensic science?

What Plagues Forensic Science?

Four main things currently dog the forensic sciences—and, by extension, crime scene investigation, which is where forensic science starts—and keep them from fully realizing their place among their sibling sciences. They are:

1. The complexity of nature and modern material culture
2. The discipline's focus on the individual
3. The perception that forensic science is "only an applied science"
4. The confounding effects of taphonomic processes

Complexity: The World Is More Complicated Than We Can Imagine

Material culture refers to the physical aspects of a society, the objects made or modified by a human. These objects surround a people and its activities and are defined by their properties, be they chemical, physical, or biological. Properties are intrinsic to an object, like shape, size, surface texture, chemical composition and organization, molecular or cellular structure, color, and weight. Objects do not sit alone in the human or natural world, however, and when an object interacts with other objects or humans, it gains meaning and develops performance characteristics, which "are defined relationally, for they refer to the capabilities of one interactor in its engagement with another in a specific real-world, not laboratory, interaction" (Schiffer, 1999, page 34). For example, think of the following two events:

1. A baseball thrown through the window of a house
2. A rock thrown through the window of an automobile

In Event 1, the materials in play are quite different, although the house and the car both have glass windows, than in Event 2. To properly describe these events, one needs to understand not only what the objects are (those outside the United States may not have encountered a baseball before), but also the nature of their components (animal hide, polyester thread, minerals, coatings, elements, etc.), the way those components were combined by natural or

---

[2] For example, see Winks, R., Ed.,1969. *The Historian as Detective*. Harper & Row, New York; Cleland, C. E., 2001. Historical science, experimental science, and the scientific method. *Geology* 29(11): 987–990; Roueche, B., 1991. *The Medical Detectives*. Truman Talley, New York; Vakkari, J., 2001. Giovanni Morelli's "Scientific Method" of attribution and its reinterpretations from the 1960s until the 1990s. *Journal of Art History* 70(1): 46–54.

human actions, and the way they interacted. This last part becomes even more complicated because it involves all the physics of the *action* (velocity, angle, rotation, surfaces, etc.) and the *interaction* (the rock, the window coating, the baseball, the plate glass) to produce the final results. These seemingly simple examples turn more complex with further consideration.

The complications that beset these two seemingly simple interactions are not so great, however, that one could not deal with them in the abstract. The problem is that not only does the CSI have to think of events abstractly ("Could a rock really have broken that auto window?") but also in the specific ("Could *this* rock really have broken *that* auto window?"); more on this in a moment. Now, consider the myriad possible combinations of interactions that occur all day long across the world and *add to that those that involve alleged criminal activities*. Not only do CSIs have to work with the world as it is but they also have to sort the signal of criminal activity, as it were, from the noise of everyday life. The combinatorial aspects of object–person and person–person interactions along with the range of "all things in the world" means crime scenes can get very complicated, very fast.

> *I have for example distinguished things, which inertly exist or just lie there from facts, which are the propositions of things in relationship….A wheel is a thing, not a fact, and a paving stone is a thing, not a fact, but if the wheel rolls over the paving stone, they both come to life as a fact. Even if it is a fact solely in his own mind. Sun is just a noun, but if the sun shines through the window, together they are joined into propositional life.*
>
> —**E.L. Doctorow,** The City of God

Individual Focus: The Tyranny of the Particular

Forensic science's focus on individual, singular things creates additional complexities unknown to other sciences. Other historical sciences work at different scales of observation. Archaeology focuses on the social, by comparison, and the unit is usually the family or household; geology has a global-to-local orientation on natural processes; astronomy views light from millions or billions of years ago. Like archaeology, it's closest academic relative, forensic science goes beyond mere study of objects and includes the cultural relationship between humans and objects, including behaviors, institutions, and ideas; unlike archaeology, forensic science works at the level of the individual, and must take personal—as opposed to social or institutional—behaviors into account. An archaeologist would, for example, analyze all porcelain ceramics or porcelains from the St. James' factory to make a larger statement about the materials or designs, but a forensic scientist would analyze *this specific* porcelain object as an object and its relation to a *specific* crime.

Most sciences don't do this. Other sciences work from the specific (observations in an experiment, for example) to the general (development of principles or laws about phenomena in the world), whereas forensic science works from the general (all automotive paints, as an example) to the specific (the paint on the automobile in the current case). Given the combinatorial aspects of the world and the science of crime scenes, the focus on the individual, whether a person or a thing, greatly confounds the interpretation of crime scenes.

Applied Science: A Book of Recipes

In the years after World War II, the United States needed to make social good out of the vast investment made in the war effort. Vannevar Bush, an advisor to the president, made the distinction between basic and applied scientific research: basic research led us to knowledge about the world, applied research led us to solutions to specific questions (Bush, 1945). This dichotomy stands today and defines funding by several governmental agencies, like the National Science Foundation (NSF).

Forensic science is often classified as applied science because of its direct applicability to solving crime. Consequently, certain funding agencies will not consider a forensic proposal because it is not "basic enough," that is, it does not lead us to a greater understanding of the world. This view is arguably wrong-headed and narrow. As an example, consider the process of cyanoacrylate fuming to visualize latent fingerprints found at crime scenes. While the process works well as a method, a procedure, the mechanisms of the process are not well understood. One study found that the primary initiator of the polymerization process is the carboxylate moiety in the glue—thus, a basic environment inhibits chain termination and an acidic environment promotes it. Although all protocols and methods use hot water as an "initiator," water cannot perform this function (Wargacki and Lewis, 2007). Is this "applied" research? Perhaps. But who's to say that it will not lead to a better understanding of the interactions between these kinds of materials? And might not this provide insights to new solutions to other problems?

While the idea of basic and applied sciences has stuck, it is too simplistic for the modern complex nature of how science really works (Bromley and Fleury, 2006; Stokes, 1997). Forensic science studies a compilation of phenomena that no other science pays attention to in a way no other science does. In many ways, this would argue for forensic science being a basic science. Unfortunately, forensic and crime scene science still has an uphill battle to fight to gain recognition as a "real" science.

Entropy and Taphonomy: The Center Cannot Hold

Nothing lasts. Ice melts, mountains erode, bodies decay, water evaporates. These processes are central to crime scene science—as a historical science, forensic science is as much concerned with *when* events occurred as it is with *what* objects were involved in those events. The events do not need to be as dramatic as those just listed and could be as simple as the sharpening of a knife before its use in a stabbing; change, no matter how seemingly incidental, is inevitable but important. Daily use, in fact, may be most important to a forensic scientist:

> Many interactions eventually modify an [object's] properties—and thus its performance characteristics. As a result, activities often affect an [object's] performances in subsequent activities. This formulation, it should be clear, applies equally to artifacts and to people. (Schiffer, 1999, page 38)

From shoes to tires to tools to individual skin cells, the increase in entropy is the lifeblood of forensic science and crime scenes. The trouble is very few study this as a process in the combination of relationships between objects and people. Physicists may study energy loss as a phenomenon of thermodynamics but they are not concerned with how a warm beer may tip off a police officer to a suspect (Houck, 2003). In many ways, forensic science is the study of material culture in the immediate past, a kind of micro- to nano-history, with crime as its context. Inroads have been made to study taphonomy, the science of what happens from the time an organism dies until it is studied, in a forensic setting (Haglund and Sorg, 1997, 2002), but this has been done mostly for human remains and not objects; still, attempts have been made (for example, see DeGaetano et al., 1992) but nothing yet as systematic as a research program or theme.

Crime Scenes as a Process

The notion of a crime scene being merely "bagging and tagging" is wrong, if it was ever accurate. Processing a crime scene is one of the most mentally challenging, physically tasking, critically important tasks a scientist can do. The old computing adage "garbage in, garbage out" applies: If the crime scene is compromised, the entire case may be jeopardized. Nevertheless, the systematic approach to the collection and handling of physical evidence at a crime scene can be sequenced as follows (Buscemi and Washington, 1973):

1. Protecting the scene(s)
2. Documentation of the location, scene, and evidence
3. Collection of the potential evidence
4. Preservation of the evidence
5. Labeling of evidence and related materials
6. Chain-of-custody considerations
7. Letter of transmittal (to the custodial agency or laboratory)
8. Collection of reference materials (known samples for comparison)

This book takes the approach that those who process crime scenes are—or should be—scientists with the requisite education and training appropriate for that kind of work. The majority of crime scenes are processed either by law enforcement officers with some level of training or personnel specifically trained for the job of collecting, preserving, and evaluating crime scene evidence; according to the NAS report, however, about two-thirds of U.S. forensic laboratories send personnel to crime scenes. Training is variable by jurisdiction or agency with few standards (although more are coming through the efforts of working groups in the United States, Europe, and Australia). Training and experience nevertheless are key to being a good crime scene investigator—but what of education? Few forensic science programs offer practical courses in crime scene processing but more are developing each year, indicating the critical nature of a solid practical education in this foundational task.[3]

Conclusion

The focus at a crime scene is the evidence, and rightly so, but this should not lead to a "bag-and-tag" mentality. Many things must be kept in mind when working a crime scene: the victim(s), the perpetrator(s), the crime scene investigator's agency, the crime scene investigator's career, along with personal and public safety (and don't forget the evidence!). Given that the crime scene is "where forensic science starts," to coin a phrase, more attention is required to educate, train, and prepare those who work diligently and professionally at them. No less is owed to those professionals and certainly no less is owed to the victims of the crime and the public depending on the CSIs to help keep them safe.

References and Bibliography

Bugliosi, V., 1997. Outrage: The Five Reasons O.J. Simpson Got Away with Murder. Island Books, New York.

Buscemi, P., Washington, W., 1973. Collection and Handling of Physical Evidence for a Forensic Laboratory. Sampling, Standards, and Homogeneity, ASTM STP 540, American Society for Testing and Materials, pp. 37–44.

Bush, V., 1945. Science, The Endless Frontier. U.S. Government Printing Office, Washington, DC.

Cahalane, C.F., 1923. The Rise of Urban America. E.P. Dutton & Co.

DeGaetano, D.H., Kempton, J.B., Rowe, W.F., 1992. Fungal tunneling of hair from a buried body. J. Forensic Sci. 37 (4): 1048–1054.

Fleury, P., Iachello, F., 2006. D. Allan Bromley: Nuclear Scientist and Policy Innovator. World Scientific Publishing Co., London.

Gaddis, J.L., 2002. The Landscape of History. Oxford University Press, Oxford, UK.

Haglund, W., Sorg, M., 1997. Forensic Taphonomy: The Postmortem Fate of Human Remains. CRC Press, Boca Raton, FL.

Haglund, W., Sorg, M., 2002. Advances in Forensic Taphonomy: Method, Theory, and Archaeological Perspectives. CRC Press, Boca Raton, FL.

[3] For a list of programs accredited by the Forensic Science Educational Program Accreditation Commission (FEPAC), visit www.aafs.org/fepac.

Houck, M.M., 2003. Trace Evidence Analysis. Academic Press, San Diego.

Houck, M.M., 2010. An Investigation into the Foundational Principles of Forensic Science, PhD Dissertation. Curtin University of Technology, Perth, Western Australia.

Hughes, T., 2005. Human-Built World: How To Think About Technology and Culture. University of Chicago Press, Chicago.

National Institute of Justice Technical Working Group on Crime Scene Investigation, 2000. Crime Scene Investigation: A Guide for Law Enforcement. Available at www.ncjrs.gov/pdffiles1/nij/178280.pdf.

Schiffer, M., 1999. Material Life of Human Beings: Artifacts, Behavior and Communication. Routledge, London.

Stokes, D., 1997. Pasteur's Quadrant: Basic Science and Technological Innovation. Brookings Institution Press, Washington, DC.

Wargacki, S., Lewis, L., et al., 2007. Understanding the chemistry of the development of latent fingerprints by superglue fuming. J. Forensic Sci. 52 (5): 1057–1062.

Wilson, C., 1975. Crime detection laboratories in the United States. In: Peterson, J.L. (Ed.), Forensic Science: Scientific Investigations in Criminal Justice. AMS Press, New York, pp. 96–108.

The Science of Crime Scene Investigation

The "Forensic Mindset"

Forensic Professionals Are Knowledge Workers

Key Terms

Knowledge workers
Cuvier's principle of
    correlation of parts
Proxy data

Knowledge worker is a term coined by Peter Drucker in 1959 to describe the then-rising group of workers whose jobs required extensive education, the application of theoretical and analytical knowledge, and continuous learning (Drucker, 1995). Knowledge work, as defined by Drucker, "is not experience-based as all manual work has always been. It is learning-based" (page 227). Knowledge work has high entry costs:

> *Knowledge work and most of services work, in their work characteristics, are nontraditional. Displaced industrial workers thus cannot simply move into knowledge work or services work the way displaced farmers and displaced domestic workers moved into industrial work. At the very least*

they have to make a major change in their basic attitudes, values, and beliefs. (page 227)

Specialization, not generalization, is what makes knowledge useful, and the more specialized knowledge is, the more useful it becomes. Increased specialization does not imply that the knowledge will become more "applied," however, as many knowledge workers with highly specialized knowledge conduct very basic research, as with high-energy particle physics. With specialization comes two follow-on features of knowledge workers: they operate in teams and they have to have access to an organization. Teams balance out the necessary specialization for knowledge to be applied properly and the organization provides the basic continuity that allows the knowledge worker's specialization to be converted into performance (Drucker, 1995). For forensic professionals, the collection of investigators, laboratory colleagues, and the larger organization constitutes one or more participatory teams.

In this context, forensic professionals, including crime scene investigators (CSIs), use their specialized knowledge to convert items of evidence into reports and testimony. Knowledge of evidence is thus the core of forensic knowledge and, in part, sets the limits of its interpretation.

Hunting as an Origin for Forensic Science

Humans and their kind have a several-million-year prehistory of hunting prey (Standford, 1999). Over the millennia, humans learned to reconstruct the shapes and traces of unseen animals from tracks, broken branches, spoors, odors, and other indicators or clues (Ginzburg, 1989). The ability to hunt and track is often cited as the basis for what could be termed a *forensic mindset* (pages 63–65). Ginzburg suggests it is "what may be the oldest act in the intellectual history of the human race: the hunter squatting on the ground, studying the tracks of his quarry" (page 105). Even Locard noted the antiquity of such a forensic mindset: "Searching for traces is not, as much as one could believe it, an innovation of modern criminal jurists. It is an occupation probably as old as humanity" (Locard, 1934, as translated in Chisum and Turvey, 2007, page 7).

The first modern document demonstrating the forensic mindset is Voltaire's novel, *Zadig ou la Destinee* (*Zadig, or The Book of Fate*, 1747), the story of a Babylonian philosopher, the eponymous Zadig, who challenges religious and political orthodoxies of Voltaire's own day through thinly veiled tales woven into one narrative. Zadig's accumulated powers of observation lead him into trouble when members of the royal household approach him in a panic. Zadig says that they must be searching for a dog and a horse, both of which Zadig describes perfectly although he claims never to have seen either. He details the method of his seemingly supernatural knowledge:

[The tracks] were those of a small dog. Long, shallow grooves drawn across tiny heaps of sand between the paw-marks told me that it was a bitch whose teats were hanging down, which meant that she had whelped a few days previously. Other traces going in a different direction, and apparently made by something brushing constantly over the surface of the sand beside the front paws, told me that she had very long ears. And as I noticed that the sand was always less indented by one paw than by the other three, I realized that the bitch [had] a slight limp. (Voltaire, 1747; pages 132–133)

Zadig goes on to describe the King's missing horse in a similar manner. The retainers decide that Zadig himself must have stolen the animals and take him to the King, with further adventures resulting. The character of Voltaire's novel stands as the conceptual predecessor of nearly every detective and forensic scientist, fictional or real. It is in this same way that modern forensic scientists and CSIs make inferences from evidence present at a crime scene.

Trifles, Traces, and Clues

Perhaps the original scientist-as-detective, Georges Cuvier (1769–1832), the founder of comparative anatomy and paleontology, used scattered, fractured bits of information to reconstruct the prehistory of Earth and its animals (Cuvier, 1832). In a 1798 paper, Cuvier wrote on his realization of the form and function of bones as it relates to the overall identifiable anatomy of an animal, leading to the recognition of the creature from which the bone originated:

This assertion will not seem at all astonishing if one recalls that in the living state all the bones are assembled in a kind of framework; that the place occupied by each is easy to recognize; and that by the number and position of their articulating facets one can judge the number and direction of the bones that were attached to them. This is because the number, direction, and shape of the bones that compose each part of an animal's body are always in a necessary relation to all the other parts, in such a way that—up to a point—one can infer the whole from any one of them, and vice versa. (Rudwick, 1998; page 36)

This has been called "Cuvier's principle of correlation of parts" and is a central tenant in biology and paleontology. Rudwick notes that Cuvier claimed to be able to *identify* an animal taxonomically from a single bone, not completely *reconstruct* it, as the preceding quote might imply. The reconstruction would only be possible with a sufficient number of bones representing the animal in question.

The same clue-based method was employed in an unlikely venue: art. In an attempt to make attributions of Italian artists' works more accurate and less susceptible to false identifications, an art connoisseur and politician, Giovanni Morelli, published essays on a novel method for the art world.

From 1874 to 1876, under the pseudonym Ivan Lermolieff, Morelli outlined a method for identifying artists based on what he considered to be incidental, unintentional indicators of the artist in the work itself. As Vakkari notes, "[o]n the basis of [Morelli's] observations, he concluded that every artist tends to repeat certain forms and shades in the same way" and these forms "were not influenced by school or tradition" (Vakkari, 2001; page 46). The forms were indicators of the artist's unconscious additions to the art, exclusive of their formal education and training. Morelli focused on unintentional details such as hands, ears, and shading.

In modern parlance, these would be clues to the artist's identity. Morelli's method, which he called *metodo sperimentale* ("experimental method"), entailed detailed, systematic perception of elements of the work with comparison to known artwork. The reference to known works was a central tenet of the method; without authenticated references, the inference of identity may be wrong. In forensic terms, this would lead to an incorrect classification or the resolution of an item of evidence into too large a class (perhaps leading to a Type II error, that is, a false negative). Having a reference collection of known materials presupposes that the provenance of those items is well characterized, accurate, and traceable. Reference collections, therefore, stand as explicit object-based examples of the inherent process that produced it. Morelli's work caused a stir in the art world during his life and for several years after because of his reattribution of hundreds of works hanging in famous European museums; over half of his reassignments were correct (Vakkari, 2001).

From Science to Art to Literature

Edgar Allan Poe may have been influenced by Voltaire's story of Zadig for the character of Auguste Dupin (Silverman, 1991), widely regarded as the first detective in modern fiction. Morelli's method also has been linked as a formative basis for Freud's analytical psychoanalysis and, interestingly, to Arthur Conan Doyle's detective character, Sherlock Holmes. Another intriguing link to Morelli's method is the suggestion that Cuvier's comparative anatomy is the basis for Morelli's method (Vakkari, 2001). Essig notes the basis for the method of the fictional detective Sherlock Holmes (the first story was published in 1887) was the historical sciences, particularly the example of Cuvier's foundational work in paleontology, and the medical sciences, especially Doyle's medical school professor, Joseph Bell (Essig, 2000). Holmes, despite being a fictional character, influenced Bertillon ("I would like to see Sherlock Holmes' methods of reasoning adopted by all professional police.") and Locard ("Sherlock Holmes was the first to realize the importance of dust. I merely copied his methods.") (as quoted in Berg, 1970; pages 447 and 448, respectively). To bring the relationships full circle, there is some evidence that Doyle was inspired by early editions of Hans Gross' groundbreaking treatise, *Criminal Investigation*, published in 1893 (Morgan and Bull, 2007). Ginzburg links Morelli, Freud, and Doyle through their medical education and training: Morelli studied medicine and Freud was a physician, as was Doyle before he became famous for his fiction. A doctor's conclusions are drawn from the external signs and symptoms of the patient much in the way a CSI must come to conclusions based on the signs left at a crime scene.

The clues of Zadig, Cuvier, Dupin, and Holmes are minor things ("trifles," in Holmes' terms) that reveal the larger truth of the investigation. The fossil of the paleontologist, the specimen of the anatomist, and the artifact of the archaeologist is what a CSI would call evidence, Freud's "slight and obscure traces." Detection, like archaeology and other historical investigations, is by definition illuminating, an uncanny act "which reveals that which should have remained invisible" (Vidler, 1992; page 12), thereby making the absent present.

Evidence Is Proxy Data

Criminal events under investigation are, by definition, history. The events themselves were not seen by the CSI and are inaccessible to present-day investigators. Imagine a scientist walking into his laboratory and finding his experiment completed for him—he would have no idea what had happened, only what results were left behind. Such residual evidence represents a more accessible kind of information because objects created in the past are the only historical occurrences that continue to exist in the present (Prown, 1982). Gaddis comments that time and space provide the field in which history occurs but it is structure and process that are the mechanism by which that reconstruction takes place:

> It's here that the methods of historians and scientists—at least those scientists for whom reproducibility cannot take place in the laboratory— roughly coincide. For historians too start with surviving structures, whether they be archives, artifacts, or even memories. They then deduce the processes that produced them. Like geologists and paleontologists, they must allow for the fact that most sources from the past don't survive, and that most daily events don't even generate a survivable record in the first place. (Gaddis, 2002; page 41)

The kind, sequence, and magnitude of the events must be reconstructed from the physical remnants of past criminal events. The concept of physical remnants—what the forensic science would now call "traces" or evidence[1]— is common among historical sciences but goes by different terminology (e.g., fossils, artifacts, symptoms, clues). A more descriptive and encompassing term, used in paleoclimatology, is *proxy data*. Surface temperature records are only available for approximately the past hundred years; therefore, indirect

---

[1] The word "traces" is primarily a European term for any type of evidence left behind, not just "trace evidence," as the phrase is used in the United States. In this book, "traces" and "evidence" will be used interchangeably.

or "proxy" indicators, such as geological patterns, flora and faunal remains, and shorelines, must be used to reconstruct earlier climatic variability (Mann, 2002). Proxy data acts as the components for a complex reality that cannot be experienced directly; invariably, the data are organized to relate the reconstruction in a narrative structure. Multiple validated proxies are useful for periods of temporal overlap and no one proxy by itself is enough to reconstruct larger events; this is also the case in forensic science, where one item of evidence rarely "makes the case."

By definition, proxy data all contain a signal (a meaning or a forensic significance) on two levels. First is the meaning of the material in its original context: a handgun, a rock, a carpet. The item's intrinsic value is established by the rarity of the materials that compose it. At this first level of meaning, forensic science typically deals in class-level evidence and leads to a sourcing of the material at some level of resolution. The second level of meaning is an added layer that the criminal activity has contributed to the item: the handgun used to shoot the victim, the rock used to break the store window, the carpet where the sexual assault took place. This level of forensic meaning can be more transient or variable, begging the issue of proper collection and preservation by the CSI.

Conclusion

A working forensic (as opposed to a legal) definition for evidence, then, is proxy data that is identified, collected, and analyzed for a legal process (civil or criminal). With this understanding of the basic unit of forensic science, the method of history now pertains more directly to a better understanding of crime scene methodology.

References and Bibliography

Berg, S., 1970. Sherlock Holmes: Father of scientific crime detection. J. Crim. Law. Criminol. Police Sci. 61: 446–452.

Chisum, W.J., Turvey, B., 2007. Crime Reconstruction. Academic Press, San Diego.

Cuvier, G., 1832. The Animal Kingdom Arranged in Conformity with Its Organization. Treater and Co., London.

Drucker, P.F., 1995. Managing in a Time of Great Change. Truman Talley Books, New York.

Eco, U., Sebeok, T. (Eds.), 1998. The Sign of Three: Dupin, Holmes, Peirce. Indiana University Press, Bloomington.

Essig, M.R., 2000. Science and Sensation: Poison Murder and Forensic Medicine in Nineteenth-Century America. Cornell University, Ithica, NY, PhD thesis.

Gaddis, J.L., 2002. The Landscape of History. Oxford University Press, Oxford, UK.

Ginzburg, C., 1989. Clues, Myths, and the Historical Method. Johns Hopkins Univeristy Press, Baltimore.

Huxley, T.H., 1898. On the method of Zadig. In: Collected Essays. D. Appleton and Co., New York, pp. 1–23.

Kirk, P., 1963. The ontogeny of criminalistics. J. Crim. Law Criminol. Police Sci. 54: 235–238.

Kirk, P., 1963. Criminalistics. Science 140: 367–370.

Locard, E., 1934. La Police et Les Methodes Scientifiques. Les Editions Rieder, Paris.

Mann, M.E., 2002. The value of multiple proxies. Science 297: 1481–1482.

Morgan, R., Bull, P., 2007. The philosophy, nature and practice of forensic sediment analysis. Prog. Phys. Geol. 31 (1): 43–58.

Prown, J., 1982. Mind in matter: An introduction to material culture theory and method. Winterthur Portf. 17 (1): 1–19.

Rudwick, M., 1998. Georges Cuvier, Fossil Bones, and Geological Catastrophes: New Translations and Interpretation of the Primary Texts. University of Chicago Press, Chicago.

Silverman, K., 1991. Edgar A. Poe: Mournful and Never-ending Remembrance. Harper Perennial, New York.

Standford, C., 1999. The Hunting Ape. Princeton University Press, Princeton, NJ.

Vakkari, J., 2001. Giovanni Morelli's "scientific" method of attribution and its reinterpretations from the 1960s until the 1990s. J. Art Hist. 70 (1): 46–54.

Vidler, A., 1992. The Architectural Uncanny. MIT Press, Cambridge, MA.

Voltaire, 1998. Candide and Other Stories. Oxford University Press, Oxford, UK.

From Scene to Laboratory to Court

The main problem of criminal investigation is therefore one of matching the dry certainty of the law to the messy, unpredictable and complex reality of the human behavior called crime. (Stelfox, 2009; pages 6-7)

Officers are called to *the* scene where *a* crime has been committed. *The* evidence is collected and *it* is transported to the laboratory. *The* case eventually ends up in court. Although singular verbiage is used to describe crime scenes, this grammatical necessity belies a powerful truth that is worth remembering: crime scenes are a *process* and not a singular *event*. What happens at the scene can affect every aspect of a case from that moment on and can even render the case unable to be investigated or prosecuted. Crime scene investigators need to be aware that what they do in a moment of weakness, exhaustion, or laziness may not only haunt them for their professional careers but has the potential to affect people's lives for years to come.

Key Terms

Fourth Amendment to the Constitution
Rule of law
Exigent circumstances doctrine
Butterfly effect
Modus operandi
Fruit of the poisonous tree

The Science of Crime Scenes

Access to the Scene

Typically, to gain access to a crime scene the police must first have permission to enter and search a location. To do so without permission, either by the owner of the premises or the demand of a judge, may violate individual rights and expose the person entering the premises to a lawsuit and legal damages. Moreover, any evidence collected might not be admissible in a court proceeding because it was obtained illegally. Law enforcement officers therefore seek legal authorization, called a *warrant*, which permits an otherwise illegal act, in this context, searching a person, place, or thing for evidence even if the person objects (the word comes from the Old High German word, *Weren*, "an authorization"). A judge, magistrate, or other official issues a warrant, which is served and executed by law enforcement officers; typically, warrants are only good for a certain amount of time and do not provide permanent permission. Warrants normally issued include search warrants, arrest warrants, and execution warrants.

Search warrants are written to specifically address the offense that has been committed, the location(s) to be searched, and what can be seized. In the United States, the need for a warrant to search is rooted in the Fourth Amendment to the Constitution, which states:

> *The right of the people to be secure in their persons, houses, papers, and effects, against unreasonable searches and seizures, shall not be violated, and no Warrants shall issue, but upon probable cause, supported by Oath or affirmation, and particularly describing the place to be searched, and the persons or things to be seized.*

This amendment has been interpreted and reinterpreted by the courts on an almost continuous basis since it was ratified on December 15, 1791. The warrant must be specific enough in the description of the incident and the items that could be collected to persuade the judge of the legitimacy of the request; it must also be broad enough in scope that whatever items are discovered during the search can be collected for later analysis.

Jurisdictions respecting the rule of law[1] and individual privacy put constraints on police powers, like warrants, even in criminal investigations. Laws vary by jurisdiction, but there are situations where a search and seizure can take place without a warrant. In the United States, for example, the *exigent circumstances doctrince* states that in certain situations, such as where people are in imminent danger, evidence may be destroyed, or a suspect will escape, a warrantless search may be conducted. For example, if a criminal flees the scene of a crime and enters a building in an attempt to evade capture,

---

[1] The *rule of law* is a legal concept that concedes that no person is above the law, that the state may not punish individuals unless they break the law, and that no one can be convicted of breaking the law unless the procedures for such prosecution are provided for by the law itself. Not all governments recognize the rule of law, the Romans and the Nazis being two historical examples.

the officer has the right to enter that property. If evidence is in plain view, the officer is within the law to seize it; for example, if an officer sees what appears to be a marijuana cigarette on the seat of a vehicle that was stopped for a traffic violation, he may seize the cigarette as evidence. Additionally, a warrantless search can be conducted on a person who is arrested by the police, largely for the officer's safety. Of course, consent can be given by a person in control of the thing or place that the police want to search.

Sensitivity to Initial Conditions

Crime scenes embody a complex, overlapping set of circumstances: the "normal" environment of the day-to-day activities of the location and the "criminal" environment that is superimposed on it during the commission of the crime. The goal of the crime scene investigator is to sort the "signal" of the criminal activities from the "noise" of the preexisting circumstances.

The interaction of the normal and criminal environments—both dynamic systems in their own rights—leads to a one-time set of results: time only goes in one direction and the outcomes of activities exhibit a sensitive dependence on initial conditions. Although the mechanics of Newtonian physics provides a deterministic view of the world—knowing the trajectory of a baseball, we can plot where it will likely land—the initial conditions of many dynamic, complex systems cannot be so accurately determined. The problem is not with our measurements—we can be as precise as our instruments allow and still be off. Small changes or differences at the outset can have large consequences later on. For example, think of a simple incline and a ball. You set the ball at the top of the incline and release it; it rolls to the bottom. Imagine doing this 100 times and tracking the course of the ball (Figure 1.1.1). The ball would exhibit differences in the path it takes to the bottom of the incline, developing a range or pattern of possible paths. Small changes in

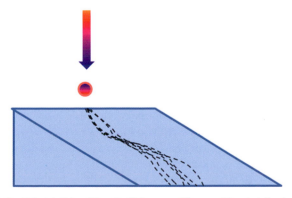

FIGURE 1.1.1 Sensitivity to initial conditions. Small changes or differences at the outset, like placement of the ball on the incline, the surface of the incline, or the surface of the ball, can have large consequences later on, such as variations in the trajectory of the ball. Crime scenes are also sensitive to initial conditions.

the ball's position, the surface of the incline, and other initial conditions can change the ball's trajectory.

The "butterfly effect," as it is known, may seem to be a strange and esoteric concept, but it is exhibited by systems as simple as the ball example and leaves falling from trees to those as complex as the weather. When systems exhibit sensitive dependence on initial conditions, they are no longer predictable to a certain extent (weather cannot be predicted with any accuracy beyond about five days, for example[2]), and determinism no longer holds. Some phenomena are more resistant to change than others and some patterns of activity (physical or mental) can act as regulators or borders of what is possible; the ball does not just roll 90° along the ridge of the incline, for example. Remember: It is not the idea that *any effect* can create a systemwide change but that a *small* one can have a *global* effect, but not just *any effect*.

What does all this have to do with crime scene investigation? No two crime scenes can ever be "the same." Think of the typical dwelling and how it might be right now, as clean or as messy as it is; freeze that thought. Now imagine all of the conditions, events, actions, external influences, and behaviors that led to that "snapshot"—the cereal bowl from breakfast, a favorite shirt on the floor that needs to be laundered, the magazine with the torn cover sitting on the coffee table. None of these things was "predictable" in any deterministic sense. They are a confluence of habits (cereal for breakfast), preferences (a favorite shirt), and timing (leisurely reading a magazine) that could have ended up different in any number of ways. Now, imagine a crime occurring in that location: Who would have predicted that the bowl, shirt, or magazine would end up as evidence? Add to this whatever the criminal brought with him (a specific pry bar to open the door and a particular pair of shoes, for example) and the actions taken to commit the crime; again, not predictable in any realistic fashion. The crime scene investigator has to deal with the totality of information at any given crime scene.

Peter Stelfox, Head of Investigative Practice at the U.K.'s National Policing Improvement Agency, calls this totality of information at a crime scene the *information profile*. He notes that each crime is committed under unique circumstances, producing a unique information profile that varies by the volume, type, and distribution of information: "The information in this case arose from the unique dynamics of that incident and it can easily be imagined how slight changes to the circumstances of the incident could have changed the level of information" (Stelfox, 2009; page 99). Even the same kind of crimes committed in the same kind of locale produces markedly different outcomes. Although there are differences between individual burglaries for various reasons (like each house and its contents are different, burglars have different levels of skill, and so on), the information profiles of burglaries committed

---

[2] Lorenz, Edward N., 1963. Deterministic nonperiodic flow. *Journal of Atmospheric Sciences*, 20: 130–141.

in houses will have some general commonalities just because of the way a burglary is carried out. By contrast, the information profile of other crimes, like a homicide or an embezzlement case, will be different from a burglary but similar to other homicides and embezzlements, respectively. Each type of crime can be thought of as having its own "activity space" because of the kinds of actions required to commit them. On an individual level, this is the *modus operandi*, or MO, of a perpetrator: a burglar who always enters through a rear window by breaking it but leaves through the front door, for example. The information profile is a key element in gaining experience in crime scene investigations, learning where to look and what to look for, as well as noting when something is out of the ordinary.

Downstream Effects

If, after reading the preceding material, it seems that crime scene investigations are a daunting matter, they are. Doing nothing because of the fear that some evidence might be damaged, destroyed, or overlooked is not an option. The scene must be processed, the evidence has to be collected, and the documentation has to be completed. It is very important, however, to remember that what happens at the scene can affect the remainder of the case. An infamous example of this is the crime scene work done in the Brown-Goldman murders (see sidebar).

Crime Scenes Affect the Entire Case: The Brown-Goldman Murders

Dennis Fung, the lead Los Angeles Police Department criminalist called out to the crime scenes of Nicole Brown and Ronald Goldman's murders, provides an example of crime scene processing affecting an entire case. Fung, an experienced professional who had worked for LAPD for 11 years and had been involved in hundreds of crime scenes, spent nearly three weeks on the witness stand, testifying about the detailed, tedious process of collecting evidence, including bloodstains, blood smears, and physical items of evidence. His extensive testimony included the paperwork and logistics of crime scenes, including the documentation, the labeling, and the storage of evidence. Fung's cross-examination by Simpson's lawyers, specifically Barry Scheck, was extensive, exhaustive, and embarrassing.

Scheck questioned Fung about key pieces of the prosecution's narrative: the Ford Bronco, the sock from the Rockingham Avenue residence, and the other sock from the South Bundy location. As an admittedly important part of the crime scene, the Bronco should have been sealed off and access restricted; it wasn't. Contamination is always an issue, either from

---

the crime scene investigators or from other evidential contacts unrelated to the crime; Fung worked both crime scenes, gloves were changed only when they appeared "dirty," and Brown's body was covered with a blanket from the house (her body was found outside). Scheck asked Fung if he had used gloved hands to collect an envelope containing Brown's glasses; Fung said yes and reaffirmed his answer when the question was repeated. The courtroom was then shown a video of Fung collecting the envelope with bare hands. Fung's crime scene notes included the questions, "Has the scene been altered?" and "If so, by whom and how?" which were answered in the notes only with question marks. Fung admitted that he placed blood samples into plastic bags, which numerous sources cautioned against.

Fung's testimony was damaging enough to the integrity of the scene and the methods used to collect the evidence. It was devastating, however, to the remainder of the trial, which dealt with all of the evidence collected from the various scenes, precisely the items that Fung and his assistant had collected. With this level of doubt planted in the jurors' minds, almost any item of evidence could be questioned.

The crime scene profession has guidelines, like the National Institute of Justice's *Crime Scene Investigation: A Guide for Law Enforcement*, that provide information about general procedures and recommendations. Agencies will have specific protocols for their investigators to follow. Knowing when to depart from protocol and documenting your reasons why is as important as following protocols the remainder of the time.

Documentation

A crime scene can only be processed once. Documentation of crime scene processing, therefore, is critical to the success and later explanation or defense of the actions taken at the scene. Documentation is a theme that will run throughout this book so it will only be highlighted here. The old adage, "If it wasn't written down, it never happened," applies to crime scene processing. Unless there is documentation, such as written notes, photographs, video, measurements, lists, or all of the preceding, it is simply the word of one person against another's. Getting into the habit of consistent and comprehensive note-taking is the best way to ensure that it will happen when things get hectic at the scene. And they will.

Chain of Custody

With the advances of technology and science, it is a safe assumption that physical evidence will be a significant part of any investigation, either as leads or as physical evidence for prosecution or exoneration. Ultimately, any useful evidence may end up in a courtroom and be offered as evidence for either the prosecution or the defense. Because of this and the critical role physical evidence now plays in the criminal justice system, it is a requirement that evidence be handled, transported, and labeled properly so that it can be determined where the items were at any point in its history.

Arguably, the singlemost important piece of paper generated at a crime scene is the *chain of custody*. This form documents the movement of evidence from the time it is obtained to the time it is presented in court. The most compelling evidence in the world can be rendered useless if inaccuracies or gaps exist in a chain of custody. The form is a historical record, a chronological document that demonstrates the custody, transfer, and disposition of evidence. Like the entire crime scene, mishandling even one piece of evidence can create problems later on in the courtroom, compromising the case for either the prosecution or the defense. Where was the evidence collected? Who had control of it and when? Who last had this item? Could it have been tampered with during the time that person had it? It may seem to be a nuisance to have to document each exchange of an item from person, to evidence locker, to person, to agency, but it is the foundation that permits evidence to enter into a courtroom.

The chain of custody also ensures that the item offered in court is the exact same item that was collected at the scene and underwent examination or analysis. It cannot be just *any* item but must be the specific one collected as evidence. The chain of custody is also a safeguard against unauthorized persons gaining access to the evidence and altering it inappropriately or even tampering with it.

Fruit of the Poisonous Tree

Gaps in a chain of custody, also called *breaks*, are an excellent example of what was not done being as important as what was done. If there is a breach in this chain, it cannot be established what was or was not done to any evidence in this unaccounted-for period, and it then becomes *tainted*. The legal concept is referred to as the "fruit of the poisonous tree." The analogy is that the original tainted or compromised situation, like evidence seized in an unjustified warrantless search, is the tree and, thus, any fruit (evidence) that comes from it is also poisonous and may not be used. Again, it is obvious that seemingly small problems at the scene can affect the entire case from the laboratory to the courtroom.

Submitting Evidence for Analysis

The jurisdictional patchwork quilt of the U.S. criminal justice system creates enormous inefficiencies in the provision of forensic services. Over 18,000 federal, state, and local law enforcement agencies exist in the United States

(Walter and Katz, 2002) with control focused at the local level; by comparison, the United Kingdom, which is one-quarter the size of the United States has only 43 police departments. These various roles and responsibilities create a fragmented, decentralized system in the United States.

The downstream effect of this is the hodgepodge delivery of forensic services, some of which overlap significantly either in services, geography, or both. In a 2005 U.S. Bureau of Justice Statistics report, 254 public forensic laboratories were recognized (U.S. Bureau of Justice Statistics, 2005); moreover, a 2009 survey identified an additional 300 forensic service providers (Childs et al., 2009). This creates an environment of extreme disaggregation. As an example, consider the Dallas–Fort Worth metroplex encompassing 12 counties with a 2010 population of nearly 6.4 million people. The City of Fort Worth has a police department forensic laboratory; the surrounding county (Tarrant) has a medical examiner's office that also has a full-service forensic laboratory. Likewise, the City of Dallas police department offers forensic services as does the Dallas County medical examiner's office. In between theses jurisdictions, the City of Arlington police department has a forensic service provision for its citizens. Overlaid on all of this is the statewide Texas Department of Public Safety's Forensic Laboratories, in addition to numerous private forensic laboratories. The various law enforcement agencies (city, county, state) throughout the metroplex have numerous opportunities for forensic service provision, some of which are contractual. Further recognizing that federal agencies may have forensic service provisions in the area (like a Drug Enforcement Administration laboratory in the Dallas area) that may offer assistance to local agencies *pro bono*, the forensic landscape becomes complicated, to say the least.

A CSI will work for one agency that will have its own protocols for evidence submission; joint-agency task groups have to negotiate about what evidence goes where. Paperwork, cataloging, and data entry may seem deadly dull but an item of evidence can be lost just as easily by being left off of a list as it can being forgotten at the scene. CSIs will be tired, dirty, and hungry; mistakes are likely to happen during transitions so special effort must be made to make the workflow smooth, validated, and straightforward. Forms, checklists, and signatures are all as necessary to finishing a crime scene as are photography, note-taking, and sealing evidence.

Conclusion: Evidence in the Courtroom

The next time the CSI sees an item of evidence will most likely be in the courtroom. The evidence will have been processed by the CSI and one or more laboratories; it may look very different than when it was collected. The evidence has been discharged from the laboratory back to the police or directly to the prosecuting attorney. It has been under the control of the police or the attorney but not necessarily in the same way as it was during collection at the scene. On direct testimony, the CSI will be asked if she recognizes the item being offered into evidence; the CSI should not take this request lightly. Carefully look at the item, note the identifying information on it, and double-check that the item being offered is the correct one based on the CSI's notes. This will be based on the labeling the jurisdiction uses, such as case numbers, item numbers, and the CSI's initials on the seal or packaging. Additional paperwork may be involved and the CSI should check for it and cross-reference it, if necessary.

References and Bibliography

Census of Publicly Funded Crime Labs, U.S. Bureau of Justice Statistics, 2005.

Childs, R., Witt, T., Nur-Tegin, K., 2009. Survey of forensic service providers. Forensic Sci. Policy Manage. 1 (1): 49–56.

Stelfox, P., 2009. Criminal Investigation: An Introduction to Principles and Practice. Willan Publishing, London.

Walker, S., Katz, C., 2002. The Police in America, fourth ed. McGraw-Hill, New York.

What Is a Crime Scene?

Introduction

Anyone who watches detective shows will know what a crime scene is: it's the area behind the yellow tape. Someone, however, had to decide where to put that tape, determining where the "scene" is, how many scenes there are, and how to manage that space. The view in this chapter will be a bit different from other books on crime scene processing—most do not spend a whole chapter on the definition of a crime scene based on spatial, behavioral, and legal information. Conceptually, however, this is the core of the discipline and the start of every investigation: *Where is the scene?*

Crime scenes can occur anywhere, in busy urban areas or on lonely rural tracts of land, inside a house or under water, involving one person or thousands. The seemingly endless variety may make it appear that deciding *how* to define a crime scene is impossible; the typical pattern of criminal behaviors may make it seem that defining a crime scene is easy. This is the paradox of a crime scene: each one is different somehow, each one is the same in some way. All bank robberies have similar patterns to them and yet each one happens at a different bank, is committed by a different robber, or, at the very least in the case of the dogged recidivist, on different days.

Bank Robbery Patterns

All crimes have some sort of pattern to them; for the offender(s), this pattern of behavior is called the *modus operandi*, or "method of operating." There is no corresponding term for a category of crime but they nevertheless have similarities based on the nature of the crime, the space occupied by the targets, history, and the way humans think.

The Australian Institute of Criminology analyzed trends in bank robbery from January 1998 through May 2002. Of the 808 bank robberies that occurred in that time, 55% were committed by lone offenders, 25% by pairs, and 20% by three or more robbers. Unarmed lone offenders committed 28% of robberies, caused the least number of injuries to victims (1% of all victims' injuries), were the type of robber who most often used a note to threaten bank staff (so-called "note jobs," 46% of all their robberies), and failed most often in their robbery attempts (33% failure). Unarmed gangs inflicted the most injuries to victims (51%) and failed the least in their robbery attempts (6% failure). Armed robbers used a disguise more often compared to unarmed robbers, with armed pairs employing disguises most often (59%).

Although each crime scene is unique, it is important to study crime scene "spaces" and (criminal) human behavior for patterns that may help lead the CSI to otherwise undetected evidence.

Source: Borzycki, 2003.

Human activities, like crimes, happen over time and in space; they change the space in which they occur. Much like physical evidence—normal objects of which the meaning increases because of their involvement in a crime (the fireplace poker *becomes* a murder weapon, while remaining a fireplace poker)—locations also become transformed into crime scenes, locations with increased meaning. The job of the CSI is to sort the normal meaning of a location from the *criminal* meaning of the place, the layer of illegal activities that sits on top of (or sometimes inside of or underneath) the normal accumulation of noncriminal activities. In this way, crime scenes are like aboveground, open-air archeological sites. The ordering of the space, both legal and criminal, defines the purpose of it—what has happened, what was the space used for, how has it changed, what was the criminal purpose of the space? It is the (re)ordering of the space by the criminal that designates its criminal purpose.

A Definition

Technically, a crime scene is a location where an illegal act occurred; for purposes of the CSI, it is also the location from which physical evidence is retrieved. It is not necessarily where the crime was committed, however. A location linked to the commission of a crime, such as where preparations were made, where a body or weapon was discarded, or intermediate locations, can also be thought of as crime scenes.

Some experts classify crime scenes as "primary," "secondary," "tertiary," and so on, to reflect the order of importance to the criminal activity. This can be misleading: The most important evidence may be found not at the primary site but elsewhere. For example, a kidnapper may abduct the victim from her home (first scene), force her into a stolen vehicle (second or the true first scene, because the criminal had to steal the vehicle before the kidnapping), drive her to a deserted location (third scene, either way it is counted) to assault her, and then perhaps on to another location where he discards either the car and steals a new one or commits murder and dumps the body (fourth scene). The numbering approach can quickly become cumbersome.

Another way to classify crime scenes is by the type of offense that has occurred there: "murder scene," "robbery scene," and so on. While less clumsy than the ordering approach, it is also less descriptive. A single "murder scene" can cover a wide variety of situations, ranging from single deaths to multiple ones, covering more than one area (is it, for example, only where the body is found or is it where the person was killed?). Additionally, if the offense changes, say from "homicide" to "manslaughter," then what?

A novel (as far as the authors are aware) approach is to think of scenes as a matrix of people and locations, both single and multiple, as follows:

- **One person**: one individual, either victim or suspect, is the direct focus of the investigation; a dead body found in a wooded area, for example.
- **One place**: one location constitutes the crime scene; a bank that has been robbed, for example.
- **Multiple people**: more than one person is the direct focus of the investigation; a gang of drug manufacturers, for instance.
- **Multiple places**: more than one location constitutes a crime scene, thus there are multiple scenes; the kidnapping example offered earlier describes this situation.

If these categories are arranged in a matrix (Figure 2.0.1) then the complexity of the combinations becomes evident. A one person/one location scene is the easiest scenario to deal with in terms of scope, time, and personnel.

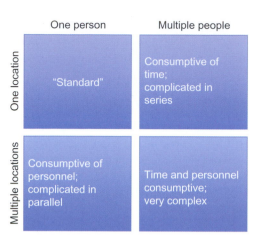

FIGURE 2.0.1 A matrix of crime scene categories.

The next most complicated would be either one location with multiple people or multiple locations with one person because more variables are introduced that must be accounted for. Given a situation with multiple locations with one person (say, a dead body that has been dismembered), not only does each location have to be accounted for (likely by determining first the MNI, or minimum number of individuals present—two left hands indicate at least two people, for example—at each site and then determining if the parts found at each site catalog together properly to account for the same person), the number of considerations increase, as does the time (traveling to and processing each locale) and resources (gasoline, supplies, etc.). Likewise, multiple people at one location directly indicates increased human (and, therefore, criminal) activity, such as the clandestine drug laboratory or a mass shooting. Scenes like these are consumptive of personnel (more people are needed to process) and they become complicated to work at the same time (in parallel). The most complex scenes are those that involve multiple people and multiple locations; regrettably, examples abound, from a shooting spree across a metropolitan area to a string of bank robberies to coordinated terrorist attacks, like the July 7, 2005 London subway bombings, which killed 56 people and injured many more (Figure 2.0.2).

The experienced CSI, or even perhaps the casual observer, might ask, "Aren't all crime scenes ultimately about multiple people and multiple locations?" If taken literally, then, yes, each scene has at least one victim and one suspect and, unless both are at the place where the crime occurred (a murder/suicide, for example), there are multiple locations (the scene, the victim's person, the suspect's person). This matrix description is not meant to be an exclusive, categorical taxonomy of crime scenes but, rather, a way to delineate them based on complexity, resources, and what the CSI might need to plan for to process them properly.

(a)

(b)

FIGURE 2.0.2 (a) The four men named as having detonated bombs in the London subway and on a bus on July 7, 2005, captured at Luton train station on CCTV; (b) ambulances at Russell Square (a subway station), London, after the bombings. *Sources: (a) BBC News; (b) Wikimedia Commons.*

Staged Crime Scenes

Not all crime scenes are "real." Although they are an extreme rarity (one study estimates less than 1%; Gerbeth, 2010), there are numerous reasons why a person or a criminal would stage a crime scene. The biggest challenge for the CSI is recognizing that a scene has, in fact, been staged; sometimes, as with arson, the staging is there to cover up the actual crime, such as murder, or misguide the police, as with insurance fraud. Staging is often caught in one of two ways: detection of a gap in logic or events or a vague perception that something is amiss. The former is easier to prove outright, the latter is more difficult until additional evidence is attained or examined. The best bet is to follow leads, gathering objective evidence until the fraud can be proven. In circumstances like this, a systematic approach to crime scenes truly serves the CSI to providing a solid basis for their claims. Some indications of staging include:

- No sign of forced entry or the entry is forced beyond what would be required to gain access.
- Only one specific item was stolen.
- No search for any valuables is apparent in a burglary or no items have been stolen.
- The ransacking is excessive and destructive or too careful of specific items (some may have been set aside to protect them).
- The victim is posed to suggest/cover up a sexual assault.
- Survivor of an attack has minor wounds only on the side of the body opposite their own handedness (self-inflicted).
- Wounds are consistent with being self-inflicted.

The entry or exit is the most common area to be staged, trying to draw attention to the false criminal act. Attendant evidence, such as fibers, blood, fingerprints, or shoeprints, should be present (see the discussion on the

Exchange Principle in Chapter 2.1). Likewise, if a deceased body has been moved after it has sat, rigor or livor mortis may not match the body's current position, indicating that the body was moved.

Interestingly, regardless of whether a crime was *actually* committed, legal concepts involving the usefulness of evidence in court (such as *Brady* issues or admissibility challenges) still apply to the recovery of what is considered at the time to be evidence.

Conclusion

Defining the crime scene is a key stage in an investigation. Because crime scenes can occur anywhere, be of any size, and include any number of natural or manufactured items, defining one may seem difficult. It is important to remember that each scene is different but each has similarities depending on the type of crime, including staged ones.

References and Bibliography

Borzycki, M., 2003. Bank Robbery in Australia. Australian Institute of Criminology, Canberra.

Gerbeth, V., 2010. Crime scene staging: An exploratory study of the frequency and characteristics of sexual posing in homicides. Invest. Sci. J. 2 (2), http://www.investigativesciencesjournal.org/article/view/6236.

Goodchild, M.F., 2010. Twenty years of progress: GIScience in 2010. J. Spat. Inform. Sci. 1: 3–20.

Hillier, B., Hanson, J., 2003. The Social Logic of Space. Cambridge University Press, Cambridge, UK.

Crime Scene Intelligence: Connecting People, Places, and Things

Crime is terribly revealing. Try and vary your methods as you will, your tastes, your habits, your attitude of mind, and your soul is revealed by your actions.

Agatha Christie, The ABC Murders

The word "intelligence" refers to the ability to solve problems, whether it is a person or an agency doing the solving. This intelligence can occur at various levels:

- **Tactical**: supports the investigation of a particular case or suspect; a bank in a particular location that was robbed on a specific day, for example.
- **Operational**: supports the management of resources to solve a group of related problems; a string of bank robberies that all share similar patterns of execution, for example.
- **Strategic**: supports broad approaches to improving policies and strategies; an agency may, for example, allocate funds to train personnel to better process documents—like bank robbery notes—for fingerprints.

Key Terms
Intelligence
HUMINT
SIGINT
GEOINT
OSINT
MASINT
The intelligence cycle
Transfer
Persistence
Classification
Common source
Individualization
Known items
Questioned items

The intelligence community (or the IC, as it's called), relies on a variety of sources to feed their analyses at these three levels:

- People (human intelligence or HUMINT)
- Electronic transmissions (signals intelligence or SIGINT)
- Geographic and geologic (GEOINT)
- Public or open sources (open-source intelligence or OSINT)
- Measurements and signatures (MASINT)

Properly, forensic evidence from a crime scene would be considered MASINT but it poses a puzzle as it combines aspects of all the above areas and may deserve its own subcategory (FORINT, perhaps). The intelligence cycle (as it's called) consists of five steps:

1. **Planning and direction**: determining the needs of the consumer and prioritization of resources.
2. **Collection**: gathering raw data from various sources.
3. **Processing**: converting the collected information into a usable format.
4. **Analysis and production**: analyzing the processed information and turning it into finished intelligence; resolving data conflicts; and producing reports, evaluations, reliability statements, and other analytic services—hence the use of the term *production*.
5. **Dissemination**: distributing intelligence reports to consumers.

As can be seen, intelligence work and crime scene processing have much in common. The crime scene cannot be processed without a plan on how to approach the scene and what is potentially important as evidence. The evidence is collected and then processed to make it useful for later analysis; sometimes the processing and even the analysis can occur at the scene. Reports are generated and then distributed to police, scientists, and attorneys. Crime scenes provide information (not just evidence), which can be applied to improve an investigation's accuracy, focus, and chances for success. Thus, the majority of the time, crime scene intelligence occurs on the tactical level. The information provided helps the investigators, scientists, and others involved in the case to make better decisions and use their resources more effectively;

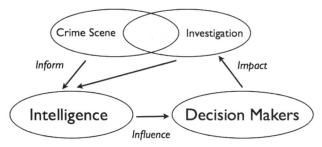

FIGURE 2.1.1 A model of how crime scene information generates intelligence, which assists those working the case to make better decisions. The crime scene has specific information based on physical evidence that can help focus the case in ways other sources cannot. *Adapted from Ratcliffe, 2009, page 9.*

for example, if a suspect is eliminated by a forensic exam, the police no longer need to spend time and money pursuing that person (Figure 2.1.1). The decisions that affect the investigation may come from the detective or officers involved, their superiors, or whoever is informed by the intelligence and has authority over the people involved (operational level).

The idea of using physical evidence to assist intelligence and criminal investigations is not new but it has yet to be gathered together as a codified field of thought and practice. This chapter will provide an outline for the use of crime scene information and evidence to aid investigations by linking (or unlinking) people, places, and things.

Connections through Contact: Transfer and Persistence

One of the fundamental principles in forensic science is the Exchange Principle. The concept was explained by Edmund Locard, a French forensic scientist in the early part of the 20th century. Locard recognized that when two things come into contact, they exchange information, even if the traces are not identifiable or are too small to be found (Locard, 1930). The results of such a transfer are the physical remnants of that transaction; this has been called proxy data, because the remnants are a "stand in" for the actual transfer. The interactions of people, places, and things at crime scenes result in a dizzying series of networks of transfers, cross-transfers, and subsequent transfers. Regardless of the kind of evidence, it is the *transfer* that is the mechanism of revealing the relationships between those involved in a criminal activity. The evidence itself relates more to the specificity and resolution of the statements that can be made: Everyone has extraneous fibers on their clothing, for example, but how many have fibers that are analytically indistinguishable from those that make up the victim's sweater? It is safe to say that essentially *all evidence is transfer evidence* and the form of evidence relates to *what can be said about the transfer*. Table 2.1.1 lists some examples of evidence types and their transfers.

Many conditions affect what kinds of evidence are transferred and how much of each is moved and retained. These conditions include:

- The pressure applied during contact
- The number of contacts (many contacts between two objects should result in more transferred material than one contact)
- How easily the item transfers material (liquid blood transfers more readily than does dried blood, for example)
- The form of the evidence (solid/particulate, liquid, or gas/aerosol)
- How much of the item is involved in the contact (a square centimeter should transfer less than a square meter of the same material)

When evidence is transferred from a source to a location with no intermediaries, that is, it goes from Source A to Location B, it is said to have

TABLE 2.1.1 Examples of Transfer Evidence

Item	Transferred *From* (Source)	Transferred *To* (Target/Location)
Drugs	Dealer	Buyer's pocket or car
Blood stains	Victim's body	Bedroom wall
Alcohol	Glass	Drunk driver's blood stream
Semen	Assailant	Victim
Ink	Writer's pen	Stolen check
Handwriting	Writer's hand/brain	Falsified document
Fibers	Kidnapper's car	Victim's jacket
Paint chips/smear	Vehicle	Hit-and-run victim
Bullet	Shooter's gun	Victim's body
Striations	Barrel of shooter's gun	Discharged bullet
Imperfections	Barrel-cutting tool	Shooter's gun's barrel

All evidence is transfer evidence in that it has a source and moves or is moved from that source to a target/location. Different kinds of evidence have different levels to their specificity; from the fundamental (striations on the barrel-cutting tool) to the specific (the bullet in the victim's body identified by the striations).

undergone direct transfer. Indirect transfer involves one or more intermediate objects—the evidence transfers from Source A to Intermediate B to Location C. Indirect transfer can become complicated and poses potential limits on interpretation. For example, consider Person A, who owns a dog and, before he goes to work each day, pets and scratches the dog. At work, he sits in his desk chair and does his work. Person A has experienced a *direct transfer* of his dog's hairs from the dog to his clothes. The chair, however, has received an *indirect transfer* of the dog's hairs—the dog certainly has never sat in the office desk chair. After returning from getting a cup of coffee, he finds a colleague, Person B, sitting in his desk chair waiting to tell him some news. Person B, after sitting in the chair, has also experienced an indirect transfer of anything on the chair, except for any fibers originating from the chair's upholstery, which would be a direct transfer (the chair being the source of those fibers). The interpretation of that situation could be difficult—how would the dog hairs on the colleague's clothing be interpreted without the knowledge that Person B sat in the chair?

Indirect transfers can be complicated and potentially misleading. It may be more accurate to speak of direct and indirect *sources*, referring to whether the originating source of the evidence is the transferring item, but the "transfer"

The Five-Second Rule

If a piece of food is dropped on the floor, how long can it sit there and still be edible by the rules of safety or society? The prevailing popular joke is five seconds, leading to "The Five-Second Rule." Scientists, however, took this to heart and decided to test it. Dawson and coworkers (2007) found that bacteria (*Salmonella*) survived on wood, tiles, and carpet after 28 days. After exposing the surfaces to the bacteria for 8 hours, the researchers found that bread and bologna were contaminated in under five seconds; after a minute, the contamination increased significantly (longer contact results in more transfer).

What does this have to do with forensic science? The Five-Second Rule is a popular example of the Locard Exchange Principle, that information is transferred when two things come into contact. The rule also shows how the underpinnings of forensic science exist throughout other sciences. When critics claim that forensic science is not a "real" science or is only an "applied" science, think of The Five-Second Rule or some of the other examples offered in this textbook.

Sources: "The Five-Second Rule" at Wikipedia, www.wikipedia.com; Dawson, P., Han, I., Cox, M., Black, C., and Simmons, L., 2007. Residence time and food contact time effects on transfer of *Salmonella Typhimurium* from tile, wood and carpet: Testing the five-second rule. *Journal of Applied Microbiology*, 102: 945–953.

terminology has become fixed in the literature. Very rarely can the difference between secondary (one intermediary) and tertiary (two intermediaries) transfer be distinguished, let alone the difference between direct and indirect transfer.

The second part of the transfer process is persistence. Once the evidence transfers, it will remain, or persist, in that location until it further transfers (and, potentially, is lost), degrades until it is unusable or unrecognizable, or is collected as evidence. How long evidence persists depends on:

- What the evidence is (such as fibers, blood, toolmarks, chemicals)
- The location of the evidence (on the surface, in a pocket, under water)
- The environment around the evidence (dry, cold, wet, hot, moving)
- Time from transfer to collection (seconds, minutes, days, years, decades)
- "Activity" of or around the evidence location (a tire on a moving car versus a deceased individual)

Some evidence is more temporary than others, in that it is very fragile to these conditions. Fragile or temporary evidence, like trace materials such as hairs or fibers, should be collected first; other types of evidence, like dried blood stains, will persist far longer and can be collected at the end of the processing. The delicacy of the evidence should drive the order of evidence processing and collection at the crime scene. This planned collection order, however, may change under emergency circumstances, like sudden weather, fire, or other calamitous situations.

Classification and Resolution

All things are considered to be unique in space and time and no two objects are absolutely identical (if for no other reason than there are *two* of them). Take, for example, a mass-produced product like a polo shirt. A manufacturer may produce thousands of shirts of a particular type each year. Because consumers demand consistency of products and their performance, the manufacturer's goal is to produce shirts that all look and perform the same. In forensic work, this consistency serves two purposes:

- First, the consistency *between* similarly manufactured objects makes it easy to separate one item from another (this red polo shirt is different from this white one).
- Second, the consistency *within* objects made by the same manufacturer makes it difficult to distinguish items with many of the same characteristics (two red polo shirts).

Think about two white polo shirts that come off of the same production line one after the other—other than labeling them "#1" and "#2," it could be very difficult to separate them once they were placed together. Now consider if the two shirts are exactly the same except for color: one is white and one is red. Although they can be easily distinguished (the red one; the white one), can it be said they are in same category? Compared with a blue dress shirt, the two polo shirts would have more in common with each other than with the dress shirt. All the shirts, however, are more alike than any of them are compared to, say, a shoe.

A similar line of thinking applies to biological items; the production facility, however, is nature and not a factory. An organism is the combination of its genotype (the genetic material that is encoded in its DNA) and its phenotype (the expression of its genetic potential in a given environment). In some ways, biological specimens are far more specific than manufactured ones, identifying a suspect or a missing person by their DNA profile, for example. In other ways, however, some forms of biological information are more like manufactured items, at least as far as forensic methods go: the wood from one oak tree will look more similar to another oak tree than it would to a maple, for example.

In forensic examinations, the word "identification" is used to describe the result of the examination of the chemical and physical properties of an object; the results of the examination categorize the object as a member of a group. What the object is made of—its color, mass, and/or volume—and many other traits go into identifying it as being a particular thing. For example, examining a white powder, performing one or two analyses, and concluding it is cocaine is identification. Determining that a small colored chip is automotive paint is identification. Looking at debris from a crime scene and deciding it contains hairs from a black Labrador Retriever is identification (of those hairs). All of the characteristics used to identify an object help to refine that object's identity and its membership in various groups.

The aforementioned crime scene debris has fibrous objects in it and that restricts what they could be, most likely hairs or fibers rather than bullets, to use an absurd example. The microscopic characteristics indicate that some of the fibrous objects are hairs, that they are from a dog, and the hairs are most like those from a specific breed of dog. This description places the hairs into a group of objects with similar characteristics, called a *class*. All black Labrador Retriever hairs would fall into a class; these belong to a larger class of items called *dog hairs*. Further, all dog hairs can be included in the class of *nonhuman hairs* and, ultimately, into a more inclusive class called *hairs*. Going in the other direction, as the process of identification of evidence becomes more specific it permits the analyst to classify the evidence into successively smaller classes of objects. Class is a scalable definition. Little else beyond the fact that they are dog hairs may be needed in an analysis if the investigators are looking for human hairs or textile fibers or whatever. Analyzing the dog hairs beyond this point would be a waste of time and effort; *relevancy* is central to forensic investigations.

The same set of items can be classified differently, depending on what they are and what questions are being asked about them. Sharing a class identity may indicate two objects come from a common source. Because forensic science reveals and describes the relationships between people, places, and things involved in criminal activities, this commonality of relationship may be critical to a successful investigation. Commonality can show interactions, limitations in points of origin, and increased significance of relationships. What is meant by a "common source" depends on the material in question, the mode of production, and the specificity of the examinations used to classify the object. For example, take an automotive paint chip: What's the common source for this? Options include:

- The manufacturer (to distinguish it from other similar paints)
- The factory (to determine where it was made)
- The batch or lot of production (to distinguish it from other batches at the same factory)
- All the vehicles painted with that color paint
- The vehicle painted with that color paint involved in the crime in question

All of these options, and they are not exhaustive, could be the goal in an investigation of determining whether two objects had a common source. Paint is a coating and is considered as a "whole" and not as individual units. Consider another example, this time of shoes. Because shoes come in pairs, finding one at a crime scene and another in the suspect's apartment could be considered useful to the investigation. The forensic examinations would look for characteristics to determine if the two shoes were owned by the same person (the common source, in this case). If the question centered on identifying the production source of the shoes, then the factory would be the common source.

Another example is fibers found on a body left in a ditch that are determined to be from an automobile. A suspect is developed and fibers from his car are found to be analytically indistinguishable in all tested traits from the crime scene fibers. Is the suspect's car the common source? For investigative and legal purposes, the car should be considered as such. But certainly it is not the only car with that carpeting—other models from that car manufacturer or even other car manufacturers may have used that carpeting, and the carpeting may not be the only product with those fibers. But given the context of the case, it may be reasonable to conclude that the most logical source for the fibers is the suspect's car. If the fibers were found on the body but no suspect was developed, part of the investigation may be to determine who made the fibers and track what products those fibers went into in an effort to find someone who owns that product. In that instance, the common source could be the fiber manufacturer, the carpet manufacturer, or the potential suspect's car, depending on what question is being asked.

This section may seem to belabor the point of common source but it is central to any investigation and especially to one involving forensic evidence. Establishing connections between people, places, and things involved in crimes, like playing the game of "six degrees of separation," is what forensic science does (see the following sidebar).

Six Degrees of Separation (Plus or Minus)

Everybody has encountered that unexpected connection between people (a "friend of a friend"). The popular way of describing this is "six degrees of separation." But what does that mean? The phrase, popularized by a play written by John Guare and a subsequent movie by that title, suggests that each person on Earth is only six steps or people away from anyone else on the planet on average. The idea was originally authored by a Hungarian, Frigyes Karinthy, who wrote of the notion in a work of fiction (*Everything Is Different*). The idea was passed around between colleagues and academics until the concept was approached systematically by several researchers, including de Sola Pool, Koche, and Milgram.

One paper by de Sola Pool and Koche laid the foundation for social networks in mathematical terms and included the measurement of the degree of connectedness. Milgram's research involved sending letters to individuals around the United States asking them if they knew one or more target people listed in a letter. The recipient was asked if he knew the target person; if so, the letter was to be sent directly to that person and, if not, the letter was to be sent to someone who the initial recipient thought might know the target person. Milgram calculated the connectedness and found that the average path length (the technical term for a measure of connectedness) was 5.5 or, rounding, 6. Milgram never used the phrase "six degrees of separation." Other research has found varying levels of connectedness, from about 3.5 to 12, depending on the mode of interaction.

In forensic science, this network analysis could apply to the various hypotheses offered for what happened at the crime scene. The prosecutor is, in essence, saying that there is a path length of 1 between the victim and the suspect relating to the crime; that is, they had contact. The defense attorney, on the other hand, typically tries to demonstrate that the path length is greater than some number larger than 6, indicating that the evidence that might link them is "random" and occurred by chance; alternatively, he may concede that the path length is less than 6 but meaningless to the crime (the interaction is either consensual and expected, or confounding, and is being mistaken for the real criminal interaction). With the search for ways to explain and interpret forensic science results to the public and stakeholders, network analysis may be a rich topic to explore.

Sources: de Sola Pool, I. and Kochen, M.,1978–1979. Contacts and influence. *Social Networks* 1(1): 5–51; Newman, M., Albert-László, B., and Watts, D.J., 2006. *The Structure and Dynamics of Networks.* Princeton University Press, Princeton, NJ; and Travers, J. and Milgram, S., 1969. An experimental study of the small world problem. *Sociometry*, 32(4): 425–443.

Individualization of Evidence

If an object can be classified into a group with only one member (itself), it is said to have been individualized. An individualized object has been associated with one, and only one, source—it is unique. The traits that allow for individualization depend, in large part but not exclusively, on the raw materials, manufacturing methods, and history of use. To that extent, individualization is the logical extension of classification. The concept of individualization rests on two assumptions:

1. All things are unique in space and time.
2. The properties by which a thing is classified are constant over time.

These two assumptions come with baggage, however. The assumption of uniqueness of space is an inherently nonprovable situation. The population size of "all things that might be evidence" is simply too large to account for; think of all the fingerprints on all of the surfaces all over the world. Therefore, forensic science is relegated to making interpretive statements based on *statistical* methods because it deals with so many uncertainties. Forensic science deals with the ultimate uncertainties in the real world of criminal activities with varying physical objects. The gap between the controlled laboratory and the real world is central to forensic science's fundamentals—uncertainty is everywhere. Even in DNA analysis, where each person's genetic material—except for identical twins—is known to be unique, statistics are used. Statistics are, in fact, what give forensic DNA analysis its power.

Relationships and Context

The relationships between the people, places, and things involved in crimes are critical to deciding what to examine and how to interpret the results; these relationships also feed the intelligence work of the current investigation and related ones. For example, if a sexual assault occurs and the perpetrator and victim are strangers, evidence of contact will be more relevant than if the two knew each other or, even more so, were sexual partners. Strangers, by definition, have not met and, therefore, would have not transferred evidence to each other prior to the crime. Casual cohabiting people have many opportunities to transfer certain types of evidence (head hairs and carpet fibers from the living room, for example) but not others (pubic hairs, semen, or vaginal secretions). Spouses or sexual partners, having the most intimate relationships, would share a good deal more materials. The interaction of these evidence environments is shown in Figure 2.1.2.

Stranger-on-stranger crimes beg the question of coincidental associations, that is, two things that previously have never been in contact with each other have items on them that are analytically indistinguishable at a certain class level. Attorneys in cross-examination may ask, "Yes, but couldn't [insert evidence type here] really have come from *anywhere*? Aren't [generic class-level evidence] very *common*?" It has been proven for a wide variety of evidence that coincidental matches are extremely rare. The variety of mass-produced goods, consumer choices, economic factors, and other product traits create a nearly infinite combination of comparable characteristics for the items involved in any one situation. Some kinds of evidence, however, are either quite common, such as white cotton fibers, or have few distinguishing characteristics, such as indigo-dyed cotton from denim fabric. "Common," however, is a word to be used with caution, and even then only after a thorough knowledge of how that material is produced, either naturally or artificially, and how it varies. Even materials that are thought to be "common" can have a high variance (Figure 2.1.3).

Victim and **Criminal** only interact at a **Crime Scene** unfamiliar to both
Ex. Sexual assault in an alley

Victim and **Criminal** interact at a **Crime Scene** familiar to both
Ex. Spouse kills cohabitating spouse

V
C
S

Victim and **Criminal** interact at a **Crime Scene** familiar only to the **Criminal**
*Ex. Kidnapping and assault in **Criminal's** house*

Victim and **Criminal** interact at a **Crime Scene** familiar only to the **Victim**
Ex. Home invasion

FIGURE 2.1.2 The relationships and context between the subject, the victim, and the crime scene dictate what evidence will be of the most use in establishing connections between them.

FIGURE 2.1.3 Forensic scientists need to learn the details about the materials they study and analyze as evidence—even something perceived to be very common, like sand, can have a wide variation. Top to bottom: Rodeo Beach, Marin County, CA; Agate Beach, OR; Daytona Beach, FL; Bermuda; Santorini, Greece; Ayers Rock (Uluru), Australia; Sahara Desert, Mauritania; Old Course Beach, St. Andrews, Scotland. *Source: Holman, R., 2009. Many worlds in tiny grains.* Science *323: 1291.*

It is important to establish the context of the crime and those involved early in the investigation. This sets the stage for what evidence is significant, what methods may be most effective for collection or analysis, and what may be safely ignored. Using context for direction prevents the indiscriminate collection of items that clog the workflow of the forensic science laboratory. Every item collected must be transferred to the laboratory and cataloged—at a minimum—and this takes people and time. Evidence collection based on intelligent decision making, instead of fear of missing something, produces a better result in the laboratory and the courts.

Known and Questioned Items

In a hit-and-run incident, a motorist strikes a pedestrian with his car and then flees the scene in the vehicle. When the pedestrian's clothing is examined, small flakes and smears of paint are found embedded in the fabric. When the automobile is impounded and examined, fibers are found embedded in an area that clearly has been damaged recently. How should this evidence be classified? The paint on the victim's coat is questioned evidence because the *original* source of the paint is not known; likewise, the fibers found on the damaged area of the car are also questioned items. The co-location of the fibers and damaged area and the wounds/damage and paint smears are indicative of recent contact. When the paint on the clothing is analyzed, it will be compared to paint from the car; this is known evidence because it is known where the sample originated. When the fibers on the car are examined, they will be compared to fibers taken from the clothing, which makes them known items as well. Thus, the coat *and* the car are sources of *both* kinds of items, which allows for their reassociation, but it is their *context* that makes them questioned or known. It is important to keep these types of relationships clearly in mind when processing crime scenes.

Conclusion

The work of the intelligence community and CSIs is very similar in some ways and very different in others. It is of primary importance for a CSI to have a plan on how to approach the scene, select what is and is not important as evidence, and prioritize resources to efficiently take on the task at hand. But crime scenes provide information as well as evidence and this information can be applied to improve an investigation's accuracy, focus, and possibility for success.

CSIs must think beyond the tactical, task-oriented needs of the current case. The information developed at *this* scene helps others involved in the case to make better decisions now and at *future* scenes. Operational information like this improves all of an agency's investigations and uses their resources more effectively. Forensic intelligence is only now becoming a routine approach for police agencies worldwide but, in many ways, it is the future of forensic science and policing.

References and Bibliography

Houck, M.M., Rockwell, L.R., in press. Forensic Intelligence: From CIA to CSI. John Wiley and Sons, New York.

Houck, M.M., Siegel, J.A., 2010. Fundamentals of Forensic Science. Academic Press, San Diego.

Houck, M.M., Siegel, J.A., 2010. Fundamentals of Forensic Science, Second Ed. Elsevier, Amsterdam.

Locard, E., 1930. The Analysis of Dust Traces. Am. J. Police Sci. 1 (3): 279–298.

Locard, E., 1930. The Analysis of Dust Traces (Second Part). Am. J. Police Sci. 1 (4): 401–418.

Locard, E., 1930. The Analysis of Dust Traces (Conclusion). Am. J. Police Sci. 1 (5): 496–514.

Ratcliffe, J.H. (Ed.), 2009. Strategic Thinking in Criminal Intelligence. The Federation Press, New South Wales, Australia.

Ratcliffe, J.H., 2008. Intelligence-Led Policing. Willan Publishing, Portland, OR.

Ribaux, O., Girod, A., Walsh, S., Margot, P., Mizrahi, S., Clivaz, V., 2003. Forensic intelligence and crime analysis. Law, Probab. Risk 2 (1): 47–60.

Ribaux, O., Margot, P., 2003. Case based reasoning in criminal intelligence using forensic case data. Sci Justice 43 (3): 135–143.

Ribaux, O., Walsh, S., Margot, P., 2006. The contribution of forensic science to crime analysis and investigation: Forensic intelligence. Forensic Sci. Int. 156 (2–3): 171–181.

Ribaux, O., Baylon, A., Roux, O., Delemont, O., Lock, E., Zingg, C., et al., 2010. Intelligence-led crime scene processing. Part I: Forensic intelligence. Forensic Sci. Int. 195: 10–16.

Ribaux, O., Baylon, A., Roux, O., Delemont, O., Lock, E., Zingg, C., et al., 2010. Intelligence-led crime scene processing. Part II: Intelligence and crime scene examination. Forensic Sci. Int. 199: 63–71.

Personnel and Procedures

Personnel

It is unlikely at the crime scene of a quadruple homicide to have a single CSI arrive and take charge; document the scene in notes, sketches, and photographs; recognize, preserve, and collect all the evidence; and subsequently present his or her findings in court. In today's complex forensic world, even Sherlock Holmes would have to utilize a team-based approach to accomplish the task of capturing the maximum amount of information at the crime scene.

Although the team concept is advocated, well-trained CSIs with their scientific approach will be the centerpiece of a successful crime scene investigation. What makes CSIs so special? To be even considered as a possible employee of a modern forensic service provider, a CSI typically must have a minimum of a four-year degree in science; many have advanced degrees and even internships with forensic agencies. With the improvements in forensic science

Key Terms

Crime scene investigator (CSI)
Post-traumatic stress
Contamination
High-performance workplace organizations

education in the last few years (such as the Forensic Science Education Programs Accreditation Commission, FEPAC), recent forensic graduates may go directly into a job working crime scenes entirely in the field.

To become a CSI, a new employee will need time, experience, and training. The training will be a mixture of in-house and external training. The latter is vital to make sure the employees are current in the latest techniques, understand the trends in the profession, and have an outside check against traditional but unsupportable methods. The training needed to become a CSI is varied, encompassing instruction in areas including firearms and ammunition recognition, gunshot residue, toolmarks, trajectories, bloodstain pattern analysis, latent blood visualization, DNA collection, clothing damage assessment, drug recognition, hairs, fibers, paint, glass, plastics, metals, shoeprints, tire tracks, latent print development, crime scene reconstruction, and report writing. The training has to be continuous, as the field of forensic science, and, consequently, the science of crime scenes, changes constantly.

Forensic Scientist Focus

In agencies where laboratory personnel share crime scene responsibilities, it is rare that a forensic scientist becomes a CSI immediately upon being hired; they usually spend three to four years in the laboratory working in one of the core forensic disciplines, such as microanalysis (trace evidence analysis), DNA, firearms, or chemical (drug) analysis. In that time, they learn about, and must master, the topics of evidence transfer, chain of custody, evidence preservation, visualizing latent material, instrumentation, microscopy, how to follow protocols (and what happens if you don't!), and testifying in court. Not only must they become proficient in these topics, they must channel their knowledge and bring it to bear on the analysis of unknown material. Forensic scientists, after being established as an expert in their core discipline, may be considered as a potential CSI. It is typical that they attend crime scenes as an apprentice initially; they contribute immediately in cases that concern their core discipline but it is a rare crime scene that is confined to, say, DNA only.

When forensic scientists have finally achieved the status of CSI, can they relax? No, they have two areas where they are expected to do casework. They might attend crime scenes on Monday and analyze a rush paint case in the crime laboratory on Tuesday, then drive 150 miles to go to court on Wednesday and spend 18 hours at a crime scene on Thursday. They need to get their paint case and crime reports written on Friday but their supervisor tells them overtime has been canceled because of budget cuts, and that they will have to come back on Monday, when, even if they didn't go on any other crime scenes on the weekend, they are still playing catch-up when they return. Sound hectic? It is. Toss in a major incident over that weekend and the personal, scientific, and administrative pressures all come to a head.

Project Management in the Laboratory

Any activity that has a stated goal and defined start and end times can be considered a project; the term has a broader meaning than a child's "science project" for a class. A *project*, in the field of project management, is any temporary set of activities intended to achieve a stated (usually beneficial) goal within a set timeframe and under resource constraints (money, personnel, space, etc.); therefore, a crime scene, a case, or an investigation could all be thought of as projects. Managing a project is not like managing a factory line or a grocery store, for example, where the overall work is ongoing, repetitive, and permanent.

What makes project management a challenge is achieving the goal within the limitations that exist, usually defined in terms of *scope, time*, and *cost*. This is referred to as the *project management triangle* (see Figure 3.0.1). For example, three forensic personnel may arrive at a scene that is assessed to require eight professionals and no backups or additional people are available. How can the constraint of personnel and time be adjusted so that the scene can still be processed effectively? Or consider that time is the limiting factor (say, because of impending weather): How should the scene be parsed to assign people to those parts most in danger and process them before it rains? Changing one side of the triangle affects the other two sides. Quality could be considered an overarching fourth constraint, as compromising any of the other limitations could affect quality.

CSIs and other forensic professionals benefit from learning about project management; books, websites, and courses—some of which lead to certification—are all available on this topic.

FIGURE 3.0.1 The project management triangle.

Sources: Campbell, C. 2006. *The One-Page Project Manager: Communicate and Manage Any Project with a Single Sheet of Paper*. John Wiley and Sons, New York; Lock, D. 2007. *Project Management*. Gower Publishing, Surrey, UK.

Forensic scientists who also respond to crime scenes often experience guilt because they feel that their laboratory work suffers at the expense of their crime scene work, and vice versa. They may also feel guilty that their laboratory coworkers have to cover for them too much while they are at crime scenes. The responder's laboratory superiors need to be aware of these feelings and work with all of their employees to stress the importance of a balanced casework/crime scene workload. This requires constant monitoring, adjustment, and compromises.

CSIs at a crime scene see the horrors one human being can inflict on another. These sights are extreme and not seen by the average person, certainly not repeatedly. Police departments, whose officers are also subjected to viewing the same horrors, have become more aware of potential problems associated with cumulative stress disorder. Officers may have a mandatory psychological debriefing after a particularly harrowing fatality; in follow-ups the officer may be asked if she has experienced flashbacks. CSIs are different: If they answer this question in the negative, they might want to bring up that in preparation for writing their crime scene report, they might have to review the images of the scene many times, mentally subjecting themselves to the horrors over and over. Not every forensic scientist is mentally equipped to become a CSI and, if they think they are not, they must be honest with themselves and report to mental professionals if they are experiencing any signs of cumulative stress disorder. It is because of such issues that crime responders should consider with their supervisors a finite time for their crime scene commitment; it has been shown that rotating assignments can moderate or even reduce stress. One such plan would be, two years as a trainee, two years as a primary responder, and one year to train your replacement. Operational necessity and availability of replacement personnel may prolong this time, but it should be seriously considered.

Post-Traumatic Stress

Traumatic events and their psychological and emotional aftermaths have been classified in psychiatry as post-traumatic stress disorder (PTSD) and acute stress disorder (ASD). Medicine and medical specialists who focus on occupational health and safety have focused upon observable injury and illness caused by single events; that is, harm done on the outside. However, "many health and welfare concerns with far-reaching effects within organizational environments may be psychological, social and complex in nature and have enduring effects over a considerable span of time." The attention paid to these potentially serious conditions is ongoing and is being refined by research, clinical studies, and a greater understanding of the human psyche to traumatic events.

Some researchers feel that, instead of focusing on the pathology of trauma, a better concept is that of resilience—the ability to withstand, process, and rebound from traumatic events. Resilience may be enhanced through validated selection and screening of employees and institutional support systems. The latter element may be key, providing that "degrees of support, connection and affirmation within the organizational context will contribute to recovery." Importantly, research indicates that "the emotional component of single-session interventions termed as psychological debriefing (PD) should be avoided, suggesting that in many situations practical and pragmatic support provided by an informed peer group is both necessary and sufficient for an intervention."

Each employee experiences trauma differently, based on their personal history, environment, nature of the event, and subsequent, cumulative events. Organizations should develop strategies to identify "at risk" employees, assess employees' level of stress, and reduce exposure through, for example, rotating assignments. Recognizing that no prediction can be completely accurate, early intervention or treatment is crucial.

Ongoing research into the human response to trauma and an individual's resilience continue, addressing questions such as:

- "Does resilience lie within the individual?
- Can it be sustained and developed through environmental supports?
- Do organizations have a responsibility to manage environments that serve to mitigate the cumulative effect of stressors?
- How do the roles of occupational health practitioners and physicians dovetail with organizational responsibilities under health and safety jurisdictions, and what is the evidence base for effective intervention?
- Where do individual organizations and workplaces lie on the continuum from preventive to reactive responses to the occurrence of trauma?"

As researchers and employers refine and expand their understanding and treatment of post-traumatic stress disorders, they "need to develop a strong understanding of the relationship between cumulative stress, resilience and the impact of traumatic events."

Source: Adamson, C. 2007. Post-traumatic stress disorder: Overview. *Occupational Medicine (London)* 57(6): 397–398.

CSIs who have gone to crime scenes for many years may not exhibit outward symptoms; mental fatigue, at the very least, may be present. Later, after some number of crime scene responses and accumulated stress, it may be time to consider, with the help of mental health professionals, a change of duties or perhaps careers. Police officers who work as detectives for many years can have similar feelings, and many opt to go back to driving a patrol vehicle; these situations are similar for firefighters and emergency medical technicians, who all face the stresses of dangerous and shocking situations. If either group decides to return to their first line of work, they will have benefitted greatly from their crime scene experiences. Their way of thinking about what happens "in the field" has changed forever. They are much better equipped to do their job.

Time and Money

At a perfect major crime scene, the resources of time, personnel, and money would be endless. Unfortunately in today's unstable economy, someone will ask, "Can we really afford to take so much time when everyone knows that time is money?" This shortsighted view is more common than one would suppose. Many small police departments face potential financial difficulties if major multiple homicides occur within their jurisdiction—who could have budgeted for these situations? It is a natural reaction of management to try to curtail overtime and limit supplies to try to make ends meet. Before the reader concerned with scientific truth decries such practices, this is usually born from the laudable motive of trying to prevent layoffs of trained personnel and preservation of public services. In the United States, until recently, cities with fiscal problems asked the state for help and sometimes even the federal government. Neither the state nor the federal government have much to spare for law enforcement, so departments are increasingly forming local agency task forces to try to share the financial burden. These task forces, however, are usually dedicated to high-profile crime, such as narcotics or gang activities, and few task forces are devoted to crime scene investigation.

There was a time when detectives collected everything at a crime scene and then tried to work it all out later: those days of "bagging and tagging" are long gone (if they ever really existed). Taking time to do the job correctly and intelligently will cost money initially; it will *save* money in the long run. Everyone associated with the investigating agency, elected or otherwise, must be on board with this concept. The importance of not rushing the crime scene must become part of the culture of the investigating agency. This change in culture will not occur overnight; culture is one of our slowest "technologies" to change. It will be a long process involving many meetings of the principals involved and hopefully successful investigations where crime scenes are approached scientifically with a view to optimizing the evidence. Unfortunately, the only time when culture change is rapid seems to be in crime scene investigations where the media perceives that collection of evidence or the scene was somehow mishandled (whether it really was or not). Committees of inquiry will be set up, the offending agency will have to reevaluate how they approach crime scenes, and administrative changes go into overdrive. Changes in this type of environment are often rushed, ill-thought-out, and lack vision. No one wants to see bungled investigations and it is important for forensic scientists to take a leadership role and educate the agencies they work with on the benefits of a scientific approach, one that is developed over time with validity and reflection.

Depending on the seriousness and/or the complexity of the crime scene(s), the numbers of CSIs, and their experience, knowledge, diversity, and degree of specialization can vary widely. At major crime scenes, in addition to the first officer on the scene you may have forensic scientists, a lead detective, a scene detective, and an evidence officer as well as specialists such as a medical examiner, an entomologist, an anthropologist, a forensic odontologist, trackers and cadaver dogs, and a prosecuting attorney.

Contamination

Having a large number of people at a crime scene greatly increases the probability that evidence will be inadvertently deposited at, and removed from, the crime scene. Indeed, according to Edmond Locard, "*toute action de l'homme, et a fortiori, l'action violente qu'est un crime, ne peut pas se dérouler sans laisser quelque marque,*" which translated means "any human action, and particularly if that violent action is a crime, cannot take place without leaving a trace." Hence, it is inevitable that such transfers take place even if someone— the criminal or an "official" visitor to the scene—does not mean for them to. So a key element of the crime scene is the management of team personnel and resources to minimize the loss of evidence. This begins with the basics:

- Limiting attendance at crime scenes to absolutely only the essential responders
- Making sure everyone wears protective clothing that is also designed to limit transfer of evidence, such as booties, head covers, vinyl gloves
- Using disposable evidence collection tools such as plastic forceps
- Using disposable pens and writing materials; thoroughly cleaning cameras and other documentation equipment between crime scenes.

Just wearing vinyl gloves is not enough. Lounsbury and Thompson (2006) state:

> Glove protection protocols to avoid latent print contamination is critical. Either a double glove should be worn or cotton gloves should be worn underneath the vinyl glove shell. The double glove method may be less comfortable because of the amount of heat it generates. Both the double glove method and the wearing of a cotton under-glove proved effective in keeping inadvertent latent prints by the crime scene personnel from contaminating the crime scene. Single glove wear, and in particular, vinyl examination glove wear, could significantly contaminate fingerprint evidence that is handled by crime scene processors at the scene.

Again, everyone at the crime scene must work constantly to promote an environment of minimizing contamination.

Logistics

Large numbers of personnel at a crime scene will create logistical problems involving transportation, food, water, sanitation, and adequate rest. It is also the 21st century with its attendant ever-present communication technology, so large numbers of people will attract the media, amateur and professional alike. The investigating agency must have an advance plan to cope with these contingencies. To return to the Sherlock Holmes theme, he was his own boss and did not feel the need to inform the authorities of his activities. He also did not have to deal with today's instant media. Informing the chain of command and the media of what is happening at the crime scene is essential, and with tact and diplomacy can be used to best advantage.

Building the Team

Consider the following definitions:

- *Team*: two or more people who are working together.
- *Ego*: your sense of your own value and importance; the part of the mind that is responsible for your sense of who you are.

Individuals need to sufficiently supress their egos to the team's ultimate goal of a successful prosecution of the perpetrator. However, the investigation of major crimes, at least for the foreseeable future, will be performed by humans, so hurt feelings, bruised egos, and perceived lack of respect will continue, if the personality component of a major crime scene team is not addressed.

The police, CSIs, forensic scientists, medical examiners, and the other specialists who attend crime scenes are all used to people asking for their opinions and giving them respect. However, as Clint Eastwood as Dirty Harry once said, "A man's got to know his limitations."[1] A lead detective with 20 years' experience is not going to want to hear the opinion of a rookie CSI on how to collect evidence. The medical examiner that has the jurisdiction over the body of the deceased may have to be convinced to release the shirt to the CSI, who in his capacity as a bloodstain pattern analyst does not wish the shirt to go into the body bag of the deceased, where the stains will be altered by other blood and body fluids. Egos, however, should be checked at the entrance to the scene so that the group can cooperate on achieving the necessary goals. Too much "ego" can quickly turn a smoothly running crime scene into a catastrophe of arguing, mistakes, and grudges.

In a team-oriented crime scene philosophy, each team member contributes to the success of investigation. Each has a specific role and may not be employed by the investigating agency, but you must work with the other team members

---

[1] *Magnum Force*, Warner Brothers Pictures, Malpaso Company, 1973.

to accomplish the overall objectives. Each member of a crime scene team, be it a forensic scientist, an evidence officer, or a medical examiner, is normally very detail oriented in his or her daily job, if he or she is to be personally successful. At crime scenes, while being detail oriented, these individuals must never lose sight of the bigger picture. Crime scene teams are high-performance work organizations, in modern business parlance, and their structure and performance needs to be considered in a new light (see the "High-Performance Workplace Organizations" sidebar).

High-Performance Workplace Organizations

The challenge for companies nowadays is to deliver quickly and flexibly new quality products and services, in order to be able to respond to greater and changing demands from clients. Standardization and specialization characterize traditional work organization; the work is divided into different segments, from preparation to support roles, in which workers specialize in order to maximize productivity. Specialization, control, and routine are suitable when a constant demand for standardized products applies. However, for a fast changing demand, this method does not seem to work as well, and may lead to coordination problems and rigidities. Thus, companies started to look for new forms of work organization.

A high-performance workplace focuses on increasing people's influence on the business as well as the impact of processes, methods, the physical environment, and the technology and tools that enhance their work. [The high-performance workplace organization] also implements a so-called holistic organizational approach, which means featuring flat hierarchical structures, job rotation, self-responsible teams, multitasking and a greater involvement of lower-level employees in decision-making. A high-performance workplace invests in its human resources and supports both their technical and innovation skills and their social skills; this promotes good interpersonal relationships in the workplace from which the company can also benefit. This type of organization is different from the [mechanistic, repetitive] work organization, which is characterized by task specialization, a pyramid hierarchical structure, and a centralization of responsibilities.

Source: European Foundation for the Improvement of Living and Working Conditions, 2007. *Teamwork and High Performance Work Organisation*. Dublin, Ireland (edited for clarity).

The investigator in charge has to define the team to be built and clearly communicate the expectations for the team, and individual expectations to each member, in a precise, clear manner. The investigator in charge occupies a pivotal role in a crime scene investigation both as a team builder and a deliverer of final results. He will be ultimately responsible if something goes wrong; sadly, he may receive little praise if everything goes right.

Conclusion

Having a well-educated, cohesive, organized crime scene team will go a long way toward having a successful investigation, yet all the skills and ability of the team will mean nothing if the scene is compromised at the beginning by the first officer on the scene. The actions of the first officer on the scene, in the moments after the crime has been discovered, will have long-lasting effects on the subsequent crime scene investigation.

References and Bibliography

Katzenbach, J., Smith, D., 2003. The Wisdom of Teams: Creating the High-Performance Organization. Harper-Collins, New York.

Locard, E., 1934. La Police et Les Methodes Scientifiques. Les Editions Rieder, Paris.

Lounsbury, D., Thompson, L.F., 2006. Concerns when using examination gloves at the crime scene. J. Forensic Ident. 56 (2): 179–185.

National Institute of Justice, 1999. Crime Scene Investigation: A Guide for Law Enforcement. U.S. Department of Justice, Office of Justice Programs, Washington, DC.

United Nations Office on Drugs and Crime, 2009. Crime Scene and Physical Evidence Awareness for Non-forensic Personnel. Laboratory and Scientific Section, United Nations Office on Drugs and Crime, United Nations, New York.

First Responder on the Scene

The first responder at the scene of a major crime is typically a fireman, a police officer, or an emergency medical technician (EMT). Although the same general principles outlined below apply to all three categories as well as to CSIs, this chapter concentrates on the actions that the first official on a scene should carry out.

For a successful crime scene investigation, it is essential that the scene be preserved in as close to the original state as possible. Of course, given the natural entropy we humans generate in any situation, the chance of a pristine crime scene for subsequent investigators is remote. A primary goal for investigators at a crime scene is to minimize the loss of useful information and evidence.

Key Term
First responder

Consider a police officer on patrol who receives a call from the dispatcher that a woman has called to say she has been shot in the abdomen by her boyfriend who has fled the apartment.

When you hear the address, you recognize it as an apartment complex that has had several recent violent incidents. As you turn on your siren and drive to the scene, many things rush through your mind. You are the closest responder to the scene and, with recent cutbacks, it may be a while before you receive backup from other officers. The boyfriend is presumably still at large and is probably armed and dangerous. Has he really left? Will he return? Will the shot woman still be alive? Are there any other family members or people in the apartment? All these questions and more rush through your mind. Your heart races, adrenaline flows; you force yourself to breathe deeply.

As you arrive at the apartment, two women run toward you screaming, "She's been shot, she's been shot!" as they point to an upstairs apartment. You push through a crowd of onlookers and up the stairs. The front door is open. As you carefully enter the apartment with weapon drawn, you shout "Police!" several times. You hear a cough and as you look through the doorway of the kitchen you see a young woman slouched on the floor wearing a blood-soaked nightdress. She is speaking into a cellphone; as she looks at you, she says, "There's an officer here now." You hear noise from the stairs below and several EMTs are on their way. A bedroom door opens and a 20-year-old man emerges. You raise your weapon and shout, "Police! Raise your hands now!" You see a towel in his hand. Tears roll down his face as he tells you that it is his sister who has been shot, and that he needs to help her. The injured woman screams that this is true. You tell the young man and the EMTs not to move. You go from room to room in the apartment. When you verify that it is safe, you motion the EMTs to come in. You calm the victim's brother and tell him his sister is in good hands. You lead him and the onlookers outside. Your heart rate slows and you momentarily relax.

Your mind races. Why did the EMTs enter the apartment when it wasn't secure? You are about to ask them what were they thinking when you remember the priority now is to try to limit access to only essential personnel. Are two EMTs enough or not enough? If others arrive, should you let them in? As your head clears, it is only then that you recall that one-hour lecture at the Police Academy 10 years ago, something about evidence and preserving the scene.

This example is not fanciful; it is what a police officer will encounter several, if not many, times in his or her career. Any police officer can be put into the position of being the first responding officer to a crime scene. In fact, almost any public servant who responds to emergencies, like police, firefighters, EMTs, and others, can technically be "first on the scene"—what if the EMTs in the preceding example had arrived before the officer? What then?

Initial Response/Receipt of Information[1]

Principle: One of the most important aspects of securing the crime scene is to preserve the scene with minimal contamination and disturbance of physical evidence. The initial response to an incident shall be expeditious and methodical. Upon arrival, the officer(s) shall assess the scene and treat the incident as a crime scene.

Policy: The initial responding officer(s) shall promptly, yet cautiously, approach and enter crime scenes, remaining observant of any persons, vehicles, events, potential evidence, and environmental conditions.

Procedure: The initial responding officer(s) should:

a. Note or log dispatch information (e.g., address/location, time, date, type of call, parties involved).
b. Be aware of any persons or vehicles leaving the crime scene.
c. Approach the scene cautiously, scan the entire area to thoroughly assess the scene, and note any possible secondary crime scenes.
d. Be aware of any persons and vehicles in the vicinity that may be related to the crime.
e. Make initial observations (look, listen, smell) to assess the scene and ensure officer safety before proceeding.
f. Remain alert and attentive. Assume the crime is ongoing until determined to be otherwise.
g. Treat the location as a crime scene until assessed and determined to be otherwise.

Summary: It is important for the initial responding officer(s) to be observant when approaching, entering, and exiting a crime scene.

Crime scenes are sensitive to initial conditions and small events at the start can have repercussions for months or years. How the first responder acts in the initial moments after arriving at the crime scene can set the tempo for the subsequent investigation. The most contagious disease known to humankind is panic. If the first responder panics and makes rash and hasty decisions, then this will affect everyone who enters that scene. Professionals may feed off these emotions, become anxious, and their work will suffer. Thankfully, most police officers are trained to react calmly in tense situations.

Competing Responsibilities

Approach the scene in a way that reduces risks of harm to themselves and others. As mentioned before, survey the scene for dangerous persons—not

---

[1] This and other sidebars in this chapter, except where noted, are from National Institute of Justice, 1999. *Crime Scene Investigation: A Guide for Law Enforcement*, U.S. Department of Justice, Office of Justice Programs, Washington, D.C.

just the possible perpetrator! The first responder should make sure that no immediate threat exists to themselves or to other responders. Check the surrounding area for sights, sounds, and smells that may present danger to personnel (for example, natural gas). If the scene poses specific threats to life and limb (such as a clandestine drug laboratory, chemical spills, explosive materials, or others), the responder should contact the appropriate personnel prior to entering the scene. Other personnel should be contacted for support ("backup") and further assistance.

The dual responsibilities of the first responding officer of rendering aid and securing the scene often compete. In the previous example, a dangerous suspect may have been loose in the area and an unknown young male was at the scene, who may or may not have been the suspect. Officer and public safety concerns obviously take first priority. An injured victim who needs immediate medical aid comes first, always. In this case, EMTs were on site. However, the officer always has to consider whether the scene is safe enough to allow EMTs access to the injured victim. Rendering aid to the victim is vital, but allowing a situation to occur where more victims may be created is worse.

Safety Procedures

Principle: The safety and physical well-being of officers and other individuals, in and around the crime scene, are the initial responding officer(s)' first priority.

Policy: The initial responding officer(s) arriving at the scene shall identify and control any dangerous situations or persons.

Procedure: The initial responding officer(s) should:

a. Ensure that there is no immediate threat to other responders—scan the area for sights, sounds, and smells that may present danger to personnel (e.g., hazardous materials such as gasoline, natural gas). If the situation involves a clandestine drug laboratory, biological weapons, or radiological or chemical threats, the appropriate personnel/agency should be contacted prior to entering the scene.
b. Approach the scene in a manner designed to reduce risk of harm to officer(s) while maximizing the safety of victims, witnesses, and others in the area.
c. Survey the scene for dangerous persons and control the situation.
d. Notify supervisory personnel and call for assistance/backup.

Summary: The control of physical threats will ensure the safety of officers and others present.

Most professionals in the role of first responder are certified first aid responders. Standard procedure is to check victims for vital signs; several of these methods will involve touching the victim to attempt to detect a pulse. These are competing priorities: render aid or prevent contamination (in this case, introducing fingerprints and DNA through touching the victim). This choice is easy: choose life. Remember, though, to document where the victim was touched and by whom; this documentation must be specific. The notation, "touched victim on left side of neck to check for carotid artery pulse," is far superior—and may be required—over the vague, "checked for vital signs."

If the victim is not deceased, perform first aid until he is stabilized, later making specific notes of the steps that were taken. If EMTs attempt resuscitation efforts on the victim, note what the body position and the condition of the clothing of the victim were before these efforts, if possible. If the victim is deceased, however, the procedures take a different track. Look for obvious signs of wounds. Do not attempt to turn the victim over or touch the deceased in any way. If the victim has any weapon in his hand or close by, photograph it from several angles. If the weapon is a firearm, do not attempt to render the gun safe at this time unless there is a danger that onlookers may enter the scene. The firearm will have to be rendered safe sooner rather than later, but it is better to make that decision with the help of trained personnel, who may be able to collect transient evidence from the weapon before it is removed from the scene.

Emergency Care

Principle: After controlling any dangerous situations or persons, the initial responding officer(s') next responsibility is to ensure that medical attention is provided to injured persons while minimizing contamination of the scene.

Policy: The initial responding officer(s) shall ensure that medical attention is provided with minimal contamination of the scene.

Procedure: The initial responding officer(s) should:

a. Assess the victim(s) for signs of life and medical needs and provide immediate medical attention.
b. Call for medical personnel.
c. Guide medical personnel to the victim to minimize contamination/alteration of the crime scene.
d. Point out potential physical evidence to medical personnel, instruct them to minimize contact with such evidence (e.g., ensure that medical personnel preserve all clothing and personal effects without cutting through bullet holes, knife tears), and document movement of persons or items by medical personnel.
e. Instruct medical personnel not to "clean up" the scene and to avoid removal or alteration of items originating from the scene.

f.   If medical personnel arrived first, obtain the name, unit, and telephone number of attending personnel, and the name and location of the medical facility where the victim is to be taken.

g.   If there is a chance the victim may die, attempt to obtain "dying declaration."

h.   Document any statements/comments made by victims, suspects, or witnesses at the scene.

If the victim or suspect is transported to a medical facility, send a law enforcement official with the victim or suspect to document any comments made and preserve evidence. (If no officers are available to accompany the victim/suspect, stay at the scene and request medical personnel to preserve evidence and document any comments made by the victim or suspect.)

Summary: Assisting, guiding, and instructing medical personnel during the care and removal of injured persons will diminish the risk of contamination and loss of evidence.

As a result of rendering aid and securing the scene, some physical evidence will be lost or altered in some way—it is inevitable. Accepting this fact is difficult for new crime scene investigators. With experience, this loss of evidence or alteration will lessen until it rarely happens. Documentation of what was altered will at least account for that evidence when investigators begin the work of crime reconstruction. There will be times, however, when the actions of the first responder on the scene change the crime scene dramatically: they may accidentally step in a pool of blood in a dimly lit house where a person has been stabbed, they may inadvertently remove or smear fingerprints when opening doors to secure the scene, they may knock something over as they move through the scene. As before, the officer must document what took place. Like all mistakes, inadvertent or not, the best that can be done is to remember and learn from them; as the saying goes, "Mistakes are okay, just don't repeat them." In the case of crime scenes, there is the responsibility to document any mistakes.

Timing is everything. In police dramas (and sometimes westerns), when characters come across a person who has been hanged, someone will always say, "Give me some help cutting him down." No one ever asks, "Why now?" A deceased person who has been hanged isn't going anywhere and all the evidence associated with the body is still in place. No matter how much it offends human sensibilities to have a person suspended above you on the end of a rope, it is better for the subsequent investigation to leave that person hanging until a thorough investigation of the body is performed *in situ*.

After the crime scene has settled down it is not only easy, but natural, to relax. Until now the first responder has been dealing with competing priorities of rendering aid and securing the scene. However, now there is only one priority: prevent the destruction of or the diminishment of the utility of evidence that may lead to the apprehension of the criminal or the solution of the crime.

Securing the Scene

Once the scene has been stabilized, it should be secured to prevent unauthorized people from entering the area and contaminating or adulterating it. This typically involves using some type of indicator, such as caution or crime scene tape, to indicate the limits of public access. The extent to which the scene is taped off will depend on the scene or scenes, their size and connectedness, and environmental conditions. If a person has been murdered in a house, it is not sufficient to merely stretch across the front and back doors. Remember that the suspect had to enter and leave the house and *then* continue his escape; therefore, consider extending the taped area to natural entrance and exit points, such as the front gate and the back alley. When a body is discovered outdoors, the area to be cordoned off may be large. Again, do not be constrained by the terrain and resist the temptation to extend the crime scene tape between trees or objects located conveniently nearby. The first responder should err on the side of taping off as large an area as possible. A good rule of thumb is to consider the distance from the scene that you think is appropriate to stretch the tape, then double that distance. It is always easier to constrict a scene's proportions than to expand them. Later, investigators, with more information, will reevaluate the area to be cordoned off.

Boundaries: Identify, Establish, Protect, and Secure

Principle: Defining and controlling boundaries provide a means for protecting and securing the crime scene(s). The number of crime scenes and their boundaries are determined by their location(s) and the type of crime. Boundaries shall be established beyond the initial scope of the crime scene(s) with the understanding that the boundaries can be reduced in size if necessary but cannot be as easily expanded.

Policy: The initial responding officer(s) at the scene shall conduct an initial assessment to establish and control the crime scene(s) and its boundaries.

Procedure: The initial responding officer(s) should:

a. Establish boundaries of the scene(s), starting at the focal point and extending outward to include:
   - Where the crime occurred
   - Potential points and paths of exit and entry of suspects and witnesses
   - Places where the victim/evidence may have been moved (be aware of trace and impression evidence while assessing the scene)

b. Set up physical barriers (e.g., ropes, cones, crime scene barrier, tape, available vehicles, personnel, other equipment) or use existing boundaries (e.g., doors, walls, gates).

c. Document the entry/exit of all people entering and leaving the scene, once boundaries have been established.

d. Control the flow of personnel and animals entering and leaving the scene to maintain integrity of the scene.

e. Effect measures to preserve/protect evidence that may be lost or compromised (e.g., protect from the elements (rain, snow, wind) and from footsteps, tire tracks, sprinklers).

f. Document the original location of the victim or objects that you observe being moved.

g. Consider search and seizure issues to determine the necessity of obtaining consent to search and/or obtaining a search warrant.

Note: Persons should not smoke, chew tobacco, use the telephone or bathroom, eat or drink, move any items including weapons (unless necessary for the safety and well-being of persons at the scene), adjust the thermostat or open windows or doors (maintain scene as found), touch anything unnecessarily (note and document any items moved), reposition moved items, litter, or spit within the established boundaries of the scene.

Summary: Establishing boundaries is a critical aspect in controlling the integrity of evidentiary material.

As the first responder at the scene is waiting for the lead investigator to arrive, he should remain vigilant. Anyone with only a passing familiarity of humans and our curious nature knows that taping off the crime scene is no guarantee that people, including some fellow professionals, may attempt to enter the crime scene. Perversely, it may tempt them more than if the tape were not there. The first responder must tactfully, but insistently, keep everyone, and that includes superior officers who should know better, from entering the scene. As Don Sachtleben, a former FBI Special Agent and explosives expert who worked nearly every major explosion scene of the last few decades, suggests, the "crime scene" is the area you can reliably control.

Secure and Control Persons at the Scene

Principle: Controlling, identifying, and removing persons at the crime scene and limiting the number of persons who enter the crime scene and the movement of such persons is an important function of the initial responding officer(s) in protecting the crime scene.

Policy: The initial responding officer(s) shall identify persons at the crime scene and control their movement.

Procedure: The initial responding officer(s) should:

a. Control all individuals at the scene—prevent individuals from altering/destroying physical evidence by restricting movement, location, and activity while ensuring and maintaining safety at the scene.
b. Identify all individuals at the scene, such as:
   - Suspects: Secure and separate.
   - Witnesses: Secure and separate.
   - Bystanders: Determine whether witness; if so treat as above, if not, remove from the scene.
   - Victims/family/friends: Control while showing compassion.
   - Medical and other assisting personnel.
c. Exclude unauthorized and nonessential personnel from the scene (e.g., law enforcement officials not working the case, politicians, media).

Summary: Controlling the movement of persons at the crime scene and limiting the number of persons who enter the crime scene is essential to maintaining scene integrity, safeguarding evidence, and minimizing contamination.

The first responder may be tempted to pick up the defibrillator pads, gauze, and latex gloves left by EMTs or to "tidy up" a bit before more personnel arrive. The first responder may also become curious and want to venture outside the crime scene to check on vehicles or to monitor the status of the witnesses. These temptations must be avoided. The first responder must provide security and also help to maintain the chain of custody of any items of evidence that will be collected later. These moments should be used as an opportunity to review notes and make additions as they come to mind.

Establish a clear route into and out of the scene for all personnel. Conduct a quick search of the scene to ensure no physical evidence will be disturbed and then delineate a path so that later responders know where to walk.

First Responder Training

Training for responding to crime scenes is critical because of the nature of the situations: They are stressful, hazardous, and easy to damage. They can occur anywhere, at any time, and can be of any size. A single fiber on a decedent could constitute "the scene." On the other extreme, the Vancouver, Canada, serial killer, Robert Pickton, was convicted of the murders of 6 women, charged in the deaths of 20 more women, and confessed to 49 murders. He disposed of the bodies at his 10-acre pig farm through various means; archaeological methods and excavation equipment were required to search the farm for human remains over the course of *two years*.

Because crime scenes are not predictive, it is imperative that *agencies budget for annual training for all crime scene personnel*. All too often, training budgets are the first cut for agencies to make, but this cheats their professional employees of the chance to improve their skills—the very skills that will keep their agency out of the newspaper headlines. What is that worth?

Preserving the Scene

After you have collected images of the scene you should begin documenting the condition of the scene as it was upon your arrival, and what has happened since. Begin a crime scene log of who enters the crime scene, and for what purpose. You should keep notes on the significant times involved in responding to the crime scene including time dispatched to scene, time arrived at scene, time EMTs were contacted, the arrival and departure times of the EMTs, time of announced death, etc. Make a note of what furniture the EMTs may have moved to gain access and remove the victim.

The officer will now start to assess the situation, taking pains to disturb things as little as possible. The mental notes he made earlier will now be recorded permanently. Transient evidence such as odors and open doors and windows should be recorded. As backup officers arrive, remember that they, like others, will bring trace evidence into and remove trace evidence from the scene, if they enter. It is better if these officers do not enter the scene; briefly inform them of the events. These officers should contact the people who may have entered or been at the scene. These individuals should be separated and detained, then written statements taken from each. In the scenario at the beginning of the chapter, one of the officers should go with the victim to the hospital, record any statements made en route (for example, "dying declarations"), and collect her clothing as evidence.

FIGURE 3.1.1 First responders from St. John Ambulance and local fire departments assist paramedics during an exercise near Thunder Bay, Ontario, Canada, in November 2008. *Source: Wikimedia Commons.*

Document Actions and Observations

Principle: All activities conducted and observations made at the crime scene must be documented as soon as possible after the event to preserve information.

Policy: Documentation must be maintained as a permanent record.

Procedure: The initial responding officer(s) should document:

a. Observations of the crime scene, including the location of persons and items within the crime scene and the appearance and condition of the scene upon arrival.
b. Conditions upon arrival (e.g., lights on/off; shades up/down, open/closed; doors or windows open/closed; smells; ice, liquids; movable furniture; weather; temperature; and personal items).
c. Personal information from witnesses, victims, suspects, and any statements or comments made.
d. Own actions and actions of others.

Summary: The initial responding officer(s) at the crime scene must produce clear, concise, documented information encompassing his or her observations and actions. This documentation is vital in providing information to substantiate investigative considerations.

Releasing the Scene

The first responder on the scene cannot "release the scene" (transfer authority and responsibility for it) until the lead investigator arrives. There is a tendency for the first responder to rush to get back to work, to deal with the backlog of work that has built up while responding to the crime scene. Too often, the only contact investigators have with the first responder on the scene is via a report hurriedly written by the officer two days after the incident. It is imperative that the first responder briefs the lead investigator face to face. As much as the evidence location will permit, the officer should do a walkthrough with the lead investigator. The officer must verbally relate all details about his actions that began the moment he arrived at the scene. Officers cannot assume that the witnesses interviewed at the scene will give exactly the same details to the investigator nor can they assume that what was obvious to them when they entered the scene will be readily apparent to later investigators. With today's technology, it is possible for first responders to give a copy of the images from their camera and a copy of their notes to the lead investigator before they leave the scene. Many police departments also issue body cameras to their officers; these cameras should not be overlooked as a potential source of vital crime scene information. If the first responder cannot give copies of images and notes to the investigator immediately, then he should make arrangements to do so as soon as possible.

Turn Over Control of the Scene and Brief Investigator(s) in Charge

Principle: Briefing the investigator(s) taking charge assists in controlling the crime scene and helps establish further investigative responsibilities.

Policy: The initial responding officer(s) at the scene shall provide a detailed crime scene briefing to the investigator(s) in charge of the scene.

Procedure: The initial responding officer(s) should:

a. Brief the investigator(s) taking charge.
b. Assist in controlling the scene.
c. Turn over responsibility for the documentation of entry/exit.
d. Remain at the scene until relieved of duty.

Summary: The scene briefing is the only opportunity for the next in command to obtain initial aspects of the crime scene prior to subsequent investigation.

Conclusion

Although it may seem that the first responders can never perform all the tasks needed at a crime scene, if they have the right mental attitude, are careful, and perform the tasks methodically, they can have a great positive effect on the subsequent investigation.

References and Bibliography

Bergeron, J., Le Baudour, C., Bizjak, G., Wesley, K., 2008. First Responder. Pearson, New York.

Fatah, A., Barrett, J., Arcilesi, R., Lattin, C., Janney, C., Blackman, E., 2002. Guide for the Selection of Personal Protective Equipment for Emergency First Responders, Volumes I and 2. National Institute of Justice, Washington, DC.

FirstResponder.gov provides a portal that enables federal, state, local, and tribal first responders to easily access federal web services, information on resources, products, standards, testing and evaluation, and best practices; http://www.firstresponder.gov/Pages/Default.aspx.

LeMay, J., 2011. CSI for the First Responder. CRC Press, Boca Raton, FL.

The Investigator in Charge

An investigator in charge (IIC) may be represented in the entertainment media as tough and grizzled or brilliant and quirky, but the real IIC is a very different being. First of all, in many jurisdictions, "he" is likely to be a "she" (Houck, 2009; pages 65–69). Second, and no matter who they are, the IIC must adopt many roles in varying degrees: politician, drill sergeant, project manager, supervisor, front-line worker, colleague, diplomat, and, ultimately, scientist. They must also be knowledgeable and experienced, persistent and energetic, level-headed but compassionate, open-minded yet skeptical, all while being a detail-oriented trained observer. In addition to the fundamental skills required to conduct an investigation, a lead investigator will often need advanced training in areas such as human anatomy, firearms, fingerprints, DNA, and trace evidence recovery. Additionally, the lead investigator will need a thorough understanding of criminal law and procedures and the chain of custody of evidence. Sound complicated? It is, and this is why so much emphasis is now

Key Terms
Investigator in charge (IIC)
Warrant

being placed on the science of crime scenes: Because they are sensitive to initial conditions, crime scenes are a delicate, time-sensitive balancing act.

The concept of an IIC may be just that—an idea that one person at the scene takes "the lead"—or it may be an official assignment from the authorizing agency. Jurisdictional practices and regulations vary considerably and this variation becomes more pronounced when multiple jurisdictions are involved ("We don't do it *that* way … now what?"). In some jurisdictions, the IIC may wield nearly as much control at the scene as the lead detective; in others, they may have little to none and must adapt to differing political pressures. For some agencies, like the U.S. National Transportation Safety Board (NTSB[1]), the role of IIC is a formal one that comes with overarching influence at the scene. This chapter discusses the aspects needed for leadership, however that is expressed, at a crime scene.

The required tasks vary during the life cycle of the investigation, placing different demands on the IIC and the team at different times and places; moreover, this is a dynamic situation and one change can create many difficult downstream effects and responses. In small-scale investigations with only a few team members, the IIC needs to be a domain expert who has knowledge of and experience with the investigation life cycle. In the case of large-scale investigations, the required investigation skills of an IIC are more focused on controlling, conducting, and organizing different aspects—irrespective of the phase—of the investigation cycle; domain-specific knowledge of the IIC is of secondary importance (Koning and Peters, 2006).

When the IIC gets the call that she is needed at the scene of a serious crime, she typically will be given a synopsis of events from the lead detective. This synopsis will often contain, among the hard information, many subjective statements, false conclusions, and conjecture. The IIC has to have the ability to listen to statements such as "there are buckets of blood at the scene" or "he shot the dead guy with a .38 because he was 'dissing' his girlfriend" without letting her judgment be unduly influenced. It is vital when listening to the lead detective's synopsis to not become locked in to a theory of what happened before, during, or after the commission of the crime. It is often only several months later when autopsies, forensic evidence analysis, and witness interviews have been completed before a clear picture emerges of the exact sequence of events. When the IIC is first informed of any details of the crime, she has to carefully balance an open-minded approach with a healthy dose of skepticism.

Teamwork is essential for a successful crime scene investigation. That teamwork begins the moment the IIC contacts the team members. Discussion with the team will direct what supplies and reagents may be needed and also indicate a time of arrival at the scene. This will help with the answer to the question the lead detective always asks immediately after providing the synopsis: "How soon is your crime scene team going to get here?"

---

[1] www.ntsb.gov.

In forming any team, the most basic challenge [is] getting folks to take the big step away from just being themselves (the thing we all know best) and joining something larger (the thing we fear may let us down).… Whether brought by duty or desire, once people are in the same room, they've assumed the basic stance of being a team—which is to be together. Preconceived negative opinions don't evaporate, but at least negativity can mix with positivity in the room, which by electrical principles results in the neutralizing of the respective $+/-$ charges. I now consider this the most basic concept to leading a team.

Source: Maeda, J. with Bermont, R. 2011. Redesigning Leadership (Simplicity: Design, Technology, Business, Life). MIT Press, Cambridge, MA, p. 5.

Every crime scene starts with a location, a place, and a set of coordinates. Asking "Exactly where is the main crime scene located?" may seem a simple question but it must be answered precisely if time is not to be wasted or critical evidence overlooked. There is not a year that goes by without reports of a police department forcibly entering the wrong house and their departments being sued for thousands of dollars by the innocent house owners. Police officers know their precincts intimately, so if they say to their colleagues, "The shooting was at the mom & pop store on 9th," they are aware of the location; the IIC, who is unfamiliar with the city, may have a tough time finding the crime scene when provided with such a vague description, however. The IIC must get the exact address and relay it accurately to her team members; global positioning systems (GPSs) and satellite navigation ("sat-navs") are available and inexpensive and all crime scene vehicles should be equipped with one.

After having established the exact location, the IIC should ask for guidance on avoiding hazards or obstructions in approaching the crime scene. These could include emergency ambulance or fire vehicles, media vehicles, crowds of onlookers, or blocked streets. It is useful to review these hazards on a GPS map before arriving at the scene and revise your approach if the direct route is unavailable. Typically, CSIs park as closely as possible to the crime scene to facilitate access to their supplies, reagents, and specialized equipment. The IIC should initially park at least a block away; the crime scene can then be approached by foot. A slow circuit of the block around the scene is advised. Potential physical evidence that may have been overlooked, discarded by the perpetrators, or undiscovered may be found. This area reconnaissance will also assist the IIC in determining where to place the limits of the crime scene. This is true of rural crime scenes as well, although the distances may be greater and access limited.

The next thing the IIC must verify is whether a warrant to search has been issued or if one is needed. Circumstances may arise when the IIC decides to delay or stop a search for evidence. Issues of weather, lighting, personnel, or other situations may suggest or dictate that a delay is in the best interest of the investigation and the evidence. Although the reasons may be obvious to the IIC, she should take time to outline the reasons for her decision.

Another issue that crime scene teams face, most notably in the western United States when investigating the discovery of buried human remains, is the *Native American Graves Protection and Repatriation Act*. This is a law that establishes the ownership of cultural items excavated or discovered on federal or tribal land after November 16, 1990. The act also applies to land transferred by the federal government to the states under the *Water Resources Department Act*. The act states that Native American remains and associated funerary objects belong to lineal descendants. If the descendants cannot be identified, then those remains and objects, along with unassociated funerary or sacred objects and objects of cultural patrimony, belong to the tribe on whose lands the remains were found or the tribe having the closest relationship to them (Canby, 2004; page 276). Other countries have similar laws protecting either archaeological sites for cultural or environmental reasons or for issues of native population primacy; for example, in Australia, *The Commonwealth Native Title Act 1993* covers land rights for aboriginal Australians and Torres Straits Islanders. If at any time during digging of any type at a crime scene, the IIC suspects that she is dealing with a potential archaeological or historical burial site, then further work must cease and the appropriate government representatives must be contacted so that an archaeological excavation can be performed to recover any funerary or sacred objects in a respectful manner.

Security at the Crime Scene

A discussion of security may seem puzzling when conducting an investigation for a police agency, where nearly every employee carries a firearm, but IICs must ensure that there is adequate security for their team for their entire time at the crime scene. After the scene has stabilized and after officers and detectives return to their normal duties, it is common for everyone in the police agency to breathe a collective sigh of relief, especially if an experienced crime scene team is collecting the evidence. Police commanders, as always in today's financial climate, are conscious of paying for expensive overtime; they will begin to scale back their crime scene response as soon as they can. The IIC must ensure that the police agency has enough armed personnel available to provide security and keep onlookers out of the crime scene. Besides onlookers, it is not unheard of for family members to want to get back into the crime scene to retrieve their valuables or possessions. Worse still, an armed suspect may return to (or be hiding at) the scene for any number of reasons. The crime scene team must remain focused on their task of preserving and collecting physical evidence; they cannot afford to spend time on security. Constant security is a nonnegotiable component of the crime scene team's presence at the crime scene. The IIC must be strong-willed enough to give notice that she will pull her team out of the crime scene if at any time she notices that the police agency is not providing security, for whatever reasons. This is particularly true at multiagency scenes where the CSI may not be employed by a law enforcement agency (such as when the CSI comes from a medical examiner's office).

Leadership at the Scene

The IIC must set the standard of behavior for her team: calm, even-voiced, respectful of others' talents and opinions. Decisiveness is critical; carefulness is warranted. As already stated, the IIC should not get "anchored" by any single theory associated with the crime; however, it is human nature to theorize and "fill in" details when faced with facts that do not have an obvious link. The IIC should not think out loud: someone may overhear a conjecture or supposition in a conversation between two crime scene investigators who were discussing theories in a normal collegiate manner. The wrong idea may be communicated or others may adopt this theory as the basis for their subsequent investigation.

A duty often overlooked by an IIC is as an ambassador for the forensic services section. Patrol officers rarely visit a forensic laboratory and the IIC and her team may be the first CSIs the officers have met in person. How these first interactions are handled can shape how that police agency subsequently views and works with the forensic laboratory in later investigations. The IIC should move into a teaching role and educate the officers. As most CSIs are used to explaining their work in court, the transition to a teaching mode is not difficult. If time or circumstances do not permit the IIC to answer the questions at the scene, the IIC should note the officer's contact information and arrange to provide the answers to their questions later. It is worth it for the IIC to demonstrate courteous behavior throughout the investigation and let her team see how to behave. The time spent "incidentally teaching" will bear fruit in later investigations with that police agency.

Conclusion

The IIC plays a key role in coordinating activities at the crime scene, communicating with other relevant professionals, and leading the crime scene team. The authority of the IIC may be informal or it may be a specific role designated by a particular jurisdicition. Regardless, the job of the IIC is central to successful, efficient crime scene processing.

References

Canby Jr., W.C., 2004. American Indian Law. West, St. Paul, MN.

Houck, M.M., 2009. Is forensic science a gateway for women into science? Forensic Sci. Manage. 1 (1): 65–69.

Koning, G.Th., Peters M.L.M.M., 2006. The Investigator-in-Charge, Role or Profession? Delft TopTech, The Hague.

The Forensic Team: Officers, Scientists, and Specialists

Like all successful teams, a crime scene team is most effective if the members have superior technical skills, can clearly communicate with each other, and come from diverse backgrounds. All team members should be equally valued. Forensic scientists and CSIs, with their scientific and technical skills, are experts at recognizing, collecting, and preserving physical evidence; however, they typically lack the investigative and interviewing skills that detectives are trained in. Medical examiners have great knowledge of anatomy and medical processes but usually have only rudimentary knowledge of forensic science or police investigations. Detectives, likewise, have not spent their time studying science or medicine. Even within these team categories, there may be varying degrees of knowledge; a forensic scientist with a background in molecular biology may know very little about firearms, for example.

If you have a team that can communicate well, cooperate, and show mutual respect, they will accomplish marvelous things that individuals acting alone

Key Terms
Medical examiner
Latent print expert
Photographer
Prosecutor
Forensic anthropologist
Forensic odontology
Forensic nurses
Computer forensics/ digital
Evidence
Trackers
Forensic entomologist
Gallows humor

cannot. Each team member brings their unique life experience. A seasoned investigator in charge, puzzled by rubber bands wrapped around the handle of a kitchen knife used as a murder weapon, is enlightened by the rookie team member who recognizes that rubber bands are also used by her grandmother to help her grip the knife while preparing food. A forensic scientist struggling to safely unload a weapon at the scene is helped by a CSI who happens to be a gun collector.

Communication

A little girl sat outside shivering in the cold despite her heavy winter coat. She was intently reading a library book. Her mother looked out, saw her daughter, and said, "Honey, why are you reading outdoors like this, freezing to death?" The little girl replied, "Our teacher said if we wanted to do well in school, we should do a lot of outside reading."

Misunderstandings are a necessary evil of communication. Like other accidents, they are preventable, but only if we take precautions and stay aware of possible trouble. The best idea in the world does not one bit of good if it is not communicated properly and acted on accordingly. This applies to any team, teammate, or team leader.

"Communication is the soul of management: analysis and solid decisions translated into clear messages that influence people to act and feel good about their performance."

Source: Story and quote from Booher, D. 1994. *Communicate with Confidence!* McGraw-Hill, New York, p. ix and xvi, respectively.

The size and makeup of the team is dependent on the size of the agency, the available personnel, and the nature of the crime. Some levels of effort are basic: conducting a vehicle search for physical evidence should require only two experienced forensic scientists. In contrast, a crime scene involving partially buried and scattered remains may need forensic scientists, an anthropologist, and a host of searchers and forensic specialists; likewise, a multiple homicide will require additional effort of varying specialties. For many crime scenes, however, forensic specialists may not be available and a team member may have to perform multiple tasks. This heightens the importance of continuing education for all team members so that they gain an understanding of all the aspects of crime scene procedures.

Kinds of Teams

Not all teams are alike. Think of sports teams: a rugby team is different than a bowling team.

Rugby	Bowling
Nothing significant can be accomplished without cooperation of the members.	Members can achieve significant results individually (scoring points, for example).
Team members specialize (throwing, kicking, blocking, etc.).	Every member performs the same actions.
An individual's success is linked to the team's success—a single member cannot win alone.	The performance of one member does not affect the performance of another member.

Thus, teams like rugby teams are interdependent teams; those like bowling teams are independent teams. Crime scene teams are clearly interdependent teams, then. Depending on the agency and how it is structured, a crime scene team may also be thought of as a project team, where the members are brought together for a period of time for a specific task; once finished, they are disbanded as a functional team. Some crime scene teams, however, may be permanent assignments and the members will work together again and again, only rarely bringing in outside specialists.

Interdependent teams do best when the members know each other well, both within an organization and socially. This closeness supports trust and collegiality, and creates a platform for easing tensions. Leadership in interdependent teams is tricky, because each member may be responsible for their own specific tasks and may be the best judges of their own performance. Taking a top-down, hierarchical approach (telling team members to do something "because I'm the boss") typically does not work; what does work are clearly defined boundaries of control, responsibility, and trust all focused on a clear goal. Delegation is essential; if the team members are all properly trained and trusted professionals who know their specific duties, the best thing a leader or manager can do is give them clear expectations with defined parameters and stay out of their way.

Source: Bryant, B., Noga F., and Griffiths, A. 1994. *Self-Managing Teams & Changing Supervisory Roles*. Centre for Corporate Change, Sydney.

A Forensic Team

Who are these forensic specialists and what duties do they perform? A list could include:

- First officer
- Lead detective
- Scene detective
- Medical examiner and/or coroner

- Latent print expert
- Forensic scientist
- Photographer
- Prosecutor
- Forensic anthropologist
- Forensic dentist
- Forensic nurse
- Forensic computer expert
- Trackers and cadaver dogs
- Entomologist
- Public information officer

The duties and the importance of the actions of the *first officer* on the scene have already been described. So far, the crime scene has been described in the singular. If it is defined as a location where evidence of a crime may be found, there may be, in addition to the primary scene, secondary, tertiary, and even more crime scenes. The lead detective is in charge of the entire investigation and is concerned with canvassing witnesses, interviewing suspects, being aware of all aspects of the investigation, and staying with it until its final presentation in court. As this encompasses so many tasks, the lead detective may cede police control of the crime scene(s) to the scene detective.

The *scene detective* may be the investigator in charge of the scene or someone who works with an individual who is so designated; either way, the scene detective is in charge of the overall crime scene for the police department. He has to oversee security and to make sure that the maximum amount of evidence is extracted from the scene before it is released.

Depending on the jurisdiction, either a *medical examiner* or a coroner is concerned with the body of the deceased. Medical examiners by definition are physicians who are schooled in forensic pathology; they perform autopsies and are appointed to their positions, usually in urban areas. The medical examiner will determine the cause and manner of death. Manner of death is one of five categories listed on a death certificate: homicide, suicide, natural, accidental, and undetermined. "Undetermined" is used when the manner of death cannot be determined or a distinction between two categories cannot be made. Medical examiners and their staff (often called "death investigators") will perform investigations at the scene of death, work to identify the deceased, and may identify and collect evidence. By contrast, the office of coroner is an elected position, usually in rural areas. A coroner does not have to have any medical training. Nevertheless, the coroner is responsible for identifying the body, notifying the next of kin, collecting and returning any personal belongings on the body to the family of the deceased, and signing the death certificate. Typically in the United States, the state or county will provide a pathologist to perform autopsies in counties where the coroner has jurisdiction.

As the name implies, a *latent print expert* will be skilled in fingerprint collection and comparison. They will work closely with the CSI, particularly on major crime scenes. Most police officers and CSIs have knowledge and practical experience in developing fingerprints, but it may take a latent print expert with knowledge of the myriad fingerprint development techniques to recognize the potential for developing prints on objects at the crime scene that might go unexamined by more casual latent print practitioners. At autopsies or with badly decomposed bodies, latent print experts can assist with identification of the deceased by using specialized techniques to rehydrate or otherwise render the skin to a condition in which useful fingerprints can be collected.

An expert *photographer* may be needed to best capture images or video at the scene. Low-light, infrared, or aerial photography require skills that the average CSI may not possess. Capturing transient images, such as low-level fluorescence from the use of blood visualization reagents, is something that requires training and practice to perform reliably. Photography experts are often called to piece together still images and videos from camera phones, traffic cameras, ATMs, security cameras, and other sources. These often involve the use of sophisticated enhancement software programs that require expert training and experience if maximum information is to be obtained from these various images.

It is not only useful but desirable to have a *prosecutor* at the crime scene. Many large prosecutors' offices in the United States have an on-call rotation whereby deputy prosecutors work with law enforcement at major crime scenes. Although they should not enter the crime scene, they can interact closely with the investigators, assisting with the wording of search warrants and learning about key items of evidence, the context of events, and the persons involved, to better shape the potential for prosecuting the case. This knowledge permits them to do their job more effectively in the courtroom.

Forensic anthropologists are specialists in physical anthropology, the study of human biological function and variation, particularly skeletal biology. The anthropologist's ability to understand the forms and variations of the human skeleton in individuals and populations complements the forensic pathologist's emphasis on soft tissue and body systems. Forensic anthropologists use archaeological methods to recover buried bones and human material and are often called to crime scenes involving buried or scattered human remains.

Forensic odontology is identification based on the recognition of features present in each person's dental structures; it is particularly useful when identification by the use of friction ridge skin is not possible, as in burn victims or airplane crashes. Forensic odontologists are also called upon to preserve and perform comparisons on human bite marks.

Forensic nurses provide specialized care for both victims and perpetrators of violence. They care for the physical, psychological, and social trauma that occurs in patients who have been assaulted or abused. Forensic nurses also acquire skills in injury identification, evaluation of the nature and scope of injuries, documentation of the patient's incident, and the collection and proper storage of biological and physical evidence. Forensic nurses also have a specialized knowledge of the legal system, provide medical testimony in court, and provide consultation to legal authorities.[1]

Computer forensics (also known as *digital evidence*) can be defined as the collection and analysis of data from computer systems, networks, communication streams (wireless), and storage media in a manner that is admissible in a court of law (Nolan et al., 2005). At one time, police agencies would haul off all the computers at the scene of a crime and try at a later date to recover the persistent data, which is data that is stored on a local hard drive or other medium and is preserved when the computer is powered off. However, the examination and collection of volatile data is becoming more important. Volatile data is any data that is stored in memory, or in transit, that will be lost when the computer loses power or is powered off. Volatile data resides in registries, cache, and random access memory (RAM). Since the nature of volatile data is effervescent, collection of this information will likely need to occur in real or near-real time. In addition to data from computer hard drives, forensic computer experts are becoming more in demand for their ability to recover computer data and personal records from personal phones, cameras, and memory devices. Crime scene investigators and the first officer on the scene should have basic training in how to preserve this type of evidence.

Trackers use their tracking skills to locate suspects and missing persons. They often work with various types of dogs. Search and rescue (SAR) dogs can be classified broadly as either air-scenting dogs or trailing (and tracking) dogs. They also can be classified according to whether they "scent discriminate," and under what conditions they can work. Scent-discriminating dogs have proven their ability to alert only on the scent of an individual person, after being given a sample of that person's scent. Dogs that are not scent discriminating alert on or follow any scent of a given type, such as any human scent or any cadaver scent. SAR dogs can be trained specifically for rubble searches, for water searches, and for avalanche searches. Air-scenting dogs primarily use airborne human scent to home in on subjects, whereas trailing dogs rely on the scent of the specific subject. Air-scenting dogs typically work off-lead, are non-scent-discriminating (for example locate a scent from any human as opposed to a specific person), and cover large areas of terrain. These dogs are trained to follow a diffused or wind-borne scent back to its source, return to the handler and indicate contact with the subject, and then lead the handler back to the subject.

Human remains detection (HRD) or cadaver dogs are used to locate the remains of deceased victims. Depending on the nature of the search, these

---

[1] For more information, see the International Association of Forensic Nurses, www.iafn.org.

dogs may work off-lead (for example to search a large area for buried remains) or on-lead (to recover clues from a crime scene). Air-scenting and tracking/trailing dogs are often cross-trained as HRD dogs, although the scent the dog detects is clearly of a different nature than that detected for live or recently deceased subjects. HRD dogs can locate entire bodies (including those buried or submerged), decomposed bodies, body fragments (including blood, tissues, hair, and bones), or skeletal remains. This greatly reduces the need for large numbers of searchers if only general information is available about the location of the burial site.

A *forensic entomologist* uses insects to gather information about a crime scene. They deal with the necrophagous (or carrion) feeding insects that typically occupy human remains. Given stable environmental conditions, insects follow a predictable succession of occupation on decomposing bodies. An analysis of the insects and their life stages can yield information about the time of death. All crime scene teams should have basic training about the proper collection of insects, but a trained entomologist, if available, can extract the maximum information from human remains. It is often overlooked that insects can affect blood stain interpretation. This is often seen where repeated attempts to leave the area by flies who have been feeding off the blood create small-diameter impact patterns on windows.

How Groups Become Teams

When does a group become a team? One view says groups evolve into teams in four stages:

1. Dependency and inclusion, where the members are concerned about belonging and look to a leader to make decisions, in essence identifying with the group,
2. Counter dependency and fighting, where the members push back against goals, values, and procedures, arguing among each other on what to do; they may even challenge the leader. If the group can compromise, agree on goals, and eventually trust each other, they move to trust and structure.
3. Trust and structure, where members reach more mature negotiations and agree to roles, responsibilities, and procedures.
4. Work, where the members become productive, effective, and the quality and quantity of product increases.

Getting to Stage 4 is difficult and not every group achieves that goal; remaining at Stage 4, with its effective productive work, is also difficult and, without good leadership, goals, and persistent effort, the team can backslide into a group at any of the previous levels, with associated loss of cooperation, productivity, and success.

Source: Wheelan, S., 2010. *Creating Effective Teams: A Guide for Members and Leaders.* SAGE, Los Angeles.

At car search crime scenes, only a few of these specialists may be needed, while at a complex homicide investigation many of these experts may be required. No matter what the investigation, there must be a plan for exactly when each specialist enters the scene. This would involve the investigator in charge negotiating with all the specialists so that, with due deference to Abbott and Costello, everyone would know "Who's on first?" All the experts must be in agreement with the IIC's plan, with each expert providing information and insight; the IIC should make the final decision, however, on the order in which each expert does his or her task.

It may not seem like on television, but crime scene investigation is very demanding work, both physically and mentally. Spending long hours wearing a Tyvek® suit can lead to dehydration, especially in summer. Crawling into confined spaces, ripping up carpet to look for blood, or cutting walls to find bullets, can all lead to fatigue as well as safety hazards. Adequate water and rest breaks must be built into the crime scene procedures. Crime scene documentation involves multiple measurements, tests, and observations, all of which are scrutinized for the smallest mistake by other experts later, sometimes years later. Decisions are constantly being made about which stain to test, which fingerprint to collect, how many photos to take, and which reagent to use to develop the latent blood. "Getting it right the first time" is very tiring mentally. The team must have adequate rest if mistakes are to be kept to a minimum. Food breaks are also necessary, of course, but these also provide useful opportunities for team members to outline their findings, discuss aspects of the scene informally, and seek advice on technical matters. The application of light humor (see the "Gallows Humor" sidebar) or a quiet word of praise from the IIC will go a long way toward building that sense of teamwork that is so essential.

Gallows Humor

A homicide scene cannot be realistically compared to a comedy club but gentle humor, judiciously applied, can help to relieve the stress inherent in crime scene investigation. So-called gallows humor is humor that manages to be funny during—and perhaps because of—hopeless, stressful, or life-threatening situations. The famous psychiatrist, Sigmund Freud, wrote an essay on humor and offered this insight about gallows humor:

The ego refuses to be distressed by the provocations of reality, to let itself be compelled to suffer. It insists that it cannot be affected by the traumas of the external world; it shows, in fact, that such traumas are no more than occasions for it to gain pleasure.

This is not a call to make jokes at a crime scene, far from it. Gallows humor is not a "feel good" kind of humor; it is, in most cases, almost accidental. But the psychological stresses of forensic work press on one's personality and emotions to a point that some humor is bound to escape as a "release valve" or "emotional anesthesia," as one researcher called it. In fact, it can even be a sign of a healthy personality to find humor in horrible situations. Gallows humor can strengthen morale, create a sense of team spirit, and relieve tension.

Examples:
- "Our day begins when your day ends," a common homicide or forensic phrase.
- Romeo and Juliet, Act 3, Scene 1: Mercutio is [fatally] stabbed in a swordfight by Tybalt:
  - *Romeo*: "Courage, man; the hurt cannot be much."
  - *Mercutio*: "No, 'tis not so deep as a well, nor so wide as a church-door; but 'tis enough, 'twill serve: ask for me to-morrow, and you shall find me a grave man."
- Author and playwright Oscar Wilde, lying on his deathbed in a ill-kept, cheap boarding house, is quoted as saying, "My wallpaper and I are fighting a duel to the death; one or the other of us has got to go."
- The Japanese Navy Mitsubishi G4M bomber airplane was nicknamed the *hamaki* (Japanese for "cigar") by the Japanese crews because the vehicle would typically ignite and burst into flame when hit. The American military nicknamed the G4M "the flying Zippo" after the cigarette lighter company's marketing slogan, "Guaranteed to light on first strike, every time."

Sources: Mooney, J. 2008. To break the crime scene tension, jokes. *New York Times*, January 28; Sultanoff, S.,1995. Levity defies gravity: Using humor in crisis situations. *Therapeutic Humor* 9(3): 1–2; Watson, K., 2011. Gallows humor in medicine. *The Hastings Center Report* 41(5): 37–45; Winchester, J. (ed), 2004. *Aircraft of World War II*. Thunder Bay Press, San Diego.

Conclusion

Team building also continues after the crime scene. One person may be responsible for writing the entire report or each team member may submit an individual report. All team members should see the successive drafts and express their opinions based on their own observations at the crime scene. Newer team members are often so concerned with the minutiae of learning the many techniques needed at crime scenes that they lose sight of what the evidence is telling them. Being involved with report writing is one of the primary ways that newer team members learn to focus their thoughts about what happens at crime scenes. It also helps them gain experience in crime scene reconstruction.

Reference

Nolan, R., O'Sullivan, C., Branson, J., Waits, C., 2005. First Responders Guide to Computer Forensics. CERT Training and Education, CMU/SEI-2005-HB-001.

Nonforensic Personnel: Superiors, Officials, and the Media

A surprisingly large number of people must be informed about some or all of the events at a crime scene. An even larger number think they need to be informed. The first responder must notify their superior officer about the crime scene situation as soon as possible; the superior officer then notifies the appropriate personnel in the departmental chain of command. Depending on the crime and jurisdiction, a wide variety of people may need to be informed, including the chief of police, the mayor, magistrates, and judges, not to mention all the intervening officers and officials (some of whom think they need to be informed, remember). These people may have a stake in bringing the crime scene investigation to a speedy and successful conclusion and, most importantly for the CSI, these officials can aid the investigation by freeing up resources not available to a single police department.

Key Terms

Public information officer

First Amendment of the U.S. Constitution

Information: Two Points of View

Law enforcement is an inherently political process; crime is of obvious social concern. Additionally, humans have a perverse interest in the dark side of their species' behavior. Therefore, it cannot be ignored that crime scenes can be intensely interesting to people, drawing crowds of officials and public onlookers alike. The media highlight criminal activities in their reports and persistently look for more information to feed their stories. The CSI won't have the time, training, or authority to deal directly with the media or the public and should not be concerned with directly communicating with these people. A professional, such as a public information officer (PIO), should be employed; if one is not available, then superiors in the CSI's agency should be the ones to shoulder this administrative responsibility.

PIOs in police agencies are typically experienced police officers who are educated or trained in dealing with public information and can speak well extemporaneously. They are well versed in police procedures but may know little of crime scene operations. The investigator in charge (IIC) should arrange regular tours of the forensic laboratory and answer questions about developments in forensic science. The IIC of the crime scene should have formed a good prior relationship with the PIO. Time spent educating the PIO on the realistic expectations for results at a crime scene will bear fruit during the investigation when the IIC will be concerned with hundreds of other details and have little time to inform others of his progress. The PIO, in addition to keeping superiors and officials informed, will also deal with the other major player at crime scenes, the media.

If You Have to Deal with the Media, Understand This

Immediately following a crisis, the public will want to know three things (Figure 3.4.1):

- What happened? These facts should be released as soon as the information is confirmed. Updates should be frequent and numerous.
- What does it mean to me? Place yourself in the public's shoes. Provide people with information to enhance their safety and address potential concerns they may have. Fear of the unknown is greater than fear of the facts.
- What are you doing about it? The public wants to get "back to normal" as soon as possible. Tell people what you are doing to control the situation and return order. Explain how the process will work, how long it could take, and what can be expected.

Most crises tend to follow a cycle. Media coverage will mirror this cycle in the form of news content and issues covered. Know these phases and anticipate the questions/stories the media will pursue.

What does it mean to me?

What are you doing about it?

What happened?

FIGURE 3.4.1 Crisis management triangle.

- Breaking Phase—Media arrives on scene requiring access and information; basic coverage of who, what, when, where, why, and how.
- Sustaining Phase—Media attention grows, use of subject matter experts to fill immediate information void.
- Recovery Phase—Crisis is defined, questions on cause, problems, and blame surface. A reduction in media interest may occur.
- Anniversary Phase—Spike in interest, questions on current status or lessons learned.

Any statement should consist of no more than three or four key messages you want to convey to the public. In the initial stages of a crisis, information about health and safety should constitute the primary message. Other key messages should have information to calm the public, such as what is being done to respond and recover from the crisis, commitment to solving the problem, levels of expertise involved, and statements of concern. Try to phrase your key messages in 10- to 12-word soundbites for ease of understanding. Be clear and concise— don't ramble. Keep your statements short. Phrase statements so that a 12-year-old could understand them.

Source: www.publicinformationofficer.com.

The First Amendment of the U. S. Constitution states:

> Congress shall make no law respecting an establishment of religion, or prohibiting the free exercise thereof; or abridging the freedom of speech, or of the press; or the right of the people peaceably to assemble, and to petition the Government for a redress of grievances.

This amendment, which guarantees the "freedom of the press," is mirrored by the European Charter on Freedom of the Press, which attempts to guarantee journalists access to information and protects them from government interference. Unfortunately, the media is seen by many law enforcement personnel as the enemy, quick to take inappropriate photographs and videos, pushy and eager to destroy a person's reputation given the chance. As a result, law enforcement can be unhelpful and restrict their information to the statement most hated by the media: "No comment." This adversarial view is slowly changing. More enlightened police agencies realize that the media has a job to do at crime scenes; to exercise their right to get as much information as possible to the public. Many police agencies have formed media relations departments who interact with the media, providing contact and what the media needs more than anything, information.

> Journalists and government officials both serve the public. Both need to be sure the information they disseminate is accurate, credible, timely, and relevant. Both must know that they will pay a price if they fail to do their jobs well.
> Frank Sesno, Professor of Public Policy and Communication at George Mason University and former Washington, D.C. Bureau Chief for CNN

So why has the police and the media had such a poor relationship? First, law enforcement and the media think about and report events differently. Law enforcement verbally describes events in chronological order and tends to write in the same order. The media thinks and speaks or writes based on what they—in their opinion—believe are the important parts of the story they want to tell. Historically, this practice stemmed from the fact that the newspaper editor of the story, when dealing with a deadline, often was left with limited space to print. The reporter knew this and wrote the story in order of importance, assuming that the later paragraphs had the potential to be cut by the editor. This style of editing is even more evident on television, where the reporter may have less than a minute to get their point across. This has led to the dreaded "soundbite" and the creation of verbal shorthand that uses clichéd phrases; if something is repeated often enough, it becomes accepted, and examples of this can be heard every night on the news. The reporting of a fire would not be complete without the phrases like, "thick black acrid smoke," "smoke was seen billowing," or "the fire spread rapidly." All of these phrases show a lack of knowledge of fire behavior. A scientist may testify at an inquest that "no fingerprints or DNA profiles of use were found on the murder weapon," which when later reported live by the media becomes "once again, the laboratory found no fingerprints or DNA." Such assertions introduce the potential for misunderstanding between law enforcement and the media. The forensic and police community will accuse the reporter of leaping to conclusions based on a lack of knowledge; the reporter will suspect a police cover-up.

Information is the lifeblood of the media; this is also true of police agencies, but they operate in a world where information is given out on a need-to-know basis. Police agencies who are investigating a suspect may not want details of his whereabouts released to the media for fear he will flee. This restriction of information can be seen by an overzealous reporter as interfering with First Amendment rights. Both groups have negative views of the other that are based more in ignorance than bias.

The agency's PIO will work with the media at major crime scenes, providing a separate area for the media to park their vehicles and assemble. The PIO must not forget that the media has deadlines. For TV stations, the evening and late-night newscasts are the most critical. If the PIO holds timely briefings and provides updated information then most of the media will not interfere with the crime scene or jeopardize the investigation. The PIO should provide locations and opportunities for the media to obtain file footage for their newscasts. Although restricting the media to a particular area is easier to provide security for, the media should not be barred from areas where casual onlookers are permitted. The media should not be allowed close enough to record sensitive pictures that may be embarrassing or distressing to family members of the victim. Modern crime scenes are scrutinized by circling helicopters, cameras with zoom lenses, and sensitive listening devices. IICs must be aware of this when conducting their investigations. Some investigators resort to playing a radio to provide background noise or erecting covers over the windows; companies now make collapsible barriers or shields to help police protect the privacy of victims, the accused, and employees.

The Public as Reporters

The public, via smartphones, now has the ability to record high-definition video and pictures and at a simple keystroke upload the material to social media sites for the entire world to see. PIOs and all the crime scene investigation team must act with discretion at all times as they perform their duties. An unguarded comment or a disrespectful gesture and everyone from Toledo to Timbuktu will see and hear it instantly. Recent events in Europe and the United States have shown that a "flash mob" can form in minutes simply by social site interaction or by text communication. All they need is a street address and their phone's mapping software gives them visual and audio directions; suddenly, several hundred people appear at the scene screaming at the police. This is a potential problem that cannot be ignored, particularly with officer-involved shootings. This reinforces the importance of informing superiors and officials as soon as possible in the investigation.

Another note on personal communication devices is the use of personal phones, equipped with digital cameras, by law enforcement and medical personnel. Just like in the office, personal communications should be kept to an absolute minimum. More importantly, the ubiquity of cameras and the ability to communicate images poses an enormous security threat to the CSI and his agency. Images only available to public officials at the crime scene or the morgue have been published in the media. Money, fame, or other inappropriate personal motives lead to this unethical behavior. Recent events indicate that cell phones can be hacked by unscrupulous people. If police departments and medical examiner's offices have not already written a policy forbidding officers and personnel from using their personal phones to take images at crime scenes, then they should consider introducing one as soon as possible. This should be expanded beyond taking images to the use of instant messaging, including on sites such as Facebook or Twitter. An unguarded remark on someone's smartphone, if discovered, could jeopardize the entire investigation or an agency's reputation—worse, it could compromise personal security or public safety.

Communicating to Superiors

Police agencies are hierarchical and are like the military (hence the term paramilitary to describe them) in their structure, rules, and ranks. Communicating can be difficult, communicating to a supervisor can be more difficult, and communicating to a supervisor within a paramilitary organization can be fraught with problems. Learning to provide the right information, at the right time, and to the right people is a critical professional skill. Adding to this set of potential problems is that crime scenes are stressful situations, full of confusion, complexity, and chaos, not to mention emotionally wrenching situations.

Facts about Communication at Work

- The average worker spends 50 percent of his or her time communicating.
- Business success is 85 percent dependent on effective communication and interpersonal skills.
- Forty-five percent of time spent communicating is listening.
- Writing represents only 9 percent of communication time.
- One-fourth of all workplace mistakes are the result of poor communication.
- A remarkable 75 percent of communication is nonverbal.

Source: Federal Emergency Management Agency, 2005. *Effective Communication: An Independent Study.* Washington, D.C.

Why is communicating about stressful situations so ... stressful? As Holly Weeks, an independent business communication consultant, has said, "The reason is precisely because our feelings are so enmeshed. When we are not emotionally entangled in an issue, we know that conflict is normal, that it can be resolved—or at least managed. But when feelings get stirred up, most of us are thrown off balance." Keeping your balance in these situations is difficult but not impossible. First, approach the situation with a greater self-awareness and awareness of what management expects. Are phone calls acceptable or is face-to-face communication expected? Second, rehearse the message before it is delivered. Anticipate questions, both those that will be asked and those to be asked. Write a short set of notes to make sure the necessary details are covered. Third, be careful of words, tone, and phrasing. Choosing better words and refining phrasing can help clarify information and prevent misunderstanding. Avoid cliches or euphemisms. For example, rather than saying "Stop interrupting me," try "Can you hold on a minute? I want to finish this before I lose this thought." Prioritize what needs to be communicated and avoid rambling. Keep a neutral tone in your voice. Be careful of evaluative or interpretive open-ended questions like, "Is there anything else?"; what appears as ancillary at the scene may seem significant to management, and details omitted for brevity may appear to be "covering up." Finally, make notes of the conversation—both sides—to document who said what.

Conclusion

It is in the interests of the crime scene investigators to have a plan on how to deal with the media at crime scenes. If relationships are based on a level of respect and information that can be disclosed is freely released on a regular basis, then the investigators can focus on their task of maximizing the collection of evidence at the crime scene. CSIs must also be aware of how to communicate both good news and bad to superiors as part of their normal course of duties.

Bibliography

Harvard Business Review, 2011. Communicating Effectively. Harvard Business School, Cambridge, MA.

Lemay, E., Schwamberger, J., 2007. How to Communicate Effectively at Work. Papilio Publishing, Soquel, CA.

The Technology, Education, and Design (TED) lectures, www.ted.com, are an excellent source from which to learn about public speaking and communication in general.

Weeks, H., 2001. Taking the stress out of stressful conversations. Harv. Bus. Rev. 79 (7): 112–9, 146.

General Crime Scene Procedure

In Chapter 3.1, the procedures to be followed by first responders to secure the scene and to minimize the potential loss of physical evidence during the critical initial stages of the investigation were outlined. This chapter describes general crime scene procedures employed by CSIs after the crime scene has passed to their control.

The human imagination sees to it that people kill, assault, rape, and rob other people in many creative ways; this leads to the possibility of many different types of crime scenes. A quick analysis of this statement might lead to the suggestion that investigators need to have a game plan for each of these different crime scenes. Fortunately, employing consistent scientific crime scene procedures will work for most situations. When an investigator has not encountered a particular type of crime scene before, she may have to be innovative in ensuring that the evidence is collected in as pristine a condition

Key Terms

Three R's: recognize, recover, record

as possible. However, even when being creative, experienced investigators will work to stay within the confines of scientific crime scene procedures.

Scientific crime scene procedures have been described in many previous works but all such procedures are based around the three R's: recognize, recover, and record. Each of these rules can be subdivided into techniques that, when correctly applied, will accomplish the rule. To illustrate this point: Search patterns are used when trying to recognize the presence of physical evidence, sketching and photography are used to record the crime scenes, and reagents such as leucocrystal violet and luminol, which are sensitive to the presence of blood, are used to visualize latent blood stain patterns. The techniques must be practiced over and over in the laboratory, or in similar controlled conditions, before being used at a crime scene. To answer former NBA great Allen Iverson's question, "Yes, we are talking about *practice*."[1] Of course, the practitioner must be evaluated by an experienced investigator to ensure that the techniques are being used correctly, and in the right context at the crime scene. CSIs who use chemical screening techniques to look for the presence of semen, latent blood, and other such materials are much more effective if the investigator understands the physics and chemistry of those techniques.

The three R's as described may seem simplistic, but if used correctly they are methods by which the maximum amount of information may be extracted from any crime scene by a well-trained experienced crime scene team. The remainder of this book will discuss various approaches to these three guiding principles.

It is axiomatic that crime scenes are dynamic, not static, events. Every action performed by investigators, even entering the crime scene, will change that scene irrevocably. How is an investigator supposed to "freeze" that crime scene? The first answer is, it is not easy. The second is, it can't be done, at least not completely. The best a CSI and his team can do is to minimize the loss of physical evidence and recover the maximum amount of pertinent physical evidence. Although the three R's should be followed at every scene, the techniques used will vary depending on the circumstances of the crime. Collecting fibers from the seats of a car owned by a suspect to connect him to the rape of his girlfriend in that very car or examining the suspect's underwear for the presence of his semen would not net much information of investigative value; those things would be expected to be in those locations. It is essential to establish the relationship of the victim to the suspect and obtain a chronology of events if the right techniques are to be used to recover the physical evidence (the diagrams in Chapter 2.1 on forensic intelligence described this concept).

Consider the Washington state case of a Tacoma woman who went missing in November 2002. She had been reported missing by her husband a few

---

[1] http://sportsillustrated.cnn.com/basketball/news/2002/05/09/iverson_transcript/, posted May 10, 2002.

days after her disappearance. He did not appear for a follow-up meeting with detectives and the Washington State Patrol Crime Scene Response Team was called in to assist. Before entering the dwelling, the investigator in charge asked about the interests of both the victim and the missing woman. The house had a split-level layout with a master bedroom and bathroom and two storage rooms upstairs, and a garage, bedroom, shower, and storage room downstairs. The house was very clean and tidy with no obvious signs of violence. A brief walkthrough established that, based on their respective interests, the couple inhabited different areas of the house. Upstairs were multiple statues, pictures, and framed inspirational works, all depicting angels; this had been a primary interest of the missing woman. Downstairs were numerous fishing poles, nets, lures, fishing tackle boxes, and pictures of the husband with caught fish.

The daughter of the missing woman had said her mother was very proud of her four-poster bed with its elaborate canopy and the bedspread embroidered with angels. When the investigator in charge entered the master bedroom, several things were readily apparent. The canopy was missing from the bed and the bedspread had designs not of angels but of fish! In addition, a strong smell of pine-scented cleaner was apparent in the same room. The smell of the cleaner and the missing bedspread suggested that an attempt to clean up something had occurred, possibly on the bed or the surrounding area. The dark brown synthetic carpet on the floor beside the bed was damp. Several swabs from the surface of the carpet were tested with phenolphthalin reagent, a presumptive test for blood, with negative results. As the lead investigator was a former trace evidence analyst, he was aware that even if the carpet was cleaned with water, and blood was removed by mechanical action from the surface, the synthetic fibers would repel any blood/water and the mixture would be pushed through the carpet to the foam carpet lining underneath. When the investigator pulled back the carpet, a large stain that tested presumptively positive for blood was observed on the yellow carpet liner. When the yellow foam lining was pulled back, a stain over 15 inches in diameter was seen on the wooden floor. This stain also tested presumptively positive for blood.

The missing woman was found stuffed in a blue recycling bin several days later by hunters near Mount Rainier. At autopsy, it was ascertained that she had been bludgeoned to death. Serial numbers on the recycling bin were tracked by police to the victim's nextdoor neighbor; the victim's own recycling bin had been delivered to the neighbor by mistake. The victim's husband was later convicted of his wife's murder.

Later when relating the details of the case to his colleagues, the investigator, unlike many inexperienced investigators, resisted the temptation to say that he had a "gut feeling" that something violent had happened in that master bedroom. In reality, he relied on the provided information about the victim and suspect, and used his observational skills coupled with his experience of human nature to lead him to search in the right place for the physical evidence. He also held to the maxim that "it is not only what is present that is important but also what is not present."

Garbage Truck Forensics and Opportunity Costs

Fear is not a good strategy and yet it is out of fear of missing evidence that some police agencies or CSIs collect every possible item of potential evidence at a crime scene and submit it to the laboratory thinking, "They're the smart scientists; they can sort out the important stuff." This brings to mind the image of a large garbage truck dumping evidence into the laboratory while hapless scientists look on, hence the term "garbage truck forensics." While it may make sense to the uninitiated, this type of unconsidered evidence submission creates numerous problems up- and downstream in the criminal justice system; one of these problems is called an opportunity cost.

An *opportunity cost* is the cost of doing something measured in terms of the value of *not* doing the next best thing (the second best choice). In economics, it is characterized as the essential relationship between scarcity and choice. Opportunity cost can be measured in money (typically) or in anything of value, like time. If someone wanted to go to two sporting events that were scheduled for the same time, they can only go to one. The opportunity cost of going to the basketball game would be the cost of *not* going to the hockey game. If they recorded the hockey game (assuming it was televised) and went to the basketball game, the opportunity cost would then be the time spent watching the hockey game later. Likewise, when dining out with friends, the cost of choosing the cheaper entree includes the cost of *not* ordering a steak or lobster—for example, missing out on the luxury and taste of the more expensive meal is part of the cost.

For a police officer or CSI, there are opportunity costs involved in submitting evidence. If a "garbage truck" of evidence is submitted to the laboratory, it will take the scientists that much longer to sort thr9ough all of the items, process them, and then choose which ones to analyze. The time they spend doing this keeps them from working other items in other cases, possibly ones that were submitted by the very same CSI. Therefore, the opportunity cost of submitting everything and hoping the laboratory will sort it out is *increasing the time to process the next case submitted*. This cost is largely invisible to the submitter, other than increasing delays in receiving reports. Complaints may be voiced about how slow the laboratory is without realizing the CSIs and officers in the field are directly contributing to the wait.

When speaking of recovering physical evidence, it is important to ensure that what is actually recovered is really needed to answer questions that arise from the investigation. This can be taken to the extreme by certain police agencies that collect everything at the scene that might be considered physical evidence, label it, and try to assess the significance later or hope that the forensic laboratory will sort it out. This "garbage truck" approach (see the "Garbage Truck Forensics and Opportunity Costs" sidebar) has one advantage in that the agency can state with certainty that they showed due diligence and collected *all* the physical evidence. However, with so much evidence, they will have to perform the extraordinary (and time-consuming) job of measuring, photographing, and documenting every single item they have collected. Whoever then has to sort out the significance of all the evidence, and how all the evidence is related, will be working long hours, and at completion they will still be unaware of the answers to many crime scene reconstruction questions. On the other hand, if vital evidence is either not collected or not properly preserved, the outcome will be the same, and the investigation will not be successful. This reinforces the importance that systematic methods must be used to recognize and recover physical evidence that is relevant to the investigation while excluding unnecessary material.

"Freezing" the Scene and the Three R's (Recognize, Recover, and Record)

The dream of every CSI is to walk into a crime scene, press the button on a clock, and have time stand still, "freezing" the scene until it is completely and properly processed. Being a historical science, forensic science is time dependent, both forward and backward. The crime is over and cannot be changed; the fact that the future is "coming" cannot be stopped, but perhaps only delayed. Thus, at a crime scene, the CSI is in a race, and sometimes a fight, against time. Balanced against this race are available resources and quality. The best option is to record as much as possible, document extensively, and process the most time-sensitive materials first. The goal is to recognize, recover, and record any physical evidence at the crime scene to uncover what happened and in what order: These are the first steps toward crime scene reconstruction. Approaching a crime scene to uncover the last known chronology of events and, if possible, the identity of the people present at the

Key Terms
Three R's
"Freezing" the scene
Strip or lane search
Grid search
Spiral search
Trail search

crime scene when the incident took place, and their interrelationships, will provide the CSI with the best scope of the work to be done.

Death Investigations

In a death investigation case, it is important that the crime scene investigation team know the manner in which the victim died as soon as possible after the death. Remember this is only a preliminary manner of death finding, as the official manner of death finding will be released by the coroner or the medical examiner (depending on the jurisdiction) usually soon after the autopsy report is issued. There are only five manners of death: natural, accidental, homicide, suicide, undetermined. The cause of death is the disease or injury responsible for the lethal sequence of events.

Without moving or touching the body in any way, the investigators can do a visual inspection for the presence of any wounds. The projectile from a discharged firearm produces a special kind of blunt-force trauma. Gunshot wounds can provide useful information; as before, this is only preliminary information, and at autopsy the nature of the wounds, the bullet trajectory, and the distance from the muzzle of wounds will all be confirmed. Entrance wounds where a bullet entered the body are usually, but not always, smaller than the exit wound. They may be relatively clean and well defined and there may be blackening around the edges; often little blood is associated with this wound. Exit wounds are larger and more irregular in shape, with more associated blood. The presence of tattooing or stippling that occurs when gunpowder is deposited beneath the skin can help to determine that the muzzle of the weapon was in close proximity to the skin when the gun was discharged.

The hands and arms can be viewed to find defense wounds. These are wounds caused during a struggle between a victim and the attacker. The victim may have many slashing wounds to the fingers or puncture wounds to the rest of the hands as a result of trying to ward off numerous knife stabbing attempts. In cases where a victim defends himself from a beating, there may be defense wounds in the form of abrasions or bruises on the forearms.

Sometimes the manner of death may be homicide but the cause of death is not what it seems initially. Consider the case of an elderly woman who was found dead by her son at her apartment near the Space Needle in Seattle, Washington. Her home had been ransacked and many of her valuables were missing. When called the initial officers observed that she was lying on the floor and had a purple towel wrapped around her head with an eight-inch kitchen carving knife protruding at an angle from the area of her neck. Bloodlike stains could be seen on the towel. Even though it was summer the heat was turned up to a high setting and she was wearing multiple layers of clothing—not unusual circumstances for an elderly woman, who probably had bad circulation. She had a blanket and a white sheet across her thighs and

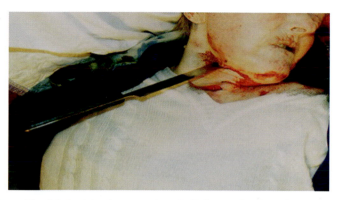

FIGURE 4.1.1 Wounds in the victims that were not immediately obvious to the police at the scene.

lower legs. The son stated he had done this to preserve his mother's dignity; situations like this are understandable but complicate matters for the CSI. Officers pulled back the towel (not a good idea) and noticed open gashing wounds on her throat and that blood had dried around her neck (Figure 4.1.1).

When detectives arrived, they quickly interviewed the son and, with their experience, they decided that he was not a likely suspect. When they contacted the CSIs, they reported that the elderly woman had had her throat cut. The CSIs searched the apartment and could find blood nowhere other than in the bedroom around where the victim was found. They considered that her throat had been cut in the bedroom but could find no signs of a struggle, or any projected bloodstains or drip patterns. They waited for the medical examiner and then assisted him in removing the towel and looking at the bloodstains on the victim's body and clothing. Again, very little blood was evident on her body or clothing; certainly nothing would suggest that she had had her throat slashed. Their suspicions were confirmed when the medical examiner removed the outer clothing to inspect the neck wound: not only were there wounds to the side of the neck where the knife protruded but the other side of her neck indeed had been cut open to the extent that the carotid artery was clearly visible (Figure 4.1.2). There was, however, no bloodstain evidence to support the contention that the victim was alive at the time the wounds were made to her throat. The medical examiner quickly agreed with the crime scene investigators that these wounds had been made postmortem.

At autopsy it was determined that the victim had died by strangulation. A transient who was arrested several days later when trying to cash checks from the victim admitted to the crime.

Preliminary Search

To further assist with establishing a chronology of events, the following information should be looked for before any major attempts are made to

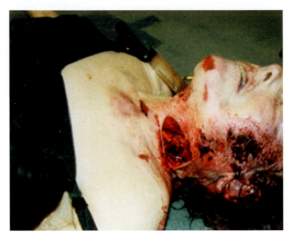

FIGURE 4.1.2 The wounds to the victim's neck were more extensive than previously thought but did not generate significant loss of blood.

recover any physical evidence. This information will later be used as data for crime scene reconstruction analysis. Visually identifying the presence of obvious physical evidence will direct the method of searching for less visible evidence. Points of entry and exit should always be checked for signs of fingerprints, shoeprints, and toolmarks from forced entry. There should be a search for any evidence that helps to establish how many people were present: This goes beyond the Hollywood plot where a man is found dead in an empty house but there were two wine glasses, one with lipstick, on the coffee table, and this sets our detective off on a hunt for the *femme fatale*. In addition to using fingerprints and DNA in relation to alcohol and cigarettes, look for signs of items or objects that look out of place.

To illustrate this concept, consider a case from Redmond, Washington, where a middle-age woman, who lived alone, had gone missing. Her apartment appeared to be very clean and tidy. Her container for municipal recycling was in the middle of the kitchen floor and the contents had been deposited in the apartment complex recycle bin. Although she was a smoker (who invariably smoked a particular brand), she always smoked on her balcony and never in the apartment. Investigators found two cigarettes (of a different brand) floating in urine in the toilet bowl; the toilet seat lid was up. The latter information suggested that the person who smoked two cigarettes then urinated in the toilet was a male. In addition, a dirty towel was lying on the rack in the same bathroom; this towel was collected. After a week or so a suspect was developed. He lived with the victim's daughter, who was also the mother of his two children. He worked as a low-skill polisher and grinder in a metalworking company nearby. The police had insufficient evidence to arrest him. Two months later, he was the last person seen with a female childhood friend before she too went missing. The bodies of both missing women were discovered outdoors several months later. When the trace evidence from the towel and other items from each outdoor scene were analyzed at the laboratory, metals of the appearance and elemental composition associated with polishing and grinding were found to be common between the items. This metals evidence, fiber evidence, and a fingerprint from one scene were important in finding the suspect guilty of both murders.

Look for signs of struggle, like knocked over furniture, broken fixtures and lamps, broken glassware and bottles, or broken windows. All should be left undisturbed initially and photographed thoroughly. Although the presence of such disturbed items suggests violence has occurred, the possibility of a staged crime scene cannot be discounted. Where staging is suspected, the glass remaining in the broken windows, if carefully marked as to inside and outside, can be examined at the laboratory and the direction it was broken from can be ascertained. Even if staging is not suspected, the broken glass in the window pane should be examined for fibers and possible blood. The glass on the ground beneath the broken window should also be examined carefully for the presence of shoeprints.

Signs of drinking alcohol can give investigators clues about events; this is very important when people have left the scene before police arrive. This investigative technique was used following an incident at a New Year's Eve party in Bellevue, Washington, that was attended by reportedly up to 50 people. At midnight, several of the partygoers celebrated the new year by firing their guns into the air. A fight subsequently broke out and one man was shot. Someone called the police but, by the time they arrived, only the victim and his girlfriend remained. Due to language and cultural differences, the officers were unable to learn the names of any of the partygoers. There were obvious signs of heavy alcoholic drinking and some recreational drug use. The bottles, glasses, and drug paraphernalia, when checked for latent prints, led, after investigation, to the arrest of several gang members. DNA from cigarette butts collected at crime scenes can also lead to identification.

Transient evidence like odors, from products like cleaning solvents and bleach, are often encountered, particularly in scenes involving the cleanup of bloodstains.

When encountering possible abandoned or stolen vehicles, measure the distance from the seat to the pedals: if the car of a missing woman who is 5′3″ tall is discovered and the seat is pushed back to the maximum, where she could not reach the pedals, she may not have been the last person to drive the car. The steering wheel can be swabbed for DNA different from the victim's. A different driver will likely adjust the rearview mirror and the door mirrors (if they are able to be adjusted manually); these mirrors (or their interior controls) should initially be checked for fingerprints, before DNA swabs are taken.

This list could continue, but to summarize, there are things that investigators can look for that will greatly assist and direct them before they begin their systematic search for physical evidence.

Recognizing Evidence

Before you begin any systematic search for physical evidence, you must first be able to recognize the evidence. Physical evidence can be everything from a 500-pound engine block dropped on someone's head to microfibers that are 10 microns thick to latent fingerprints or touch DNA that cannot be seen. Unfortunately, sometimes the situation may best be described by the phrase, "It's hard to find something when you don't know what you are looking for." To search for physical evidence, the CSI's eyes, nose, and ears are the best detectors. The best tool known for solving crimes is the human brain. To successfully search for physical evidence, the CSI needs a thorough grounding in all the forensic disciplines, including firearms, DNA, fire debris, drug analysis, document examination, and trace evidence. The latter discipline requires knowledge of many subdisciplines such as glass, hair, fibers, paint, explosives, and soil. Ambient and apparently incidental information, like weather conditions, cars, human behavior, and whatever else, may be of use. Not everyone can be an expert on everything, however, and very often a phone call can be a lifeline at a crime scene. It is always better to admit ignorance, but know who to call to find out the answer. Call on the assistance of one of the other specialists that attend crime scenes. No matter what the situation the search must be systematic and coordination and communication are required for success.

> Dr. Amy Mundorff, a forensic anthropologist who was in charge of the anthropological examinations of the victims of the September 11, 2001 attacks on New York, was once asked what was the one thing she had now that she wished she'd had when working on that case. She answered, "My phone contact list."

Recovering Evidence

There are several different methods of systematically searching for evidence (see Figure 4.1.3). The most important are the following:

- Strip or lane search method
- Grid or checkerboard method
- Spiral method
- Trail method

Which of these is employed principally depends on the type of crime scene you have, and the manpower available.

Strip or lane searches are often used for outdoor searches with large groups of searchers. They involve setting up lanes or strips where each strip is searched by one person. The lanes can be marked by tying string to a set of stakes at

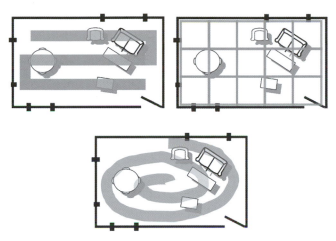

FIGURE 4.1.3 Three of the four search patterns: strip (or lane), grid, and spiral.

uniform lane widths apart, placed at either end of the area to be searched. Typically this lane width is an arm's length on either side of the searcher. The search group should be thoroughly briefed before the start of the search on what type of evidence items they may encounter. Each searcher should be supplied with a supply of flag markers, which are brightly colored plastic flags mounted on wire staffs often used by utility companies for the aboveground marking of underground wires. The searchers should be instructed to place a marker beside any object they see of interest. The searchers should not make an assessment of the object but leave this to the crime scene investigators who come behind them. As the searchers move down their lanes they will invariably do so at different speeds. An investigator must act as a coordinator to regulate the pace of the search. If a following investigator assesses that a marked object is an item of evidence that needs to be collected, he should signal the coordinator who will stop the search temporarily. The searchers will be briefed on the evidence item so they can get an understanding of the type of item they are looking for when the search is resumed.

The grid or checkerboard method is basically the repeat of the strip method at 90 degrees; in other words, if you complete a strip search in an east-west direction, you follow it with a strip search in a north-south direction. Each square in the grid can be searched separately. A single investigator or a team of investigators can use this search pattern in an indoor scene. A team could use this search method to assign a room in a house to each investigator. The room could be described as a cube and each investigator could do a subzone search of the six sides of the cube by systematically searching the four walls, the ceiling, and the floor. This type of search works very well when ensuring that all bloodstains in a room are accounted for.

A spiral search can be conducted from a point at the scene, like a body, a point of entrance or exit, or a gunshot hole, outwards in increasingly larger curves.

This can be useful to find specific items of evidence (like a fired cartridge casing).

A trail search is often used outdoors for the discovery of scattered remains. Animals that live in thick brush or forest areas tend to move along well-defined trails and bones or items that have been dragged off from the site of the body are often found on these trails.

Recording Evidence

For future court proceedings, note-taking is the most important task for the investigator at a crime scene. Notes must be:

1. Chronological and continuous
2. Detailed and specific
3. Complete
4. Legible and permanent

Chronological and continuous: The notes begin before entering the scene. The opening notes will contain details such as which investigators are present at the scene, the scene location, the time and date the investigator was contacted, the time the investigator arrived at the scene, the names and contact information of the detectives who contacted the investigator, and lastly a brief synopsis of the information given to the investigator before he enters the scene.

As the investigator does his walkthrough of the scene, brief notes should be taken in each room of a house or in each distinct area in an outdoor scene. These notes will be expanded upon later as each room or area is thoroughly searched. This is the section of the notes where general comments are made about topics such as indoor cleanliness, the condition of the entrances and exits, the appearance of overturned objects, the signs of a struggle, the outdoor environmental conditions, and the other topics for consideration in the preliminary search described before.

After the plan for systematic searching is agreed upon, the reasons for the adoption of this plan must be noted. As the search proceeds, the notes must be continuous.

Detailed and specific: Descriptions such as "There was blood on the light switch" provide little information. The notes must have the detail and the specificity to leave no room for ambiguity about what is being described and where it is located. Compare the previous description to an experienced investigator's notes on a homicide: "The white plastic light plate inside the front door has two bloodlike smears. These smears tested presumptively positive for blood with phenolphthalin. The smears are on the upper edge of the plate, 47½ inches from the floor and 16 inches from the north end of the east wall. A sample of the bloodlike smear on the north side of the plate was collected as item TMCA-6."

Complete: The notes must describe every observation, every action, every result of testing, and the collection of every item of physical evidence that occurs. The author cannot be selective about what results are recorded; every result, positive or negative, must be noted. Before the investigator leaves, the disposition of every evidence item must be noted, with descriptions of the packaging and seals applied to each.

Legible and permanent: The style of chicken scratch you have perfected as your signature will not cut it for recording written notes. The notes must be written in such a way that they can be easily read by anyone. They must be written in permanent ink so that changes are not easily made. In the very cold areas of North America in the winter where it is impractical to use a pen, the notes can be made in pencil, but they must be transcribed using a pen as soon as possible after the scene. Any errors to the notes that are noticed should be crossed out using a single strike-through, and the author's initials and date noted beside the strike-through. Another thing to be remembered is that the notes will potentially be scanned and photocopied many times by defense investigators, attorneys, defense experts, and others. The more organized and easily read the scene notes are, the less likely there will be any misunderstandings about meaning or content.

Conclusion

All crime scene procedures are based around the three R's: recognize, recover, and record. Each of these rules can be subdivided into techniques that achieve each goal. Practice is central to successful execution of the methods at the scene. Indiscriminant collection of evidence is *not* a good crime scene method, however, and rampant collection of all evidence hoping the laboratory will sort it out only delays everyone's work.

The Chain of Custody

What is the single most important thing to come out of a crime scene? It's not the physical evidence. It is a document that records the movement of every item of evidence from its moment of collection to its ultimate disposal: the chain of custody. The *chain of custody* can be defined as the order of places where, and the persons with whom, physical evidence was located from the time it was collected to its submission at trial. Anyone even remotely familiar with court proceedings knows that it is central to the criminal investigation.

To illustrate how important the chain of custody is, consider a bloodstain sample that is collected on a swab by a forensic scientist at a crime scene. The sample will subsequently undergo extensive serological and DNA testing in the laboratory. The results indicate the chances of the bloodstain being from a person other than the suspect is 1 in 27 billion. During testimony, the scientist is asked if a tested sample was under her control at all times during her testing. To this seemingly routine question, the scientist answers, "Yes."

Key Term
Chain of custody

The laboratory is internationally accredited and the science associated with the DNA testing has undergone quality check after quality check; the scientist has checked and rechecked her statistics. The case file has been technically peer-reviewed by another scientist who agrees with her statistics and the conclusions in her laboratory report that was submitted to the court. The work is solid and the scientist is ready to answer any and all questions about forensic DNA analysis and the samples in this case. What the scientist does not realize is that, while she was waiting in the hallway to testify, the detective who worked the case is asked the same question: Was the DNA sample under your control at all times? The detective says it was. The attorney then points to the chain of custody, which shows the DNA sample being collected by the CSI and then transferred to the detective, followed by a period where it disappears off the chain until it comes into the possession of the forensic scientist in the laboratory. Based on this official documentation, the DNA sample was unaccounted for over a period of hours. Was it tampered with? Where was it? Who had access to it? Could it have been contaminated? Although commonsense would dictate that the DNA sample was in the packaging and was transferred to the laboratory with the other evidence, the official record does not confirm this. The integrity of this evidence will now be questioned and may affect the outcome of the case.

It may not seem fair that a small error of writing or a signature can change the course of a case. While the preceding scenario does not happen often, when it does, the consequences for any break in the chain of custody can be disastrous. As an experienced investigator at a crime scene you will employ all your skills to recognize and recover items of physical evidence. You and everyone who subsequently handles the items of evidence are responsible for ensuring that there is an unbroken record of where the physical items are and who has custody of them at all times (Figure 4.2.1). No one in that chain of custody can afford to be sloppy in their documentation of the disposition of that evidence.

When is something in your custody? Samples and data are considered to be in your custody when:

1. They are in your physical possession.
2. They are in your view, after being in your physical possession.
3. They are in your physical possession and then secured so that tampering cannot occur.
4. They are kept in a secured area, with access restricted to authorized personnel only.[1]

Chains of custody may be a simple paper document (as in Figure 4.2.1) that is filled out by hand and signed by each party in the evidence exchange. With modern computerized evidence tracking systems, the chain may be created

---

[1] Chain of custody procedures for samples and data. United States Environmental Protection Agency. http://www.epa.gov/apti/coc/.

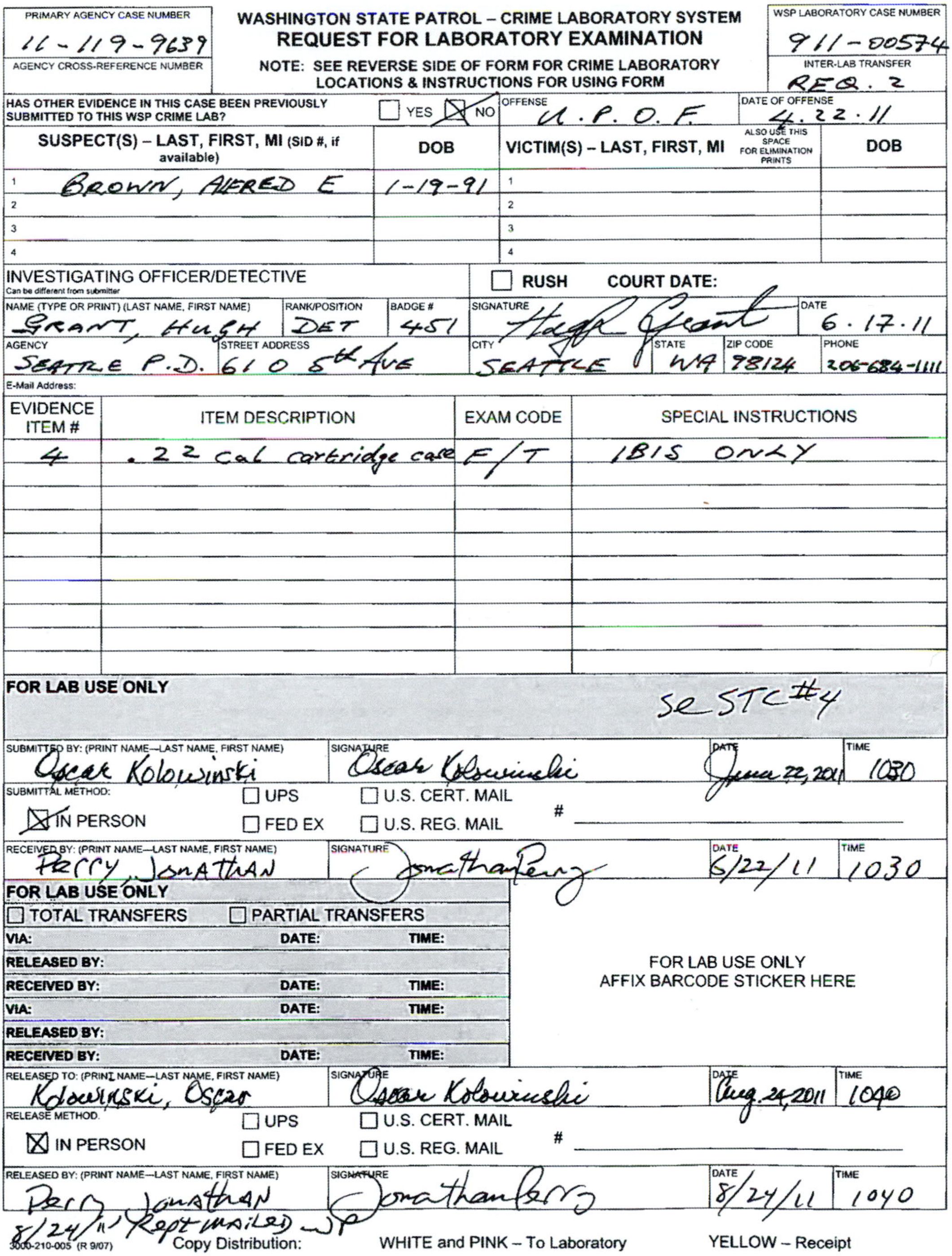

WASHINGTON STATE PATROL – CRIME LABORATORY SYSTEM
REQUEST FOR LABORATORY EXAMINATION
NOTE: SEE REVERSE SIDE OF FORM FOR CRIME LABORATORY
LOCATIONS & INSTRUCTIONS FOR USING FORM

PRIMARY AGENCY CASE NUMBER: 16 - 119 - 9639
AGENCY CROSS-REFERENCE NUMBER:

WSP LABORATORY CASE NUMBER: 911 - 00574
INTER-LAB TRANSFER: REQ. 2

HAS OTHER EVIDENCE IN THIS CASE BEEN PREVIOUSLY SUBMITTED TO THIS WSP CRIME LAB? ☐ YES ☒ NO
OFFENSE: U.P.O.F.
DATE OF OFFENSE: 4.22.11

SUSPECT(S) – LAST, FIRST, MI (SID #, if available)	DOB	VICTIM(S) – LAST, FIRST, MI	ALSO USE THIS SPACE FOR ELIMINATION PRINTS	DOB
1 BROWN, ALFRED E	1-19-91	1		
2		2		
3		3		
4		4		

INVESTIGATING OFFICER/DETECTIVE
Can be different from submitter
☐ RUSH   COURT DATE:

NAME (TYPE OR PRINT) (LAST NAME, FIRST NAME)	RANK/POSITION	BADGE #	SIGNATURE	DATE
GRANT, HUGH	DET	451	Hugh Grant	6.17.11

AGENCY	STREET ADDRESS	CITY	STATE	ZIP CODE	PHONE
SEATTLE P.D.	610 5th Ave	SEATTLE	WA	78124	206-684-1111

E-Mail Address:

EVIDENCE ITEM #	ITEM DESCRIPTION	EXAM CODE	SPECIAL INSTRUCTIONS
4	.22 cal cartridge case	F/T	IBIS ONLY

FOR LAB USE ONLY

se STC #4

SUBMITTED BY: (PRINT NAME—LAST NAME, FIRST NAME)	SIGNATURE	DATE	TIME
Oscar Kolowinski	Oscar Kolowinski	June 22, 2011	1030

SUBMITTAL METHOD:
☒ IN PERSON   ☐ UPS   ☐ FED EX   ☐ U.S. CERT. MAIL   ☐ U.S. REG. MAIL   # _____

RECEIVED BY: (PRINT NAME—LAST NAME, FIRST NAME)	SIGNATURE	DATE	TIME
PERRY, JONATHAN	Jonathan Perry	6/22/11	1030

FOR LAB USE ONLY
☐ TOTAL TRANSFERS   ☐ PARTIAL TRANSFERS

VIA:	DATE:	TIME:
RELEASED BY:		
RECEIVED BY:	DATE:	TIME:
VIA:	DATE:	TIME:
RELEASED BY:		
RECEIVED BY:	DATE:	TIME:

FOR LAB USE ONLY
AFFIX BARCODE STICKER HERE

RELEASED TO: (PRINT NAME—LAST NAME, FIRST NAME)	SIGNATURE	DATE	TIME
Kolowinski, Oscar	Oscar Kolowinski	Aug. 24, 2011	1040

RELEASE METHOD:
☒ IN PERSON   ☐ UPS   ☐ FED EX   ☐ U.S. CERT. MAIL   ☐ U.S. REG. MAIL   # _____

RELEASED BY: (PRINT NAME—LAST NAME, FIRST NAME)	SIGNATURE	DATE	TIME
Perry, Jonathan	Jonathan Perry	8/24/11	1040

8/24/11 Rept Mailed WSP

3000-210-005 (R 9/07)
Copy Distribution: WHITE and PINK – To Laboratory   YELLOW – Receipt

FIGURE 4.2.1 An example of a handwritten chain of custody. (The names used above are fictitious.)

INTERNAL CHAIN OF CUSTODY

LABORATORY CASE #: 911-000574
Submission: SEA002
Evidence Description: sealed envelope stc item 4

FROM	TO	Time
Kolowinski, Earl ( ) [ ]	Perry, Jonathan (SEA) [X]	6/17/2011 10;30;00AM
Perry, Jonathan (SEA) [X]	NON DRUG BOX (SEA) [ ]	6/17/2011 12:45:23PM
NON DRUG BOX (SEA) [ ]	Perry, Jonathan (SEA) [X]	6/23/2011 08:45:32AM
Perry, Jonathan (SEA) [X]	Stevens, Elizabeth (SEA) [X]	6/23/2011 08:45:39AM
Stevens, Elizabeth (SEA) [X]	Collins, Michael (SEA) [X]	6/25/2011 01:26:17PM
Collins, Michael (SEA) [X]	NON DRUG BOX (SEA) [ ]	6/25/2011 01:26:24PM
NON DRUG BOX (SEA) [ ]	Perry, Jonathan (SEA) [X]	8/24/2011 10:40:52AM
Perry, Jonathan (SEA) [X]	Kolowinski, Earl ( ) [ ]	8/24/2011 10:40:59AM

NOTE: [X] indicates a secured transaction (a PIN was entered)
12/23/2011 12:5pm

Page 1 of 1
R-2009-02-03

FIGURE 4.2.1 (Continued).

electronically using personal identification numbers (PINs), badges, or some other identification device; at the end of the case, a paper copy can be printed out and stored in a hard copy file.

Whenever students in undergraduate forensic science classes are introduced to the subject of chain of custody, they quickly understand the concept and opine that it is so obvious, how could anything go wrong? This is because they have not been exposed to the documentation that is involved to show an unbroken chain of custody. To illustrate this, it is useful to follow an item of physical evidence as it travels from the crime scene through many hands before it finally ends up in court. At the conclusion of the description of this evidence trail, those new to a chain of custody are often surprised how many checks are made by each person associated with the evidence.

A Chain of Custody Example

A CSI observes a hair in the sink in a bathroom at a scene. He documents in his notes the exact location and physical appearance of the hair, then carefully places the hair into a paper envelope. The investigator seals the envelope with evidence tape and writes his initials across the evidence tape seal. He assigns an exhibit number, such as TMCA-1, to the hair; he labels the envelope with this exhibit number, a description of the contents, the time it was collected, and the location from which it was collected. He then hands the envelope to the scene evidence officer from the police agency that is investigating the incident. The CSI documents in his notes how the item was packaged, the name of the scene evidence officer, and the time he transferred the item to her.

The evidence officer checks the seal, and adds the item to her evidence log before transporting it back to the police station. At the police station, the scene evidence officer will verify the assigned incident number and will enter details of the evidence associated with it into the property management computer system. The system will generate a bar code that the evidence officer will affix to the envelope. The envelope containing the hair will be transferred by the scene evidence officer to the police agency property management officer, who will also check the seals and the exhibit number, and verify if the label on the envelope matches the details that have been entered into the property management computer system. The time of the transfer, and the identity of the property management officer to whom the hair was transferred, will be logged using a bar code scanner. The property management officer will place the envelope containing the hair in an assigned location in the police agency evidence vault.

Several weeks later, after speaking with the deputy prosecutor and the lead detective, the property management officer will take the envelope containing the hair and other sealed evidence items and drive to the forensic laboratory. There, the property management officer will complete a request for laboratory examination form listing the envelope containing the hair and any other evidence items associated with the case and the type of testing needed on these items. The laboratory property and evidence custodian verifies that the items submitted are all present on the request and checks the seals on the items. The property and evidence custodian assigns a laboratory case number and enters the details of the evidence into the laboratory information management system (LIMS) using her PIN. The bar codes that LIMS generates for each item of evidence are affixed to the outer packaging by the property and evidence custodian who then places them into the laboratory evidence vault.

Some time later, as caseloads allow, the scientist who is assigned to analyze the case comes to the evidence vault where, using her PIN, the property and evidence custodian performs a secure transfer of the envelope containing the hair to the scientist. The scientist checks and notes the appearance of the packaging and the condition of the evidence seals. The scientist's notes will contain whatever analyses that he performed on the hair. Whenever the scientist is not working on the hair for any extended period, he will secure it in his personal evidence locker that is only accessible by the scientist and the laboratory manager. When his analysis is complete he will reseal the hair inside the envelope. Several days later, he will return it to the property and evidence custodian in the laboratory vault by secure transfer.

One week later, when a laboratory report of results of the testing on the hair has been signed, the report and the envelope containing the hair will be transferred from the laboratory vault to the laboratory property and evidence custodian, and subsequently to the police property management officer. The police property management officer will sign laboratory documentation indicating that he has taken possession of the hair. The laboratory property and evidence custodian will print out an electronic chain of custody and place it in the case file. This electronic chain of custody lists the evidence, the locations where the evidence was stored, and the names of laboratory members of staff who had the evidence in their possession. This links any evidence transfer to a specific second in time.

The police property management officer returns to the police station and replaces the hair in the station vault.

Perhaps a year later the police property management officer signs the evidence over to a court administrator for the court proceedings. It is a legal requirement that before physical evidence is introduced into court it must be identified as the same item that was collected at the crime scene. When the scientist goes into court to discuss the results of his analysis on the hair, he must first be able to demonstrate that the seals he put on the evidence envelope containing the hair are intact, and that the packaging is in the same condition as when he sealed it. The scientist often produces the electronic chain of custody from when the evidence was in the laboratory. It is then and only then that that the hair will be entered into evidence (assuming the defense attorney does not object).

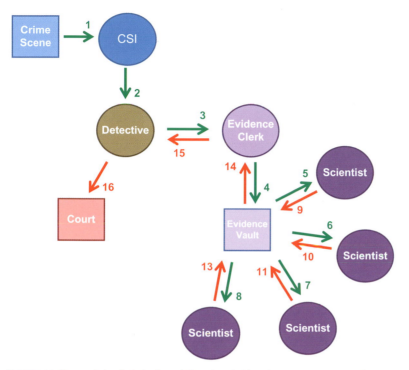

FIGURE 4.2.2 The complexity of a chain of custody for a piece of evidence increases as more personnel access it, and this complexity is compounded by each additional piece of evidence cataloged in a case. Here, a single item of evidence is diagrammed. First it is collected at the scene (1) and handed off to the detective by the CSI (2), who submits it to the evidence clerk at the laboratory (3). The clerk transfers the evidence to the vault (4), from which four scientists retrieve the item of evidence for each of their analyses (5–8), returning it after they are done (9–13). When all exams are completed, the evidence is taken from the vault by the clerk (14) and returned to the detective for storage (15) until trial when it is presented in court (16). In this hypothetical example (chain of custody protocols vary by jurisdiction), this one item of evidence has 16 exchanges associated with it, all of which must be documented.

This process of movement, verification, exchange, and receipt occurs for every piece of evidence collected at a crime scene! If there were a hundred items collected, each would need to have a chain of custody for it—the set of relationships between the items and who had them when is very complex (Figure 4.2.2).

Problems with Chains of Custody

Now that we are very aware of the importance of the chain of custody what are the potential problems that might arise for crime scene investigators in this area? The first and probably greatest problem is inappropriate packaging: When evidence is recovered it must be protected against deleterious change. If the forensic scientist does not package the evidence herself, then with her greater scientific knowledge, she has a responsibility to clearly explain to a police agency with whom she is working what the optimum packaging is for each piece of evidence. So, in the case of a shirt that is dripping with blood, she must tell the agency to thoroughly dry the shirt while it is lying flat, and then put it into paper packaging, which must be properly sealed, before it is submitted to the lab. It is good practice on items that the forensic scientist is not sealing at the crime scene to leave specific written instructions on how to package these items at a later date. Putting the shirt into a paper bag when wet could cause blood to leak through the bag losing evidence and contaminating other items.

Packages that are inadequately sealed are another potential problem. Gaps in the evidence seals or holes in the packaging can lead to a loss of evidence or the introduction of contamination. The evidence will not be in the same condition when it was collected.

Losing recovered items or having them be unaccounted for is another potential problem at the crime scene or even later. After seven hours at a crime scene the crime scene investigators are tired and want to go home. They have collected a total of 67 bloodstain, hair, fiber, and glass samples; they want to just hand a bag containing all the recovered evidence over to the scene evidence officer and go home. This is almost a sure way to lose items. The primary crime scene investigator must spend the time to make out a list of the recovered items, and then review that list with the scene evidence officer item by item, and have the officer sign for each item to ensure that no items are lost.

Conclusion

Chain of custody is not a difficult idea to grasp but procedures must be employed to ensure that the chain is unbroken. Maintaining the chain of custody can take a lot of time but, to quote Homer Simpson, "Do you want the job done right, or do you want it done fast?"

Recording the Scene: Sketching, Photography, and Video

Chapter 4.1 offered the three R's as guiding principles in crime scene investigation. Their order, overall, is important: recognize, recover, and record. This chapter on recording is presented first, out of order, because teaching is different than doing: Knowing how information will be documented and recorded *beforehand* is important to properly recovering any recognized evidence.

In real estate, when speaking of the value of a property, the phrase "location, location, location" is often used. A comparable phrase, "documentation, documentation, documentation," can be applied to crime scenes. It cannot be stressed enough that crime scene documentation is the key to a successful crime scene investigation.

Crime scene documentation includes written notes of the investigator's observations, photography, videotaping, and sketches. Measurements are a further important component of documentation and must be included in the investigator's notes. As the science of crime scene investigation evolves, and many practitioners and their parent agencies move toward personal certification and institutional accreditation, the one constant is that there can never be too much documentation. It is by the practice of comprehensive documentation that the crime scene investigator captures the original

Key Terms
35 mm film
Digital camera
Secure digital (SD) memory cards
Secure digital high-capacity (SDHC) memory cards
Pixel
Megapixel
High-dynamic range (HDR) processing
Inverse square law
Rectangular technique
Triangular technique
Polar technique
Geographical information system (GIS)
Crime mapping

condition of the crime scene and subsequently chronicles the changes in the scene as evidence items are recovered. Documentation is the foundation of any final crime scene reports. It can be simply stated: Without adequate documentation, crime scene reconstruction is not possible.

Although documentation may seem at first view a passive activity with little impact on the content of the crime scene, the actions involved in documenting the scene will themselves alter that scene (a kind of Heisenberg Uncertainty Principle[1]). Even the simple act of walking through the scene to photograph or videotape the scene in its initial state increases the likelihood that evidence will be disturbed or altered. In their pursuit of the laudable goal of "capturing the scene exactly as it was," unsuspecting investigators may alter or damage shoeprints that may only be visible using oblique light or after the use of fluorescent or staining chemicals as they capture the images of the crime scene. On TV crime scene investigation shows, crime scenes are either brightly lit from all angles and the investigator can stride straight in the front door and walk directly up to the body of the victim, or amazingly dark and the characters scout around in the inky blackness looking at everything with a flashlight. In reality, crime scenes can take place in dimly lit, double-wide trailers, where the drug and alcohol abuse lifestyles of the inhabitants make it very unlikely that they have employed a cleaning service every week. The clutter and unsanitary conditions associated with these scenes greatly increase the chances of evidence being disturbed during the initial photography and videotaping stages. They also occur outdoors in bright sunlight, in shopping malls, or anywhere people have been, objects have accumulated, and evidence can be overlooked.

Written notes of the investigator's observations, photography, videotaping, and sketches cannot all take place at once. The individual nature of each crime scene will dictate the order in which they are performed, but in general, initial observations are recorded first, followed by videotaping and photography, then sketches and measurements. As evidence is discovered and recovered, evidence-specific photography is needed, followed by more measurements. The involved nature of these activities reinforces the need for the team-based approach to documentation that was espoused in Chapter 3.3.

Crime Scene Photography

The only time car owners may open the owner's manual is when they have to reset their clock twice each year; most owners of today's point-and-shoot

---

[1] A principle in quantum mechanics, published by Werner Heisenberg in 1927, that states that the more precisely one property is measured, like speed, the less precisely another can be determined, like position.

digital cameras never even get that far. While such cameras are very useful for the initial responder, they are totally inadequate for the rigorous demands of evidence photography.

To get the most out of your photographic equipment, it is essential to understand the process by which the image is captured and how light and time of exposure affect the final image. Modern digital cameras on automatic setting can capture adequate images in many crime scene situations but photographing scenes in extremes of lighting, such as very dark or very bright situations, will necessitate specialized techniques that will require the user to understand the camera's capabilities and use the manual settings. Individual investigators and police departments should invest in crime scene photography courses. At a minimum, crime scene investigators must familiarize themselves with their camera, flash, and other photography equipment. They have to practice with their equipment repeatedly before they use it at a crime scene. It is the corollary to the three-part phrase this chapter started with: "practice, practice, practice." A homicide scene is not the place to learn to use the camera for the first time.

Many times forensic scientists are contacted by attorneys or detectives to consult about crime scenes where the scientist is asked to perform a reconstruction based solely on photographs taken by a local forensic unit. Too often, the supplied photographs are poorly lit and out of focus. The scientist may be asked what she can tell about a shoeprint pattern that is visible in a photograph; she then has to diplomatically explain that as the shoeprint was taken from 20 feet away, at an acute angle, and without a scale, she can't say much about the print at all. Making assessments from other peoples' photographs is a potentially dangerous situation for everyone involved and is to be avoided.

Well-respected books on crime scene investigation published in recent years devote much space to how to achieve good 35 millimeter (mm) film crime scene photography. This chapter concentrates more on digital photography; however, a thorough knowledge of the principles and practices of 35 mm photography is an excellent grounding for good digital crime scene photography. In addition, there are special instances that may require the use of different format cameras or film that is sensitive to infrared or ultraviolet regions of the spectrum, where a digital camera (at present) is not applicable.

The advent of widespread high-quality digital cameras has revolutionized crime scene photography. Experienced investigators can identify with world-renowned crime scene investigator Ross Gardner, who as recently as 2005 stated, "City managers and police chiefs are often quick to complain about the costs of film and film processing, but remember that the technician has only one chance to process the scene. *Film is the cheapest thing at a crime scene!*"

(Gardner, 2005; emphasis in original). Today, there should be no such reason to skimp on the number of photos taken at a crime scene, as memory is even cheaper.

The biggest difference in the operation of the traditional 35 mm camera and a modern digital camera is in the storage medium. With a 35 mm camera, to capture images you expose a plastic film, which is coated with a layer of light-sensitive material, to a timed light exposure. When you capture an image with a digital camera, the light strikes a digital sensor array. The digital sensor is made of millions of tiny sensor points called "pixels," which is short for "picture elements." The 35 mm camera typically has a maximum of about 36 exposures before you have to rewind the film, open the back, and insert another film roll. With digital cameras you might be able to shoot hundreds of images before changing the small memory card that inserts into a slot in the camera body. The images on the memory card (secure digital (SD) or secure digital high-capacity (SDHC) cards are used most) can be quickly transferred to a computer for further processing; the card is electronically reformatted and can be used again. Digital cameras also have the advantage that they usually have a large image viewer on the back of the camera, which enables the user to immediately see the image he has just captured. Compare this to 35 mm cameras where you take a picture, and hope the picture turns out. Image quality of the final image from digital cameras is determined by a number of factors, foremost of which are the quality of the camera lens and the number of pixels of the camera image sensor.

Most cameras from well-known camera manufacturers will have compatible high-performance lenses that will perform well in crime scene situations. A megapixel (MP) is one million pixels and is a term used not only for the number of pixels in an image, but to express the number of image sensor elements of digital cameras or the number of display elements of digital displays. For example, a camera with an array of 3872×2584 sensor elements is commonly said to have 10 megapixels ($3872 \times 2584 = 10,005,248$). Although there is some controversy between camera enthusiasts, a 10 MP or 12 MP camera will capture an adequate resolution image.

Where digital photography really outshines 35 mm photography is in its ability to integrate with other technologies and media and share images cheaply, quickly, and repeatedly. Digital cameras can integrate with GPS systems to apply a location tag to each image. When the images are downloaded to a computer that can be easily linked to TV monitors or projectors, they are ideal for courtroom displays. Images can be wirelessly transmitted to printers for direct printing. When loaded onto a computer, it is a simple matter to share images via email or on CD to other investigators or attorneys. Another important property of digital images is the ability, by use of mathematical algorithms, to perform photo enhancement. This permits cropping, magnifying, brightening, darkening, adjusting the color balance, and making many other enhancements to the image. To perform such image manipulations with 35 mm film, a chemical darkroom is needed.

Forensic science students often ask, "How many images do you need to take at a crime scene?" The answer to this question can be expressed mathematically as

$$N = n + 1$$

where

> $N =$ the number of images that should be taken at a crime scene
> $n =$ the number of images that were taken at the crime scene

In other words, you can never take enough images; and when you are reviewing your case file later, there is always an image that you wish you had taken.

Crime scene images are used to record the location of the scene and the condition of the scene before any processing for evidence occurs, to record the location and orientation of any evidence items that are recovered, to document the spatial relationship between areas and evidence items in the scene, and lastly to help to attorneys and jurors see the crime scene as the investigators viewed it. To accomplish these tasks, three types of images are captured:

1. Long-range, overall images that set the scene and give perspective and scope.
2. Medium-range, evidence-establishing images that show the location of things within the scene.
3. Close-up evidence images, intended to show the detail of individual items.

Long-range, overall images are taken first. These images convey the layout of the scene from various angles. When taking these overall images of a residence, the photographer should include all entrances, exits, and windows. Frontyard and backyard images that may show routes into and out of the residence should be captured. As with medium-range images, overall images can be taken so they overlap. Using image editing software the digital images can be "stitched together" to show a large area in one image. Illustrating the location of evidence in a large outdoor scene can be accomplished using aerial photography. Nighttime photography is a special technique and some training is required to conduct it properly. The nighttime scene can be "painted with light" (opening the shutter for a second or more and panning a light across the area to be photographed) or enhanced with high-dynamic range (HDR) processing, which expands the dynamic range from the lowest to the highest areas of an image. These techniques represent the best possible means of capturing the scene "as is" (albeit in the dark). If the CSI and any available personnel are not familiar with these techniques, any crime scene photography should be postponed until daylight. This postponement has the added advantage of facilitating the observation of evidence images that may not have been apparent in darkened conditions.

Medium-range, evidence-establishing images help to show the location and orientation of evidence items, and their relationships to other items in the scene. After these medium-range images have been taken, the evidence items can be marked with easily seen numbered evidence placards, then a second set of medium-range images can be captured with the evidence numbers in place.

Zoom/macro lenses on the digital camera are used to capture close-up evidence images in focus, and without distortion. They should be taken both with and without a measurement scale, with the camera back "normal" (at 90°) to the surface of the evidence item. Many images from different angles may be needed to capture all the fine detail of pertinent features of evidence items.

The inadequate or inappropriate lighting of an object is one of the most common problems in crime scene photography. Light radiates from a point in all directions and the amount of light striking an object reduces as the square of the distance from the light source. A surface 2 feet away will receive 100 times more light than that which is received on a surface 20 feet away ($2^2 = 4$, $20^2 = 400$); this is based on the inverse square law, which states that any physical quantity is inversely proportional to the square of the distance from its source. Automatic electronic flashes that compensate for the distance between the camera and the object will automatically adjust the lighting output of the flash. The integral flash mounted on the top of most cameras can lead to reflection and subsequent overexposure of items that are directly in front of the camera. This can be negated by using an offset synchronized flash on an extension cord that can be directed at any angle. The lighting output of integral flash is also designed for medium- to close-range images and is often not powerful enough to illuminate distant objects. More powerful flash units and ancillary strong lights must be used in such circumstances.

Video

Videotape provides a perspective on the crime scene layout that cannot be as easily seen in photographs and sketches. It is a more natural viewing medium to generations who grew up watching TV and is good at demonstrating the layout of the crime scene and how the evidence items relate to the crime.

A mistake often made is to make a recording too soon. It is better to assess the scene to learn what the crime is about and then formulate a plan of what you will videotape. The videographer should think out the sequence of the items of interest and move methodically through them. When each item is in focus, wait for several seconds before moving to another item. Always allow viewers time to discern what they are looking at.

Video cameras do not see or focus as effectively as the human eye. The human eye can rapidly scan from object to object back and forth throughout a room and pick up important information. If a video camera is used to capture a scene in a similar way, the resultant videotape will appear as a succession of rapid images that appear disjointed with no logical connection between them. The key to good videotaping is slow camera movement; this is why slow panning of an area is necessary. The videographer should resist the temptation to overuse the zoom or wide-angle features on the video camera when focusing on items of interest. It may seem that the needed detail is being captured but viewers of such footage will quickly experience an unsettling visual effect and the importance of such items may be lost. Even worse, when viewing this in court, the jury may lose interest.

Use restraint and avoid sensationalism. Do not record the victim(s) as the opening scene. The taping should begin with a general overview of the scene and surrounding area. Shoot the location, etc., leading up to the victim(s). If the video dwells on the wounds/trauma too much the judge may not permit its entry into evidence.

The audio function of the video camera can be used at the beginning of the recording or a placard with the scene details can be shot to open the recording. If other investigators are present it is better that they and their equipment are not captured by the video camera. After any initial remarks, audio should be turned off to prevent the recording of any inappropriate remarks or unsubstantiated theories of the crime. This also enables the videographer to focus on the visual recording without having to think of exactly what commentary to provide as he moves through the crime scene.

Modern video cameras can produce excellent still images of evidence items and a videotape viewer can assimilate the spatial relationships between rooms, doors, objects of interest, and evidence items better than with photography and sketching. Video is not, however, a substitute for photography and sketching. It is an additional documentation tool that is used when necessary to highlight items of interest at a crime scene.

Measurements

Measuring a crime provides quantitative information to back up other types of visual documentation. The accuracy will depend on the location and the purpose of the measurements; typically, small areas require more detail as the distances are shorter. Sketches are often drawn from an overhead (or plan) view; other views may be necessary to capture certain details, like bullet holes in a wall, for example. While a finished sketch can provide a useful visual for the CSI or the jury, measurements are more important now with the prevalence of drafting and reconstruction software capable of rendering quality images and drawings.

Three main techniques are used for taking measurements at a crime scene (Figure 4.3.1(a)–(d)). All measurements should be taken from fixed points

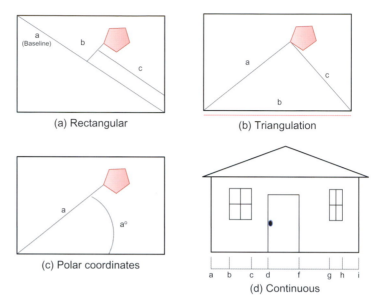

(a) Rectangular

(b) Triangulation

(c) Polar coordinates

(d) Continuous

FIGURE 4.3.1 Techniques for measuring at a crime scene: (a) rectangular with baseline; (b) triangulation; (c) polar coordinates; (d) continuous.

that are more or less permanent; a north arrow (determined from a compass) should be included in each sketch. The first, the rectangular technique, takes measurements in relation to a baseline, a central measurement from one fixed point to another. The baseline acts as a permanent referent for all other measurements. Straight lines are drawn between two points with a third perpendicular to those two lines. The second technique is triangulation, where two points at a scene are selected and then measurements are taken between them and a third point. Distance and angle can be documented using triangulated measurements, accurately placing an object in two-dimensional space. The third main technique measures the distance and angle an object is from a known point. When measuring the length of a large room or an outdoor structure, it is best to measure the distances continuously (0'0", 3'4", 7'6", 8'10", etc.) rather than from one point to another; the continuous approach leaves less chance for mistakes and accumulated errors from gaps between features.

Sketching

Sketches complement the crime scene investigator's notes and photographs. Their usefulness lies in their ability to present a lot of visual information about the scene by the omission of objects of no evidentiary value. A sketch can vary widely in complexity. It can be a rough hand drawing to give an aerial view of the crime scene (Figure 4.3.2) or an overall view of bloodstains on a dresser. When combined with measurements, a sketch can be a carefully drawn scale diagram (Figure 4.3.3). Using computer-aided drawing software, the two-dimensional scale diagrams can be transformed into an interactive

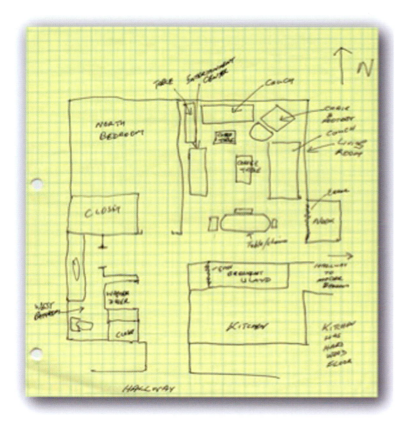

FIGURE 4.3.2 A rough hand sketch of a crime scene.

three-dimensional representation (Figure 4.3.4) that can be used to show the jury the crime scene from every angle and perspective imaginable.

Considering the time it takes to complete some investigations it is not unusual for investigators to have to use their sketches at trial several years after the event. They may have the scene details in their mind very clearly initially, but as time and memories fade away, sketches can quickly refresh the memory of investigators. Figure 4.3.2 is hardly a thing of beauty but it accurately shows the layout of an apartment where a homicide occurred. A rough sketch at the crime scene is fine for capturing the information necessary to process and document the scene; rough sketches are typically not drawn to scale. That rough sketch should be cleaned up for the CSI's notes file (intermediate quality) and drawn in a more professional fashion for a final sketch to be used in court; many software programs are available to assist CSIs with a final sketch if no artist is available in their agency.

Sketches, when drawn to scale, can show accurately the location and relationships of evidence items (Figure 4.3.3). As mentioned before these

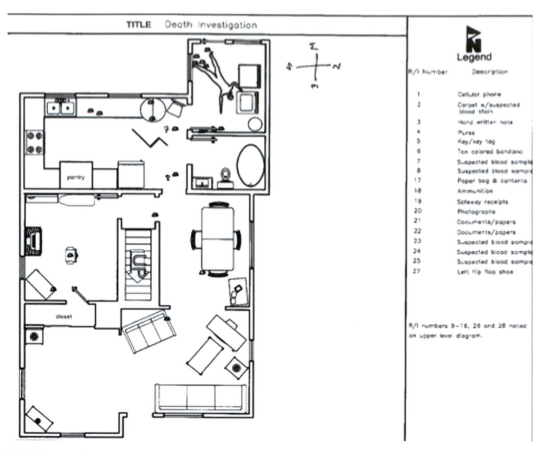

FIGURE 4.3.3 A two-dimensional scale diagram of a crime scene.

FIGURE 4.3.4 A three-dimensional diagram of a crime scene.

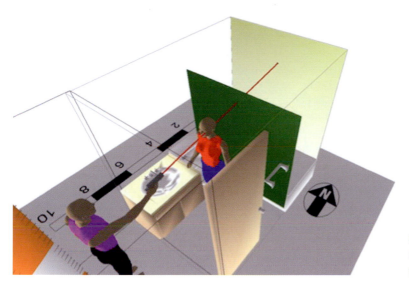

FIGURE 4.3.5 A three-dimensional diagram of a crime scene showing a theory of the crime.

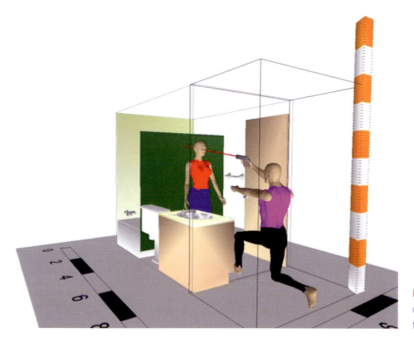

FIGURE 4.3.6 A three-dimensional diagram of a crime scene showing a theory of the crime.

scale diagrams can be used to produce three-dimensional diagrams. Such a diagram is shown in Figure 4.3.4. Three-dimensional diagrams can be used in reconstruction. Where there are competing theories of how the incident occurred, each can be applied to a scale representation and used by both prosecution and defense alike (Figures 4.3.5 and 4.3.6). Persons that are anatomically to scale can be inserted into the representations as can scaled weapons, furniture, and other items. It is not automatic that such

123

representations can be introduced into evidence to help illustrate the crime scene. The crime scene depicted in Figures 4.3.5 and 4.3.6 involved a woman in Tacoma, Washington, who was shot by her husband while she was getting out of the shower. He insisted that he was cleaning the gun when it went off accidentally. The husband was found guilty, but due to a change in the laws of appeal he was granted a second trial. At the first trial the investigator used conventional two-dimensional scene diagrams and photographs. At the second trial, due to improvements in technology, he was able to use interactive three-dimensional representations.

Prior to being allowed to show the representations to the jury the investigator had to prepare two sets of diagrams, one showing the gun being held by a male of the same height and build as the defendant, and a second set with the gun "floating" in midair without any depiction of a shooter. The bullet trajectory, shown as a red line in Figures 4.3.5 and 4.3.6, was drawn using data extracted from the bullet entry and exit wounds described at autopsy, combined with measurements of the bullet holes made successively by the bullet after it exited the rear of the victim's head, passed through the green shower curtain, and then entered the bathroom wall.

The representations were considered too prejudicial when they depicted a male shooter but were admitted into evidence in the "floating gun" format. The crime scene investigator had to demonstrate to the court, out of the presence of the jury, the precise perspectives he would later show to the jury. When the order of perspectives was agreed upon, the investigator had to practice with the mouse to make a smooth presentation to the jury. The software had the capability to make the presentation into a movie but the specific questions of counsel made it easier for the investigator to answer them by movements of the mouse, giving a visual tour of the crime scene to the jury.

Geographic Information Systems (GISs) and Crime Mapping

The combination of data, geographic information, and visualization of the space is called geographical information science. Computer systems are designed to capture, store, analyze, organize, and visualize data over space. *Crime mapping*, as it's called, is the application of GIS to reported crimes. It allows law enforcement agencies to determine "high-crime" areas, patterns, and trends. The well-known CompStat program that started in New York City applies principles of GIS; other cities have followed suit to various degrees as have social researchers (Figure 4.3.7). This type of technology will eventually trickle down to the individual CSI, if it hasn't already (see Chapter 7.3 on three-dimensional crime scene scanning). The portability of global positioning systems (GPSs) and satellite navigation systems ("sat-navs") will eventually become standard issue for CSIs, who may eventually upload images of evidence and real-time video as a matter of standard procedure (Figure 4.3.8).

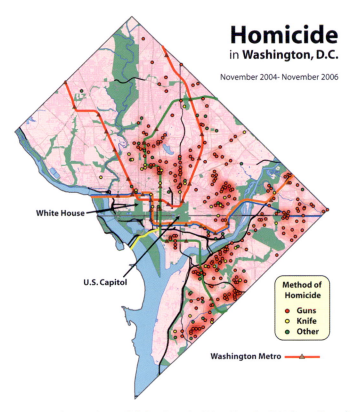

FIGURE 4.3.7   Homicides in Washington, D.C., from November 2004 to November 2006. *Source: Metropolitan Police Department.*

FIGURE 4.3.8   Portable gear for geographic information mapping (a GPS and laser rangefinder) and data collection (computer, in hand). *Source: Wikimedia Commons.*

125

Conclusion

Documenting the crime scene is so important that it is done several times over, in various modes, using sketches, photographs, video, and measurements, among others. Each mode will complement the other and act as "backup" if one of the modes fails or is destroyed. As with any area of science, technology offers new methods, such as GIS and other types of automated measurements; in time, the CSI's job will become less tedious and more attention can be spent on recognizing and recovering evidence, rather than paperwork and documentation.

Reference

Gardner, R.M., 2005. Practical Crime Scene Processing and Investigation. CRC Press, Boca Raton, FL.

Detection and Reconstruction

Searching for Evidence: Recovery

The primary purpose of a crime scene search is to recognize, locate, and collect any evidence potentially relevant to the case, such as evidence that could identify the perpetrator, exonerate an innocent person, or reconstruct the events close to the crime. It is commonsense to claim that the crime scene is at the root of forensic science: the science begins at it, informs a final result, and—with luck—answers more questions than it poses. Successful outcomes, be they legal or scientific, for the case at hand, often start with the physical evidence collected at the scene as the case begins. Lack of physical evidence could jeopardize the whole criminal procedure or at least decrease the relevance of the various investigative hypotheses. It is often said that "absence of evidence is not evidence of absence," and there are several possible reasons for a lack of physical evidence:

- The perpetrator has committed the "perfect crime" involuntarily. This hypothesis can be rejected out of hand, as it would violate Locard's Exchange Principle, which is paradigmatic and at the core of our science.

Key Terms

Evidence

Trace

Locard's Exchange
  Principle

- The perpetrator has taken protective countermeasures to conceal the presence of his or her own traces at the scene; in that case, "absence of evidence" is an indication of his or her actions.
- The CSIs did not detect any critical evidence for various reasons, including time since transfer, degradation of the evidence, scope of the material (too small, for example), or human factors on the CSI's part, such as lack of training or inattention to details.

A moment's consideration of the three aforementioned hypotheses to explain an "absence of evidence" unfortunately supports the last reason as being subjectively more probable than the first two. Recent academic works tend to support this conjecture, as many more traces are found on serious criminal cases or when a criminal commits a series of crimes than on minor or serial-but-unlinked ones, even if they are more "tracegenic" (rich with traces under Locard's Exchange Principle, like a car theft, where the perpetrator was active in the stolen car for some time as he was driving). A commonsense solution is to bet on experience to correct this "weakest link" of the investigation, to recognize, document, collect and preserve physical evidence. This more holistic approach initially looks relevant, but is not the only answer. First, experience only illuminates the events and phenomena so far encountered; as two cases are never exactly the same and as unexpected and deceptive actions are always possible, the idea of experience as pure "experimental" knowledge should be avoided. Moreover, an active investigation can hardly be assimilated into a relevant experience from the scientific and epistemological point of view only. Thus, a systematic and structured approach is the best method to decrease the risk that relevant evidence is left behind. At the very least, this provides a secure, systematic crime scene management approach that could explain, months or years later, why now-awaited evidence from the scene was not collected at that time. Questions like this and others could be either corroborated or dismissed by the evidence logbook and documentation.

This chapter will cover what constitutes evidence at a crime scene, what it takes for evidence to be relevant and exploitable, what kinds of evidence are useful, the constraints of the crime scene environment, and how to approach a crime scene systematically without losing sight of the "bigger picture" while optimizing the search. The next chapters of this section will present general concepts of evidence detection, collection, preservation, and submission.

From Trace to Proof, or Why Only Finding a Trace Is Not Sufficient

Relevant traces, marks, prints, signs, clues, and exhibits for the case under investigation are commonly considered evidence (see Table 5.0.1). It could be macroscopic (visible to the human eye), microscopic (minute and impossible

TABLE 5.0.1 Examples of Distinctions between Specimens Collected, Comparisons, and Controls to Be Collected at Crime Scenes

Specimen	Comparison or Reference Samples	Controls
Physical		
Fingerprints	Known ten print card	Fingerprints on relevant materials from the crime scene
Shoeprint development or cast; photograph	Shoes and inked prints of those shoes	Not applicable
Toolmark or cast of it, with photographs	Suspected tools	Not applicable
Cartridge case	Suspected weapon, other cartridges known to have been fired by it	Not applicable
Bullet	Suspected weapon, other bullets known to have been fired by it	Not applicable
Glass fragments	Glass found at scene	Pieces of the known broken glass
Biological		
DNA	Suspect's mouth swab or blood sample	Sterile cotton pad used for swabbing
Bloodstain photograph	If available, piece of bloodstain substrate; if not, descriptions and other photographs	Camera settings, establishing photographs
Digital		
Mass memory storage	All other available mass memory storage and the suspected central units	Similar devices on the market (for memory)
Printed document	Any other similar printed document found during a search	Similar printers on the market (for memory)
GSM (or parts like SIM cards)	Any other similar and compatible GSM slotting devices	Similar devices on the market (for memory)
Chemical		
Explosives swab on the neutralized bomb or nearby the blast	Swabs on suspect's hands; collection of clothes, chemicals, or accelerants found during a search	Environmental chemicals identified through interview of the suspect or explanatory hypotheses
Arson swab	Burned or exploded material	Original unexploded or unburnt materials similar to the ones at the crime scene

(a) (b)

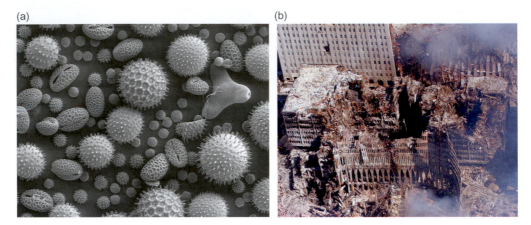

FIGURE 5.0.1 Anything can become evidence, large or small, living or dead, solid, gas, or liquid, from pollen grains ((a): 500x; the bean-shaped grain in the lower left corner is about 50 micrometers long) to entire cities ((b): the September 11, 2001 World Trade Center attacks on New York City). *Sources: Wikimedia Commons and U.S. Navy photo by Chief Photographer's Mate Eric J. Tilford, respectively.*

to see without aid), living or dead, solid, liquid, or gas. Literally, anything can become evidence (See Figure 5.0.1).

But, whatever its property, a trace is the residue or the vestige of a presence or an action; recall the discussion of proxy data in Chapter 1.0. A trace's form can be thought of as occurring in a variety of forms, described variously as marks, signs, or clues. Traces may be in such a small quantity that the CSI cannot choose the "best" one; they must work with what they find. Other times, however, there may be too many and the problem then becomes one of choosing (or sampling, in statistical terms). Regardless, there is a low degree of freedom in selecting pieces of evidence. Because of the scant materials that may be available of the criminal action or source, inherent weaknesses of the evidence may have to be addressed:

- How was this trace found?
- Has intentional deception or staging been eliminated?
- Were other traces searched for nearby?
- Could it have been left by an action other than the criminal one(s)?
- Are there other alternatives than the perpetrator as the source of this trace?
- Does the other evidence support the relevancy of this trace?

Just as collecting evidence is critical to a case, collecting controls and known samples is also important. Forensic examinations are centered on comparison as a method; this requires not only something to compare the crime scene sample to but also against to ensure the actual comparison is valid, accurate, and relevant. Moreover, as the following forensic analyses will necessarily interpret the collected questioned items in the specific case at hand, other materials should be collected as controls at the scene. What is collected, and how, will also depend on the protocols adopted in the laboratory, including known limitations of chemical or analytical tests (false positives and negatives). Known, blank, and control evidence collection can be easily incorporated into crime scene protocols in regard to the specimens collected at the crime scene.

As the CSI has only one chance to collect evidence at the crime scene, there should be no hesitation to contact post-scene forensic capacities (forensic laboratories, individual experts, forensic scientists, etc.) to identify clearly in the field what could be relevant to assist the forensic process, including avoiding false positives and negatives.

Which Evidence Is Useful?

Coming back to the wider concept of evidence, which covers all of the different types of relevant materials to be collected at the scene, an item of evidence constitutes the basic unit of a crime scene; these units can (Horswell and Fowler, 2004) (See figure 5.0.2):

- Confirm that a crime was committed
- Describe the circumstances in place at the time of the crime
- Establish what happened (reconstruction)
- Link the victim(s) to the scene of the crime
- Link the perpetrator(s) to the scene of the crime
- Link the victim(s) to the perpetrator(s)
- Link different scenes of crimes to each other (through operative forensic intelligence)
- Identify the author of a crime, but also link it to another criminal event

Remember, if the potential physical evidence cannot be recognized and collected, no forensic testing can be conducted. If the first step of the forensic process—recognition—is not done, then the whole process is affected and

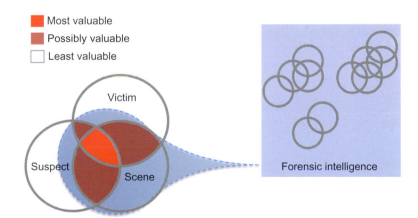

FIGURE 5.0.2 Evidence, the basic unit of a crime scene, has the ability to establish linkages between the various actors involved in one crime; it also has the ability to establish links between multiple crimes. The suspect, victim, and the scene all share some level of relationship, whether shared before the crime or only during that event. Likewise, evidence collected at the current scene may provide information for forensic intelligence about other crimes, by the same perpetrator, through a similarity of victims (elderly pensioners, for example) or a location (dark alley, for example).

FIGURE 5.0.3 The systematic
structure of the search process.

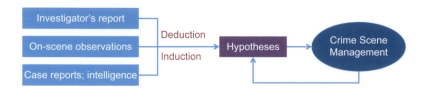

the crime scene investigation may fail, which could lead to an unsolved case and, worse, more crimes committed by a criminal not yet caught.

Collecting everything that could be construed as evidence, however, is not possible or even desirable for various reasons:

- Theoretically, it is senseless, as the scene itself is still modified by the very presence of the first officers, investigators, and forensic scientists, not to mention the previous precrime actors on the scene. Hence, collecting everything also means collecting items unrelated to the forensic investigation.
- Practically, the entire scene cannot be fully collected; doing so would also modify the scene, anyway.
- Operationally, the forensic facilities in charge of analyzing various items of evidence would be rapidly overwhelmed with the vast majority of collected items having no probative value. Notwithstanding the waste of time and resources, this type of practice could induce legal and investigative problems.

Hence, a moment's reflection by the investigator in charge of the crime scene will reveal how important it is to collect only the relevant pieces of evidence, as he realizes that he is operating between, on the one hand, the fact that collecting everything is illogical (garbage truck forensics!), and, on the other hand, the fact that forgetting or ignoring a piece of evidence could be disastrous. Thus, a system must be proposed to recognize and locate relevant physical evidence, while excluding irrelevant material. Stop for a second and realize that collecting is not submitting. Therefore, items that might be relevant should be collected, recorded, and preserved but submitted only to support or refute investigative hypotheses (Figure 5.0.3).

This requires that crime scene investigators understand the goals of a crime scene search within the immediate investigative hypotheses and other alternatives assessed from their observations, and process the crime scene effectively to address the scene as comprehensively as time and resources allow. The whole process would then define a systematic structured search process.

The Search for Evidence

The search for evidence should be legal, scientific, systematic, and complete (Lee et al., 2001). The search itself is generally ruled by a criminal procedure code, under the control (either immediate, as in the inquisitorial justice system, or final, as in the accusatory one) of a magistrate or judge. The combination of human resources, technical skills, and expensive detection and development techniques are intended to secure the actions of the CSI and her colleagues as a legal process to avoid any rejection of the evidence by the court. One of the means for defense counsel to devalue forensic evidence is either to claim it was obtained illegally or that scientific requirements (collection, preservation, or even interpretation) were not met, making it not presentable in court. Because of that, a constant awareness of the chain of custody should stay in the mind of all personnel at the crime scene. Photographing each and every step of the search from general viewpoints to particular ones offers a security that what was recorded was actually conducted at the scene; this will then be verified through other documents, like notes, scene logs, etc. Videotaping also provides assurance and support for specific actions or observations that may have to be described later. Note that photography has here a legal purpose complementary to scientific photography, which will be dealt with later.

Investigators should use relevant scientific methods and understand analytical sequences to increase the detection and development of evidence traces. Nondestructive means, such as optical detection and developments, should be preferred to, or at least applied before, any chemical, physical, or destructive ones. Hence, a thorough understanding of optical phenomena should be mastered by the CSIs; specific knowledge of chemical reactions with various evidence types will be of great help both at the scene and during later testimony. Finally, scientists should use Locard's Exchange Principle in the field to confront the different proposed hypotheses at hand, and focus specifically on points of contact to help describe the sequence of events. The Exchange Principle, in this context, is not a passive rule but an active tool to help focus a scene investigation. Using the a priori information available, the CSI should analyze the status of the to-be-collected evidence, and be aware of potential deception, bias, or relevancy within the context of the case at hand.

The systematic method of search chosen should follow a recognized scheme to avoid neglect of evidence through oversight. The system thus becomes a rubric, a habit, a regular procedure that acts as a safety net during complicated, long, or difficult investigations.

Finally, remember that processing a crime scene is "careful destruction" and can only be managed once. Even if an item of evidence seems marginally relevant but is in danger of being destroyed by weather, activity, or other means, it is best to collect and preserve it regardless of whether it becomes relevant. Completeness is a product of caution.

Practical Search: Focal and Ancillary Points

But where should a systematic search begin? Crime scene investigators should take the lead to focus immediately on precise points of the crime scene, as indicated by their observations and hypotheses.

- How far may I track the path used by the suspect to and from the scene? This path search should focus on shoeprints, tireprints, or even animal traces.
- How did the suspect enter and exit the scene itself? Signs of forced entry should help find toolprints, paint chips, fingerprints, shoeprints, blood, hair, fibers, and other evidence types.
- What kind of materials is the scene composed of? A thorough review of the environment of the crime scene should be completed to diagnose the types of traces probably transferred to the suspect or victim (originating from the crime scene itself), such as vegetation, pet hair, fabrics or fibers, paint chips, glass debris, or other materials.
- Was evidence moved at the crime scene? How was the victim handled? These necessary points of contact are the best areas to search for traces, such as fingerprints, blood, fibers, hair, or other transfers.

Main areas should be rapidly identified as focal points and ancillary ones for trace searches. Within these scenes, focal points are defined as areas having the highest probability of containing relevant pieces of evidence, such as the points of entry and exit, the paths suspected of having been used by the perpetrator, and the points of contact with the victim or the crime scene:

- Which drawer of the kitchen cupboard was opened?
- Which room hid the stolen goods?
- Where was the safe?
- Which areas have been obviously damaged, looted, visited? Why?
- Which specific location of this area was of interest?

Once these focal points have been identified, if not fully exploited, ancillary points can be better identified as areas plausibly accessed by the perpetrator to complete or conclude the crime: Did the weapon come from the victim's house? Was it recovered? Which area would have been used by the perpetrator to dump the gloves, ski mask, or weapon? Did the perpetrator stay long enough at the scene or nearby to have eaten, showered, or performed other activities? Pathways between these different areas should also be preserved as ancillary points.

The search should finish with a general search in the neighborhood of the crime scene, in locations such as trash bins, other dwellings, and other places where evidence may be located based on the inferred routes of the participants in the crime. Identification of the points of interest and systematization of the search do not guarantee proper collection of all relevant pieces of evidence. A reasoned process, however, should capture the scene as comprehensively as possible, and ensure that the search is not just focused on a single type of evidence (fingerprints or DNA, for example).

Optimizing the Search: Applying Locard's Theory

Sets of items can be targeted depending on the potential source of transferred material suspected to have been in contact with the other evidence (Gallop and Stockdale, 2004). For example, knowing the shirt worn by the perpetrator could increase the chances of finding those "target" fibers on the victim's clothing or on a broken window.

Recent technological advances have changed the way crime scenes are processed. The methodologies discussed have been developed with certain types of evidence in mind. Trace DNA analysis, for example, can yield a DNA profile with only the discovery of a few cells; however, the potential for contamination is exceedingly high. Notwithstanding the interpretation process involved and its acceptance both by the scientific and the legal authorities, the sensitivity level of trace DNA should remind the crime scene officer to carefully evaluate a scene before implementing various search methods at each single area of interest.

Controlling Contamination

Contamination of a scene can occur as soon as the crime is over. Any non-crime-related activity that compromises the scene once criminal activity ceases can compromise or destroy the environment set by the criminal actors. Crimes like arson or explosions greatly complicate the investigation because they destroy so much evidence. First responders, investigators, and forensic personnel could, understandably, contribute to this problem. For these reasons, controlling the crime scene provides a protection from trace contamination by anyone allowed to enter the scene:

- Anyone entering the scene should wear disposable coveralls that cover hair, gloves, and shoes. All personal protective equipment should be collected when leaving the scene to prevent the transfer of materials.
- A unique path of entry to the scene for the CSIs and other professionals should be identified, different from the most probable pathway used by the perpetrator. Unfortunately, this entry path is frequently decided by patrol officers, first responders, or SWAT teams.
- Identities of any stakeholders at the scene should be recorded to collect reference samples for future shoeprints, fingerprints, DNA, and other traces later found in the evidence for elimination purposes.

Moreover, understanding each chronological layer of the evidence, the CSI should work to unveil each level of evidence top down and epicenter out (or in). Shoeprints, for example, are of initial interest less for their identification capacity (depending on their condition) than for their ability to evaluate the number of persons involved and their positions or directions during the crime. Making the various authorized CSIs in the investigation aware of the need to protect shoeprints will enhance this first, delicate layer of information. Similarly, areas that would have been touched, like handles, weapons, or doorknobs, need to be dealt with cautiously to avoid damaging suspect latent prints. Trace evidence, bloody stains, and other biological material should then be collected, followed by gunshot material (residues and shooter's hand detection). Finally, processing and development of any fingerprints at the crime scene can begin, as this stage involves chemical products that may contaminate the scene.

Conclusion

Do not leave the scene until all available methods relevent to recovering evidence have been used. Maintaining the integrity and security of the scene is the responsibility of the police, but the scene should not be released until all viable evidence has been collected. The scene(s) may be kept under restricted access for some time to preserve it for any additional examinations. Before leaving, make sure that all collected evidence is under control, that photographs and memory cards are secured, and that the crime scene logbook is kept safe (Green, 2000).

References and Bibliography

Barnett, K., 2004. Marks and impressions. In: White, P.C. (Ed.), Crime Scene to Court: The Essentials of Forensic Science, second ed. Royal Society of Chemistry, Cambridge, UK, pp. 82–114.

Caddy, B., Cobb, P., 2004. Forensic science. In: White, P.C. (Ed.), Crime Scene to Court: The Essentials of Forensic Science, second ed. Royal Society of Chemistry, Cambridge, UK, pp. 1–20.

Crispino, F., 2010. Thesis. Le principe de Locard est-il scientifique? Ou analyse de la scientificité des principes fondamentaux de la criminalistique. Defended on May 5, 2006. University of Lausanne, School of Criminal Sciences. Institute of Forensic Sciences, Switzerland. Published under the title "Le principe de Locard est-il scientifique? Ou analyse de la scientificité des principes fondamentaux de la criminalistique." Editions Universitaires Européennes.

Gallop, A., Stockdale, R., 2004. Trace and contact evidence. In: White, P.C. (Ed.), Crime Scene to Court: The Essentials of Forensic Science, second ed. Royal Society of Chemistry, Cambridge, UK, pp. 56–81.

Green, M.A., 2000. Preservation of evidence. In: Siegel, J., Knupfer, G., Saukko, P. (Eds.), Encyclopedia of Forensic Sciences, in three volumes, pp. 1172–1177.

Horswell, J., 2004. Crime scene investigation. In: Robertson, J. (Ed.), The Practice of Crime Scene Investigation. CRC Press, Boca Raton, FL, pp. 2–45.

Horswell, J., 2004. Management of crime scene investigation. In: Robertson, J. (Ed.), The Practice of Crime Scene Investigation. CRC Press, Boca Raton, FL, pp. 82–94.

Horswell, J., Fowler, C, 2004. Associative evidence—The Locard Exchange Principle. In: Robertson, J. (Ed.), The Practice of Crime Scene Investigation. CRC Press, Boca Raton, FL, pp. 46–56.

Lee, H.C., Palmbach, T., Miller, M.T., 2001. Henry Lee's Crime Scene Handbook. Academic Press, New York.

Martin J.-C., 2002. Investigation de scène de crime. Fixation de l'état des lieux et traitement des traces et d'objets. Presses polytechniques et universitaires romandes.

Robertson, J., 2004. Crime scene investigation: Key issues for the future. In: Robertson, J. (Ed.), The Practice of Crime Scene Investigation. CRC Press, Boca Raton, FL, pp. 389–424.

Weston, N., 2004. The crime scene. In: White, P.C. (Ed.), Crime Scene to Court: The Essentials of Forensic Science, 2nd edition. Royal Society of Chemistry, Cambridge, UK, pp. 21–55.

Detecting

As the previous chapter dealt with the general approach of evidence collection at the operational level, this one will treat the general detection of traces at a tactical level. Commercially available technology, equipment, and resources, such as canine teams to track a perpetrator or a victim or to detect corpses, accelerants, explosives, or drugs; chemical sniffers; trace or metal detectors; and three-dimensional (3D) computer-aided reconstruction techniques to support ballistic findings and trajectory determination, are of interest to enlarge the existing toolbox for detecting traces and selecting collection areas. Many of them are only technical devices; others require specialized skills and training.

Understanding the different activities that may have occurred given the different hypotheses and assumptions made so far in the criminal investigation invites the eye to explore specific places for evidence. That is, indeed, the core issue of the CSI, whose findings will be mainly interpreted in the light of the various hypotheses covering the case at hand. It should be

Key Terms
Electromagnetic radiation
Wavelength
Frequency
Hertz
Luminescence
Fluorescence
Alternate light sources
Forensic light sources
High-pass filters
Band-pass filters
Specular reflection
Coaxial episcopy

remembered that the discovery of contact traces depends upon (Gallop and Stockdale, 2004; Horswell, 2004):

- The nature of the surface onto which the material has been transferred. For instance, fabric surfaces will retain fibers better, but are poor collectors of fingerprints.
- The time and weather since the contact.
- The way evidence has been handled since the commission of the crime, and once collected, the methods employed to avoid losing traces on it.

But the very first detection tool at a crime scene is the eye of the investigator itself. Special attention should be paid to optical artifacts (things that look like a reaction or item of interest but are not) and phenomena with a good understanding of light and its interaction with matter. This chapter is, therefore, a forensic review of the basic theory of light and an explanation of the types of evidence that can be detected with common forensic light sources. Physical and chemical tests that develop (or visualize) latent evidence are of interest, but:

- They are of use only in specific areas, suggesting that some kind of detection process already took place and indicated these areas be processed.
- Their detection properties are identical to their enhancement properties, and are specific to the matter and substrate searched.

Although some photographic tips will be presented here, the reader is invited to refer to any of the excellent books on forensic photography, for example, Russ (2001).

What Is Light and How Do We See an Object?

Electromagnetic radiation refers to energy in the form of waves. Humans and animals are visually sensitive to certain kinds of radiation; this is referred to as light. Light radiation strikes the optic nerves of the eyes and is sensed as color; different wavelengths of the light register in the brain as different colors. Different kinds of matter react with different waves of light. The matter absorbs more or less of the radiation causing one or more responses, some of which are useful in crime scene investigations.

Electromagnetic radiation can be thought of as existing in sine waves irradiating out from a source in all directions. These waves come in many sizes or lengths; thus, waves can be described by their wavelength (λ), which is the distance between corresponding points on two adjacent waves. Some types of radiation, such as X-rays, have extremely short wavelengths; others, like radio waves, can be very long.

Sometimes it is more convenient to measure light in terms of its frequency (ν), which is the number of waves that pass a given point in one second, measured in cycles per second or hertz. Since light travels very fast and the wavelengths are generally very short, the number of waves that pass a given point in one second is generally very high and most light has high values of cycles per second.

The continuum of electromagnetic radiation that we are aware of and can measure is depicted in Figure 5.1.1(a). At the far left of this electromagnetic spectrum are gamma rays; these are very energetic, can pass through matter, and therefore can be dangerous because they can damage or destroy living cells. Next in the spectrum are X-rays, which can also pass through most matter but are deflected by denser materials, such as bones. The X-rays reflect off bone and other dense tissue and are detected while they pass through soft tissue. The next region of the electromagnetic spectrum is called the ultraviolet-visible region, which contains ultraviolet and visible light. These two regions are spoken of together ("UV-Vis," pronounced "yoo-vee-vez") because both UV and visible light have similar effects on matter. Electromagnetic radiation in this region is not energetic enough to pass through matter; instead, when a molecule absorbs this light, electrons are shifted within the material and some are absorbed and others emit photons as excess energy (such as luminescence). As the frequency of visible light decreases, the light changes from violet to red at the lowest frequencies (Figure 5.1.1(b)). Only certain types of molecules will absorb ultraviolet light; most substances do not.

Figure 5.1.1(b) should grab the attention of CSIs: The human eye is most sensitive at around 550 nm and can be deceived by other colors where it is not so sensitive. For instance, a fingerprint in blood on a dark surface may not be clear to the unaided eye but will look good on a camera, as the CCD (or the film) is more sensitive than the eye on these regions. Moreover, as blood absorbs violet light, it could show contrast with its substrate; darkening the conditions for the eye could become an enlightening one for forensic devices.

Below the red region of visible light is the infrared region (infra means "below"; IR is a shorthand way to refer to it). This type of light causes bonds between atoms in a molecule to vibrate. Every substance absorbs light in the infrared region; the vibrations of the molecules are different for every substance. IR light is useful as a tool for the identification of a substance. At still lower frequencies than infrared light is the microwave region, which causes molecules to rotate or spin and therefore heat up (like in a microwave oven), and radio waves, which have very long wavelengths and thus very low frequencies with relatively little energy. These last two types of radiation have little use in forensic science.

Luminescence

Luminescence can be subdivided into phosphorescence, which is characterized by long-lived emission, and fluorescence, where the emission

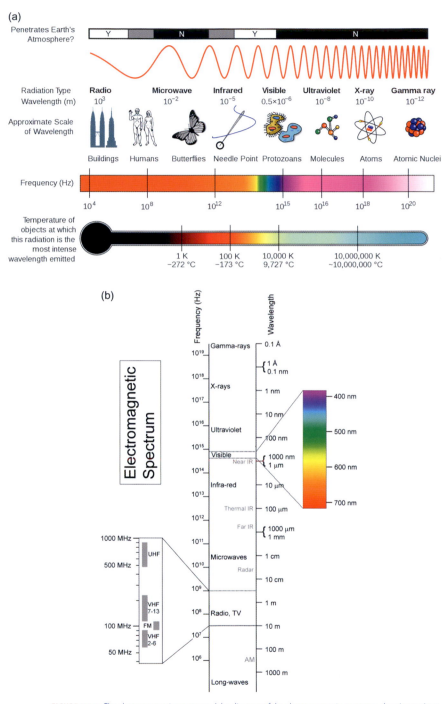

FIGURE 5.1.1 The electromagnetic spectrum: (a) a diagram of the electromagnetic spectrum, showing various properties across the range of frequencies and wavelengths; (b) the electromagnetic spectrum highlighting the visible range. *Source: Wikimedia Commons.*

stops when the excitation stops (Figure 5.1.2). The wavelength of the emitted fluorescence light is longer than that of the exciting radiation. This happens because, when the radiation of relatively high energy falls on a substance, the substance absorbs a specific range of the energy; most of the energy not absorbed by the substance is reemitted. Compared with the exciting radiation, the fluorescence radiation has lost energy and, therefore, its wavelength will be longer than that of the exciting radiation. A substance can be excited by near-UV radiation and, if it contains fluorescent components (fluorophores), fluorescence is seen in the visible range. The exciting wavelength is controlled using a band-pass filter, which, as its name implies, allows certain bands (or wavelengths) to pass and blocks or attenuates wavelengths outside that range (Figure 5.1.3). Part of the light striking the object is absorbed by the specimen and reemitted as fluorescence. To enable the comparatively weak fluorescence to be seen, despite the strong illumination, the light emanating from the object is filtered out by a secondary filter placed between the specimen and the eye (Figure 5.1.4). The second filter is called a barrier or emission filter, which has a well-defined band-pass region that transmits fluorescence emission wavelengths collected from the specimen by the objective lens while blocking residual excitation

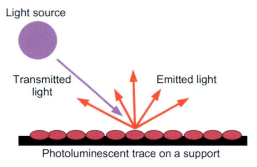

FIGURE 5.1.2 Fluorescence occurs when light of a higher energy strikes a material that absorbs some of the energy, emitting the rest as light (wavelength).

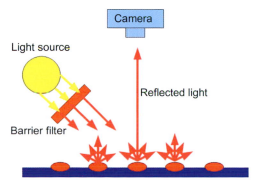

FIGURE 5.1.3 An excitation filter restricts the light wavelengths striking a sample. *Source: Champod et al., 2004.*

143

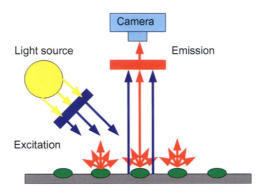

FIGURE 5.1.4 A barrier or emission filter restricts the light striking the detector (eye or camera) and filters out all the wavelengths except those of interest; the signal is typically weak and is difficult to see without this filter to reduce the background brightness. *Source: Champod et al., 2004.*

light. The barrier filter blocks any reflected excitation light and transmits only the fluorescence from the object of interest. The barrier filter is positioned in front of the viewing device, whether that is the eye or any kind of camera. The fluorescent object is, therefore, seen as a bright image against a dark background.

Once these properties are understood, it becomes obvious that light sources are the first materials to be used at a crime scene: they are powerful, sensitive, specific, and nondestructive. The general functioning of these devices will be explained before proposing steps to detect various untreated traces on-site.

From Theory to Practice: The Forensic Light Source

The first articles on light sources for use at crime scenes were published in the late 1970s, mainly focusing on lasers, as they offered, at that time, the only light source of sufficient intensity to reveal untreated traces. High-intensity filtered sources (with bulbs) appeared in the 1980s and were called alternate light sources (ALSs) to distinguish them from the original forensic light sources (FLSs) based on lasers. ALSs took the lead because of their power, portability, practicability for crime scene conditions, cost, and ease of safe use. They are provided with various colored goggles, which are not only protective, but are also used as transmission filters to let the reflected or emitted light pass.

To be selective, such lamps provide narrow slices (called bands) of wavelengths over the spectrum (including near UV, but excluding IR, because the heat could damage the filters and the illuminated object), but with a strong intensity on each of the desired bands. ALSs currently on the market offer bandwidths from 30 nm for very specific wavelengths, larger for general screening, and finally a very strong white light. Generally, the light operates

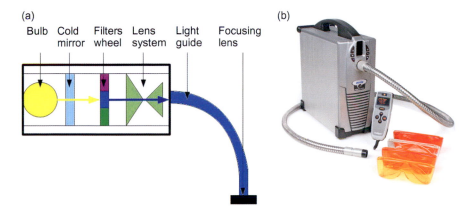

FIGURE 5.1.5 (a) Schematic of an ALS; (b) an ALS.

around a strong white light (over 300 W, such as a Xenon arc lamp), in front of which a selection of filters is placed to transmit only the relevant bandwidths (Lennard and Stoilovic, 2004). Some ALSs use high-quality filters (multilayer interference filters), which enables fine control of bandwidths (down to 5 nm, usually to their central value) by tilting the filter's axis on the path of the light beam. This construction is of great help when the photoluminescence of the background interferes with one of the targets.

Between the bulb and the filter, a cold mirror neutralizes any IR radiation. A lens system collates the colored beam onto the tiny entry spot of the light guide, which guides the beam to the final focusing lens (if available) to yield a uniform light field on the target. The guide can be moved closer to or further away from the target; note, however, that this could lead to a loss of intensity of the incident beam. The illumination of the target should be uniform to provide even detection and to minimize artifacts and shadows. Figure 5.1.5 gives the schematic concept of an ALS (Champod et al., 2004). Simpler (and cheaper) devices may also be found on the market, at the cost of effectiveness and sensitivity, but the lighting principles are still the same.

General Crime Scene Screening

Table 5.1.1 gives some examples of optimal excitations and emission settings, keeping in mind that environmental parameters (contamination, substrate, etc.) may interfere with the signal of interest; the CSI is cautioned not to simply apply "recipes" without awareness and thought. CSIs should understand the use of both emission filters and goggles and why they work in combination; the combinations also should be validated with known samples.

Crime scene detection frequently requires screening the entire light spectrum to find traces. Darkening the environment can help the CSI to better see and interpret contrasts; darkness is mandatory to detect luminescence. Because of the weak signal strength, background light will input noise in the emission light beam.

TABLE 5.1.1 General Forensic Use of Light

Wavelengths	HBW*	Application	Emission Filters	Goggles
All (white)		General searching, particularly visible fingerprints, stains, 3D impressions, 2D impressions on smooth surfaces	400–420 460–480 490–520 530–570 560–580 580–600 600–650 620–650	Clear Yellow Yellow Orange Orange Red Red Red
350	Between 50 and 80 nm	Traces on UV luminescent surfaces, especially fingerprints, semen, GSR, fibers, paint chips, lubricants		
415	Between 30 and 40 nm	Dried blood, bloody fingerprints, semen, GSR, fibers, lubricants		
450	Between 60 and 100 nm	General searching for photoluminescence (fingerprints, semen, GSR, fibers, lubricants)		
500	Between 30 and 50 nm	Semen, GSR, Ruhemann purple selective absorption (ninhydrin-treated fingerprints)		
550	Between 30 and 50 nm	Semen, Ruhemann purple selective absorption		
600	Between 30 and 50 nm	Selective absorption for stained bloodmarks		

HBW stands for "half-bandwidth," which measures the width of the band-pass region at half-power of maximum transmittance peak.

Care should be taken with any ALS, because the high intensity of the beam could damage the unprotected eye. Reflective surfaces are also potentially dangerous given the intensity of the beams.

White Light and Selective Absorption

Once the areas of interest to be screened are selected, strong white light should be used first with various incident angles (45° on specular; low-angle and oblique light on smooth surfaces). With a 45° angle, high-pass filters (HPFs), which pass through wavelengths above a specific value, can be used

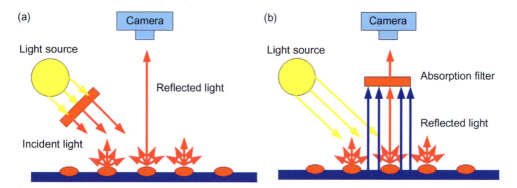

FIGURE 5.1.6 Two ways to obtain selective absorption: (a) contains an absorption filter, and (b) shows a barrier filter. *Source: Champod et al., 2004.*

to increase the amount of signal detected. A band-pass filter (BPF) can be used to enhance contrast; choosing a color similar to the surface will lighten it, and choosing a color opposite to it will darken it. A visible trace on a surface can then be seen easier due to increased contrast.

Another way of applying selective absorption is to analyze the color of the surface and to darken it with incident light of a complementary color to the surface. This incident light can be obtained by selecting the relevant wavelength of the ALS (Figure 5.1.6(a)) or with a filter in front of the white light (Figure 5.1.6(b)). As the half-bandwidth (HBW) of such ALS filters also decreases the intensity of the transmitted light, full darkness is mandatory for this solution. But for the same reason, the ALS filter might better distinguish the trace on its substrate if their colors are close. An enterprising CSI might want to combine both techniques, but should remember to integrate the loss of intensity at each step.

Film or a camera diode is much more sensitive than the human eye, and provides better contrast even in the violet, blue, and red regions of the visible spectrum. Another way to increase the contrast is to play with the different physical properties of the evidence and its substrate through diffuse reflection.

Reflections

A trace on a flat, dark, shiny surface will likely produce a diffuse reflection of the incident beam, as the background will create specular reflection. The incident light will arrive at 45°, and enter the eye or camera positioned parallel to the trace; due to specular reflection, some diffuse rays emitted from the trace will reach it and, hence, the trace will appear light on a dark background (Figure 5.1.7).

This approach can work for greasy fingerprints or dusted shoeprints, for example. As the difference of the light paths is based on the different reflections of the incident light, tuning the incidence angle (45°±) can easily

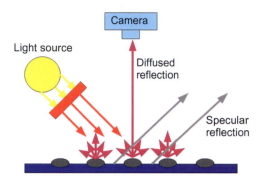

FIGURE 5.1.7 Diffuse reflected rays captured as specular ones miss the camera. *Source: Champod et al., 2004.*

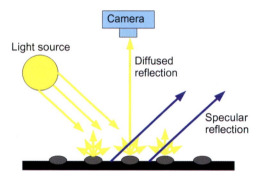

FIGURE 5.1.8 Diffuse/specular reflections on a colored support, darkening it with the opposite color of the incident beam. *Source: Champod et al., 2004.*

improve the result. Once this illumination configuration is understood, it becomes easy to set the optimal conditions to repeat it on a colored substrate or trace (Figure 5.1.8).

Coaxial Episcopy

An upgrade of the reflective effect can be implemented with a tool called coaxial episcopy, sometimes provided with the ALS. Its principle consists of directing a beam alongside the lens axis of the camera to the trace/ substrate. The incident angle is then 90°, providing all the specular rays with a privileged pathway to the camera; this is because only a few diffuse rays from the trace will take the path back. Hence, the trace will appear dark on its now whitened substrate. Some adjustments are needed to create this illumination (Figure 5.1.9). The incident light is initiated by placing the light source at 90° from the lens axis, redirecting the beam down to the substrate with a semitransparent mirror on the camera. A semitransparent mirror transmits only 50% of the incident light and lets the rest pass through it. A black background facing the light source but opposite the mirror can absorb the light that passes through to avoid background noise. Due to the position of the mirror, the reflected rays will reach it once again, half

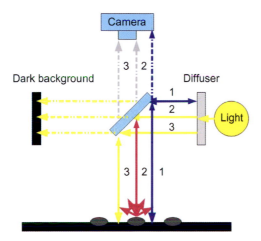

FIGURE 5.1.9 Schema explaining coaxial episcopy, looking at three different rays (1, 2, 3) after the diffuser. Ray 1 (blue): half of it is sent to the matrix, hitting the (specular) support; half of its result crosses the mirror (the other half is sent to the bulb), but is not detected by the camera. Ray 2: half of it is sent to the matrix, hitting the (diffuse reflective) trace; only a few reflected rays can return to the mirror, and half of their intensity is transmitted to the camera. Ray 3: half of it is sent to the matrix, hitting the (specular) support; half of its result crosses the mirror again, to be detected by the camera.

being sent to the light source, half going through the mirror to enter the camera. Therefore, only a quarter of the light source will reach the camera for specularly reflected objects. The few rays of diffuse light reaching the mirror will be cut by half, darkening the objects being diffusely reflected.

Because of this loss of intensity, tight white spots of light should be avoided; placing a diffuser in front of the light bulb will soften the light beam and, as a result, the trace appears dark on a bright background.

Photoluminescence

When the photoluminescence of a trace is optimized at a specific excitation wavelength, its emitted light will be captured within a specific bandwidth (by either a band-pass filter or selective goggles). These filters lower the intensity of the response, which makes it mandatory to work in full darkness with this technique. Working in the dark with yellow or orange goggles, the CSI should begin to screen with a large excitation blue band (in an interval covering 450 nm), labeled "CS Blue," or a low-pass filter (LPF), selecting wavelengths under a specific threshold. As soon as a signal is detected, various excitation wavelengths should be tested to increase the signal. At its peak, an emission filter with a more selective bandwidth could be tested to reduce as much as possible the background luminescence. Once the best combination of excitation-emission filters is found, the trace can be photographed. The luminescent trace will appear clear on a dark background.

Because of the weak signal from the evidence, long exposures are necessary to record the image. Moreover, as modern microchips in digital cameras average the white balance through an evaluation of about 75% of the frame, if the photoluminescent object does not cover enough area on the frame, the whole image will be lightened and the area of interest overdeveloped. The forensic examiner should try to cover at least 70% of the frame with the photoluminescent trace, which can be done using a macrolens.

Closing the aperture will sharpen the edges of the trace and its details but also increase the exposure leading back to the previous problem. Hence, an aperture setting at f8 is a good compromise to work with, exposure time being the parameter to adjust. Beginning at 1 second, and doubling the time to reach 32 seconds of exposure (i.e., six photographs at 1, 2, 4, 8, 16, and 32 seconds each) should provide at least one good image. Another solution would be to trust the metering system of the camera, take the first photograph (exposure compensation set on 0), and add bracketed snapshots at corrections of +1 (twice the original settled exposure), +2 (four times the exposure), −1 (half the exposure), and −2 (quarter the exposure).

UV Techniques

The first thing to understand about UV rays is that they are not only dangerous because of their high energy, but also because they are invisible to the human eye; the eyes should be protected by glass or plastic goggles and the skin should be covered as well when using UV light. Short-wavelength UV lights also generate ozone, which is poisonous to humans. Finally, the shorter the UV wavelengths, the more hazardous its use, including for evidence (DNA could be irreversibly damaged, for example). Two kinds of UV have been identified: UV-A rays from 300 to 400 nm, and UV-B rays from 200 to 300 nm that are more energetic.

Because of its upper energy in the light spectrum, UV illumination can be used as excitation light for luminescence, but UV detectors allow also UV-A reflectance techniques to be used (Keith and Runion, 1998). In darkness, UV-A-Vis photoluminescence is helpful for traces or objects such as dyed fibers, paper, paint chips, semen, some gunshot residue (GSR), or stains on white luminescent areas. Blood also absorbs UV-A, which can be exploited through selective absorption based on the background substrate. UV-A incident light has also been shown to be effective to detect untreated fingerprints and shoeprints.

UV-A reflection techniques and UV-B–UV-A luminescence require special materials to record the rays (expensive quartz lenses are needed for wavelengths shorter than 320 nm). The Baader Venus® filter is recommended to reduce all visible and IR noise (Sanfilippo et al., 2010).

Specific devices using the UV-A reflection property have been marketed, like the RUVIS® or the Camcorder. With their intensifier CCD, fingerprints appear clear on a dark nonporous surface, as soon as the substrate absorbs the UV-B or UV-A. Midinfrared and Fourier transform infrared (FTIR) spectroscopic imaging is also a promising tool to locate fingerprints on porous surfaces but it requires knowing where the print is beforehand (Tahtouh et al., 2005, 2007; Crane et al., 2007; Plese et al., 2010). In the same vein, IR illumination also looks promising as a technique to detect blood under layers of dark paints on nonporous surfaces; it requires a special camera for IR photography (Howard and Nessan, 2010).

Specific Crime Scene Screening

Table 5.1.1 describes the visible spectrum and the related evidence that could be detected at each position. White light and CS Blue light are better used for general screening, then switching to other more specific wavelengths when a trace has been detected to further enhance it. Another way to use the ALS is to directly target some specific evidence with the appropriate illumination. Table 5.1.2 proposes such approaches for different traces.

Fingerprint Detection

Latent fingerprint secretions are not visible under normal lighting conditions. Heavily sebaceous prints can be detected and captured with coaxial episcopy. After screening with a strong white light at 45° and at low angle/oblique incidences, more specific lighting techniques could be applied on areas of interest. Photographs should be taken before any further physical (powder) or chemical (say, ninhydrin) treatment.

Selective absorption depends on the colors of both the contaminant and the support. Knowing or inferring a contaminant (as blood, paint, etc.) would lead the crime scene examiner to choose the best optical protocol. Otherwise, scanning the entire spectrum (Table 5.1.2) will be required.

Fingerprints are not photoluminescent on their own; any potential luminescence of fingerprints is caused by contaminants on the finger (grease, food, chemicals, etc.). During the search in a dark environment, the spot size of the incident light should be very small (not more than 10 cm diameter) and the beam strong enough to induce luminescence, which will be detected as a white mark on a dark background when viewing through orange goggles that cut the blue ALS incident light. Once detected, the luminescence could be improved with various excitation and emission filters.

Earmark Detection

Earmark detectors are very greasy; hence, after a strong white light screening at 45° and low-angle incidences, relevant photographs could be taken after black or luminescent powder treatment.

TABLE 5.1.2 Proposed Illumination and Wavelengths for Various Types of Marks

Evidence	Technique	Incident	Barrier	Goggles	Remarks
Fingerprint	Absorption Luminescence	UV-A	—	White Yellow	See also the section "Fingerprint Detection"
Earmark	Absorption Luminescence	UV-A	—	White	See also the section "Earmark Detection"
Blood	Absorption	LPF 420 CS Blue	— —	White	Black edges on reflecting background; see also the section "Blood"
Semen	Absorption Luminescence	CS Blue UV-A	— 530–570	White Yellow	See also the section "Semen"; caution: long UV exposure could damage DNA
Saliva	Absorption Luminescence	CS Blue UV-A	— 530–570	White Yellow	Caution: long UV exposure could damage DNA
Urine	Absorption Luminescence	CS Blue UV-A	— 530–570	White Yellow	Caution: long UV exposure could damage DNA
Bones, tooth fragments	Luminescence	445 nm CS Blue	580–600 580–600	Orange Orange	
Bites, scratches	Absorption Luminescence	LPF 420 CS Blue 530–570 UV-A	530–570 580–600 HPF 600 —	Yellow Orange Red White	
Fiber, hair	Luminescence	UV-A LPF 420 CS Blue	— 580–600 580–600	White Orange Orange	See also the section "Fiber, Hair, Glass"
Glass	Luminescence	UV-A CS Blue	— 460–480	White Yellow	See also the section "Fiber, Hair, Glass"
GSR	Luminescence	455 CS Blue	580–600 580–600	Orange Orange	See also the section "Gunshot Residue"
Grease, lubricants	Luminescence	CS Blue	To be optimized	Yellow Orange	
3D impressions (shoemark, toolmark, etc.)	Absorption and luminescence	White and all available	— 400–420 460–480 490–520 530–570 560–580 580–600 600–650 620–650	White Yellow Yellow Orange Orange Red White White White	See also the section "3D Impressions"

Blood

Dried blood absorbs at an optimal wavelength of 415 nm, but also diffusely reflects at other wavelengths. Hence, absorption at 415 nm is recommended for a colored or luminescent substrate, which will then appear bright while the blood will appear black. Because the human eye is not highly sensitive in this violet region, darkness is mandatory. By daylight or artificial light, a picture can be acquired with an LPF 415 in front of the camera, and the trace will be lightened with a strong white beam.

On dark-colored and shiny substrates, bloody stains will appear brighter through diffuse reflection with a beam of greater wavelength than the optimal peak, like CS Blue or one of an opposite color of the substrate. Varying the incident angle of the light beam would improve the contrast.

Semen

Dried semen shows a very strong luminescence with excitation varying from 300 to 500 nm with the optimal peak at 400 nm. Its respective emission varies from 450 to 540 (emission around 500 nm for an excitation at 400 nm). Hence, CS Blue can be a good alternative to detect semen stains in dark conditions with yellow goggles. Because the substrate can interfere, a more optimal protocol can be proposed:

- UV-A excitation, white goggles: If the substrate is luminescent, go to the next step, or else the stains will appear bright blue.
- LPF 415 excitation, yellow goggles: If the substrate is luminescent, go to the next step, or else the stains will appear bright yellow.
- CS Blue, yellow goggles: If the substrate is luminescent, go to the next step, or else the stains will appear bright yellow (see also with orange goggles).
- Excitation at 500 nm, orange goggles: If the substrate is luminescent, go to the next step, or else the stains will appear orange.
- Excitation at 550 nm, red goggles: The stains will appear bright red.

Whatever the optical detection, further biological or chemical tests should be conducted to confirm the presence of semen.

Fiber, Hair, Glass

Due to fibers' optical brighteners or their own fluorescent dyes and the coating layers for glass, many fibers and glasses are luminescent. Interestingly, this may also be the case with blond and red hairs, or hairs that have been dyed. Darkening the scene will optimize observation. Low-angle white light could also be used on smooth, shiny substrates. Moreover, individual fibers or glass fragments can be discriminated between each other in the field because of their various emissions under different excitations; caution should be exercised, however, and the CSI should not collect only those that emit as many fibers as they may not luminesce at all.

Gunshot Residue

Unburned or partially burnt propellants may show weak luminescence. Despite the huge number of particles deposited after a discharge, their weak luminescence requires a dark scene to detect them. Because of the transient nature of such small particles, surfaces should be observed and recorded with care before collection or packaging. A similar but shorter protocol to the protocol used for semen luminesence can be used:

- UV-A excitation, white goggles: If the substrate is luminescent, go to the next step, or else the particles will appear bright blue.
- LPF 415 excitation, yellow goggles: If the substrate is luminescent, go to the next step, or else the particles will appear bright yellow.
- CS Blue, yellow goggles: If the substrate is luminescent, particles will appear bright yellow (see also with orange goggles).

3D Impressions

Strong white light is best for a general search for two-dimensional (2D) patterns on smooth surfaces and 3D impressions (e.g., shoeprints); selective absorption can improve the result by darkening the background. If the mark is contaminated, photoluminescence could improve the image; therefore, the protocols proposed for blood and semen could be applied to such traces. For 3D impressions, low-angle/oblique light should be optimized to create shadows highlighting the structure of the trace: the deeper the trace, the higher the ALS should be above the support. Place the tripod over the evidence so that the lens is parallel to it, then rotate the light source at different angles parallel to the trace to capture different views from the trace in the same position. These images can later be integrated within dedicated imaging software using addition and subtraction.

References and Bibliography

Barnett, K., 2004. Marks and impressions. In: White, P.C. (Ed.), Crime Scene to Court: The Essentials of Forensic Science, second ed. Royal Society of Chemistry, Cambridge, UK, pp. 82–114.

Champod, C., Lennard, C., Margot, P., Stoilovic, M., 2004. Fingerprints and Other Ridge Skin Impressions. International Forensic Science and Investigation Series. CRC Press, Boca Raton, FL.

Crane, N.J., Bartick, E.G., Perlman, R.S., Hufman, S, 2007. Infrared spectroscopic imaging of noninvasive detection of latent fingerprints. J. Forensic Sci. 52 (1): 48–53.

Dalrymple, B.E., Duff, J.M., Menzel, E.R., 1997. Inherent fingerprint luminescence— Detection by laser. J. Forensic Sci. 2: 106–115.

Gallop, A., Stockdale, R. 2004. Trace and contact evidence. In: White, P.C. (Ed.), Crime Scene to Court: The Essentials of Forensic Science, second ed. Royal Society of Chemistry, Cambridge, UK, pp. 56–81.

Horswell, J., 2004. Crime scene investigation. In: Robertson, J. (Ed.), The Practice of Crime Scene Investigation. CRC Press, Boca Raton, FL, pp. 2–45.

Horswell, J., Fowler, C, 2004. Associative evidence—The Locard Exchange Principle. In: Robertson, J. (Ed.), The Practice of Crime Scene Investigation. CRC Press, Boca Raton, FL, pp. 46–56.

Howard, M.C., Nessan, M., 2010. Detecting bloodstains under multiple layers of paint. J. Forensic Identification 60 (6): 682–717.

Keith, L.V., Runion, W., 1998. Short-wave UV imaging casework applications. J. Forensic Identification 48 (5): 563–569.

Lee, H.C., Palmbach, T., Miller, M.T., 2001. Henry Lee's Crime Scene Handbook. Academic Press, New York.

Lennard, C., Stoilovic, M., 2004. Application of forensic light sources at the crime scene. In: Robertson, J. (Ed.), The Practice of Crime Scene Investigation. CRC Press, Boca Raton, FL, pp. 95–121.

Plese, C.A., Exline, D.L., Stewart, S.D., 2010. Improved methods of visible hyperspectral imaging provide enhanced visualization of untreated latent fingerprints. J. Forensic Identification 60 (6): 603–618.

Russ, J.C., 2001. Forensic Uses of Digital Imaging. CRC Press, Boca Raton, FL.

Sanfilippo, P., Richards, A., Nichols, H., 2010. Reflected ultraviolet digital photography: The part someone forgot to mention. J. Forensic Identification 60 (2): 181–198.

Tahtouh, M., Kalman, J.R., Roux, C., Lennard, C., Reedy, B.J. 2005. The detection and enhancement of latent fingerprints using infrared chemical imaging. J. Forensic Sci. 50 (1): 1–9.

Tahtouh, M., Despland, P., Shimmon, R., Kalman, J.R., Reedy, B.J., 2007. The application of infrared chemical imaging to the detection and enhancement of latent fingerprints: Method optimization and further findings. J. Forensic Sci. 52 (5): 1089–1096.

Collection

Traces have been detected, recorded, and protected. The CSI is then confronted with a dilemma: either improve the signal of the traces, which could lead to other undetected traces, or secure the already-detected traces by collecting them. For those traces that have already been optimized, they should now be collected. A few considerations should be reviewed prior to proceeding:

- Traces are fragile by nature, some (fibers) more than others (DNA). Laboratory forensic capacities offer a better controlled environment and more specific methods than are available in the field, so a safe solution would be to collect any substrate with the traces instead of developing them on-site. Moreover, the CSI should manage any chemical development in awareness of and in conjunction with any processes that will be conducted in a laboratory, where a full sequence of enhancements can be better applied.

- Easily lost or transient evidence (like flies, wastewater, odor, temperature, etc.), or even potential evidence that has to be moved to process the rest of the crime scene, should be collected after being documented before any further detection methods are applied.
- Forensic analytical methods are able to deal with minute traces, down to the molecular level, as with DNA. Mishandling a piece of evidence, or erring about the development protocol to apply, could lead to a loss of relevant information for the investigation. Hence, it is better to collect, package, and preserve rather than dealing with an imperfect field development technique that forbids other enhancements and having to sort out possible contamination later, which could prevent the laboratory from fully developing the value of a piece of evidence.
- Finally, for the CSI who chooses to develop in the field, protocols are presented elsewhere in this book. Nevertheless, this choice should be made mainly for surfaces or objects that cannot be brought to the laboratory.

The ideal solution would be to assign one CSI the role of evidence officer, who is in charge of packaging, marking, sealing, preserving, and later tracking evidence. In the French Gendarmerie, a deputy crime scene examiner is in charge of this task, or even a crime scene coordinator on serious cases; other jurisdictions have similar arrangements. Officially assigning this important duty will help prevent the loss or contamination of collected evidence and secure the legal process.

As specimens, comparison (or reference), and control evidence were explained previously in Chapter 5.0, a brief inventory of the kind of materials to collect will be addressed first, along with the types of sampling to conduct. Second, materials and containers most suited for evidence packaging will be described. Third, the available techniques are addressed. Finally, a survey of the different pieces of evidence to collect will be presented, along with the relevant protocols.

Types of Evidence to Collect

Collecting materials in excess is better than "saving" containers and letting an investigation fail because of a lack or insufficient quantity of evidence. Remember: A crime scene can be processed only once! Moreover, collecting does not mean analyzing, and submitting the evidence to the laboratory should be considered within the context of the investigation, like supporting one hypothesis over another one (Horswell, 2004). Control materials are necessary to perform the analysis, for example, to determine if the substrate could interfere with the evidence signal, as in arson cases. Similarly, enough reference or comparison materials should be sampled to allow the analyst to evaluate the intravariability of the potential source; this is especially the case for microtraces (soil, fibers, hair, glass, etc.).

FIGURE 5.2.1 Many evidence types are solids, which are easily packaged.

For scientific, but also legal, reasons, each piece of evidence should be packaged and sealed separately, to avoid cross-contamination, to ease its exploitation by laboratories, and to limit, as much as possible, opening and closing the seals to retrieve parts of the collected items. Many evidence types are solids and these can be easily packaged in containers that avoid friction to optimize trace retrieval and minimize contamination (Figure 5.2.1). Storage and preservation of such containers are determined by the type of evidence they protect.

- Liquid pieces of evidence have to be packaged in unbreakable, leakproof containers.
- Liquid or solid exhibits that could evaporate should be stored in clean, unused, watertight, and waterproof cans, jars, or jars like the ones used for paints or solvents.
- Explosives, fire debris, and other similar evidence that could diffuse low-carbonate vapors should be enclosed in watertight nylon 6 × 6 bags or airtight metallic containers, to avoid contamination of nearby evidence from the current case, but also in evidence storage rooms or on laboratory shelves.

Many problems arise with biological evidence (blood, plants, insects, etc.) or moist, wet materials. These could be removed from the crime scene in temporary seals and later allowed to dry, then repackaged in proper containers. Plastic bags should be avoided as much as possible for temporary seals; if used, they should be quickly replaced with proper packaging to avoid rotting of the evidence. After repackaging, the original package should be sealed with the final repackaging to insure the chain of custody. In case the CSI faces some trouble with the collection of any evidence (for instance, underwater or chemical, biological, radiological, and nuclear (CBRN) evidence), the CSI should stop the processing and request a specialist.

Materials and Containers

It is convenient, if not mandatory, to have a variety of collecting, marking, and packaging materials close to the crime scene for the CSI. The best place for storage and disposal is generally at the entry point of the crime scene. This provides ease of processing: The containers are collected at the entry, the evidence is packaged at the point of collection, and the container is labeled and closed. Sealing should be done outside the scene, but as soon as possible after the time of collection to avoid problems during the transportation to the police and later to the laboratory. Sealing involves tamper-evident tape, which is delicate but very sticky; handling it can be difficult with gloves (Figure 5.2.2).

Basic materials to be used for crime scene collection could include (Green, 2000; Horswell, 2000):

- Various sizes of containers such as paper envelopes, plastic zipper storage bags, pillboxes, clean unused metal paint cans, and cardboard boxes (including preformed ones for weapons such as rifles, guns, and knives).
- Various sizes of paper sheets, even in rolls, on which to shake evidence, or to wrap collected items like clothes. These various papers (large roll, A3, A4, letter, and legal sizes) could be prepared beforehand and sealed outside the crime scene.
- Sterile and one-use swabs, cotton gazes, pipettes, test tubes, eyedroppers, and glass jars and bottles.
- Clear tape to collect various microtraces from surfaces, but also evidence tape to seal the various containers; labels and markers.
- Gel lifters, plaster, or dental polymers as Mikrosil® with dedicated containers for mixing.

FIGURE 5.2.2 Tamper-evident tape, used to seal evidence packaging, is very sticky but very delicate; any attempt to open breaks the seal. *Courtesy ForensicSource.*

- Various one-use paint brushes, a dustpan, and a broom to sweep traces hidden in constricted areas.
- Steel tweezers to collect microtraces (fibers, hair, etc.) and one-use plastic tweezers to avoid damaging evidence with steel tweezers. One-use plastic tweezers are also to be used when collecting biological traces (DNA or bloodstains on a distilled water–moistened gauze, for instance).
- Small doses of distilled water and rubbing alcohol to moisten either gauzes or detected stains.
- One-use scalpels; a steel spatula.
- A small dental mirror to observe hidden places and reflect light, a 5× magnifying glass to better see microtraces on substrates, and a rubber-coated magnet to attract iron and steel particles without damage.
- Specific kits, either commercial or prepared by the laboratory, could also be of some use, such as DNA, blood collection, GSR, explosives, sexual assault, drugs, or postmortem fingerprint kits.
- Positioning and sketching materials, such as a compass to indicate north, retractable tape measure (30 m, 3 m), various rulers for scales in photographs, and graph paper for drawing.
- An ALS and an electrostatic lifter with sheets.

Any evidence exiting the scene should be protected in a container, be it a temporary or the final sealed one. The information documented on packaged evidence (the container) will vary by agency but generally should include:

- A unique identifier ("item #23," for example)
- Date and time of collection
- Location of collection
- Brief description of the item
- Initials of the collector

It is important that each agency have a system for uniquely identifying items of evidence. A crime scene may consist of hundreds of items of evidence and each one has to be able to be identified, cataloged, and retrieved without error. A cumulative numbering system works well; better yet is a decimal system that shows relationships between items. For example, given a coat from a suspect (item #1), the following evidence could be developed and enumerated:

1 Coat
   1.1 Cigarette lighter (right pocket)
   1.2 Switchblade knife (left pocket)
      1.2.1 Swabbing from knife blade
   1.3 Sunglasses
      1.3.1 Fingerprint lift from front lens
   1.4 Debris from coat (tapelifts)
      1.4.1 Fibers from debris
      1.4.2 Glass particles from debris
   1.5 Known fiber sample from coat
   1.6 Swabbing from stains on coat front

The numbering system allows all of the derivative evidence from the coat to be associated with the coat but still with each item having its own unique identifier. The numbers on the derivative (also sometimes called subsidiary) evidence can be assigned later in the field or in the laboratory to save time while actively processing the crime scene.

Available Techniques to Collect Evidence

Various techniques described here do triple duty: prevent damage of the substrate of the evidence, and hence of the potential trace itself; limit contamination of the evidence; and protect the CSI from hazardous materials. There is no routinely or exclusively better technique over any others available in any circumstance; indeed, evidence collection is very dependent on the local context of the scene. The best tool the CSI brings to the scene is the CSI's education, training, and intellect.

Whole Substrate Collection

The easiest solution to collect detected traces is to remove the whole object: a shoe, a shirt, whatever. Indeed, this technique is the one to be used when:

- The substrate contains different types of evidence, and where collecting one type in preference to the others might damage or contaminate them.
- Chemical or physical enhancements that should be processed in an identified development sequence are better managed in the laboratory.
- The observation and collection of evidence cannot be processed on the spot, such as the victim's or suspect's clothing; each item should be packaged as found in large paper sheets, separately if possible.
- The pressures of the case are such that the CSI cannot process evidence at the scene.

Nevertheless, whole substrate collection requires dedicated large containers. This could take time and special packaging to reduce loss or contamination of evidence. Specialized commercially available off-the-shelf (COTS) packaging may be a resource to agencies that can afford it. Notwithstanding storage problems at the police station, the laboratory, and the courtroom, a more selective collection of evidence is also a sign of the observation skills of the crime scene examiner on-site.

Tweezing

A set of two to three different sizes of tweezers is a good idea, as each of them would be convenient to collect various sizes of microtraces. Tweezers are highly selective tools to recover microtrace evidence like hairs, fibers, glass fragments, and other minute physical traces. Their high selectivity also provides specificity because the CSI can explain exactly where and why these traces were collected in regard to the case. It also provides relevance and priority to further analytical procedures in the laboratory, where scientists can concentrate on the submitted evidence, facilitating the interpretation, instead of sorting through hundreds of items looking for microscopic evidence.

Plastic one-use tweezers are preferable to steel ones, as they limit damage to the collected evidence. They should be replaced each time there is a chance of contamination, which mainly appears with DNA sampling, such as cigarette butts. This principle also proscribes the container policy at the crime scene: one dedicated container for any one set of single source evidence. Thus, cigarette butts in an ashtray should be collected individually, one per envelope, because the CSI is not able to distinguish smokers based only on the appearance of the cigarette butts. Contamination is also the motivation to systematically clean steel tweezers (and other steel sampling tools) with distilled water and organic solvent between collections.

Small materials collected, like hairs, fibers, soil, or other particulates, should not be placed directly into stationery envelopes, as the corners are not always sealed (Figure 5.2.3) and the contents can leak out. They should be stored in a paper bindle or "pharmacist's fold" first, which is sealed, and then placed in an envelope, if necessary.

FIGURE 5.2.3 Stationary envelopes are not always sealed at the corners and small evidence should not be placed directly into them as it could leak out.

Tapelifting

Tapelifting is a reliable method to collect microtraces on fabrics and garments. When using a roll of collection tape, dispense and discard the first 10 cm of the tape to avoid contamination, then dispense around 10–20 cm of tape and cut it. Place the piece of tape on the surface of interest, press down along the length of it, and repeat with an adjacent area. The tape can be used several times until it becomes loaded with debris. Place the full tape onto clean acetate sheets to sandwich the debris and protect it from contamination or loss. Each acetate sheet should represent a particular surface; for example, for a car interior, two acetate sheets at least for the front and rear seat areas. The locations collected from should be relevant to the situation of the crime. In this example, for instance, it may be important to collect from the front seat separately from the rear. Once covered and labeled, each acetate sheet should be stored in a plastic bag.

Vacuuming

Another means to collect microtraces on large, flat surfaces is vacuuming. Prior to using a collection vacuum (which is different from a household vacuum), carefully consider the following:

- Vacuuming makes for difficult trace extraction in the laboratory; the debris has to be sorted under a stereoscope, by hand.
- This kind of collection is very effective—some think too effective—but not selective. It collects everything, not only what is on the surface, like taping would collect.

Nevertheless, vacuuming is good for processing large areas, like rugs, or difficult areas, like automotive interiors, where taping would be too physically demanding. A forensic useful vacuum device has a stainless steel or one-use plastic nozzle that is easy to clean or change between different surfaces (Figure 5.2.4). Cleaning applies not only to the outside of the nozzle, but also inside up to the front of the filter. Cleaning the nozzle is best done with a bottlebrush and hot soapy water, then rinsing with distilled water and leaving it to dry. Once clean and dry, the nozzle should stay enclosed in a sealed plastic bag, to prevent incidental contamination.

A one-use nozzle should be packaged with the container it was used with to collect. A clean one-use filter paper or cotton gauze is placed between the nozzle and the vacuum chamber, which catches the debris that is sucked into the vacuum. The filter is supported by a perforated plate. A blank filter should be run in the air for about 30 seconds before evidence collection on any substrate. It should be removed, packaged, and stored separately as a check against contamination.

Microtaping

Some microscopic traces can be lifted by using very small tapelifts, such as on a suspected shooter's hands or bullet entry holes. Commercial microlifts are about 10–20 mm^2 round surfaces covered with a glue, protected by a plastic

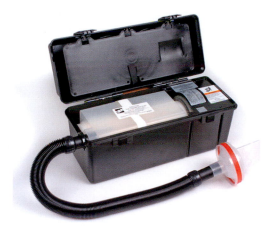

FIGURE 5.2.4 A trace collection vacuum. *Courtesy ForensicSource.*

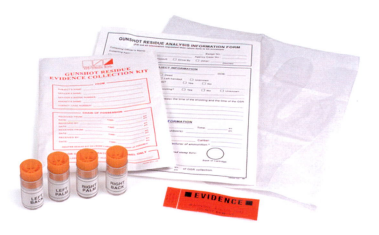

FIGURE 5.2.5 Gunshot residue collection kits use microlift stubs to collect small particulates.

cover sheet. A blank sample should be set aside for each set collected. These microlifts are often in small aluminum stubs used for electron microscopy and the analysis of gunshot residue (GSR). The stubs with adhesive tape are packaged in small plastic containers with caps to protect the now evidence-laden tape surface. Due to its high selectivity, a microlift should be used for each surface under question; for example, collecting from the hands of a suspect would require at least five individual lifts: two hands times two surfaces (back and palm surfaces of each hand), plus a blank stamp (Figure 5.2.5).

Pipetting

Fresh liquids and body fluids can be easily sampled by pipettes or syringes; disposable ones are preferred. Care should be taken that the suction bulb is never in contact with any fluid. As soon as there is any suspicion that this might have occurred, the pipette should be thrown away. Each pipetting requires a new pipette or syringe.

Swabbing

A dry cotton gauze or cotton swabs are useful to collect liquids or even solid particles; for the latter, first the gauze or cotton swab has to be slightly moistened with distilled water or acetone, depending on the kind of specimen to be collected (inorganic and body fluids or, respectively, organic solvents and compounds). Once again a blank gauze or cotton swab should be collected as a control.

Sweeping

Using a brush to access difficult areas to collect evidence is useful, as long as the brush is clean and no cross-transfer is suspected. Having a set of new, disposable (and inexpensive) paint brushes can be useful. A few threads of the brush, taken prior to use, can be provided as a control.

Lifting

An electrostatic lifter (ESL) (Figure 5.2.6) is a commercial device consisting of a high-voltage power supply, a grounding plate, and a metalized lifting sheet. A low-tension, high-voltage charge is applied to the lifting sheet, rendering the grounding plate positively charged. Any dust (now positively charged) is transferred to the lifting sheet in an exact mirror image of the original print. Both horizontal and vertical surfaces can be processed by this method. The print should be photographed (with a scale) as soon as possible and handled carefully; it is delicate and the ESL print will dissipate over time. Unused pizza delivery boxes make excellent ad hoc storage containers for lifting sheets.

FIGURE 5.2.6 An electrostatic dust lifter.

Scraping

Solidified materials, like paint drops, can be collected on to a clean paper sheet or in a container by scraping them with a one-use scalpel or razor blade. For health and safety reasons, materials suspected of being dried biological materials, like blood, should **not** be scraped without the CSI wearing the appropriate personal protective equipment.

Casting

Three-dimensional marks, like shoeprints, toolmarks, and tireprints, can be cast with materials like Duplicast for big prints, or dental stone or a polymer, like Mikrosil®, for small ones. Even impressions in snow can be molded using various methods, like sulfur casting or, preferably, snowprint wax.

Collection Guidelines

Another way to understand the different collection techniques is to propose guidelines for the collection of the various evidence types (Tables 5.2.1 to 5.2.10). A systematic collection, documented with photographs at each of the various stages, can help determine what has been done and what is left to be completed.

TABLE 5.2.1 Collection Guidelines for DNA

Type	State	Support	Collect	Container
DNA	Solid	Cigarette butt Chewing gum Hanky	Use new plastic tweezers (or new gloves) for each item, packaged separately.	Double envelopes (a crystal one within a paper one)
		Cloths Balaclavas Caps Hats	Use new tweezers (or new gloves) for each item. Let dry.	Paper envelope
	Liquid	Bottlenecks Drinking glasses Bitten food Blood Saliva	Sterile water swab. Let dry.	Swab sampling kit, or paper envelope
	Trace DNA	Steering wheel Earpiece Glasses	Sterile water swab, roughly applied on the potential support of trace to dig out the cells.	Swab sampling kit, or paper envelope
	Miscellaneous	Victim's fingernails	Wrap the victim's hand in paper bags, if deceased; else scrape under each fingernail with a one-use swab and store each swab in a small crystal envelope.	Paper bag

TABLE 5.2.2 Collection Guidelines for Blood

Type	State	Support	Collect	Container
Blood	Stains	Walls, ceiling, floor	Clusters of bloodstains should be identified at the scene, in regards to various patterns (impact, cast-off, transfer, and wipe). Perpendicular photographs should then be taken, with a ruler on each (see Chapter 6.2).	None
	Liquid (wet)	Pool	If possible as a whole (pipetting) or use a piece of sterile cotton linen allowed to dry at room temperature, not in sunlight. Note: Refrigerate as soon as possible, but do not freeze.	Glass tube or paper envelope. Do not use plastic containers.
		Live individual	For victims, either check with the hospital to collect blood, or collect blood-stained garment and dry at room temperature. Note: Refrigerate blood as soon as possible.	
	Solid (dry)	Bloody cloth	Collect whole object. Dry with adequate ventilation. Note: If the stain is demarcated on a big support, cover the stain with clean paper scotchtape on the edges to avoid contamination.	Paper bags. Do not use plastic containers.
		Wall or object impractical to move	Swab the stain with a *dry* cotton swab.	Tube

TABLE 5.2.3 Collection Guidelines for Other Human Fluids and Products

Type	State	Support	Collect	Container
Semen	Stains	Cloth, blanket, sheets	Collect the object (whole collection or cutting). Let it dry. Package individually.	Paper bag
	Seminal liquid	Victim	Intimate sample can only be done by a pathologist. Sexual assault kits exist. Follow the instructions (see also ASTM 1843 standard).	Kit storage or paper bag
Saliva	Liquid (wet) or trace (dry)	Porous support	Collect the whole support or cut the relevant surface. Let it dry at room temperature. Note: Refrigerate as soon as possible.	Paper bag
		Nonporous support	Sterile gauze pad or swab. Allow to dry at room temperature. Note: Refrigerate as soon as possible.	Paper bag
	Bite mark	Victim's skin, food	Clean the surface with a moistened piece of cotton with distilled water and clean the surface. Let dry at room temperature.	Paper bag
Urine, feces	Liquid	Toilets	If possible collect as a whole (pipetting) or use a piece of sterile cotton linen allowed to dry at room temperature. Note: Refrigerate as soon as possible.	Glass tube or paper envelope. Do not use plastic containers.
	Solid (stain)	Porous support	Collect the whole support or cut the relevant surface. Let it dry at room temperature. Note: Refrigerate as soon as possible.	Paper bag
		Nonporous support	Sterile gauze pad or swab. Allow to dry at room temperature. Note: Refrigerate as soon as possible.	Paper bag
Hair, fingernails		Any support	By hand or with plastic tweezers. Place all recovered hair in a piece of white paper, later folded and sealed in a larger envelope or paper bag. Note: If hair is attached, such as in dry blood, or caught in materials, do not attempt to remove it. Seal the whole object.	Paper bag
	Victim	Head, pubic region	Comb with a cotton wool seeded comb to collect foreign hair.	Paper or crystal envelopes
		Reference sample	Plucking a *minimum* of 25 hairs is required from all representative areas; more is better.	Paper or crystal envelopes

TABLE 5.2.4 Collection Guidelines for Marks and Casts

Type	State	Support	Collect	Container
Fingerprints, earprints, bare footprints	Latent	Porous and nonporous movable small supports	Touch as little as possible and only on areas unlikely to have been touched. Gloves are not enough to secure traces, as they could be wiped off or smeared.	Paper bags or envelope
		Porous and nonporous movable large supports	Place on wood or heavy cardboard and fix the evidence on it to prevent shifting and any contact.	Cardboard or wooden box
Impressions	Latent	Hard, flat surface	Powdering like fingerprints, then gel lifting	Gel envelope or large paper envelope
	Dust trace	Any surface, including soft or carpet	Electrostatic dust lifter	Paper envelope or unused pizza box
3D impression			Casts for toolmarks can be packaged in plastic bags; casts for shoe-prints or tireprints have to be fixed in a cardboard box. A photograph should be made of the trace beforehand with a scale.	Plastic bags or cardboard box

TABLE 5.2.5 Collection Guidelines for Microtraces: Paints and Fibers

Type	State	Support	Collect	Container
Microtraces	Paint	Contact surface	If possible, cut around the mark, to preserve both paint and the impression; else, the scraped specimen should contain all layers.	Cut support could be stored in plastic bag. Folded paper sheet to collect the specimen, enclosed finally in a paper envelope.
		Tool	Protect the contact surface of the tool with a wrapped sheet of paper to avoid losing attached coatings of the damaged surface. Fix the tool in a cardboard box.	Cardboard box
		Chips	Collect each layer with plastic tweezers, or a clean scalpel when scraping is required, onto a prefolded paper sheet. Take reference samples of each color, ensuring they are scraped down to the base color.	Place the folded sheet in a paper envelope.
		Reference samples	Scrape over a prefolded paper sheet.	
	Fabric, fibers	Questioned fibers	Best to collect the entire item; otherwise, use gloved fingers or tweezers, and place them in a piece of prefolded paper. Tapelifting is also possible for unmovable objects, fixing the tapes on an acetate sheet.	For a whole wrapped object or prefolded paper, use a paper bag. For acetate, use a transparent plastic bag.

TABLE 5.2.6 Collection Guidelines for Microtraces: Glass, Bulbs, and Soils

Type	State	Support	Collect	Container
Microtraces	Glass	Broken projected glass	Collect all recovered pieces along the projection or moving axis (for instance, hit and run). Collect glass from different locations in different bags.	One bag per location. Plastic bags should be set into a rigid plastic container, to be sealed.
		Broken windows	If small, send the whole item; if large, recover several samples across the window. If potential physical match (fracture matches), send the whole window.	Adapted plastic bag. For big collection, secure the whole window to prevent breaking remaining parts.
		Shoes and clothing	Wrapped in paper	Plastic bags
	.	Vehicle glass and headlights	Collect remaining glass in the shell, including removing changed headlights or mirror to search for previous lens.	Plastic bags
		Bottles, other glass	Collect item	Plastic bags
	Bulb, filament	On a car, or at the scene of the crime	Wrap each of them in paper, then seal in plastic bags.	Place in a small plastic bag. Collect all parts of the lamp, including the lamp socket, glass envelope, and sealed beam.
	Soil	Under shoes, tires	Scrape or brush over a prefolded sheet of paper.	Seal the folded sheet in a paper envelope.
		Large quantity (scene of crime, reference)	Collect in a jar; one jar per location to differentiate.	Plastic bag
		Small quantity (scene of crime, reference)	Pick up, sweep, brush, vacuum. Collect in prefolded paper.	Seal the folded sheet in a paper envelope.

TABLE 5.2.7 Collection Guidelines for Firearms

Type	State	Support	Collect	Container
Firearms	Solid	Weapon	Never: • Fire with an evidence firearm. • Seal a loaded or charged firearm, even secured. • Clean the bore, chamber, or cylinder. • Pick up a firearm with a stick in the end of the barrel. Record model, caliber, and serial number. If other evidence is attached to the weapon, wrap it in clean paper. Fix the weapon in its container to avoid movement.	Dedicated or manually fitted cardboard box or wooden box
		Cartridge magazine	Gloved hands	Plastic bag, if no other evidence traces on it; else, paper bag
		Unfired cartridge	Could be left in the magazine	Plastic bag, if no other evidence traces on it; else, paper bag
		Projectile	Do not: • Mark on it. • Clean it before sending. Occasionally, let it air dry if wet or bloodied (including extracted from a body).	Wrap in a small plastic bag. Seal the various bags in a rigid plastic container.
		Cartridge case	Wrap in a small plastic bag, with the aim of protecting the breech clock from any damage.	Wrap in a small plastic bag. Seal the various bags in a rigid plastic container.
		Ammunition	If in a box, seal it; else, see cartridge case.	Wrap in a small plastic bag. Seal the various bags in a rigid plastic container.
	Shot pattern	Clothes or other fabrics	Wrap the clothes carefully in clean paper, limiting folding as much as possible to avoid dislodging of particles.	Paper bag
	GSR	Clothes, hands of the suspect	Use the GSR stamping kit.	Dedicated container for the stamp

TABLE 5.2.8 Collection Guidelines for Drugs, Arson Materials, and Explosives

Type	State	Support	Collect	Container
Drugs of abuse	Bulk	Pills, tablets, powder	Pipetting, tweezering, sweeping, brushing, and so on; also collect any prescription paperwork. In the case of drugs of addiction, sampling, weighing, and storage should be done with the assistance of a sworn police officer to avoid any challenge regarding the integrity of the crime scene examiner.	Paper envelope to be sealed and marked. When there is an evaporation risk (strong odor), seal in a nylon bag. Any documents should be placed in paper envelopes.
	Liquid	Bottles, tubes	Use the original container. Take also any prescription paperwork attached.	Locked glass or plastic vial in plastic bags. Any documents should be placed in paper envelopes.
Explosives and arson materials	Liquid	Poured or spilled on the scene	Flammable fluids do not all have characteristic odors, and can easily escape detection without sniffers (e.g., alcohols, some kerosene, charcoal lighter fluid). Techniques to collect could be pipetting, or swabbing on sterile gauze for arson materials. For explosives, one organically wet (acetone) sterile gauze and another wet distilled water gauze.	Avoid absolutely plastic containers and rubber-lined lids. Package in glass vial with an airtight seal. For explosives, let the gauze dry and package them separately in nylon bags.
		Reference sample (flammable liquids or products stored at the scene)	In their containers	Seal in nylon bags to avoid cross-contamination.
	Solid	Suspected burnt or unburnt support of accelerant (soil, cloth, paper, mattress, wallboard, rugs, wood pieces of furniture, etc.)	Sampling can utilize tweezers, sweeping, or even by picking up the evidence with protected hands. Indicate the support of the evidence on the package.	Clean metal cans immediately sealed for small items, nylon bags for big ones. Save one empty nylon bag as blank.
		Reference samples (suspect clothing, rags)		Clean metal cans immediately sealed for small items, nylon bags for big ones. Save one empty nylon bag as blank.

TABLE 5.2.9 Collection Guidelines for Document Examinations

Type	State	Support	Collect	Container
Questioned documents		Paper	With tweezers or gloved hands. Place in an open acetate folder to let authorized persons read it, without touching.	Paper envelope
		Money	With a sworn witness or police officer, double-count all the money seized. Staple it in step, note by note, on a paper sheet, indicating on it the values. Each note should be visible when having a look on the full paper sheet, which should then be packaged in a transparent plastic sheet.	Plastic sheet
Comparison		Paper	To collect existing documents of the same period (for signatures, handwriting comparison, etc.), same protocol as for questioned documents. Additional standards could, nevertheless, be requested. In the case of additional standards or creation of comparison documents, duplicate as much as possible the surrounding conditions of the original document: similar paper (quality and color), similar handwriting tools, similar style (capital or block letters), etc. Protocols include: • Writing name, addresses, and personal history 2–5 times. • Writing the text dictated by the crime scene examiner about 10 times. Other materials available to collect (depending of the case): rubber stamps, virgin and commercially printed papers, inks.	Generally, paper envelopes. For rough materials (cartridges, stamps, etc.), plastic bags are available.

TABLE 5.2.10 Collection Guidelines for Anthropology, Entomology

Type	State	Support	Collect	Container
Anthropology	Skeleton	Any	Avoid steel tools. Let dry in open air, if possible.	If dry, paper bags; if moist, in cadaver bag with refrigeration.
	Single bones or teeth			Paper bags
Entomology	Insects	On, under, and hidden areas around the body up to 1 meter away	Collect about 50 living specimens from each position.	Dive all individuals in a 70% V/V ethanol/water solution in a glass container; one glass for each location (on, under, and around).
	Pupae	On, under, about 1 m around, also about 30–50 cm in the soil in the vicinity of the body	Tweezers	All in one paper envelope.
	Maggots		Collect two samples of about 50 individuals each: • One with some flesh to let grow. • One in a 70% V/V ethanol/water solution.	Glass sealed containers (but not airtight for the first one)

References and Bibliography

Green, M.A., 2000. Preservation of evidence. In: Siegel, J., Knupfer, G., Saukko, P. (Eds.), Encyclopedia of Forensic Sciences, in three volumes, pp. 1172–1177.

Horswell, J., 2000. Packaging. In: Siegel, J., Knupfer, G., Saukko, P. (Eds.), Encyclopedia of Forensic Sciences, in three volumes, pp. 432–440.

Horswell, J., 2004. Crime scene investigation. In: Robertson, J. (Ed.), The Practice of Crime Scene Investigation. CRC Press, Boca Raton, FL, pp. 2–45.

Wolfe, J.R., 2008. Sulfur cement: A new material for casting snow impression evidence. J. Forensic Identification 58 (4): 485–498.

Xiao, R., Zhao, X., Zhu, X., Zhang, L., 2010. Distinguishing bloodstains from botanic stains using digital infrared photography. J. Forensic Identification 60 (5): 524–531.

Preserving

Traces and evidence are fragile and subjected to alteration and damage, if not destruction, from before their detection to after they are sealed. Once collected and sealed, evidence is under official control, and should, as far as possible, be in a similar condition to that when it was collected. This is important not only for scientific analyses but also for the legal process. Thus, forensic analyses should generally be nondestructive to allow for reanalysis by experts, either prosecution or defense. The final disposition of evidence is a legal situation and may be beyond the control of the CSI or the CSI's agency.

This chapter will discuss the different risks that threaten evidence, from detection through storage; preservation solutions and conditions will also be addressed (Green, 2000; Horswell, 2000, 2004).

> **Key Terms**
>
> Bloodborne pathogens
> Material safety data
> sheet (MSDS)

Threats to Evidence

Damage

Any detected evidence should be immediately protected from deterioration and damage, either by human or natural actions. This threat can be countered

FIGURE 5.3.1 Evidence should always be protected against damage or loss. *Courtesy ForensicSource.*

by clearly indicating both the pathway to be used by authorized persons to enter and walk through the crime scene and flagging the various pieces of evidence as soon as they are discovered. Also, protect any detected traces or stains, particularly when they are outdoors; wind, rain, and sometimes the sun are enemies of evidence preservation (Baldwin and Puskarich-May, 2000). Although various makeshift approaches will work, given supplies and resourcefulness, companies make off-the-shelf protective supplies for crime scene work (Figure 5.3.1).

Deterioration

Biological materials can be very fragile in hot and wet conditions. Quickly collecting and transmitting the evidence to the laboratory might be the best option to secure these kinds of traces; a cooler with ice might help retard degradation in very hot conditions.

Contamination

The potential for contamination of evidence begins immediately after its deposition. CSIs are responsible for reducing this risk by applying protective measures at the crime scene, such as wearing white one-use-only coats with hoods completely covering the hair; gloves, mouth masks, and goggles are also recommended. The more latent, microscopic, and "invisible" the trace is, the greater the potential for contamination. For better or for worse, forensic analyses are becoming more sensitive, which means it takes increasingly less to contaminate a sample of evidence. Therefore, greater care and precautions should be taken as traces get smaller. But collecting, packaging, and sealing evidence does not completely prevent contamination: Improperly packaged items can be contaminated by foreign materials, and can also contaminate other pieces of evidence, for example, by leaking on the storage shelves at the evidence depository or even in the laboratory. Hence, the CSI should evaluate the vicinity of the questioned and known materials at the scene. For example, transporting a suspect in the same car that carries pieces of evidence should be avoided; if it cannot be prevented, one solution would be to suit the suspect in a white protective coat prior to transport. Avoiding contamination may take ingenuity and creativity.

Infestation

Materials collected from the crime scene or from an outdoor location can easily contain insects. Likewise, if any of the persons of interest have poor hygiene, their personal items may be infested. Therefore, the CSI needs to take precautions when handling and collecting these pieces of evidence; additional countermeasures may be necessary to limit the damage caused by maggots or beetles.

Although they may be samples for forensic entomological purposes, insects may need to be killed to prevent destruction of evidence. Insects can be killed by two techniques: either deep freezing the material until the insects are dead, or placing a few drops of ethyl formate inside a sealed and airtight container for about an hour. Infested clothing can be handled and examined after freezing, for example, taking care not to damage other evidence in the process.

Unused and unsealed evidence collection tools that are not disposable should be washed once a month with bleach or autoclaved.

Decomposition

Time moves forward; entropy typically increases, reducing things to simpler levels of organization. The ceaseless progression of time can be viewed in two ways: useful information (as in estimating time of death) or degradation. Degradation of evidence is to be avoided because the evidence needs to remain in its "time of crime" state for as long as possible. Therefore, extremes should be avoided, depending on the evidence: too cold, too hot, too wet, too dry can each be detrimental to different kinds of evidence. In general, for biological materials, too dry is better than too wet, as too cold is better than too hot. Air drying in a protected area before packaging will preserve most types of biological or water-soaked evidence. Fragile items, like charred documents, should be protected from decomposition by placing them on a soft, noncontaminating substance in a dedicated container and carefully transporting them.

Loss

Tracking evidence once it is collected is of critical importance; the need for assurance in the chain of custody is paramount throughout the entire process. Losing a piece of evidence due to an administrative error is bad enough; the tiny size of many kinds of evidence must be taken into account when choosing their packaging and method of sealing. Traces like hairs, fibers, paint chips, soils, pollen, pupae, and so on can be lost through the poorly closed flap of an envelope or even the corner of one; evidence should be contained in paper folds (bindles) or other leakproof packaging before being placed in envelopes. Vapors or liquids can leak out of improperly sealed containers.

Tampering

As soon as the evidence is collected, it is the responsibility of the CSI to safeguard its integrity, against innocent or purposeful tampering. Items of evidence may have economic value in addition to their evidential value, such as jewelry, firearms, or drugs. Even when sealed, pieces of evidence should not be left unattended. Personnel at the crime scene should be assigned the duty of watching over the collected and sealed evidence.

Safety at the Scene

Preserving the evidence at the scene is not the only thing that needs to be taken care of: A crime scene is one of the most hazardous locations a CSI can go (Figure 5.3.2). Chemical, biological, and physical threats abound. The list of threats is extensive, from explosives to blood to firearms. Considering most of the (criminal) activities are over with and the CSI probably does not have full knowledge of the events, it can be easy to happen upon a hazardous situation or material. Terrorist scenes multiply these dangers because of the prospect of explosives manufacture or use of chemical or biological agents.

The increase in bloodborne pathogens (AIDS and hepatitis, for example) and other pathogens that may be encountered at crime scenes (like the Hanta virus) has made law enforcement and CSIs more aware of personal protection

FIGURE 5.3.2 First responders collect evidence from a potential hazardous crime scene during a training exercise at the Center for Domestic Preparedness (CDP). During CDP training emergency response personnel, regardless of specialty, learn the importance of preserving crime scenes when responding to all-hazards, mass-casualty events. *Source: Shannon Arledge/FEMA.*

when responding to crime scenes. Although the risk of infection to CSIs is exceedingly low, precautions are typically mandated by individual agencies' protocols. Additionally, federal laws or regulations from one of several health agencies may be applicable to crime scene personnel.

On the Web: Safety

Occupational Safety and Health Administration, www.osha.gov
The mission of the Occupational Safety and Health Administration (OSHA) is to save lives, prevent injuries, and protect the health of America's workers. To accomplish this, federal and state governments must work in partnership with the more than 100 million working men and women and their 6.5 million employers who are covered by the Occupational Safety and Health Act of 1970.

The Centers for Disease Control, www.cdc.gov
The Centers for Disease Control and Prevention (CDC) is recognized as the lead federal agency for protecting the health and safety of people at home and abroad, providing credible information to enhance health decisions, and promoting health through strong partnerships. CDC serves as the national focus for developing and applying disease prevention and control, environmental health, and health promotion and education activities designed to improve the health of the people of the United States.

The Morbidity and Mortality Weekly Report, www.cdc.gov/mmwr
The Morbidity and Mortality Weekly Report (MMWR) Series is prepared by the CDC. The data in the weekly MMWR are provisional, based on weekly reports to CDC by state health departments. The reporting week concludes at close of business on Friday; compiled data on a national basis are officially released to the public on the succeeding Friday. An electronic subscription to MMWR is free.

National Institute for Occupational Safety and Health, www.cdc.gov/niosh
The National Institute for Occupational Safety and Health (NIOSH) is the federal agency responsible for conducting research and making recommendations for the prevention of work-related disease and injury. The Institute is part of the CDC. NIOSH is responsible for conducting research on the full scope of occupational disease and injury ranging from lung disease in miners to carpal tunnel syndrome in computer users. In addition to conducting research, NIOSH investigates potentially hazardous working conditions when requested by employers or employees; makes recommendations and disseminates information on preventing workplace disease, injury, and disability; and provides training to occupational safety and health professionals. Headquartered in Washington D.C., NIOSH has offices in Atlanta, Georgia, and research divisions in Cincinnati, Ohio; Morgantown, West Virginia; Bruceton, Pennsylvania; and Spokane, Washington.

Sources and Forms of Dangerous Materials

Inhalation

At a crime scene, airborne contaminants can occur as dust, aerosol, smoke, vapor, gas, or fumes. Immediate respiratory irritation or trauma might ensue when these contaminants are inhaled—some airborne contaminants can enter the bloodstream through the lungs and cause chronic damage to the liver, kidneys, central nervous system, heart, and other organs. Remember that some of these inhalants may be invisible!

Skin Contact

Because processing a crime scene requires the physical collection of items, skin contact is a frequent route of contaminant entry into the body. Direct effects can result in skin irritation or trauma at the point of contact, such as a rash, redness, swelling, or burning. Systemic effects, such as dizziness, tremors, nausea, blurred vision, liver and kidney damage, shock, or collapse, can occur once the substances are absorbed through the skin and circulated throughout the body. The use of appropriate gloves, safety glasses, goggles, face shields, and protective clothing can prevent this contamination.

Ingestion

Ingestion is a less common route of exposure. Ingestion of a corrosive material can cause damage to the mouth, throat, and digestive tract. When swallowed, toxic chemicals can be absorbed by the body through the stomach and intestines. To prevent entry of chemicals or biological contaminants into the mouth, wash hands before eating, drinking, smoking, or applying cosmetics. Also, do not bring food, drink, or cigarettes into areas where contamination can occur.

Injection

Needle sticks and cuts from contaminated glass, hypodermic syringes, or other sharp objects can inject contaminants directly into the bloodstream. Extreme caution should be exercised when handling objects with sharp or jagged edges.

Universal Precautions

The U.S. Occupational Safety and Health Administration (OSHA) issued regulations regarding occupational exposure to bloodborne pathogens (BBPs) in December 1991.[1] Those occupations at risk for exposure to BBPs include law enforcement, emergency response, and forensic laboratory personnel (Title 29 CFR, 1991). Fundamental to the BBP standard is the primary concept for infection control called Universal Precautions. It requires employees to

---

[1] The European Union has a similar agency, the European Agency for Safety and Health at Work (http://osha.europa.eu), as does Australia, the Office of the Federal Safety Commissioner (http://fsc.gov.au).

treat all human blood, body fluids, or other potentially infectious materials as if they are infected with diseases such as hepatitis B virus (HBV), hepatitis C virus (HCV), and human immunodeficiency virus (HIV). The following protective measures should be taken to avoid direct contact with these potentially infectious materials (Title 29 CFR, 1991):

- Use barrier protection such as disposable gloves, coveralls, and shoe covers when handling potentially infectious materials. Gloves should be worn, especially if there are cuts, scratches, or other breaks in the skin.
- Change gloves when torn, punctured, or when their ability to function as a barrier is compromised.
- Wear appropriate eye and face protection to protect against splashes, sprays, and spatters of infectious materials. Similar precautions should be followed when collecting dried bloodstains.
- Place contaminated sharps in appropriate closable, leakproof, puncture-resistant containers when transported or discarded. Label the containers with a BIOHAZARD warning label. Do not bend, recap, remove, or otherwise handle contaminated needles or other sharps.
- Prohibit eating, drinking, smoking, or applying cosmetics where human blood, body fluids, or other potentially infectious materials are present.
- Wash hands after removing gloves or other personal protective equipment (PPE). Remove gloves and other PPE in a manner that will not result in the contamination of unprotected skin or clothing.
- Decontaminate equipment after use with a solution of household bleach diluted 1:10, 70% isopropyl alcohol, or other disinfectant. Noncorrosive disinfectants are commercially available. Allow sufficient contact time to complete disinfection.

In addition to Universal Precautions, prudent work practices and proper packaging serve to reduce or eliminate exposure to potentially infectious materials. Packaging examples include puncture-resistant containers used for storage and disposal of sharps.

Chemical Safety

A wide variety of health and safety hazards can be encountered at a crime scene. Awareness of these hazards comes from the information contained in a material safety data sheet (MSDS) and appropriate training.[2] The MSDS provides information on the hazards of a particular material so that personnel can work safely and responsibly with hazardous materials; MSDS sheets are typically available through a vendor's website. Remember, when working with chemicals, be aware of hazardous materials, disposal techniques, personal protection, packaging and shipping procedures, and emergency preparedness.

---

[2] For example, www.msdssolutions.com or http://siri.uvm.edu.

Personal Protective Equipment
Hand Protection

Hand protection should be selected on the basis of the type of material being handled and the hazard or hazards associated with the material. Detailed information can be obtained from the manufacturer. Nitrile gloves provide protection from acids, alkaline solutions, hydraulic fluid, photographic solutions, fuels, aromatics, and some solvents. It is also cut resistant. Neoprene gloves offer protection from acids, solvents, alkalies, bases, and most refrigerants. Polyvinyl chloride (PVC) is resistant to alkalies, oils, and low concentrations of nitric and chromic acids. Latex or natural rubber gloves resist mild acids, caustic materials, and germicides. Latex will degrade if exposed to gasoline or kerosene and prolonged exposure to excessive heat or direct sunlight. Latex gloves can degrade, losing their integrity. Some people are allergic to latex and can avoid irritation by wearing nitrile or neoprene gloves.

Gloves should be inspected for holes, punctures, and tears before use. Rings, jewelry, or other sharp objects that can cause punctures should be removed. Double-gloving may be necessary when working with heavily contaminated materials; double-gloving is also helpful if "clean" hands are needed occasionally. If a glove is torn or punctured, replace it. Remove disposable gloves by carefully peeling them off by the cuffs, slowly turning them inside out. Discard disposable gloves in designated containers and, it should go without saying, do not reuse them.

Eye Protection

Safety glasses and goggles should be worn when handling biological, chemical, and radioactive materials. Face shields can offer better protection when there is a potential for splashing or flying debris. Face shields alone are not sufficient eye protection—they must be worn in combination with safety glasses. Contact lens users should wear safety glasses or goggles to protect the eyes. Protective eyewear is available for those with prescription glasses and should be worn over them.

Foot Protection

Shoes that completely cover and protect the foot are essential—no sandals or sneakers! Protective footwear should be used at crime scenes when there is a danger of foot injuries due to falling or rolling objects or to objects piercing the sole and when feet are exposed to electrical hazards. In some situations, shoe covers can provide protection to shoes and prevent contamination to the perimeter and areas outside the crime scene.

Other Protection

Certain crime scenes, such as bombings and clandestine drug laboratories, can produce noxious fumes requiring respiratory protection. In certain crime scenes, such as bombings or fires where structural damage can occur, protective helmets should be worn.

Transporting Hazardous Materials

Title 49 of the U.S. Code of Federal Regulations codifies specific requirements that must be observed in preparing hazardous materials for shipment by air, highway, rail, or water. All air transporters follow these regulations, which describe how to package and prepare hazardous materials for air shipment. Title 49 CFR 172.101 provides a Hazardous Materials Table, which identifies items considered hazardous for the purpose of transportation, special provisions, hazardous materials communications requirements, emergency response information, and training requirements. Training is required to properly package and ship hazardous materials employing any form of commercial transportation.

Conclusion

Traces and evidence are fragile things and can be altered, damaged, or destroyed during careless collection and packaging. Evidence submitted postcollection should be in as close as possible to the same condition as it was when collected. This is not only scientifically important but also legally important: the final disposition of evidence is a legal matter despite how it is used in the laboratory.

References and Bibliography

Baldwin, H.B., Puskarich-May, C., 2000. Preservation. In: Siegel, J., Knupfer, G., Saukko, P. (Eds.), Encyclopedia of Forensic Sciences, in three volumes, pp. 440–443.

Green, M.A., 2000. Preservation of evidence. In: Siegel, J., Knupfer, G., Saukko, P. (Eds.), Encyclopedia of Forensic Sciences, in three volumes, pp. 1172–1177.

Horswell, J., 2000. Packaging. In: Siegel, J., Knupfer, G., Saukko, P. (Eds.), Encyclopedia of Forensic Sciences, in three volumes, pp. 432–440.

Horswell, J., 2004. Crime scene investigation. In: Robertson, J. (Ed.), The Practice of Crime Scene Investigation. CRC Press, Boca Raton, FL, pp. 2–45.

Submitting Evidence to the Laboratory

In one sense, this book can be said to be focused on the methods for the collection of physical evidence at a crime scene that will be analyzed in the forensic laboratory. The results of this analysis will help to determine the degree of association between the victim, the suspect, and the crime scene. This section will deal with the best practices for submitting evidence to the forensic laboratory.

Every local, state, and national forensic laboratory has laboratory submission guidelines of some sort that outline their preference for how items of various types should be submitted. They all share the common goal of providing guidance to their client police-submitting agencies in how to best preserve the physical evidence before it is submitted to the forensic laboratory. That way the forensic laboratory can do the best job of determining that degree of linkage between the victim, the suspect, and the crime scene.

Key Terms
Physical match
Latent prints
Lift cards

The Science of Crime Scenes

What follows are general guidelines for the submission of evidence to a full-service laboratory. Such a laboratory is one that performs forensic analysis in the principal disciplines of firearms, DNA, trace evidence, latent prints, and controlled substance analysis, among others. Police agencies must check with their local laboratories for the correct submission of physical evidence involving document examination, toxicology, and any other forensic discipline.

General Submission Guidelines

Physical evidence can be submitted in person at most forensic laboratories or shipped by commercial carriers. Commercial carriers often supply forensic laboratories with software that enables the laboratory to check on the chain of custody at any given moment of any item in transit. No matter what the type of physical evidence, choose a suitable evidence container so that the evidence will be preserved during shipping. Each evidence item must be separately packaged (if possible), uniquely identified, and sealed to avoid contamination. The seal on the evidence packaging is typically marked with a case number, item number, the date when sealed, and the sealer's initials (Figure 5.4.1). Evidence packages are properly sealed if the evidence inside is protected from loss or contamination and any attempt to enter the package would be easily noticed. Staples on envelopes or paper bags do not constitute proper seals; staples also present the possibility of puncturing or otherwise damaging the evidence inside the packaging. The open flaps of envelopes must be sealed with tape and each strip of tape must be initialed. Bottles and jars must be capped tightly to avoid leakage and then sealed with tape. The tape must extend across the top of the lid and down both sides of the body of the container.

FIGURE 5.4.1 Properly sealed evidence containers have tape across the entire opening and the sealer's initials over the tape onto the package.

The general rule is to submit the evidence in the same condition as when collected, if possible. Anything with high water content such as biological stains and vegetable matter must be thoroughly dried before submission. Bacterial action, mold, sunshine, moisture, and warm temperatures can damage the evidentiary value of biological evidence due to the damage or destruction of DNA. After drying, this type of evidence is best stored in clean paper containers. If it is not obvious what type of container or packaging to use for material after it has been thoroughly dried, paper is always a safe bet. The use of paper wrapping, clean paper bags, envelopes, cardboard boxes, or some other breathable packaging material avoids the accumulation of moisture inside the package. Do not use plastic bags or containers. The presence of moisture enhances bacterial growth.

Each item, including each article of clothing, should be packaged separately. Make the size of the package larger than the item being put into it. This may seem axiomatic, but large bulky items such as comforters or pillows, if stuffed into a small sack, will, when opened, shoot out as if they were propelled by a coiled spring. Trace evidence may be lost as a result. Having a larger package reduces the risk of losing evidence and makes it easier to reseal.

Syringes and needles are not accepted directly or by mail by many forensic laboratories. Call the local laboratory for assistance with such items.

Do not submit large quantities (greater than about one teaspoon) of suspected explosives or active explosive devices to the local forensic laboratory. Active devices, including blasting caps, should be dismantled, deactivated, or discharged in some way before submission to the laboratory. Call the local bomb squad to deactivate the device. Make note of what method was used to deactivate the device (a water cannon, externally detonated, etc.), and provide this information when submitting the evidence.

Biological Evidence

For an item, such as a firearm, which might have latent fingerprints, DNA, or other types of evidence such as gunshot residue, call the laboratory before the item is submitted to discuss the circumstances of the case; this helps make sure that the forensic services needed are performed in the right order to maximize the amount of forensic information that can be extracted from the item.

Evidence items, stains, and swabs must be thoroughly dried at room temperature without the use of heat. Partially dried items will be subject to bacterial action and mold, destroying their value as evidence. Generally, the best way to preserve biological evidence is dry and frozen. Although freezer storage is preferred, DNA typing results can be obtained from properly dried evidence stored refrigerated or at room temperature for an extended period of time. If freezing is not an option, biological evidence should be stored in a cool, dark, dry place.

The best way to collect an item of biological evidence is to collect the entire item. This method of collection allows the laboratory to process the evidence with the potential involvement of latent prints, trace evidence, and other forensic disciplines. As with every physical item of evidence, always change gloves both before picking up the item for the first time, and after placing it in the container/packaging. It is critical to collect articles of clothing worn immediately after a sexual assault in which the suspect has deposited body fluid evidence on the victim, remembering that these may not be the clothing the victim wore to go to the hospital. If the item, or part of the item, cannot be collected, the visible stain may be transferred from the object by swabbing or scraping. Scraping consists of using a new scalpel or razor blade and scraping the dried stain onto a clean piece of paper; scraping biological materials may constitute a health hazard and proper personal protective equipment should be worn. Fold and tape the paper closed.

Any reference samples must be taken from an individual by law enforcement, medical staff, or correctional staff for control purposes. A chain of custody must be maintained on the sample from the time of collection. The DNA typing profile obtained from the reference sample is compared to any profiles from the evidence items. The reference samples that should be submitted are dependent on the case circumstances reference/known samples should be submitted from the victim(s) and suspect(s). References may also be used for elimination purposes (a consensual partner of a sexual assault victim, for example); in missing person's investigations, references may be requested from family members.

Metal objects, such as guns, knives, rocks, aluminum baseball bats, etc., should not be frozen, as condensation forms upon removal of these objects from the freezer. These objects should be stored in a cool, dark, dry place.

Glass tubes containing blood that are packaged for shipping must be cushioned and protected from breaking (this includes tubes used to store sexual assault swabs) (Figure 5.4.2). Wrap the tube in absorbent material and tape the top edges together with evidence tape. Place the bag into a second bag and seal, and then place this into a Styrofoam mailing container and seal

FIGURE 5.4.2 Protective tubes should be used to store sharp objects. *Courtesy ForensicSource.*

the container. Blood tubes should never be frozen; they may be refrigerated. If liquid blood tubes are included in a sexual assault kit, they should be removed when the kit is placed in freezer storage.

Trace Evidence

The trace evidence category of analysis contains the most subdisciplines of any of the forensic disciplines. Some of these subdisciplines may not be listed here, but as with all types of physical evidence, call the local forensic laboratory with any questions.

Hairs

For hairs, as with all physical evidence, make detailed notes showing date, time, and location of the collected questioned hairs. Photograph if necessary. Hairs that are found in the same specific location can be combined. Do not combine hairs that are collected from different locations. Place the hairs from each location in separate paper containers or plastic bags. Place these small containers into larger manila envelopes, properly seal and label, and submit to the forensic laboratory. If hair is firmly attached or embedded in an object, do not remove the hair. Send the object with the adhering hair to the forensic laboratory, if possible. Pubic hair combings in sexual assault cases are collected by medical personnel. It is important that the medical personnel have a sexual assault kit that contains materials for the collection of pubic hair combings, and head and pubic hair controls as well as other necessary samples.

Glass

Homicides, burglaries, hit-and-run cases, and assault cases often provide useful glass evidence. Glass taken from a broken window at a burglary scene (control sample) may be compared with glass fragments found on a suspect's body or clothing; glass from a broken windshield may be compared with pieces of glass found on a hit-and-run victim's body or to glass found at the scene. These types of cases involve comparison of the glass samples to determine if they could have a common origin. With larger pieces of glass, it may be possible to physically fit the questioned glass to larger pieces of the control sample of glass. These examinations require the complete collection of the control glass pieces. The way the glass is broken and the position of the glass fragments may reveal the direction of a projectile and potentially the order in which several projectiles penetrated a glass pane or window.

If the direction of force that broke the glass is to be determined, all of the glass must be retrieved. Glass remaining in the window frame must be marked so the surfaces can be identified as "inside" or "outside," and may need to be taped to prevent loss or further breakage. The amount of glass on the ground or floor on each side of the frame should be noted and collected separately.

Photographs of the window frame should be taken prior to collection of the complete frame. Carefully package and submit all of the glass recovered. Submission may require hand delivery to the forensic laboratory.

If projectile holes, such as bullet holes, are to be examined, the entire pane of glass should be submitted intact. Care must be taken not to disturb any possible gunshot residue on the surface of the glass. The glass may have to be taped on the exit surface to hold it together. If the exit side cannot be determined, consult with the forensic laboratory. When a high-speed projectile, like a bullet, passes through a piece of glass, a crater forms in the glass; this crater is larger on the exit side and this may indicate the direction of the projectile. Radial cracks will form on the side of the glass opposite the side of the impact, radiating (hence the name) out from the point of impact. Concentric cracks may form on the side of impact.

If glass fragments are suspected to be on clothing, do not attempt to remove the glass at the scene. Handle the clothing carefully so that the fragments are not lost or transferred to other items. Wrap each article of clothing in clean paper and package them in separate paper bags.

Glass fragments are often embedded in the soles and heels of shoes as one walks over broken glass. Do not remove the glass from the shoes. Wrap the shoes in clean paper and place them into separate, clean paper bags. Control samples collected at the scene should be submitted separately.

Care should be taken to preserve any other trace evidence such as hairs, fibers, paint, shoeprints, or stains that may be adhering to the glass.

Glass found in different areas must be packaged separately. Small pieces of glass should be placed in a paper fold, sealed, labeled, and packaged in a small rigid container (a pill box or metal vial, for example). The container must also be sealed and properly labeled. Large pieces of glass should be packaged in rigid containers. Use packing material such as cardboard or part of a corrugated carton to avoid breakage and to protect the edges. Hand delivery is the preferred way to submit large pieces of glass, as it avoids the task of extensive packaging and reduces the risk of breakage. Package so that if a container opens or tears during shipping, the glass is not lost and does not leak out and contaminate other glass evidence or pose a safety hazard.

Submit control samples from each source of broken glass. Samples from both panes of a double-pane window must be submitted.

Glass such as that found in the frame of a window or remaining in a headlight rim are the best control samples, preferred over glass samples from a floor or roadway.

Clothing and Fibers

The transfer of fibers and fragments of cloth can be the result of such actions as violence to a person with a weapon or with a vehicle, clothing being snagged and/or torn, or the contact of clothing with another article of clothing. Microscopic examinations of fibers, yarns, cordage, and clothing can reveal many characteristics, which can be further supported by chemical and physical analyses. The type of fiber, color, dye characteristics, thread count, twist, and cross-section can be determined. The piece of cloth may be physically fitted into a garment, showing a common origin.

Comparison of questioned and control fibers and threads cannot conclusively establish that they are of common origin. However, the forensic scientist can determine the color, type, and generally the product use of the fibers. Pieces of fabric, threads, or fibers may be found adhering to the front or underside of a vehicle that hit a pedestrian. They may be part of a fabric impression. Photograph the impacted fibers and the entire fabric impression prior to collection.

Transparent tape can be used to pick up fibers from surfaces. The adhesive surfaces of Post-it® notes are also useful for collecting fibers. Since fibers can be difficult to see, surfaces likely to have come into contact with fibers of interest should be tape-lifted routinely. The adhesive surface of the tape or Post-it® should be placed on a clean glass slide or a clear plastic sheet protector. Vacuum cleaning is not a desirable collection procedure, since it picks up so much dirt and other extraneous material. It should be used as a last resort to collect trace evidence. It is best to collect the loose fibers or threads on a clean piece of paper and then fold, seal, and label. Place the folded paper into an envelope or paper bag, seal, and label. Do not put loose fibers in the outer evidence envelope. Since fibers, threads, and fabrics can be easily lost, care must be taken to seal each container. The corners and flaps of an envelope must be sealed with tape.

All clothing that may be involved in the case must be collected for comparison with the collected questioned fibers. Representative samples of possible sources of the collected questioned fibers, such as rugs, blankets, and upholstery, or the entire item itself must be submitted as the control samples. Take control samples that represent the entire source, such as color, fabric, worn areas, etc. The forensic laboratory should be contacted for assistance and information on the collection of the control samples.

If carpet fibers are involved or suspected, a representative sample of carpet must be submitted. The sample should be a piece of the carpet or good representative samples pulled from the carpet, including areas of worn and nonworn carpet. Carpets can consist of several types of fibers, so it is imperative to collect samples from various areas of the carpet.

Paint

Fragments of protective coatings, such as paint, varnish, lacquer, enamels, and plastics, can often be found at the scenes of hit-and-run cases and burglaries involving forced entries. A transfer of paint can occur when two vehicles collide. Fragments of paint at the accident scene or on the victim's clothing may produce information regarding the year, make, and model of the vehicle that fled the scene. The paint fragment from the scene may be a physical match to a particular object or vehicle. Traces of paint on burglary tools may connect these tools to the burglary scene.

Paper folds and plastic or paper envelopes can be used to collect the paint samples. Paper is preferred over plastic because of the static electricity buildup problems of plastic. Small samples of material should be collected on a clean piece of paper. The paper fold is then labeled, sealed, and placed in an envelope, which in turn is labeled and sealed. A convenient method of collecting paint scrapings is to tape a clean sheet of paper just below the sampling area. Hold the paper open and scrape the paint samples loose, allowing them to fall onto the paper. Be sure the paint samples contain all the layers of paint down to the underlying surface. Use a new, clean blade for sampling each particular area. Tape the corners and seams of the envelope or use folded paper. If the item containing the paint or paint smear is small enough, the entire item should be submitted to the laboratory. Do not attempt to remove the paint. If an item is too large to submit to the laboratory, control paint chips or the questioned paint fragments representing all of the layers must be submitted. Do not scrape off the sample in such a manner that the paint chip sample contains only a partial number of layers. The forensic scientist will examine a cross-section of the chip to determine the number, depth, and color of each layer.

Each of the recovered items must be packaged separately, properly labeled, and sealed. If a vehicle is involved, labeling should include the location on the vehicle, make, model, year, vehicle identification number (VIN), and license plate number. Envelopes must be sealed on the corners with tape to ensure that no leakage occurs. Put the paint chips into a folded paper packet and label, and then place the packet into a second envelope, also labeled properly.

Tools with paint smears must be protected to avoid loss or contamination of the questioned paint. The area containing the paint smear should be protected with soft tissue paper, and the tool packaged securely into an appropriate container (a box, for example).

If paint fragments are to be submitted for a possible physical match, they must be packaged so that the chips do not break. The fragments must be protected with tissue paper or cotton and placed in a small, rigid container. In all cases, the control samples must be taken from an undamaged area immediately adjacent to the area of damage or of interest. The collected fragments must contain all of the layers down to the underlying surface. If a physical match is possible, all paint from the damaged area must be collected or the item submitted.

When investigating a hit-and-run collision, control samples should be taken from each vehicle. The samples should be taken from the undamaged area on the same panel immediately adjacent to the damage. Similar control samples must be taken from the suspect vehicle when it is apprehended. Different body panels or parts may have different paint or layer structures. Samples from each damaged panel must be taken (the fender and door, for example).

Impression Evidence

Wherever a crime has been committed, someone has had to enter and exit the scene. In the process, shoeprints, footprints, and tire tracks can be left. This evidence is often overlooked by initial responders and subsequently lost through contamination as more responders arrive. Impression evidence also includes fabric impressions and latent prints. The latter category will be discussed here.

Impression evidence can show class characteristics, wear characteristics, and individualizing characteristics. Class characteristics include such things as the overall pattern of a shoe outsole, the weave of a fabric, or the number of ribs and grooves in a tire track. Wear characteristics are those due to the erosion of the surface of the item being examined and are reflected in the impression. Individualizing characteristics are a product of random events that occur to that one item, such as cuts in a shoe outsole, a flaw in the weave of a fabric, or a stone in a tire's tread. When present in sufficient quantity and detail, the individualizing characteristics in an impression allow it to be identified to a specific source.

Shoeprints can be examined to obtain information as to possible manufacturer, type of footwear (boot, athletic, dress), and approximate size (Figure 5.4.3). Tire tracks can be examined to obtain information as to possible tire manufacturer, design name, and type of tire (automobile, truck, off-road vehicle). Fabric impressions can be examined to determine the type of weave and possible sources.

The impression needs to be photographed both with and without a scale/ruler, using lighting that highlights the impression (usually several oblique or side lighting shots). The camera must be placed directly over an impression so that the entire impression is clearly in focus and no size or focus distortions result. Use of a tripod to hold the camera steady is necessary. The scale must be in the same plane as the impression so that both are in focus simultaneously. The camera should be positioned as close as possible to the impression (fill the frame with the impression).

Whenever possible, the entire object that has the impression should be submitted to the laboratory. Positive identification of the source of the evidence is more likely when the original impression can be examined. The evidence has to be packaged in a manner that protects the impression from contact with any other surface.

When the impression cannot be submitted to the laboratory, the impression should be documented using photography. It should then either be cast or

FIGURE 5.4.3 Shoeprints can contain class information, such as sole design, type of footwear, approximate size, and brand symbols that identify the manufacturer, as shown here. *Courtesy ForensicSource.*

lifted. Dust impressions are best lifted using an electrostatic dust print lifter. An impression can sometimes be lifted with fingerprint tape, a trace evidence lifter, or a gel lifter. The use of electrostatic dust print lifters and gel lifters require practice and should really only be used by laboratory personnel. Impressions in soil should be cast with dental stone (plaster should be avoided as it gives less detail and forms a softer cast). Impressions in snow and underwater require special handling, and again the forensic laboratory should be contacted to recover impressions in these situations.

Be aware of clothing impressions on car finishes, bumpers, undercarriages, etc. The opportunity may exist to compare the impressions to the clothing items. Care should be taken to preserve any trace evidence such as hairs, fibers, or paint in the impression.

Although impression evidence examinations can be done using only photographs (correctly taken), lifts or casts should also be taken. The important individualizing characteristics required to identify the source of an impression are often not visualized in a photograph. Also, for impressions in soil and snow, there is three-dimensional information that is lost in photographs.

Impressions and dust print lifts of impressions should be secured in cardboard boxes in a manner that prevents anything from coming into contact with the impression or lift. Plastic should never be used to package impressions or dust print lifts of impressions since the plastic can actually develop an electrostatic charge, which can then remove portions of the impression or lift.

FIGURE 5.4.4 Casts of tires should be taken while the tires are still on the vehicle.

The amount of information that can be determined from an impression without a direct comparison to a source is limited. If a suspect pair of shoes is provided, then the forensic scientist can give a much more definitive answer as to elimination or positive identification of the crime scene impression. All evidence submitted should be clearly labeled as to the source.

The test impressions (exemplar prints) of tires are best made while the tires are on the vehicle (Figure 5.4.4). These can be made by preparing pieces of white poster board the length of one full rotation of the tire's circumference. A clean board is evenly rolled with fingerprint ink and the tire is rolled across this inked board. The tire is then rolled across a clean length of second poster board (also the length of the tire's circumference). The starting and ending position and the direction of the tire roll must be marked with chalk or crayon on the tire and the poster board. The tire information (position on vehicle, inside and/or outside edge, manufacturer, design name, size, and serial number) should be written on the poster board. A point that investigators are often unaware of, until it happens, is the possibility of the rear tires running over the impressions that have been made by the front tires. The steering wheel should be turned to move the vehicle in a gentle turn. The tires should be removed from the vehicle after the test prints have been made.

Explosives

Debris from an explosion may be scattered over a wide area, buried, or burned. Pieces of an explosive device may be thrown farther from the site of an explosion than one might think. A friend of one of the authors had a car window handle fall through the skylight of his house in Northern Ireland after the explosion of a car bomb that took place over a mile away. An extensive search of the surroundings and painstaking sifting through rubble may be required to obtain important evidence. This evidence may include fragments of the explosive device itself (pipe fragments, blasting caps, electrical components, for example) or chemical residues deposited on objects near the explosion. Forensic laboratory analysis can often determine what explosive material was used in the device and may sometimes provide information about the general construction of the device and how the device was initiated. In some cases, unusual or distinguishing characteristics of the explosive or the device can be linked to materials in a suspect's possession.

Components of explosive devices may include tape, glue, containers, pipes, fuses, wires, blasting caps, timing devices, or remote controls. Many everyday items can be used in the construction of an explosive device, and their diversity is only exceeded by the imagination of the bomb maker. When found together with bulk explosives, or when found partly assembled, the particular combination of materials found may provide intelligence into how these materials were combined in an explosive device.

Unexploded devices, and the individual components of a device, will often provide the best evidence to link an individual to a bombing attempt. Fingerprints will often be intact, tape and glue will not have burned away, wiring and fusing will be undisturbed. In such cases, chemical analysis along with trace examination and fingerprinting can provide a more complete picture of the device, and there is a much greater chance of connecting the device to an individual.

Items with sharp or jagged edges should not be packaged in paper envelopes. Use sturdier containers such as clean metal paint cans (Figure 5.4.5). Paint cans are also used to hold high explosives, dynamite, nitroglycerin, or C4 that contain components that are volatile and will evaporate over time.

Whenever possible, submit control samples in a separate package along with the evidence. For example, if soil from a blast site is submitted, also collect a sample of similar soil from an area away from the seat of the blast.

Porous materials or objects with cracks and ridges tend to collect a large amount of useful residues. Materials from near the blast site, such as foam, rubber, pipe threads, cardboard, or any rough-surfaced items, will often be useful items to collect.

Due to the volatile nature of explosive vapors, surfaces and people can be easily contaminated. Smaller local police agencies often have neither the expertise nor the logistical support to handle large explosion incidents. For such incidents in the United States, it may be necessary to contact the local Bureau of Alcohol, Tobacco, Firearms, and Explosives (ATF) or Federal Bureau of Investigation (FBI) office. The ATF and FBI can provide scene response,

FIGURE 5.4.5 Clean, unused metal paint cans can be used to store arson or explosive samples. *Courtesy ForensicSource.*

investigative assistance, and laboratory services in cooperation with local agencies and the state forensic laboratories.

Physical Match

Physical match examinations consist of the examination and comparison of broken, cut, or torn items to determine if two or more pieces were at one time one item. Examples are plastic tail light pieces that match a damaged vehicle that left the scene, plastic bags, broken glass, or torn edges of duct tape. Prematurely "fitting" pieces together can alter and/or destroy fine tips, shards, detail, etc. on the side edges of the pieces. These features are an important part of the examination and can add significant weight to conclusions when they are present and "match" into the other piece. Documentation of such features is needed before the final "fitting together" is conducted and documented. Each item of evidence is examined visually to determine the correct orientation of the pieces. After the pieces are marked for identification and "sided," the contours, edges, colors, surface markings, etc. are used to help align pieces correctly. Scratches, stains, and/or defects that traverse the broken, cut, or torn edge serve to reinforce the physical fit conclusion. Matching conchoidal marks and defects may be seen in glass pieces and serve to reinforce the physical fit conclusion. Matching fabric pieces involves examination of general size and shape, weave, fiber type, twist, colors, long versus short threads, and thread counting, etc.

If possible, collect the entire item that may be used in a fracture match. If this is not possible, it may be required to deconstruct all or part of a larger item such as a car or a wall. Each of the recovered items must be packaged separately, properly labeled, and sealed. If a vehicle is involved, labeling should include the location on the vehicle, make, model, year, VIN, and license plate number. Containers must be sealed to ensure that no leakage occurs. Put the material into a folded paper packet or paper container and label, and then place the packet into a second container, also labeled properly.

Package so that if a container opens or tears during shipping, the material is not lost and does not leak out and contaminate other evidence or pose a safety hazard.

Firearms Evidence

Laboratory examination of firearms evidence may reveal data about the firearm, ammunition, or components; information regarding the target object; and may contribute information that helps reconstruct the events surrounding the firearm incident. The examination may determine:

- The caliber of the fired ammunition
- The type of firearm by examining the recovered bullets and expended cartridge cases
- If the recovered bullets and expended cartridge cases were fired from a particular firearm; any malfunctioning of a submitted firearm
- The entrance and exit bullet holes in clothing; the approximate distance from muzzle to target
- Any obliterated serial numbers
- Bullet trajectories

Do not, as often seen on TV, pick up the firearm by placing a pencil or some other object in the barrel or the trigger guard. Always handle the evidence with gloves and pick it up by the grip with two fingers placed where it would not likely have been previously touched. Handle the firearm carefully, even if the safety is on or the firearm is not cocked; the safety may be faulty or the trigger pull may be very light. Place the firearm into a box (preferred), paper bag, or envelope for transport back to the workstation (Figure 5.4.6). If the firearm is loaded, it must be unloaded before shipping to the forensic laboratory. If, for some reason, the firearm cannot be unloaded, the submitting agency must call the forensic laboratory and determine when and how to hand deliver the firearm to the laboratory.

To unload a revolver, mark a line on the cylinder on each side of the top strap with a pencil or felt-tip pen prior to opening or moving the cylinder. This will inform the examiner which chamber was at the top. While pointing the barrel downward, open the cylinder; before moving the cylinder or removing the cartridges, make a diagram of the cylinder. Number the chambers, starting at the top and going clockwise; note any cartridge in each chamber, whether the cartridge has been fired, and the headstamp information, indicating

FIGURE 5.4.6 Firearms should be packaged and transported using cardboard boxes, many of which have specialized construction to safely secure the weapon to the container and to allow viewing of the item without breaking the security seal. *Courtesy ForensicSource.*

the manufacturer. Each cartridge or cartridge case that is removed must be placed in individual containers. The number of the chamber from which it was removed must be noted on the container.

The firearm and cartridges must be marked prior to packaging and shipping. A tag is a good method of marking the firearm. Unfired cartridges should be marked with an indelible felt-tip pen along the case. Fired cartridge cases should be handled in a similar fashion as cartridge cases collected at a scene. Note that a mark made with a permanent marker may be removed during examination. Never mark the base of a fired or unfired cartridge.

To unload a semiautomatic pistol, remove the magazine. Handle the magazine with care if it is to be processed for latent prints or DNA. Do not remove any cartridges. Mark the magazine. Package the magazine in a paper envelope, small box, etc. Seal and label the container. Submit it with the firearm. Remove the live cartridges, if any, from the chamber. Mark the cartridge, indicating that it was removed from the chamber, place it in a container, and seal and label the container. Submit it with the firearm. Note the serial number of the firearm for proper identification.

Black-powder firearms are unloaded differently depending on the type of firearm. For percussion cap revolvers, remove the percussion caps from the cylinder and then remove the cylinder from the frame. Do not attempt to unload the individual cylinder cavities. For percussion cap rifles, remove the percussion cap. Do not attempt to unload the firearm. For flint lock pistols and rifles, remove the flint and any powder in the flash pan. Again do not attempt to unload the firearm.

If a firearm or other metal object is recovered from fresh or salt water, it should be placed in a container of fresh water immediately. Immersion in fresh water will slow the oxidation process and remove the corrosive action of the salt water. Do not clean the firearm before submitting. Do not attempt to fire the firearm before submitting.

Proper labeling of evidence includes the contents, source, date, time, item number, agency case number, and the name or initials of the collector.

Elemental analyses of gunshot residue, typically for unique gunshot residue particles containing the presence of lead, barium, and antimony, are conducted by some laboratories. The suspected samples must be carefully collected and precautions taken against sample contamination. Commercial GSR sampling kits are available. The attempted association of a specific fired bullet to a specific discharged cartridge case is not normally conducted; neither is the elemental analysis of lead bullets or bullet cores for identification to a lot or box of ammunition.

Descriptions of firearms should include the serial number (do not confuse with part numbers), make, model, caliber, and the condition when found (that is loaded or unloaded, cocked or uncocked, safety on or off, etc.). The area of recovery should be measured, sketched, and photographed, showing the positions of the item. Unload the firearm, if possible. Handle carefully to preserve trace evidence. Do not remove the trace evidence unless the entire object cannot be submitted. Before removing, describe the location of the trace evidence and photograph or sketch the evidence in place.

Each bullet or fragment recovered from the crime scene should be put in a pill box or envelope. Seal and label the container. The fine striations on the bullet must be protected. Do not use any cotton material for wrapping; it may be confused with fibers from clothing involved in the case.

If a bullet is buried in a wall or other object, cut around the bullet. Remove the material containing the bullet. Do not probe the hole or try to dig out the bullet; it may damage the bullet. Wrap the item, place in a carton, and seal and label the carton.

Do not touch recovered bullets unless clean protective gloves are being worn. Shot pellets should be collected and submitted in the same manner as bullets. Search for shot shell wads and shot cups whenever a shotgun is involved. Shot patterns should be measured, sketched, and photographed. If possible, the surface containing the shot pattern should be recovered.

Bullets and fragments recovered at an autopsy should be carefully rinsed and dried. Wrap them in tissue paper and place them in a small carton or envelope. Seal and label the container.

Fired cartridge cases at a scene should be placed in a small carton or envelope. Make sure the packing is appropriately labeled. Do not mark the cartridge case on the base or on the side.

If fired at close range, a firearm will discharge partially burned and unburned gunpowder particles onto the target surface. If the pattern is on skin, 1:1 color photographs of the wound and entire pattern should be submitted, before and after the wound area is cleaned. A scale or ruler must be included in the photographs. Close-up photos of the entry and exit wounds should be submitted as well as close-up photos of typical gunpowder particles in the pattern. Some of the particles should be picked off and folded in a piece of clean paper. The paper should be sealed, labeled, and placed in an envelope. Seal and label the envelope.

The laboratory should be informed of the locations of the entry and exit wounds found on the body. Copies of autopsy or medical reports are helpful in the course of the analysis and should be submitted to the laboratory.

The suspect firearm and the same type of ammunition must be submitted. The gunpowder pattern on the proximity test target material is then compared to the patterns visible on or chemically developed on the submitted clothing. In the case of black-powder firearms, the unknown factors of powder type and amount will be limiting factors in trying to establish distances between the firearm and target.

It is important to collect any and all firearm parts found at the crime scene. It may be possible to reassemble the firearm for testing; a firearm type and manufacturer may be identified. All of the collected parts may not be from the same firearm. The parts may be packaged in a box, a paper bag, or an envelope. Parts packaged in a box may be strapped down to prevent shifting during transport. The packaging should be marked with the appropriate identifying marks, such as agency case number, item number, and description of the item.

The serial number on a firearm may be obliterated to conceal ownership. Chemical processing can often restore the number. Do not wipe or abrade the surface. Package the firearm in a suitable box (preferred), paper bag, envelope, etc. Firearms packaged in a box may be strapped down to prevent shifting during transport. The packaging should be marked with the appropriate identifying marks, such as agency case number, item number, and description of the item.

All firearms must be unloaded before being shipped or hand-carried to the laboratory. If the firearm is difficult to unload, contact the forensic laboratory for assistance.

Toolmark Evidence

A toolmark is a mark made by one object on the surface of another softer object. Although these marks are generally made at the entry point of a burglary, various kinds of toolmarks can be found elsewhere, such as fractured knife blades, cut marks on wire, abrasions left on a vehicle, cut marks on a padlock, machine marks on a metallic surface, and even saw marks on bone.

Some toolmarks only show the basic shape of the tool. This type of toolmark lacks specific detail that can single out a particular tool; only the general shape and size of the tool can be determined. The toolmark that is of more value is the type that consists of striations (a series of narrow, fine grooves, some of which are microscopic) and indentations that show the individual characteristics of the tool. These marks can often lead to the identification of a particular tool.

Do not attempt to fit a suspected tool into the questioned mark. The toolmark may be damaged, the tool may be altered, and trace evidence may be lost or contaminated. In the case of cut wire–type materials, mark the end of the wire–type material cut by an agency representative during the retrieval of the evidence with paint or permanent marker, or wrap with tape, indicating this is a cut produced by a known tool. This provides information to the laboratory as to which end of the wire–type material is to be compared with the suspected tool. Care must be taken to protect the suspected tool so that the face of the tool is not damaged, thus changing the toolmark it will produce. Protect the face of the tool with soft tissue paper. Handle the tool with gloves, as DNA might be recovered from a tool left at the scene.

Protect any trace material on the face of the tool. Paint, metal particles, and other materials from a surface frequently adhere to the tool. The trace material can be compared with samples of the surface containing the toolmark. Samples of the surface adjacent to the toolmark must be taken. Later, when the suspect tool is recovered, trace materials on the tool can be compared to the samples taken at the scene. This information can be very valuable, particularly if the toolmark comparison is not definitive. When possible, submit the object containing the toolmark. It is important that the toolmark be kept clean and dry. An exception is when a toolmark on a metal surface is subject to rusting; to retard rusting, coat the toolmark with a light film of oil.

Close-up photos that include a scale must be made if the object containing the toolmark cannot be submitted. The film plane should be parallel to the toolmark. Oblique lighting will increase details visible in the photo.

At crime scenes, burglary tools may break during the commission of the crime. Fragments of the broken tool may be found near the scene or even in the toolmark itself. Since these fragments may be very small, a flashlight held obliquely to the floor surface is helpful. A magnet may also be used to locate the fragments that contain iron. The recovered fragment may be fitted to the suspect's broken tool and constitute what is called a physical match. The physical match may identify the tool as the one used at the crime scene.

Latent Prints Evidence

Latent prints are perhaps the most common form of physical evidence and one of the most valuable. They relate directly to the objective of every criminal investigation and that is the identification of the offender. Because latent prints are fragile and susceptible to destruction, proper collecting, handling, and packaging of the evidence are very critical.

In homicide and death investigation cases, the agency should make every effort to obtain postmortem prints. The laboratory should be contacted if assistance is needed.

A combination of powder and chemical applications is used to develop latent prints on the adhesive and nonadhesive side of tape. Attention must be given to perform trace evidence collection prior to latent print processing. Special care must be taken not to contaminate or lose any small particles of evidence. If possible, place the tape lightly onto a sheet protector or a sheet of heavy plastic. Avoid "wadding" the tape and packaging in paper containers.

Lift Cards

After a powder-developed latent print has been lifted and placed on a card backing, that card should be properly identified. Written information should include the date, crime type, case number, crime scene location, name of the person who made the lift, location of the lift, and the type of object. A simple sketch of the object to describe the location from where the lift was made can be an addition to written information. Using small directional arrows is helpful in orienting the placement of a latent print. Any of the officer's prints appearing along the edges of the tape should be crossed out and initialed. Inked elimination prints are prints of those persons having legal access to an area. If these prints are placed on a card backing, properly mark the cards as "elimination prints" and seal them for submission as evidence.

Evidence Types and Enhancement

One can imagine the path of evidence from collection to analysis in the laboratory as being linear: identify, collect, package, preserve, label, and submit. It can be considered highly desirable to simply collect untreated traces and evidence as they are found and send them directly to the forensic laboratory for analysis. Simple "bagging and tagging" ignores, however, the intrinsic information that some evidence types have that can lend enormous value to the investigation at the scene. Moreover, information developed at the scene can help direct immediate evidence discovery and recovery, as well as help focus investigations by supporting or rejecting certain hypotheses. Finally, in some instances, the substrate the evidence is on may not be able to be collected or the evidence may have more value being analyzed in place; more pragmatically, many optical detection methods can only be applied after a chemical or physical treatment in the field. Thus, in reality, the process of evidence is nonlinear and depends on many factors, with each evidence item possibly subjected to many and varied tests.

The Science of Crime Scenes

Chapters 6.1–6.4 will briefly detail the nature of these various pieces of evidence, introduce chemical or physical enhancements for each of them, and discuss the forensic interest they represent and the relevant questions to answer first.

Chapter 6.1 starts by presenting chemical evidence enhancement as applied to bulk materials, a process often used to determine the existence of a crime through the detection of illegal substances, like drugs or explosives. Because gunshot residue (GSR) detection, determination of the shooter's hand, and

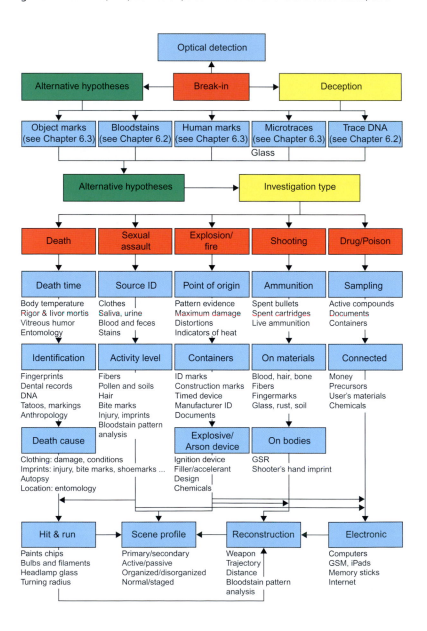

FIGURE 6.0.1 Scheme for crime scene management.

serial number restorations are essential chemical processes, they will also be addressed in this chapter.

Biological evidence will be summed up in Chapter 6.2. This subject deals with blood, semen, saliva, urine, feces, hair, and miscellaneous potential DNA sources, like fingernails. Addressing this approach after chemical evidence underlines that, despite its widespread and legitimate importance over other evidence due to its scientific specificity, DNA is not necessarily the first (and certainly not the only) evidence to focus on. Chapter 6.3 covers the various two-dimensional and three-dimensional visible and latent impressions called marks, such as fingerprints, footprints, shoeprints, tire tracks, and toolmarks. Finally, Chapter 6.4 closes with microtraces (paints, fibers, soils, glass, etc.), including some special biological samples, such as botanical evidence (pollen, leaves), insects, diatoms, and human remains.

The protocols proposed here should be integrated first in a holistic scene of crime management to optimize detection and collection, which should itself refer to and be compatible with further, more effective techniques in the laboratory. These methods should be familiar to the crime scene examiner.

Chemical Evidence

This chapter discusses chemical evidence enhancement as it can be applied to bulk materials, such as drugs, explosives, or fire debris. The simple presence of some of these materials, like illegal drugs, could also immediately inform the detectives of the criminal nature of the investigation; eventually, it could also provide intelligence about other factors or crimes, like distribution routes or manufacturing sites. Because gunshot residues detection and serial number restoration are primarily chemical processes, they will also be addressed in this chapter.

Key Term
Scanning electron microscopy (SEM)

Drugs

A drug is a natural or manufactured substance that affects physiological or psychological behavior. Many are legally prescribed for therapeutic or medical purposes. Reacting to the widespread diffusion of drugs within western societies from the mid-1960s onward, many governments enacted laws prohibiting the manufacture, distribution, sale, and consumption of certain drugs. Powerful drugs, like stimulants or depressants, have addictive qualities; others, like heroin, have little therapeutic value but are highly intoxicating. Drugs present a particular crime scene problem, in that they may occur in amounts ranging over orders of magnitude, from a few grams (or even at trace level) to kilos. Sampling, therefore, is central to drug collection.

Drugs may present themselves as plants, powders, tablets, pills, liquids, and gases. Their chemical structure is the first key to classify these substances and they can be classified according to their physiological and psychological effects (depressant, stimulant, or hallucinogenic). Another way to distinguish them is by alkaloid and nonalkaloid compounds. The word "alkaloid" comes from the original extraction of compounds, which were found to be basic or alkaline, from plants at the end of the 18th century; examples of alkaloids include nicotine, morphine, cocaine, and atropine. In large doses they act as poisons. Table 6.1.1 gives a broad classification of common licit and illicit drugs found during police investigations.

Finding the active compounds or physiological remnants of drugs in tissues, such as blood, urine, saliva, sweat, or hair, is the toxicologist's affair. The CSI, on the other hand, is confronted with bulk material in solid form to sample and occasionally to presumptively test. Large amounts of drugs pose the question about sampling raised earlier. In the field, a positive presumptive test is required for seizure, but how much is required to be tested? Starting with the hypothesis

TABLE 6.1.1   Commonly Encountered Drugs of Abuse Classified According to Their Effects

Effect	Drug Class	Examples
Depressant	Barbiturates	Butalbital, pentobarbital, phenobarbital
	Benzodiazepines	Diazepam, oxazepam, flunitrazepam, nitrazepam, temazepam
	Opiates	Heroin, morphine, codeine
	Miscellaneous	Ethanol, fentanyl, dextropropoxyphene
Stimulant	Cocaine	Cocaine, crack, ice
	Amphetamines	Metamphetamine, amphetamine
	Designer drugs	DOM, DOB, MBDB, MDA, MDE, MDMA
	Others	Phenmetrazine, cathinone, methcathinone, khat
Hallucinogenic	Phenylethylamines	Mescaline
	Tryptamines	DMT, psilocybin, psilocin
	Ergot alkaloids	LSD
	Cannabinoids	Hashish, marijuana, cannabis
	Others	PCP

DOM: 2,5-dimethy-4-methylamphetamine; DOB: 2,5-dimethy-4-bromolamphetamine; MBDB: N-methyl-1-(3,4-methyledioxyphenyl)-2-butanamine; MDA: methylenedioxyamphetamine; MDE: methylenedioxyethylamphetamine; MDMA: methylenedioxymethylamphetamine; DMT: dimethyltryptamine; LSD: lysergic acid diethylamide; PCP: phencyclidine.

that the bulk of material consists wholly of either illicit drugs or no illegal substances at all, one positive result out of five random samples from the larger population is enough to state with a high degree of confidence that at least half of the seizure is either a genuine drug or not (Nordgaard, 2005). Additional sampling can take place in the laboratory under more controlled conditions than those in the field; this means that the laboratory must have sufficient room to receive and securely store large amounts of drugs.

Presumptive spot tests offer the opportunity to immediately provide objective leads to the investigator; these need to be confirmed by the laboratory. Spot tests also help with investigative hypotheses of links with similar cases encountered over a short period of time or in the same area. Commercial kits, like NIK® tests, provide a flowchart to identify the presumptive drugs encountered. A similar scheme is presented in Figure 6.1.1, focusing on the main illicit substances encountered (opium, cocaine, heroin, amphetamines and derivates, cannabis, and barbiturates) through a step-by-step presumptive spot test approach (Baselt, 1978; UNIDCP, 1994; Jungreis, 1997; Liska, 2000; O'Neal et al., 2000; Biermann et al., 2003). Syntheses and protocols of these tests (blue boxes in Figure 6.1.1) are listed in Table 6.1.2.

As well as confirmatory testing, the laboratory can also perform drug profiling (Esseiva et al., 2002, 2007), which aims to provide forensic intelligence by tracing the synthesis route of drugs, such as cocaine or heroin (Esseiva, 2004) and ecstasy (Zingg, 2005), using their trace solvents, additives, diluents, and adulterants to link seizures with each other. In essence, this is backtracking the supply and production chain of the drugs to their sources.

Arson

Fire scene examination aims to detect the cause of the fire, the point of ignition, any accelerants or ignitable liquids that may have been used, and the pattern of the damage (Figure 6.1.2). Fire can only occur and persist in the presence of three parameters: heat, fuel, and oxygen. Smoke-staining patterns, burn patterns, and melted or discolored materials provide useful evidence to be documented. Charred wood, cracked glass, and soot are harder to analyze and should be left for the interpretation of the fire scene experts, as too many parameters can affect the appearance of materials attacked by fire. Many myths abound about fire scene indicators, like crazed glass or "fire trails"; CSIs should dedicate themselves to documenting the scene as much as possible and leave the scene interpretation to the fire scene experts.

Fires are dynamic events and can be affected by many situational factors, such as wind, rain, and firefighting techniques. The main objective of the crime scene investigation is to locate the point(s) of ignition; this can be difficult because, logically, the point where the fire started has burned the longest and so should be the most damaged. Malicious actions to accelerate the fire, such

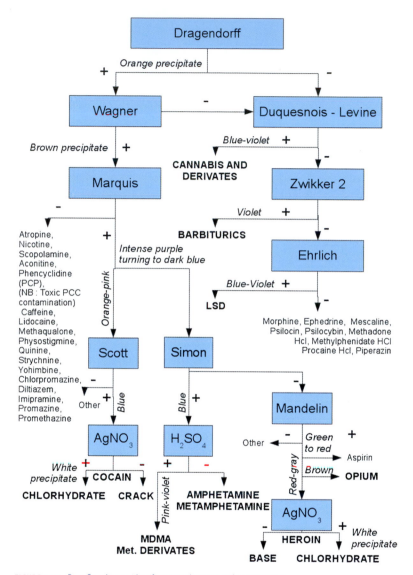

FIGURE 6.1.1 Drug flowchart to identify active substances at the crime scene.

as using gasoline, can create even more damage. Relevant clues to infer the site of ignition include:

- The area of maximum damage
- Depth of charring to wood as compared with different places with similar wood
- Spalling of plaster combined with a smoke pattern on the underlying wall; spalling without the smoke pattern could be due to firefighting techniques

TABLE 6.1.2 Drug Presumptive Spot Tests

	Synthesis	Application	Observation	False Positives
Dragendorff reagent	Sol. 1: Dissolve in 50 ml 20% aqueous acetic acid: 0.85 g bismuth subnitrate. Sol. 2: Dissolve in 20 ml distilled water: 8.0 g potassium iodide. 7 volumes of sol. 1 and 3 volumes of sol. 2 make up the reactant.	Several drops of reactant solution into 1–2 mg test sample in a test tube.	Precipitate should be considered as a positive reaction.	Alkaloids giving negative tests with Dragendorff reagent: Caffeine, Ephedrine, Lysergide, Mescaline, Psilocin, Psilocybin. Nonalkaloids giving positive tests with Dragendorff reagent: Lidocaine HCl, Meperidine, Methadone HCl, Methapyrilene HCl, Methaqualone, Pentazocine HCl, Pencyclidine HCl, Propoxyphene Napsylate.
Wagner's reagent	Dissolve in distilled water: 1.27 g iodine. 2 g potassium iodide. Bring water volume to 100 ml.	Several drops of reactant solution into 1–2 mg test sample in a test tube or a test plate.	Brown precipitate should be considered as a positive reaction.	Alkaloids giving negative tests with Wagner's reagent: Ephedrine, Lysergide, Mescaline, Morphine, Psilocybin. Nonalkaloids giving positive tests with Wagner's reagent: Lidocaine HCl, Meperidine, Methapyrilene HCl, Methaqualone, Pentazocine HCl, Pencyclidine HCl, Propoxyphene Napsylate. Also: Henne (arabic tattoo stains), red vineyard, barbital, and butobarbital.
Marquis reagent	Mix 10 ml conc. sulfuric acid with 8–10 drops of 40% formaldehyde solution.	2 drops of reactant solution into 1–2 mg test sample in a test tube or spot plate.	Positive (opiates) if presence of intense purple turning to dark-blue violet. Cocaine will give a orange-pink color.	False positive with nonopiates: Ephedrine Sulfate, Methapyrilene HCl, Amphetamine Sulfate, Meperidine, Metamphetamine HCl, Cannabinol, MDMA.
Scott reagent	Sol. 1: Dissolve 2 g thiocyanate in 40 ml ultra-pure water Sol. 2: Concentrated chlorohydric acid. Sol. 3: Chloroform.	Pour 5 drops sol. 1 on 1–2 mg question sample in a test tube. Add 1 drop sol. 2. Add 6 drops sol. 3.	Cocaine gives a blue stain of the sol. 3 (chloroform) layer.	False positive: Heroin.

(Continued)

TABLE 6.1.2 (Continued)

	Synthesis	Application	Observation	False Positives
AgNO$_3$ reagent	Mix 5 g AgNO$_3$ in 30 ml ultra-pure (18 MΩ) water.	Add 1 to 2 mg question sample in a test tube with 2–3 water drops. Shake. Add 5 drops Sol. 1.	Positive test: White precipitate.	False positive: Mercury ions, bromides, iodides, cyanides, sulfides and thiocyanates.
Simon reagent	Sol. 1: Dissolve 1 g nitroprusside in 50 ml distilled water and add 2 ml acetaldehyde while stirring. Sol. 2: Dissolve 2 g sodium carbonate in 100 ml distilled water.	Add 1 drop sol. 1 on a 1–2 mg question sample in a test plate. Mix and add 2 drops sol. 2.	MDMA and metamphetamines give a blue color.	False positive: Tobacco.
H$_2$SO$_4$ reagent	H$_2$SO$_4$ concentrated: 50 ml H$_2$SO$_4$ concentrated 96%.	Add 1 drop on 1–2 mg question sample in a test plate.	A pink-violet stain indicates presence of amphetamines derivatives (like MDMA), but no reaction with amphetamine itself or methamphetamine.	False positive: Henna (Arabic tattoo stains).
Mandelin reagent	Pour 10 ml sulfuric acid on 0.1 g ammonium vanadate.	Add 1 drop of reagent onto 1–2 mg of test sample on a plate. Wait for 30 seconds.	Stable red-brick color: Ephedrin sulfate. Orange changing to yellow or green color: Mescaline HCl. Blue-green changing to red-violet color: Aspirin. Stable red-violet color: Benzocain. Red-gray stain: Heroin. Brown stain: Rough opium.	False positive: Crack (base cocaine) and Henna (Arabic tattoo stains).

Reagent	Procedure	Result	False positive
Duquenois Levine reagent	Sol. 1: Cautiously add 0.8 ml acetaldehyde on 0.5 g vanilin. Add 24 ml 95% ethanol solution. Sol. 2: Chlorohydric acid. Sol. 3: Chloroform.	Add 1 ml sol. 1 on a question sample in a test tube. Shake for 1 minute. Add 1 ml sol. 2. Wait for 1 minute. Add 1 ml sol. 3.	A blue-violet satin appears in the low layer of chloroform, in case of cannabis or derivatives presence.	False positive: Henna (Arabic tattoo stains).
Zwikker 2 reagent	Sol 1: Dissolve 0.25 g pentahydrated copper (II) sulfate in 50 ml distilled water. Sol. 2: Add 2.5 ml pyridin to 47.5 ml chloroform.	Dissolve question sample in methanol. Add an extract on a test plate. Add 1 drop sol. 1. Add 1 drop sol. 2.	Barbiturates (including barbital, butobarbital, pentobarbital, phenobarbital) give a violet stain.	No known false positive.
Ehrlich reagent	5 ml methanol on 0.5 g p-(dimethylamino)-benzaldehyde (p-DMAB) in a 15 ml tube.	Add 2 drops reactant on 1–2 mg question sample on a test plate. Wait for 5 minutes.	LSD gives a blue-violet stain.	No known false positive.

FIGURE 6.1.2 Arson scenes can be impressive because of their size, requiring a rigorous methodology. *With permission, courtesy Francis Hebrard, 2002.*

- Distortion to glass (700–900°C), plastic (130–400°C), PVC (60–120°C), metalwork (300–1,000°C, depending of the type of metal) may also be relevant, as well as damage to concrete floors, like holes, and ceilings
- Residual heat in a lower-level burning region (as fire generally spreads upwards)
- A V-funnel pattern

Table 6.1.3 gives some relevant temperatures of fusion and inflammation for solids and gases, and functioning for various devices that could act as sparks.

Notwithstanding human intervention (such as the preparatory acts of the arsonist or the techniques used by firefighters to combat the fire), transmission of fire occurs through:

- Radiation (heating surrounding materials—fuel—to the point of ignition)
- Convection (hot air climbs)
- Projection (inflamed debris can ignite fires in disconnected areas)

All these types of transmission can act as new sources of energy.

Once potential areas of ignition have been located, the collection of evidence can begin (Figure 6.1.3). Clean reference materials, similar to those that have been burned, should also be sampled at the scene, such as carpets, painted woods, or flooring, because combustion products can interfere with chemicals suspected to have been used as accelerants.

If a point of entry to the scene is identified, the CSI should attempt to detect traces at that location; criminals will set fires away from the point of entry so they can escape safely once the fire is set. Fingerprints, shoeprints, toolmarks, and microtraces (fibers from a coat or shirt caught on a broken windowpane, for example) are all potential evidential materials to be collected. The main

TABLE 6.1.3 Various Temperatures of Interest in Degrees Celsius

Matter	T° of Fusion	Matter	T° of Fusion
Tin	230	Lead	327
Zinc	420	Magnesium	650
Aluminium	660	Bronze	699–1032
Brass	854–1038	Silver	961
Gold	1064	Copper	1083
Steel	1200–1500	Iron	1200–1500
Cast iron	1200–1500	Glass	1350–1500
Nickel	1462	Platinum	1769
Chrome	1875		
Matter	**T° of Inflammation**	**Matter**	**T° of Inflammation**
Hay	150	Wood	150–250
PVC	370–390	PET	410
Polyester, nylon	500	Melamine	790
Animal wool	600	Cotton	400
Hydrogen	400	Butane	404
Propane	450	Natural gas	482–632
Ethylene	490	Ethane	515
Methane	540	CO	605
Ammonia	649	Freon	734
Possible Spark	**T° of Functioning**	**Possible Spark**	**T° of Functioning**
Light bulb	50–200	Filament	2,500
Halogen glass	700	Short cut	4,000
Bad wiring	600	Cigarette	300
Matches	900		

Courtesy X. Gargasi, arson and explosives private expert, Bordeaux, France.

difficulty in detecting these traces is soot; suggestions for removing soot are listed in Table 6.1.4 with their associated fingerprint development methods.

Absorene® and Mikrosil® are trademarks, the former being a type of soft plastic with absorption capacities, the latter a polymer mold generally used for dentistry (but also for casting toolmarks or to lift black-powdered fingerprints). The protocols proposed for fingerprint development are in Table 6.1.5.

FIGURE 6.1.3 The point of ignition is quite easy to locate for small fires. *With permission, courtesy Francis Hebrard, 2003.*

TABLE 6.1.4 Soot Removal Process and Proposed Fingerprint Developments

Surfaces	Process	Proposed Fingerprint Development
Loose soot and debris	Light brushing	
Heavy soot	Pencil eraser	
Nonporous surfaces	Lifting tape in conjunction with sodium hydroxide washing	BPS, black magnetic powder; if not wet: superglue and BY40
Complex-shaped nonporous surfaces	Silicone rubber casting (like Mikrosil®)	BPS, black magnetic powder; if not wet: superglue and BY40
Porous surfaces	Absorene®	DFO, physical developer (PD)
Bloody nonporous surfaces	Silicone rubber casting (like Mikrosil®)	Vacuum metal deposition technique
Bloody fabric or bloody porous surfaces	Absorene®	Acid violet 17, acid black 1, acid yellow 7
Porous surfaces (large ones), even bloodstained	Latex spraying and removing	Any development on porous surfaces (see Chapter 6.3 and contact the lab)

Source: Bradshaw et al., 2008; Larkin et al., 2008; Moore et al., 2008.

It should be noted that physical developer is better used in the laboratory because of requirements for materials and chemicals; for example, silver amine stock solutions and REDOX stock solutions have a short shelf life once prepared.

The CSI should also be aware that arson is often not a crime committed only for its own sake. It frequently is used to obscure another criminal activity that

TABLE 6.1.5 Fingerprint Development Protocols Relevant to Arson Scenes

	Synthesis	Application	Observation
BPS (black powder suspension)	5 g of precipitated magnetic iron oxide (Fe_3O_4). 5 ml Kodak Photo-Flo 600. 50 ml distilled water. Pour Fe_3O_4 in a glass beaker, add Photo-Flo. Progressively add distilled water and mix to form a runny paste.	Paint on the surface to be treated. Leave for 15 seconds. Wash off using running water.	White light. FP appears dark on bright background.
BY40	Stock solution: 0.1 g BY40. 40 ml acetonitrile. 60 ml 2-propanol. Working solution: 5 ml stock solution in 95 ml petrol ether. Stable solution in dark bottle.	Apply solution with a pipette or by drowning on superglue-developed FP for at least 24 hours. Wash with water the sample (use a pipette).	Luminescence: Excitation at 440 nm. Emission at 490 nm.
DFO	Stock solution: 1.9 g DFO dissolved in 120 ml chloroform. Add 240 ml methanol, and 140 ml acetic acid. Working solution is obtained with 100 ml stock solution completed to 1,000 ml with petrol ether.	Rapid drowning, let dry in the air for a few seconds. Second drowning. Let the paper completely dry and place it in a 100°C oven for 20 minutes (excepting plastic windows documents: 1 hour at 60°C). A dry iron (without vapor) can also be used. If luminescence disappears, another heating is sufficient.	Absorption: Maximal absorption at 560 nm, for a purple color of the fingerprint. Luminescence: Excitation at 430–580 nm (max. at 555–560 nm). Emission at 550–650 nm (max. emission at 575–580 nm).

(Continued)

TABLE 6.1.5 (Continued)

	Synthesis	Application	Observation
PD (physical developer)	Silver amine stock solution: 12 g silver nitrate + 500 ml water + ammonia liquor. REDOX stock solution: 8 g ferric nitrate nonahydrate + 20 g ferrous ammonium sulfate hexahydrate + 20 g citric acid + 750 ml distilled water. Working solution: 250 ml silver amine stock solution + 750 ml REDOX stock solution. Add silver nitrate in water and stir until all the crystals are completely dissolved. Working solution available 48 hours. Add a few drops of ammonia liquor to maintain no deposition. Add ferric nitrate nonahydrate to water and stir until all the crystals are completely dissolved. Add ferrous ammonium sulfate hexahydrate and stir until all the crystals are completely dissolved. Add citric acid and stir until all the crystals are completely dissolved. Store in a black bottle. Add silver amine solution to REDOX one and stir. Store in a black or amber bottle.	Immerse and agitate samples in the working solution for 5–10 minutes. Rinse with distilled water to remove all excess of PD. Air dry the samples.	FP appears light gray on dark gray. Dry and store the supports far away from light. FP should be photographed immediately after drying.

TABLE 6.1.6 Bloody Traces or Prints Developments Relevant to Arson Scenes

	Synthesis	Application	Observation
Acid violet 17 (also known as Coomassie Brilliant Blue)	Staining solution: Coomassie Brilliant Blue R250: 0.44 g. Glacial acetic acid: 40 ml. Methanol: 200 ml. Distilled water: 200 ml. Destaining solution: Glacial acetic acid: 40 ml. Methanol: 200 ml. Distilled water: 200 ml.	Note: Fire does not need to denature bloody traces before treatment. Development by drowning for 30 seconds in the staining solution or by pipette dropping. Traces are washed afterward with the destaining solution, to decrease the background.	Vivid violet coloration of proteins from blood or other body fluids.
Acid black 1 (also known as Amido Black)	Staining solution: 0.2 g Amido Black 10B in 90 ml methanol and 10 ml acetic acid. Washing solution 1: Methanol and acetic acid (9:1). Washing solution 2: Distilled water and acetic acid (95:5).	Note: Fire does not need to denature bloody traces before treatment. Development by drowning for 30 seconds in the staining solution or pipette dropping. Traces are washed afterward with the two washing solutions, to decrease the background.	Blue-black coloration of proteins from blood or other body fluids.
Acid yellow 7	Staining solution: Acid yellow 7: 1 g. 99% glacial acetic acid: 50 ml. 98% (or higher) ethanol:250 ml distilled water: 700 ml. Washing solution: 99% glacial acetic acid: 50 ml. 98% (or higher) ethanol: 250 ml distilled water: 700 ml.	Note: Fire does not need to denature bloody traces before treatment. Development by drowning for 30 seconds in the staining solution or pipette dropping. Traces are washed afterward with the washing solution, to decrease the background.	Yellow fluorescent coloration of proteins from blood or other body fluids.

could be detected through the modus operandi of other suspected crimes, such as burglary or frauds. Finally, forensic intelligence is of prime importance to support arson investigation, as relevant data are dispersed throughout different services, such as firefighters, fire investigators, insurance companies, the police, and others.

Explosives

An explosive is defined as a compound able to undergo a rapid chemical change without an outside supply of oxygen, liberating a large quantity of energy, generally in the form of hot gases and a high-pressure wave. Many different syntheses exist from commercial preparations (dynamites, gelinites, nitroglycerine-containing explosives, ammonium nitrate fuel oil, slurry, blasting gelatine, detonating cords, etc.) to military explosives (TNT, RDX, tetryl, PETN, HNS, TATB, C4, Semtex, HDX, HMX, etc.), the proportions of which depend on the desired effect (strength, fragmentation, incendiary, etc.) and manageability (pliability, size, shock sensitivity, safety, expertise of the person constructing it, among others) for the explosives. Improvised explosive devices (IEDs) are not necessarily well-fabricated, as the name would imply. Indeed, the criminal need for an explosion overpowers the fine, calculated efforts that are usually applied to military or industrial explosives. Nevertheless, an IED can be a very complicated, cleverly designed device; it is the immediate needs and resources of the bomber that creates the very traceability needed by the CSI—what materials were used to make the bomb, what explosives, what primers, what shrapnel, etc?

The packaging of the explosive and any potential projectiles attached to or mixed with it are part of the shrapnel and debris that create exhibits by being projected by the high pressure; the area where the bomb detonated is known as the bomb seat (Figures 6.1.4 and 6.1.5). Explosives must be detonated to become active and this is done using a smaller charge called a primer. The primer, through heat, shock, or friction, ignites and liberates the energy of the explosive charge. If an undetonated bomb is located, it is highly recommended that assistance by Explosive Ordinance Disposal (EOD) officers be immediately requested. EOD officers can also provide invaluable advice to the CSI on aspects of managing a bomb-related crime scene. The following is a short list of explosives relating to their identified compounds:

- Nitroaromatics are found in TNT, DNT, picric acid, and tetryl.
- Nitramines are found in RDX, HMX, HDX, C4, Semtex, and tetryl.
- Nitroesters are found in nitroglycerine, nitrocellulose, and PETN.
- Peroxides are easy to make but unstable explosives, such as TATP or DATP.
- Nitrates and sulfur are present in black powders.
- Urea nitrates, ammonium, and potassium are typical compounds found in explosives made from fertilizers, as are chlorates and perchlorates found in commercial pyrotechnics.

FIGURE 6.1.4 Protection of an explosion scene. *With permission, courtesy Francis Hebrard, 2000.*

FIGURE 6.1.5 Locating evidence at an explosive crime scene. *With permission, courtesy Francis Hebrard, 2000.*

- Sugar may be an indication of a chlorate-sugar IED.
- Aluminium improves IEDs by increasing the fuel rate (the heat of the blast).

As soon the scene is secured, the collection of evidence can take place, starting from the outside moving inward toward the suspected bomb seat. If, for some reason, it is necessary to go straight to the center, mark the pathway used to limit the contamination of the scene; that is, all foot traffic should only take this path. Collected evidence that may contain explosive residues should be preserved in sealed nylon bags or airtight containers (Figure 6.1.6). Any body in the vicinity of the blast should be X-rayed at the beginning of the postmortem examination to identify the various shrapnel within the body for collection during the autopsy for later analysis. Moreover, if the scene is a

FIGURE 6.1.6   Evidence collection in nylon bags before transport. *With permission, courtesy Francis Hebrard, 2000.*

FIGURE 6.1.7   Identified crater of the explosion. *With permission, courtesy Francis Hebrard, 2000.*

suspected terrorist bombing, the surrounding area, as well as bodies, need to be checked for potential booby-traps or secondary charges that have been set to harm first responders, EMTs, or law enforcement and forensic personnel. The crater of explosion requires the most painstaking search consisting of (Figure 6.1.7):

- Swabs of the immediate surfaces facing the crater
- A close search of the crater and its nearby surrounding area
- A removal of all the debris inside and around the crater
- A measure of the crater's volume
- Multiple soil samples taken around the crater

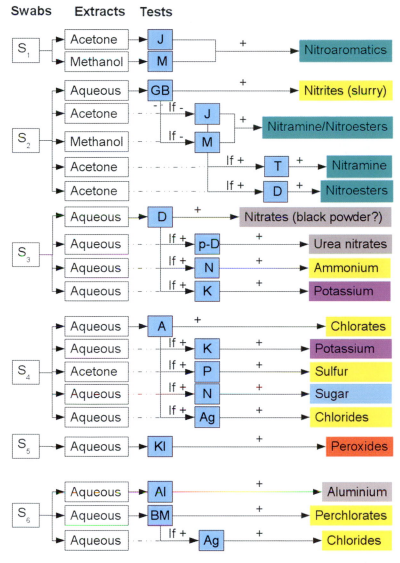

FIGURE 6.1.8 Explosives flowchart. *Sources: Jungreis, 1997; O'Neal et al., 2000; Biermann et al., 2003.*

Each of these exhibits, including the excavated soil, can help determine the size and type of the bomb used.

Spot tests for explosives are also available for the field, not only to focus on the area to search, but also to give investigators first leads for further inquiry. Such presumptive tests also could be applied to suspects' hands or other exhibits to provide some objective information to be used in interrogations or other inquiries. Commercial kits like Dropex® are available for presumptive testing; a flowchart (Figure 6.1.8) is presented above to detect the presence of nitroaromatics, nitramine, nitroesters, nitrites, nitrates, chlorates, and peroxides in explosives matrices (Parker et al., 1975; Jungreis, 1997; Yinon, 1999; Almog et al., 2005). This flowchart requires 6 different swabs (S_1 to S_6) applied to the same area, from which 13 water, 5 acetone, and 2 methanol extractions will be taken; the extractions are carried out by dropping the solvent (water, acetone, or methanol, respectively) on the swab to collect an extract on a plate.

Further laboratory analyses will confirm and identify precisely the explosives mixture involved, but gathering forensic intelligence from the presumptive tests could give first clues to the investigators to prevent coordinated attacks, share information between law enforcement agencies, and so on.

Syntheses and protocols of common tests (blue boxes in Figure 6.1.8) are listed in Table 6.1.7.

GSR

Gunshot residue (GSR) consists of unburned or partially burned gunpowder particles, soot, nitrate, and nitrites from the combustion of the powder, particles of primer (oxides of lead, antimony, and barium), and particles of the bullet or the bullet jacket (Rowe, 2000a) that are vaporized when a firearm is discharged. They are projected from the barrel in a conical cloud and they are also expelled from the various openings of the weapon such as the chamber, the ejection port, and the slide action. The various residues can help determine muzzle-to-target distance (with the error increasing with the evaluated distance), if someone is associated with the discharge of a firearm, and other information about the shooting (Rowe, 2000b). Any testing that is done, such as muzzle-to-target distance, must use the same manufacturer and brand of firearm and ammunition, among other possible factors, to accurately reproduce the variables involved.

GSR is very fragile and easily lost by even a gentle touch; contamination and cross-transfer are also a problem, particularly when police officers—who themselves discharge firearms—are involved. Scanning electron microscopy (SEM) is the only available method to confirm the presence of GSR particles; other methods, like atomic absorption, only measure the amount of bulk elements present and not their form. Hands, faces, and object surfaces (like the inside of a vehicle) can all be sampled using GSR microlift collectors. Collection kits for GSR are commercially available and are recommended for this purpose; while individual agencies can make their own kits, it is time consuming and fraught with potential contamination issues. One microlift should be used for each side of each hand (right back, right palm, left back, left palm) of any suspected shooter. Visualizing GSR around an entrance hole may require chemical treatment; this is done using the modified Greiss test, described in Table 6.1.8.

TABLE 6.1.7 Explosives Presumptive Spot Tests

	Synthesis	Application	Observation	False Positives
J stands for Janowski	Saturated potash solution: Mix 5 g potassium hydroxide with 30 ml methanol.	Put 1 ml of the acetone extract in a test tube; add 2 drops of saturated potash solution. Note: J can be combined with M as follows: Take 0.5 ml of the methanol extract; add 2 drops of potash solution. Then add 0.5 ml acetone.	Immediate appearance of a orange precipitate. Note: Mixed J/M: Coloration appears after acetone.	No false positive, but aliphatic explosives can give a colored result too.
M stands for Meisenheimer	Saturated potash solution: Mix 5 g potassium hydroxide with 30 ml methanol.	Put 1 ml of the methanol extract in a test tube; add 2 drops of saturated potash solution. Note: M can be combined with J as follows: Take 0.5 ml of the methanol extract; add 2 drops of potash solution. Then add 0.5 ml acetone.	Immediate appearance of a orange to brown coloration. Note: Mixed M/J: Coloration appears after acetone.	No false positive, but aliphatic explosives can give a colored result too.
GB stands for Griess B	0.142 g N-naphtylethyle-nediamine (Marshall). 7.5 ml glacial acetic acid. 25 ml ultra-pure (18 MΩ) water. Note: Do not expose to light.	Put 1 ml of the aqueous extract in a test tube. Add 2 drops of Griess B reagent.	A yellow to brown color points to the presence of nitrites.	No known false positive.
T stands for Thymol	200 mg thymol. 6 drops of concentrated sulfuric acid.	Test 1: Place a few mg of test materials in a test tube. Add the solution. Warm the tube for 5 min at 100°C. Add 5–10 ml ethanol. Test 2: Repeat test 1, but warm the tube at 150°C for 5 min.	Test 1 (colors): RDX: Rich blue Sugars and aldehydes: Brown HMX: Pale blue-green. Test 2 (colors): RDX: Blue HMX: Olive Test 2 is considered specific to RDX.	No known false positive.

(Continued)

TABLE 6.1.7 (Continued)

	Synthesis	Application	Observation	False Positives
D stands for DPA	0.5 g diphenylamine in 100 ml concentrated sulfuric acid.	For nitro-esters: Extract the sample with acetone. Put 1 ml of the solution in a test tube. Add 8 drops of DPA reactant. For nitrates: Pour 1 ml of the aqueous extract in a test tube and add 3 drops of DPA. Then add 2 drops of aniline and 2 drops of N-(naphtyl)-ethyldiamine.	Test 1 (colors): RDX: Rich blue. Sugars and aldehydes: Brown. HMX: Pale blue-green taint. Test 2 (colors): RDX: Blue. HMX: Olive. Test 2 is considered specific to RDX.	No known false positive.
p-D stands for p-DMAC	0.24 g p-DMAC in 60 ml ethanol (0.25% w/v).	Put 1 ml of the aqueous extract in a test tube and add 5 drops p-DMAC.	A red color appears with urea nitrate.	Some ureas also yield a red color in a very acid medium.
N stands for Nessler	Dissolve 10 g mercuric iodide and 5 g potassium iodide in 50 ml water. Mix 20 g potassium hydroxide in 50 ml water. Mix both solutions.	On a test plate, add 1 drop of Nessler's reagent to a drop of the aqueous sample.	An orange-brown precipitate is characteristic of ammonium.	Ammonia reacts also.
K stands for Potassium	28 g sodium acetate. 32.5 ml ultra-pure (18 MΩ) water. 12.5 ml acetic acid. 10 g cobalt nitrite disodium.	In a test tube, add 5 drops of K reagent to a few ml of the aqueous sample.	Orange precipitate.	Unknown.
A stands for Aniline	5 ml aniline. 100 ml distilled water. 5 ml H2SO4 concentrated 96%. Note: Do not expose to light.	Pour 1–2 ml aniline reagent in a test tube. Add carefully the same amount of concentrated sulfuric acid. The temperature rises a lot. Wait for a while, and add 10 drops of the aqueous extract.	Blue ring in the middle of the tube is characteristic of chlorates, which could be eventually seen by shaking the tube.	Unknown.

	Reagents	Procedure	Result	Notes
P stands for Pyridine	Pyridine and soda	Put 1 ml of the acetone extract in a test tube, add 4 drops pyridine. Add 4 drops soda.	A green coloration is specific to sulfur.	Other materials could be oxidized too.
Ag stands for $AgNO_3$ (silver nitrate)	Mix 4.25 g silver nitrate with 50 ml distilled water.	Put 1 ml of the aqueous extract in a test tube and add 2 drops of the solution.	A white precipitate indicates the presence of chlorides.	Mercury ions, bromides, and iodides.
KI stands for Potassium Iodide 5%	2.5 g KI in 50 ml ultra-pure (18 MΩ) water.	In a test tube, add 5 drops of KI reagent to a few ml of the aqueous sample.	A yellow-orange coloration indicates the presence of peroxides.	No known false positives.
Al stands for Aluminium	Soda. Acetic acid. Solution of ammonium salt of aurin tricarboxylic acid.	In a test tube, pour 1 ml of the extract (or the material with 1 ml water). Add 3 drops soda. When bubbling stops, add 5 drops acetic acid. Finally, pour 4 drops of ammonium salt of aurin tricarboxylic acid solution.	Red color indicates a positive result.	No known false positives.
BM stands for Blue Methylene	Methylene Blue 0.2%: 200 mg 100 ml distilled water.	Pour 1 ml of the aqueous extract in a test tube; add 1 drop of Blue Methylene solution.	A purple precipitate shows the presence of perchlorates.	Persulfates.

TABLE 6.1.8 GSR Detection

	Synthesis	Application	Observation
Detection of GSR on unmovable supports, cadavers, cloths, or shooter's hands at the scene of crime	Sol. 1: Modified Griess test (MGT): 3% sulfanilamide and 0.3% N-(1-Naphtyl)-ethylenediamine dihydrochloride dissolved in 5% phosphoric acid (AR). (Prepare "Stock papers," positive fixed photo paper, before insulation and use. Immerse Stock paper in sol. 1. Let the treated Stock paper dry in a contamination-free area, or withdraw excess with towel paper for immediate use). Sol. 2: 2% KOH in ethanol (Immerse cotton swabs in this solution. Let them dry. Store them in a closed-labeled box.) Sol. 3: 10% acetic acid solution: 20 ml concentrated acetic acid in 180 ml distilled water (stored in clean bottle). Sol. 4: 0.2% (w/v) sodium rhodizonate solution: 0.2 g sodium rhodizonate in 100 ml distilled water. Sol. 5: pH 2.8 buffer solution: 1.9 g sodium bitartrate (sodium hydrogen tartrate monohydrate) and 1.5 g tartaric acid in 100 ml slightly hot water with magnetic stirrer. Sol. 6: 10% ammonium hydroxide in distilled water. Sol. 7: Saturated rubeanic acid in ethanol.	Nitrites test: Drown one treated cotton swab in sol. 3, swab with it the four corners of the treated Stock (TS) (should become orange). Nitrites: Place a peelable adhesive (PA) (25×25 cm) on the evidence with a roller. Staple the PA on a paperboard, slightly spray sol. 2. Then place the paperboard for an hour at 100°C oven. Place TS on the tape for 1 minute at 1.3 Atm and 70°C. Lead: Spray sol. 3 on a filter paper (Benchkote 10×10 cm) stapled on a paperboard. Place the paper on the evidence at 1.3 Atm for 2 minutes. Take it out, spray sol. 4. and 5. Copper: Spray sol. 6 on a filter paper (Benchkote 10×10 cm) stapled on a paperboard. Place the paper on the evidence at 1.3 Atm for 2 minutes. Take it out, spray sol. 7.	On TS: Orange points show nitrites to be photographed with blue filters. Heavy metals residues with sol. 4 and 5: Purple spots. Copper: Olive-green spots, or around the hole.

TABLE 6.1.9 Shooter's Hands Detection

	Synthesis	Application	Observation
Detection of GSR on shooter's hands: PDT	Sol. 1: Dissolve 0.1 g pyridyl-diphenyl-triazine in 20 ml acetone. Sol. 2: Ascorbic acid 3%: 0.6 g ascorbic acid in 20 ml ethanol: water (95:5). Sol. 3: Thio-Urea 10%: 2 g thio-urea in 20 ml deionized water.	Slightly spray sol. 2 on the shooter's hands first. Wait for 1 minute. Slightly spray sol. 3 on the shooter's hands next. Wait for 1 minute. Spray sol. 1 on the hands. Available even on a dead body, if the corpse wasn't stored in a cold place.	Violet stain appears after about a minute. Color increases within a couple of hours, and a quick short UV exposure decreases the delay.
Detection of GSR on shooter's hands: 2-nitroso 1-naphtol.	Dissolve 0.1 g 2-nitroso-1-naphthol in 20 ml acetone.	Spray on the hands. Available even on a dead body, if the corpse wasn't stored in a cold place.	Deep green: Iron. Brown-red: Copper. Faded orange: Zinc. Orange: Silver.

The location of GSR on clothes can be enhanced by laying a clean piece of light-colored, clean fabric on a surface, placing the treated photographic paper (TS) face up on it, and laying the fabric face down on top of it. Over this place, in order, a thin dry towel, a towel moistened with solution 4, and another dry towel. Press a hot electric iron for 5–10 minutes on top of the area. Remove the towels. Red-orange spots indicate nitrite particles; photograph the paper immediately, since the dye may gradually fade.

Commercial products are also available for metal detection on the suspected gunman's hands, like Ferrotrace®, which indicates that the individual held a firearm with the tested hand; sometimes, even detailed information about the handgun, like the position of metal screws, grip pattern, or numbers, can be seen. Finally, identification of a hand that has held a gun without shooting can be done with one of the two formulations in Table 6.1.9 (Comment et al., 1998).

Restoration of Serial Numbers

Many manufactured goods are tagged during production for identification by the company that made them or their partner companies; some of these tags may be for the customer's reference as well. Serial numbers, a common type of tagging, help to distinguish items of similar appearance and to give information about the manufactured product itself, such as date of manufacture, type, model, etc (Figure 6.1.9). When stolen, criminals may attempt to obliterate or remove this identifying information, making tracing

FIGURE 6.1.9 Number restoration on aluminum alloy. *With permission, courtesy Francis Hebrard, 2001.*

TABLE 6.1.10 Nitric Acid Test

Nitric Acid Test	Reaction at First Minute	After 5 Minutes	10 Minutes with Water Rinse	Apply Protocol
Magnetic Metals				
Alloy steel	Black ring forms slowly	Clear drop with black ring	Gray spot	MM1
Cast iron	Black ring	Black-green drop	Black-brown spot	
Low carbon steel	Effervescence and brown drop	No change	Brown ring	
Medium carbon steel	Gray ring	Clear drop with brown-gray	Gray ring	
Nickel plate	Yellow drop	Blue-green drop	Gray spot	
Tool steel	Black ring forms slowly	Brown-green drop and mild effervescence	Black-brown spot	
Nonmagnetic metals				
Aluminum alloy	Nothing	Nothing	Nothing	AL1
Aluminum/copper	Nothing	Nothing	Nothing	
Aluminum/silicon	Nothing	Nothing	Nothing	
Brass ASTM-16	Effervescence and green drop	No change	Clean spot	NM1
Lead	Nothing	Dulled surface	Nothing	
Stainless steel	Nothing	Nothing	Nothing	NM2
Tin	Effervescence and yellow-white drop	White drop	Light-gray spot	
Zinc alloy ASTM	Effervescence and black drop	Black drop	Dark-gray drop	

TABLE 6.1.11 Restoration Chemicals to Swab, Following the Nitric Acid Test

Protocols	Preparation
MM1	90 g cupric chloride + 100 ml distilled water + 120 ml HCl
AL1	30 ml glycerin + 20 ml hydrofluoric acid + 10–20 ml nitric acid
NM1	40 g cupric chloride + 150 ml HCl + 50 ml distilled water
NM2	50% HCl + 50% nitric acid

the product or associating the thief more difficult. Methods used include new (over) stamping, scraping, sanding, or chemical processing to remove or obscure the original number (Petterd, 2000) (Figure 6.1.9).

Even if the original embossed area is concealed by the fraudulent erasing process, restoration of the prime serial number may still be possible as long as the damaged area under the marked serial number was not also removed. Chemical etching provides a slow but efficient means to reveal the original data. Various chemical solutions to wipe on the suspected area are presented in Table 6.1.10, depending of the nature of the metal to treat (which can be determined by observing one drop of pure nitric acid on a nonsensitive area of the plate).

Care should be taken when dealing with the protocols listed in Table 6.1.11, largely based on aggressive alkaline or acid compounds. The crime scene examiner should also note any number or sign appearing during the various steps of the process, as pieces of information could disappear to upgrade or develop other ones. Of course, various angles of illuminations could also optimize the optical development.

Finally, it should also be remembered that other solutions could be applied in the laboratory to restore serial numbers, such as heat treatment.

References and Bibliography

Almog, J., Klein, A., Tamiri, T., Shloosh, Y., Abramovich-Bar, S., 2005. A field diagnostic test for the improved explosive urea nitrate. J. Forensic Sci. 50 (3): 582–586.

Baselt, R.C., 1978. Disposition of Toxic Drugs and Chemicals in Man, second ed. Biomedical Publications, Seal Beach, CA.

Biermann, T., Schwarze, B., Zedler, B., Betz, P., 2003. On-site testing of illicit drugs: The use of the drug-testing device "Toxiquick1." Forensic Sci. Int. 143: 21–25.

Bradshaw, G., Bleay, S., Deans, J., NicDaeid, N., 2008. Recovery of fingerprints from arson scenes: Part 1—Latent fingerprints. J. Forensic Identification 58 (1): 54–82.

Comment, S., Bonfanti, M., Gallusser, A., 1998. Détermination de la main qui a tenu une arme sans avoir tiré. Can. Soc. Forensic Sci. J. 31 (2): 79–84.

DeHaan, J.D., 1983. Kirk's Fire Investigation, second ed. John Wiley and Sons, New York.

Esseiva, P., 2004. Le profilage de l'héroïne et de la cocaïne. Mise en place d'une systématique permettant une utilisation opérationnelle des liens chimiques. Thèse de doctorat. Institut de police scientifique. Ecole des science criminelles. Université de Lausanne.

Esseiva, P., Dujourdy, F., Taroni, F., Anglada, F., Gueniat, O., Margot, P., 2002. Les signatures chimiques à partir des signatures de produits stupéfiants. Utilité et gestion de l'information. Revue Internationale de Criminologie et de Police Technique et Scientifique 1/02: 104–111.

Esseiva, P., Ioset, S., Anglada, F., Gasté, L., Ribaux, O., Margot, P., et al., 2007. Forensic drug intelligence: An important tool in law enforcement. Forensic Sci. Int. 167 (2–3): 247–254.

Gallusser, A., Bonfanti, M., Schutz, F., 2002. Expertise des armes à feu et des éléments de munitions dans l'investigation criminelle. Collection sciences forensiques. Presses polytechniques et universitaires romandes. Lausanne.

Ide, R.H., 2000. Fire-scene patterns. In: Siegel, J., Knupfer, G., Saukko, P. (Eds.), Encyclopedia of Forensic Sciences, in three volumes, pp. 916–922. Academic Press, Waltham, MA.

Jungreis, E., 1997. Spot Test Analysis: Clinical, Environmental, Forensic, and Geochemical Applications, second ed. Wiley Interscience, New York.

Kronstrand R., Jones A.W., 2000. Drugs of abuse. In: Siegel, J., Knupfer, G., Saukko, P. (Eds.), Encyclopedia of Forensic Sciences, in three volumes, pp. 598–610.

Larkin, T.P.B., Marsh, N.P., Larrigan, P.M., 2008. Using liquid latex to remove soot to facilitate fingerprint and bloodstains examinations: A case study. J. Forensic Identification 58 (5): 540–550.

Liska, B., 2000. Drugs and the Human Body, sixth ed. Prentice-Hall, Upper Saddle River, NJ.

Meikle, P., 2000. Bomb-scene management. In: Siegel, J., Knupfer, G., Saukko, P. (Eds.), Encyclopedia of Forensic Sciences, in three volumes, pp. 745–750.

Moore, J., Bleay, S., Deans, J., NicDaeid, N., 2008. Recovery of fingerprints from arson scenes: Part 2—Fingerprints in blood. J. Forensic Identification 58 (1): 83–108.

Murray, S.G., 2000. Commercial. In: Siegel, J., Knupfer, G., Saukko, P. (Eds.), Encyclopedia of Forensic Sciences, in three volumes, pp. 750–758.

Murray, S.G., 2000. Military. In: Siegel, J., Knupfer, G., Saukko, P. (Eds.), Encyclopedia of Forensic Sciences, in three volumes, pp. 764–771.

Nordgaard, A., 2005. Quantifying experience in sample size determination for drug analysis of seized drugs. Law, Probab. Risk 4 (4): 217–225.

O'Neal, C.L., Crouch, D.J., Fatah, A.A., 2000. Validation of twelve chemical spot tests for the detection of drugs of abuse. Forensic Sci. Int. 109: 189–201.

Parker, R.G., Stephenson, M.O., Mac Owen, J.M., Cherolis, J.A., 1975. Analysis of explosives residues, Part 1: Chemical tests. J. Forensic Sci. 20 (1): 133–140.

Petterd, C., 2000. Serial number. In: Siegel, J., Knupfer, G., Saukko, P. (Eds.), Encyclopedia of Forensic Sciences, in three volumes, pp. 1205–1210.

Rowe W.F., 2000a. Range. In: Siegel, J., Knupfer, G., Saukko, P. (Eds.), Encyclopedia of Forensic Sciences, in three volumes, pp. 949–953.

Rowe, W.F., 2000b. Residues. In: Siegel, J., Knupfer, G., Saukko, P. (Eds.), Encyclopedia of Forensic Sciences, in three volumes, pp. 953–961.

Tamiri, T., 2000. Analysis. In: Siegel, J., Knupfer, G., Saukko, P. (Eds.), Encyclopedia of Forensic Sciences, in three volumes, pp. 729–745.

UNIDCP (United Nations International Drug Control Programme), 1994. Rapid Testing Methods of Drugs of Abuse. Manual for Use by National Law Enforcement and Narcotics Laboratory Personnel. ST/NAR/13/REV.1, New York.

Yapping, L., Yue, W., 2004. A new silver physical developer. J. Forensic Identification 54 (4): 422–427.

Yinon, J., 1999. Forensic and Environmental Detection of Explosives. John Wiley and Sons, New York.

Zingg, C., 2005. The analysis of ecstasy tablets in a forensic intelligence perspective. Thèse de doctorat présentée à l'Institut de police scientifique de Lausanne. Ecole des sciences criminelles. Université de Lausanne.

Biological Evidence

The advent of forensic DNA analysis has greatly increased the capacity to exploit miniscule—even molecular—amounts of evidence. The extreme specificity of DNA evidence and its origins in nonforensic molecular biology and genetics has made it the driving force in forensic investigations and the darling of forensic critics (NAS, 2009). DNA's success has, however, endangered forensic investigations by leading investigators to rely solely on this one evidence type.

Many other biological materials can constitute evidence, like blood, semen, saliva, urine, feces, hair, and bones, among others. The word "materials" is stressed here because it should be remembered that DNA is molecular-level information, while these others convey meaning based on their morphology or form. This level of information is significant for triaging evidence, generating leads, and other forms of forensic intelligence. This does not mean, however, that DNA is only useful for identifying individuals; DNA databases

Key Term

Bloodstain pattern analysis (BSPA)

are still driving significant changes in police investigative practices, feeding information for forensic intelligence–led policing (Raymond et al., 2004; Bond, 2007). Finally, it should also be remembered that collection of biological evidence can be of interest for reasons other than DNA identification, such as alcohol or drug quantification (toxicology).

DNA and Trace DNA

Dexoxyribonucleic acid (DNA) is a molecule present in every living cell, including bacteria and some viruses, which encodes the whole set of information needed for the development and the cycle of life for organisms, including inheritance during reproduction. Located in the nucleus of every cell, human DNA appears as a double helix of about 6 billion paired nucleotides (hence, each branch of this helix carries about 3 billion nucleotides), each made of a phosphate associated with a sugar on which is linked one of the following four bases: guanine (G), cytosine (C), thymine (T), or adenine (A). Bases constitute the links between the two sides of the helix chain; chemical affinities between only the T-A and C-G bases assure us that knowing the information on one side of the DNA helix (A-T-C-G-G-A-A...) is sufficient to determine the information on the other (T-A-G-C-C-T-T...). Forensic science is mainly interested in the portion of human genetic code that, as far as we know, does not produce proteins. These noncoding locations, called loci (singular locus), are chosen for ethical and privacy reasons; by choosing loci that are noncoding, no medical information can be determined from them.

The quantity of DNA present in each cell is about 6 pg ($6 \cdot 10^{-12}$ g). However, at least 0.6 ng ($6 \cdot 10^{-10}$ g) seems necessary to produce a DNA profile of good quality, which means that around 100 cells are required to avoid various technical problems arising from mutations or other problems that occur in the DNA replication process. Only 100 cells does not seem like much material, and it is not; therein lies the problem. Crime scene investigation does not occur in a clean sanitized location, and this increases the risk of DNA mixtures, loss, or modification. Even if such a small quantity of DNA is collected and later profiled, what does it mean to have found so low an amount of material? Is the DNA found relevant to the case at hand? Doesn't it pose a risk that someone unrelated to the case could have touched the item innocently, resulting in mishandling, misinterpretation, or a wrong charge or conviction (Lord Justice Thomas et al., 2009)? It also explains why further research is needed to better understand trace DNA deposition and how to improve its collection and interpretation (Phipps and Petricevic, 2007; Allen et al., 2008; Graham and Rutty, 2008; Bille et al., 2009; Wu and Chrichton, 2010).

Nevertheless, DNA deposited by simple contact can be collected at the crime scene. Porous surfaces (paper, fabric, etc.) do not present any difficulty, as cells are quite deftly trapped on such substrates. The challenge resides mainly on

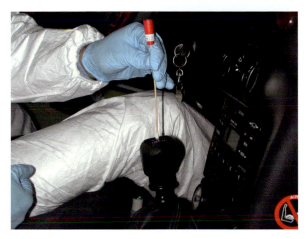

FIGURE 6.2.1 Trace DNA collection on a gear level. *With permission, courtesy Francis Hebrard, 2000.*

nonporous surfaces (like a steering wheel, a table, a weapon, etc.), for which the protocol is proposed (Wickenheiser, 2002) (Figure 6.2.1):

- Photograph any impressions, fingerprints, or other perishable pieces of information that may be destroyed by swabbing.
- Using a sterile cotton swab that has been soaked with distilled water and from which excess water has been removed, swab the surface aggressively. Rotate the swab into the direction of the swabbing action, utilizing the tip and sides of the swab.
- Document details regarding the exhibit description and area(s) swabbed.
- Air-dry in a cabinet to prevent contamination.
- Once dried, transfer the swab into a prelabeled DNA tube for processing.

Another type of DNA molecule, mitochondrial DNA (mtDNA), is also found in human cells and has forensic significance. As its name implies, it is found in mitochondria, small energy factories found in each cell, which have their own genetic material. mtDNA is the same for all mitochondria in the same cell, but has many fewer combinations than DNA does (instead of 3 billion bases, mtDNA has only about 16,569 bases). mtDNA does present two advantages despite its far weaker ability for individualization. First, about 10 mtDNA are present in each mitochondria, opposed to a single DNA packet; moreover, mtDNA is protected by a thick membrane layer and, hence, mtDNA is a hardy molecule that is sometimes the last biological vestige for molecular analysis. Second, mtDNA is inherited only from the mother during reproduction, meaning that a female lineage can be inferred from mtDNA analysis; siblings from the same mother would have the same mtDNA sequence and this would be different from their father's.

As DNA and mtDNA exist in nearly any body tissue, the next sections will focus on the chemical detection of such materials.

Blood

A human being has about 5 liters of blood. Blood is a matrix of free cells (red, white globules) and anticoagulant platelets carried by the plasma (the liquid portion). Mainly composed of water with molecules of glucose, lipids, hormones, and a few other proteins, the pale yellowish plasma is about 55% water, the remaining 45% being the cells and platelets. All of these are produced by the bone marrow. Blood is used to bring oxygen, nutrients, immune cells, and other things to tissues, and to remove refuse, such as carbon dioxide or nitrogenous waste, from the cells.

Red cells (also called erythrocytes), which compose 99% of the solid elements of blood, are not really "cells," as they do not possess a nucleus or mitochondria. Red blood cells carry oxygen using hemoglobin, a protein that contains an iron ion imprisoned at its center composed of a molecule called heme. This ferrous ion is responsible for fixing oxygen atoms, hence giving the hemoglobin the ability to transport not only dioxygen, but also carbon monoxide and dioxide. This ferrous ion is sufficiently specific to be targeted as a catalyst for any presumptive chromatic reaction for blood (Ballantyne, 2000; Lee and Pagliaro, 2000).

White cells (leukocytes) and platelets compose approximately 0.3% and 0.7% of the solid elements of blood, respectively. The former are dedicated to combating infectious agents; they are the only ones containing DNA. The latter are flat fragmented remains of cells from the bone marrow that initiate clotting.

Blood's red to brown color (depending on its level of oxidization) can be quite easily detected by the naked eye (Figure 6.2.2). Blood that is undetectable by the naked eye, because of the low quantity, or because of attempts to evade

FIGURE 6.2.2 Large blood splash encountered at crime scene. *With permission, courtesy Thierry Lezeau, 1990.*

detection, like washing or even painting over stains (Howard and Nessan, 2010), can be detected by various protein stains or using the catalyst property of the heme.

Presumptive spot tests can be carried out by soaking a cotton swab with distilled water and swabbing the edge of a suspected blood trace to avoid damaging the shape of the stain (Figure 6.2.3). In the case of clotted blood, scratch a tiny bit from the edge into a tube, add a few drops of distilled water, and allow it to dissolve at least partially before dipping the clean cotton swab in.

Various chemicals can be used as presumptive tests on suspected blood. Despite known false positives with enzymes that create a similar reaction as hemoglobin (freshly cut fruits and vegetables, iron oxide (FeO_2) and other iron salts, peroxides), a few available tests are listed in Table 6.2.1 and were chosen for their differing color reactions. Denaturation of fresh blood may be necessary before applying any treatment; spray a solution of 5-sulfosalicylic in distilled water (22 g/l) for about two minutes.

Safe for DNA analysis, Bluestar® forensic reagent, based on Luminol, is presently the most efficient commercial product for visualization of suspected blood at the crime scene; it can also be used for spot tests with cotton swabs (Figures 6.2.4 and 6.2.5). Depending on the nature of the substrate and the need to preserve DNA, other formulations to be sprayed after denaturation are listed in Table 6.2.3 (Budowle et al., 2000; Caldwell et al., 2000; Caldwell and Kim, 2002; Frejeau et al., 2000; Bergeron, 2003; Yapping and Yue, 2004; Wang et al., 2007; Marchant and Tague, 2007; Morgan-Smith et al., 2009).

Once developed, bloody traces can also provide useful information about physical traces (shoe sole, fingerprint, glove mark, etc.) (Figure 6.2.6 and Table 6.2.2). Blood actively participates in the reconstruction of a crime through bloodstain pattern analysis (BSPA) (Wolson, 2000). Any suspected

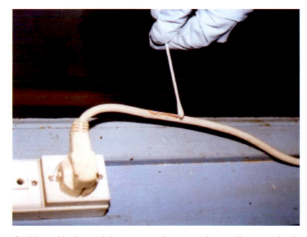

FIGURE 6.2.3 Swabbing a bloodstain while preserving other potential trace collection on the plug. *With permission, courtesy Thierry Lezeau, 2004.*

TABLE 6.2.1 Presumptive Tests for Bloody Traces

	Synthesis	Application	Observation
KM (Coquoz, 2003)	Stock and working solutions: Phenolphtalein: 2 g. KOH: 20 g. Distilled water: 100 ml. Stock solution: Reflux the stock mixture with 20 g powdered zinc for 2 hours until the solution becomes colorless. Stock solution to be stored in a dark bottle and refrigerated with some zinc added to keep it colorless.	Apply the working solution (sensitivity 1:100,000). Rinse the support with distilled water.	Pink to red color on the swab within 15 seconds.
LMG (Lee et al., 2001)	0.1 g Leuko-malachite green. Sodium perborate: 3.2 g. Glacial acetic acid: 66 ml. Distilled water: 33 ml.	Drop or fine spray of the reactant (sensitivity: 1:20,000). Development appears within 30 seconds. Dry the surface by absorption with a tissue or paper towel. Another spray could increase the contrast. Protein stains like Amido Black could be used after LMG.	Greenish blue color almost immediately on the swab. Light exposure increases the background.
OT (Coquoz, 2003)	O-tolidine: 0.1 g. Glacial acetic acid: 15 ml. Distilled water: 100 ml.	Drop or fine spray of the reactant (sensitivity: 1:100,000). Development appears within 30 seconds. Dry the surface by absorption with a tissue or paper towel. Another spray could increase the contrast.	Intense blue color almost immediately on the swab. Light exposure increases the background.

Method	Reactant composition	Application	Result
TMB (Coquoz, 2003)	Tetramethyl benzidine: 0.1 g. Glacial acetic acid: 15 ml. Distilled water: 100 ml.	Drop or fine spray of the reactant (sensitivity: 1:100,000). Development appears within 30 seconds. Dry the surface by absorption with a tissue or paper towel. Another spray could increase the contrast.	Intense blue color almost immediately on the swab. Light exposure increases the background.
LUM (Coquoz, 2003)	Distilled water: 100 ml. Anhydrous sodium carbonate: 5 g. Add 0.1 g luminol (3-aminophtalhydrazide).	Drop or fine spray of the reactant (sensitivity: 1:5,000,000). Development luminescence within 5 seconds. Dry the surface by absorption with a tissue or paper towel. Another spray could increase the contrast. Protein stains like Amido Black could be used after luminol.	Luminescent bloodstain in darkness (440 nm). Relevant to discover areas of cleaning up.
FLU (Coquoz, 2003)	Reactant solution: Fluorescein: 0.16 g. Powder zinc: 2 g. NaOH: 1.6 g. Distilled water: 20 ml. Mix for 3 minutes, to reduce fluorescein. Let it rest for 15 minutes in darkness and extract zinc by gravity. Working solution: Reactant solution: 20 ml. Distilled water: 20 ml.	Use a thickener (metrol MD or gum xanthan) to decrease flowing of the fluorescein. Apply the working solution (sensitivity: 1:500,000). Rinse the support with distilled water.	Luminescence: Excitation at 450 nm, emission with orange barrier filter.

FIGURE 6.2.4 Results of light application (left) and heavier application (right) spray on a rusted cemetery barrier, suspected to have been used for impaling a victim. *With permission, courtesy Francis Hebrard, 2008.*

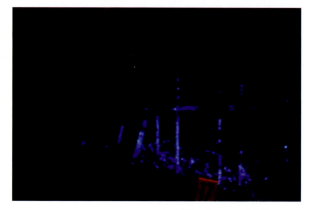

FIGURE 6.2.5 Path left by a bleeding victim after freeing herself from being impaled. *With permission, courtesy Francis Hebrard, 2008.*

bloodstain should be photographed. If the CSI is not qualified in bloodstain pattern analysis and no qualified expert is available to assist, then as many photographs as possible of the stains, spatter, droplets, etc. should be taken for later evaluation. Visual recording of the patterns can help in later reconstruction efforts and help sort out later DNA results once the "donor" of the blood is identified.

Spatter patterns can be illustrative of the points of origin and determining where they intercept a target surface. As the direction of travel can be determined by the direction of the greatest edge distortion, the mnemonics of SAADD (Wonder, 2001) could help the crime scene examiner to know what to look at:

S: Shape of the whole pattern
A: Alignment of individual spatters with respect to the whole pattern
A: Alignment of individual spatter stains with respect to each other
D: Distribution (density) of the number of spatters
D: Distribution (frequency) of spatter size ranges

TABLE 6.2.2 Priority Orders for Chemicals to Develop Bloodstains and Traces Depending on the Type of Support and the Post-DNA Analysis

Surfaces		Avoid Fading Process if DNA Required			Better Choice if DNA Required		
	AB	AV17	HR or FLU or LeuR6G		LMG	LUM	NIN
Linoleum or plastic		3	2			1	
Glass	3		2			1	
Metal	3	2				1	
Light-painted wood	2				3	1	
Dark-painted wood			2			1	
Denim jean	3				1	2	
85% polyester, 15% cotton					2	1	3
Soft tissue paper					2	1	3

Note: AB stands for Amido Black, AV17 for acid violet 17 (see Chapter 6.1), HR for Hungarian Red, LeuR6G for Leuko-Rhodamine 6G, NIN for ninhydrin. The formulations are listed in Table 6.2.3.

TABLE 6.2.3 Chemical Developers Listed in Table 6.2.2

	Synthesis	Application	Observation
AB	Stock solution: Citric acid: 38 g. Distilled water: 2 l. Combine and stir until citric acid is thoroughly dissolved. Developing solution: Citric acid stock solution: 2 l. Naphtalene 12 B (Amido Black): 2 g. Kodak Photo Flo 600 solution. Slowly add the Amido Black into the stock solution while stirring. Stir for 30 minutes. Add Photo Flo (1–2 drops). Washing solution 1: Distilled water and acetic acid (95:5). Washing solution 2: Distilled water.	Development by submersion for 30 seconds in developing solution or by pipette.	Dark-blue stain on bright blue background. Small increase of the contrast could be obtained with an orange barrier filter.
HR	Fuchsin acid dissolved at 1% in deionized water (1 g fuchsin acid in 100 ml water). Washing solution: Distilled water in acetic acid (19:1 v/v)	Blood should be dried. Apply Hungarian Red by spraying, pipette, or submersion.	Excitation at 515 and 560 nm, emission at 600 nm.

(Continued)

TABLE 6.2.3 (Continued)

	Synthesis	Application	Observation
		Let the remaining liquid evaporate. Fade it with the washing solution if necessary. A transfer in 15 minutes is available on Stocky or gelatine, and even used to better detail bloody fingerprints by successive transfers.	
LeuR6G (Yapping and Yue, 2004)	Stock solution: 2000 ml ethanol. 10 g Rhodamine 6G. 200 g powdered zinc. 100 ml glacial acetic acid. Add the different compounds. Stir with a magnetic stirrer until all crystals are completely dissolved. The solution will become colorless (leuco) soon after mixing. Continue reduction reaction for 30 minutes. Add 2.2 g sulfosalicylic acid and stir. Add 100 g mossy zinc, stir, and store in a dark bottle. Working solution: Mix 20 ml stock solution with 80 ml ethyl ether in a 200 ml beaker. Add 8–10 drops hydrogen peroxide and stir. NB: The working solution could be stored in a dark glass bottle.	Two or three sprays of LeuR6G working solution onto the blood-contaminated area. Let evaporate for 20–30 seconds. Repeat until the desired level of contrast.	Red stains.
NIN	25 g ninhydrin. 225 ml ethanol while stirring to get a slurry. Add 10 ml ethyl acetate. Add 25 ml acetic acid. Stir until a clear, yellow concentrated solution is produced. Stock solution: 25 g ninhydrin in 50 ml acetic acid, add 100 ml ethanol. Working solution: 30 ml stock, 50 ml ethanol, complete to 1 L with heptane.	Rapid submersion, development for 24–48 hours at ambient temp., in a black environment with relative humidity at 80%.	Ninhydrin-developed traces are purple (Ruhemann's purple) and contrast can be reinforced through selective absorption (415 nm or 580 nm).

FIGURE 6.2.6 Examples of invisible bloodied traces developed with Bluestar®: (a) shoeprints; (b) blood washed and brushed on a wall. *With permission, courtesy Francis Hebrard, 2009.*

TABLE 6.2.4 Spatter Groups for Quick Interpretation of Blood

Category	Impact	Castoff	Arterial Damage
Information to collect	The direction of travel is determined by the greatest edge distortion. The area of convergence is determined on the target surface as the origin of the impact through the size and shape of the drops. The reconstruction of origin is the location in 3D at right angles from the areas of convergence.	Blood accumulates prior to castoff dynamics, and stretches, deforms, and separates by gravitation or centripetal force. It can provide information on the minimum number of delivered blows, the arc of the swing, the end of the swing, the size and shape of the instrument, the quantity of blood on the instrument, and the method of swinging.	Release of blood under pressure of the heart pumping. Information provided: the directions of projected drops.
S	Origin and directions of stains distributed away from the pattern.	Linear, rectangular, or arc-shaped.	Undulation of the blood vessel (S, V, or W shapes of the pattern).
A	Outward in all directions from the convergence (rays).	Inline spatter patterns of three or more spatters of almost the same size along the direction of travel.	Parallel rows of stains.
A	Each spatter at some angle to all the other spatters in the pattern.	In line with each other or as parallel arrangements.	Stains aligned with directions of travel as parallel lines.
D	Spatter density decreases away from the origin.	Abrupt end of the stains: castoff more likely than impact.	Uniform-sized stains, secondary and satellite formation under pressure (not primary dynamics).
D	Large drops close to the origin, fine and small drops farther away, leaving round stains.	Castoff principle; fan-shaped pattern.	Uniform spacing over the whole primary pattern.

SAADD could help suggest the kind of spatter group the CSI is facing, whether impact (blunt, gunshot, exhalation, splash), castoff (drip, swing, cessation), or arterial damage (firearm, stab/cut, crush/tear) (Figure 6.2.7 and Table 6.2.4).

Nonspatter bloodstains can also be useful in reconstructing events at the scene. They can be briefly divided into transfer patterns and physiologically

FIGURE 6.2.7 (a–g) Recording of a blood spatter projection crime scene. *With permission, courtesy Francis Hebrard, 2003.*

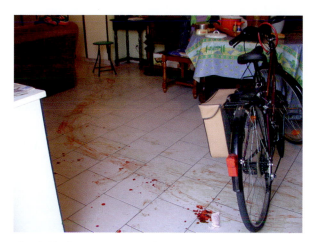

FIGURE 6.2.8 Complex blood pattern crime scene with spatter and wiping stains. *With permission, courtesy Francis Hebrard, 2002.*

altered bloodstains (PABS). The transfer patterns can determine if an obstacle existed (or still exists) between the blood projection and the target surface, or if the transfer occurred by contact of two different surfaces (one of them bloody) by swiping, wiping, or shearing (Figure 6.2.8). It is not uncommon to find what looks like fine drops that can be mistaken for aerosolized blood but in reality are flyspecks. After a fly consumes blood, it must regurgitate its own stomach fluid to equalize its aerodynamic flight balance; these tiny stains look like spatters and can vary greatly in shape (comma, pear, round), color (beige, red, black), and size (from very small to small).

Semen

Semen is a mixture of various fluids that carry live spermatozoa to the female ovule for fertilization. A fertile semen sample holds tens of millions of spermatozoa per milliliter. Various spermatozoa nutrients are immersed in the seminal fluid, such as proteins (vitamins and phosphatase), mineral salts, and a hormone (testosterone). Besides medical information that could be provided by semen (such as diagnosing sexually transmitted illness), semen can provide useful DNA evidence, due to the DNA contained in the spermatozoa head. In cases of sexual assault, statements made by the victim are strong indicators of where to search for semen. Clothing worn by the victim must also be tested for the presence of semen.

Exploitable semen for analysis can be found up to 10 days in the vagina, 19 days in the cervix, 31 hours in the mouth, 110 hours in the rectum, and 44 hours in the anus (Green, 2000). The presence of spematozoa is conclusive for sexual contact.

However, vasectomized males (surgical procedure for male sterilization), whose ejaculate leave no spermatozoa, require other tests targeting known components of semen, such as P30 or PSA (prostate-specific antigen). As expected, obtaining DNA from aspermatic samples is possible, but less successful.

UV light and ALS detect seminal stains by phosphorescence and luminescence (Calloway et al., 1973; Stoilovic, 1991; Kobus et al., 2002). Unfortunately, the luminescence of semen can be weak and difficult to see depending on the color of the substrate (Vandenberg and Van Oorschot, 2006). Therefore, chemical enhancement and detection is a complementary tool that may be necessary. Fast Blue B and MUP (Table 6.2.5) are tests based on phosphatase acid detection that can be helpful (Coquoz, 2003).

Saliva

Saliva is a biological secretion inside the mouth that is a digestive aid. It contains urea, glucose, progesterone, various traces of acids (citric, uric) and amino acids, creatinine, and more than 1,000 different proteins. Although no specific test exists for its detection, the presence of alpha-amylase strongly supports the identification of saliva (Ballantyne, 2000). Saliva is not only interesting for detecting and quantifying drugs or alcohol, but also as a carrier

TABLE 6.2.5 Presumptive Tests for Seminal Traces

	Synthesis	Application	Observation
Fast Blue B	Color reagent: Fast Blue B salt: 1 g. Sodium acetate trihydrate: 20 g. Glacial acetic acid: 2 m distilled water: 10 ml. Substrate solution: Na-alphanaphtylphosphate: 0.8 g. Distilled water: 10 ml. Before use, mix 10 volumes of color reagent, 1 volume of substrate solution, and 89 volumes of distilled water.	Swab the support surface with a paper filter or a cotton swab moistened with saline, or cut a portion of it. Place 1 drop of the working solution on the sample. Wait for 10 seconds.	The presence of sperm is revealed by a quick deep purple-pink staining. Care should be taken of false positives (although lighter purple stained) with fungi and different kinds of vegetables and fruits juices.
MUP	Color reagent: Bromochloroindolylphosphate: 500 mg. DMSO (dimethyl sulfoxide): 3–5 drops. Substrate solution: Sodium acetate trihydrate: 1.3 g. Glacial acetic acid: 0.1 ml. Distilled water: 10 ml. Mix both solutions just before use.	Swab the support surface with a paper filter or a cotton swab moistened with saline, or cut a portion of it. Place 1 drop of the working solution on the sample. Wait for 10 seconds.	The presence of sperm is revealed by a quick blue staining. Care should be taken of false positives (although lighter purple stained) with fungi and different kinds of vegetables and fruits juices.

of cells for genotyping, mostly skin cells (Fridez and Coquoz, 1996; Pang and Cheung, 2008). Hence, cells from saliva can be found on stamps, food, drinking glasses, cosmetics, pillows, and so on, including bite marks on skin. Commercial alpha-amylase detection tests exist. Swabbing the inner cheek in the mouth for DNA samples is not considered as intimate or intrusive as drawing a blood sample.

Urine

Urine, as a biological fluid, removes organic refuse from the body, mostly urea, which may carry very few DNA cells. Ninety-five percent of urine is water, the rest being salts (uric) and other waste products; these are useful for medical analysis of sugar, blood, or creatinine quantification for illness or infection, or even pollutants. A presumptive spot test is available for urine, targeting creatinine (Lee et al., 2001).

Feces

Feces is the solid organic refuse of the human body, composed of about 80% water and 20% dry material. Microscopy is the main analysis to identify feces through the various undigested cellulose fibers constituting about 90% of the dry matter (Norris and Bock, 2000, 2001); the Edelman test, based on urobilinogen (a precursor of urobilin, a waste protein) detection, is the relevant reaction to identify fecal material (Fourney et al., 2007). Urobilin gives feces substrate its characteristic coloration; note that it is also present in urine in trace amounts (Ballantyne, 2000).

Hair

Forensic hair comparison's validity as a method has been questioned for some time (Taupin, 2004; NAS, 2009). This may be partly due to the fact that microscopical human hair comparison remains one of the few fields to have been developed for forensic purposes alone (Gaudette, 2000). Most of a hair

TABLE 6.2.6 Presumptive Tests for Urine Traces

	Synthesis	Application	Observation
JAFFE	Picric acid solution: 2–3 g picric acid saturated in 100 ml distilled water. 10% sodium hydroxide: 10 g NaOH in 100 ml distilled water.	Swab the suspected surface with a paper filter or a cotton swab moistened with distilled water. Add 1 drop of picric acid solution on the sample. Add 1 drop of 10% NaOH.	The presence of urine is indicated by a dark reddish-orange color. A negative result will be indicated by the bright yellow color of the picric acid. Compare the results against the negative and positive controls.

has no nuclear cells, and thus it yields little molecular DNA (Allen et al., 1998); hairs are rich in mtDNA, however, and as little as 1 cm is required for this method. Hair morphology is nevertheless useful for species identification, body area determination, and other biological traits (Savolainen et al., 1997; Fridez et al., 1999; Houck and Bisbing, 2005). Hair roots, however, whether pulled or shed, can contain enough nuclear DNA for analysis (Hochmeister et al., 1996; Opel et al., 2008).

Hairs are collectors of various materials, both ingested and encountered, like cosmetics (Hartwig et al., 2003; Singh and Garg, 2009), drugs (Romano et al., 2003), nicotine, or even explosives (Zeichner and Levin, 1995; Sanders et al., 2002; Oxley et al. 2003, 2005, 2007); various illnesses manifest themselves in hair (Gaudette, 2000b).

Bones

Forensic anthropology is the science dealing with the identification of human remains, mainly analyzing bones and teeth. Once the species is identified and human bones or teeth recognized, race, sex, age, and stature can be assessed (Ubelaker and Scammel, 1997). Perimortem trauma, modification of bones since their disposal, and other taphonomic factors (Vass et al., 2002; Warren and Schultz, 2002; Duhig, 2003; Arany et al., 2004) can be assessed through various methods of comparative anthropometry, histology, and analytical and chemical analyses. Prosthetic devices should also be carefully collected, as they provide relevant identification data regarding their fabrication, manufacturer, and even serial numbers (Penalver et al., 1997; Warren and Schultz, 2002). DNA of both types may be extracted (Holland et al., 1995; Al-Enizi et al., 2008; Coticone et al., 2010) from almost any bones. The recovery of human skeletal remains is best left to professional forensic anthropologists and a team of specialists.

Cadaver

The body of the deceased is the jurisdiction of the medical examiner or coroner and the death investigators. Preserving and protecting the body is the CSI's first responsibility. Secure any evidence that seems transient or fragile; using paper bags to protect the hands is also a good idea.

References and Bibliography

Al-Enizi, M., Hadi, S., Goodwin, W., 2008. The development of visual and chemical methods for predicting the likelihood of obtaining a DNA profile from degraded bone samples. Forensic Sci. Int. Genet. Suppl. Ser. 1: 2–3.

Allen, M., Engstrom, A.S., Meyers, S., Handt, O., Saldeen, T., Von, Haeseler, A., et al., 1998. Mitochondrial DNA sequencing of shed hairs and saliva on robbery caps: Sensitivity and matching probabilities. J. Forensic Sci. 43 (3): 453–464.

Allen, R.W., Pogemiller, J., Joslin, J., Gulick, M., Pritchard, J., 2008. Identification through typing DNA recovered from touch transfer evidence: Parameters affecting yield of recovered human DNA. J. Forensic Identification 58 (1): 33–41.

Arany, S., Ohtany, S., Yoshioka, N., Gonmori, K., 2004. Age estimation from aspartic acid racemization of root dentin by internal standard method. Forensic Sci. Int. 141: 127–130.

Ballantyne, J., 2000. Overview. In: Siegel, J., Knupfer, G., Saukko, P. (Eds.), Encyclopedia of Forensic Sciences, in three volumes, pp. 1322–1331.

Bergeron, J., 2003. Development of bloody prints on dark surfaces with titanium dioxide and methanol. J. Forensic Identification 53 (2): 149–161.

Bille, T.W., Cromartie, C., Farr, M., 2009. Effects of cyanoacrylate fuming, time after recovery, and location of biological material on the recovery and analysis of DNA from post-blast pipe bomb fragments. J. Forensic Sci. 54 (5): 1059–1067.

Bond, J.W., 2007. Value of DNA evidence in detecting crime. J. Forensic Sci. 52 (1): 128–136.

Budowle, B., Leggitt, J.L., Defenbaugh, D.A., Keys, K.M., Malkiewicz, S.F., 2000. The presumptive reagent fluorescein for detection of dilute bloodstains and subsequent STR typing of recovered DNA. J. Forensic Sci. 45 (5): 1090–1092.

Caldwell, J.P., Henderson, W., Kim, N.D., 2000. ABTS: A safe alternative to DAB for the enhancement of blood fingerprints. J. Forensic Sci. 45 (4): 785–794.

Caldwell, J.P., Kim, N.D, 2002. Extension of color suite available for chemical enhancement of fingerprints in blood. J. Forensic Sci. 47 (2): 332–340.

Calloway, A.R., Jones, P.F., Siegel, S., Stupian, G.W., 1973. Location of seminal stains by their phosphorescence and its use in determining the order of deposition of overlapping seminal and bloodstains. J. Forensic Sci. Soc. 13: 223–230.

Coquoz, R., 2003. Preuve par l'ADN. La génétique au service de la justice. Presses polytechniques et universitaires romandes. Lausanne.

Coquoz, R., Taroni, F., 2006. Preuve par l'ADN. La génétique au service de la justice, deuxième édition mise à jour et augmentée. Presses polytechniques et universitaires romandes. Lausanne.

Coticone, S., Barna, L., Teets, M., 2010. Optimization of a DNA extraction method for nonhuman and human bone. J. Forensic Identification 60 (4): 430–438.

Dickson, S., Park, A., Nolan, S., Kenworthy, S., Nicholson, C., Midgley, J., et al., 2007. The recovery of illicit drugs from oral fluid sampling devices. Forensic Sci. Int. 165 (1): 78–84.

Duhig, C., 2003. Non-forensic remains: The use of forensic archaeology, anthropology and burial taphonomy. Sci. Justice 43 (4): 211–214.

Evett, I.W., Foreman, L.A., Jackson, G., Lambert, J.A., 2000. DNA profiling: A discussion of issues relating to the reporting of very small match probabilities. Crim. Law Rev., 341–355.

Fourney, R.M., DesRoches, A., Buckle, J.M., 2007. Recent progress in processing biological evidence and forensic DNA profiling, a review: 2004–2007. 15th International Forensic Science Symposium, Lyon, October 23–26, 2007. Individual Evidence section.

Frejeau, C.J., Germain, O., Fourney, R.M., 2000. Fingerprint enhancement revisited and the effects of blood enhancement chemicals on subsequent profiler plus fluorescent short tandem repeat DNA analysis of fresh and aged bloody fingerprints. J. Forensic Sci. 45 (2): 354–380.

Fridez, F., Coquoz, R., 1996. PCR DNA typing of stamps: Evaluation of the DNA extraction. Forensic Sci. Int. 78: 103–110.

Fridez, F., Rochat, S., Coquoz, R., 1999. Individual identification of cats and dogs using mitochondrial DNA tandem repeats? Sci. Justice 39 (3): 167–171.

Gaudette, B.D., 2000a. Overview. In: Siegel, J., Knupfer, G., Saukko, P. (Eds.), Encyclopedia of Forensic Sciences, in three volumes, pp. 999–1002.

Gaudette B.D., 2000b. Comparison: Other. In: Siegel, J., Knupfer, G., Saukko, P. (Eds.), Encyclopedia of Forensic Sciences, in three volumes, pp. 1016–1018.

Graham, E.A.M., Rutty, G.N., 2008. Investigation into "normal" background DNA on adult necks: Implications for DNA profiling of manual strangulation victims. J. Forensic Sci. 53 (5): 1074–1082.

Green, W., 2000. Sexual assault and semen persistence. In: Siegel, J., Knupfer, G., Saukko, P. (Eds.), Encyclopedia of Forensic Sciences, in three volumes, pp. 397–403.

Hartwig, S., Auwarter, V., Pragst, F., 2003. Effect of hair care and hair cosmetics on the concentrations of fatty acid ethyl esters in hair as markers of chronically elevated alcohol consumption. Forensic Sci. Int. 131: 90–97.

Hochmeister, M.N., Budowle, B., Eisenberg, A., Borer, U.V., Dimhofer, R., 1996. Using multiplex PCR amplification and typing kits for the analysis of DNA evidence in a serial killer case. J. Forensic Sci. 41: 155–162.

Holland, M.M., Fischer, D.L., Roby, R.K., Ruderman, J., Bryson, C., Weedn, V.W., 1995. Mitochondrial DNA sequence analysis of human remains. Crime Lab. Dig. 22/4: 109–115.

Houck, M., Bisbing, R.E., 2005. Forensic human hair examination and comparison in the 21st century. Comparison: Microscopy. Forensic Sci. Rev. 17 (1): 51–66.

Howard, M.C., Nessan, M., 2010. Detecting bloodstains under multiple layers of paint. J. Forensic Identification 60 (6): 682–717.

Kerrigan, S., Golberger, B.A. Body fluids. In: Siegel, J., Knupfer, G., Saukko, P. (Eds.), Encyclopedia of Forensic Sciences, in three volumes, pp. 616–626.

Kobus, H., Silenieks, E., Scharnberg, J., 2002. Improving the effectiveness of fluorescence for the detection of semen stains on fabrics. J. Forensic Sci. 47 (4): 819–823.

Lee, H.C., Pagliaro, E.M., 2000. Blood identification. In: Siegel, J., Knupfer, G., Saukko, P. (Eds.), Encyclopedia of Forensic Sciences, in three volumes, pp. 1331–1338.

Lee, H.C., Palmbach, T., Miller, M.T., 2001. Henry Lee's Crime Scene Handbook. Academic Press, San Diego.

Lord Justice Thomas, Mr. Justice Kitchin, and Mr. Justice Holroyde between Regina and David Reed and Terence Reed and Regina and Neil Garmson. Neutral Citation Number [2009] EWCA Crim 2968. Case Nos 2007/04708/B3; 2007/04710/B3; 2007/04800/D4—Royal Courts of Justice Strand. London WC2A 2LL.

Marchant, B., Tague, C., 2007. Developing fingerprints in blood: A comparison of several chemical techniques. J. Forensic Identification 57 (1): 76–93.

Morgan-Smith, R.K., Elliott, D.A., Adam, H., 2009. Enhancement of aged shoeprints in blood. J. Forensic Identification 59 (1): 45–50.

National Academy of Science, 2009. Committee on Identifying the Needs of the Forensic Sciences Community. National Research Council. Strengthening Forensic Science in the United States: A Path Forward.

Nickolls, L., 1956. The Scientific Investigation of Crime. Butterworth & Co, London.

Norris, D.O., Bock, J.H., 2000. Use of fecal material to associate a suspect with a crime scene: Report of two cases. J. Forensic Sci. 45 (1): 184–187.

Norris, D.O., Bock, J.H., 2001. Method for examination of fecal material from a crime scene using plant fragments. J. Forensic Identification 51 (4): 367–377.

Opel, K., Fleishaker, E., Nicjlas, J., Buel, E., McCurd, B., 2008. Evaluation and quantification of nuclear DNA from human telogen hairs. J. Forensic Sci. 53 (4): 853–857.

Owsley, D., Mann, R., Ubelaker, D., DiZinno, J., 1992. Unknown to positive ID: A forensic anthropological investigation. J. Forensic Identification 42: 6.

Oxley, J.C., Smith, J.L., Kirschenbaum, L.J., Marimganti, S., Vadlamannati, S., 2003. Detection of explosives in hair using ion mobility spectrometry. J. Forensic Sci. 53 (3): 690–693.

Oxley, J.C., Smith, J.L., Kirschenbaum, L.J., Shinde, K.R., Marimganti, S., 2005. Accumulation of explosives in hair. J. Forensic Sci. 50 (4): 826–831.

Oxley, J.C., Smith, J.L., Kirschenbaum, L.J., Marimganti, S., 2007. Accumulation of explosives in hair—Part II: Factors affecting sorption. J. Forensic Sci. 52 (6): 1291–1296.

Pang, B.C.M., Cheung, B.K.K., 2008. Applicability of two commercially available kits for forensic identification of saliva stains. J. Forensic Sci. 53 (5): 1117–1122.

Penalver, J., Kahana, T., Hiss, J., 1997. Prosthetic devices in positive identification of human remains. J. Forensic Identification 47 (4): 400–405.

Phipps, M., Petricevic, S., 2007. The tendency of individuals to transfer DNA to handled items. Forensic Sci. International 168 (2–3): 162–168.

Pope, S., Chapman, H., Lambert, J., 2006. The effect of bone marrow transplants on DNA profiles: A case example. Sci. Justice 46 (4): 231–237.

Raymond, J.L., Walsh, S.J., Van Oorschot, R.A., Gunn, P.R., Roux, C., 2004. Trace DNA: An underutilized resource or pandora's box? A review of the use of trace DNA analysis in the investigation of volume crime. J. Forensic Identification 54 (6): 668–686.

Romano, G., Barbera, N., Spadaro, G., Valenti, V., 2003. Determination of drugs of abuse in hair: Evaluation of external heroin contamination and risk of false positives. Forensic Sci. International 131: 98–102.

Sanders, K.P., Marshall, M., Oxley, J.C., Smith, J.L., Egee, L., 2002. Preliminary investigation into the recovery of explosives from hair. Sci. Justice 42 (3): 137–142.

Savolainen, P., Rosen, B., Holmberg, A., Leitner, T., Uhlen, M., Lundeberg, J., 1997. Sequence analysis of domestic dog mitochondrial DNA for forensic use. J. Forensic Sci. 42: 593–600.

Singh, D., Garg, R.K., 2009. Forensic analysis of oxidative hair dyes from commercial dyes and dyed hair samples by thin-layer chromatography. J. Forensic Identification 59 (2): 172–189.

Stoilovic, M., 1991. Detection of semen and bloodstains using Polilight as a light source. Forensic Sci. Int. 51: 289–296.

Taupin, J.M., 2004. Forensic hair morphology comparison—A dying art or junk science? Sci. Justice 44 (2): 95–100.

Ubelaker, D., Scammel, H., 1997. Bones, chapter 7: Sex, size, race, age at death. J. Forensic Identification 47 (3): 332–347.

Vandenberg, N., Van Oorschot, R.A.H., 2006. The use of Polilights in the detection of seminal fluid, saliva, and bloodstains and comparison with conventional chemical-based screening tests. J. Forensic Sci. 51 (2): 361–370.

Vass, A.A., Barshick, S.-A., Sega, G., Caton, J., Skeen, J.T., Love, J.C., et al., 2002. Decomposition chemistry of human remains: A new methodology for determining the postmortem interval. J. Forensic Sci. 47 (3): 542–553.

Wang, Y., Weiping, Z., Janping, M., Eosin, Y., 2007. Detection of latent blood prints. J. Forensic Identification 57 (1): 54–58.

Warren, M.W., Schultz, J.J., 2002. Post-cremation taphonomy and artifact preservation. J. Forensic Sci. 47 (3): 656–659.

Wickenheiser, R.A., 2002. Trace DNA: A review, discussion of theory, and application of the transfer of trace quantities of DNA through skin contact. J. Forensic Sci. 47 (3): 442–450.

Wolson, T.L., 2000. Bloodstain pattern analysis. In: Siegel, J., Knupfer, G., Saukko, P. (Eds.), Encyclopedia of Forensic Sciences, in three volumes, pp. 1338–1349.

Wonder, A.Y., 2001. Blood Dynamics. Academic Press, San Diego.

Wu, D., Chrichton, A., 2010. DNA wwabs from vehicles: A study on retention times, locations, and viability of identifying the most recent driver. J. Forensic Identification 60 (3): 308–319.

Yapping, L., Yue, W., 2004. Bloody latent fingerprint detection using LeuR6G. J. Forensic Identification 54 (5): 542–546.

Zeichner, A., Levin, N.J., 1995. Casework experience of GSR detection in Israel, on samples from hands, hair, and clothing using an autosearch SEM/EDX system. Forensic Sci. 40: 1082–1085.

Impression Evidence

Physical traces and impressions are still the archetypal evidence of the forensic sciences, embodied in Locard's Exchange Principle. Whether two- or three-dimensional impressions,[1] pieces, dust, smears, drops, diffusions, or stains, they epitomize the one- and two-way sharing of materials between human beings and their environment, be it criminal or innocent.

Because traces can be just that—trace remnants of transfers of almost anything—a listing of the various possible types should help the CSI to better assess not only their use as evidence, but also possible chemical or physical developments. The first part of this chapter will address direct transfer marks, the proximate "witnesses" of a person's presence. The second part of the chapter will deal with indirect indicators of such a presence, as the trace will be linked to an object, which only infers the human source.

---

[1] Properly, two-dimensional "impressions" are patterns because they do not have depth.

Human Traces

Any human traces transfer (from a bare finger, palm, foot, etc.) has the potential to carry a few cells, shed naturally from the skin. Due to today's high sensitivity of DNA analysis, only a few skin cells are required for DNA analysis. Even then, of the few potentially present cells, it may be rare to find ones that are still available for nuclear DNA analysis; shed cells are mainly from the outer layers of the skin, made of flat dead cells with few nuclei surviving (Champod et al., 2004). Even if a piece of evidence is not swabbed at the crime scene for DNA evidence, if it is handled and packaged properly, it can still be processed later in the laboratory and assist with the investigation (Raymond et al., 2004).

Human skin secretions are produced by three types of different glands: apocrine, eccrine, and sebaceous. The palms, soles, and forehead have a stronger concentration of eccrine glands than the rest of the body. Ninety-nine percent of eccrine secretions are composed of water and solvating electrolytes (mainly sodium chloride, but also potassium, calcium, copper (II), manganese (II), magnesium, and iron (II, III), as well as a variety of chlorides, sulfates, phosphates, bromides, iodides, bicarbonates, and other components). The 1% remaining are organic compounds (Reinholz, 2008; Salama et al., 2008). Apocrine glands are found under armpits, in the lower pelvic regions (genital and anal), and the chest area (mammary glands). Apocrine secretions are similar to eccrine ones with the addition of productions, lipids (as squalene, palmitoleic, and oleic acids), and proteins. Sebaceous glands are found all over the body but are in higher concentration on the face and the head. They secrete the sebum in hair follicles, which is composed of glycerides (tristearin, distearin, glycerol), fatty acids (myristic, palmitic, stearic), wax, and cholesterol esters (cholesterol, cholesterol palmitate) and squalene (Ramotowski, 2001). Quantification of these products to produce a "standard" profile is impossible, as the composition of the sebum varies with environment conditions.

Fingerprints, Palmprints, and Bare Footprints

First discovered as a means of identification in the 18th century (Berry, 1991; Quinche and Margot, 2010), fingerprints and palmprints are the impressions of ridges and furrows left on a surface touched by friction ridge skin (fingers, hands, toes, feet) (Asbaugh, 1999). Handprints and footprints are deposits of eccrine secretions, while fingerprints are a combination of eccrine and sebaceous secretions, as people generally touch their face or scratch their head, picking up the latter materials from the glands in those areas. In sexual offenses, apocrine compounds may be targeted for impressions. Finally, many environmental remnants and contaminants come to rest on our hands, adding to the impression deposit.

Little controversy exists today to admit that the friction ridge patterns on an individual are unique to that person. The morphogenesis argument to the individuality of any friction skin pattern, based on genetics and embryological development, is well recognized, if not completely researched (Hale, 1952; Asbaugh, 1992; Wertheim and Maceo, 2002; Swofford, 2008). The conclusion, however, that a fingerprint is able to individualize any past, present, or future human beings has been well falsified (Cole, 2006; Kaye, 2009; Evett and Williams, 1995; Champod and Evett, 2001). The challenge is not about falsifying the paradigm of uniqueness but recognizing that forensic science and crime scene investigation are about *traces*, that is, a potentially low-quality, frequently fragmentary impression on an uncontrolled surface, on which development choices were made to discover the mark with probable background noise attached (Taroni and Margot, 2000; Crispino, 2009). Misunderstanding the difference between a friction ridge skin on a finger and a transferred impression at a scene is the main reason for this confusion. This statement has several conclusions for the CSI. First, it is doubtful that the CSI will be able to decide at the scene which fingerprints will be useful for later development and comparison. Due to the many compounds plausibly on a print, a consistent chain of development should be understood and applied to improve and optimize the trace detection and contrast. The decision about the quality of the print will be made later by a fingerprint expert (Stoney and Thornton, 1986; Champod, 1992). Lastly, the ultimate decision of source and the weight of the evidence is made by the trier of fact, based not only on the testimony of the experts but also case circumstances (Robertson and Vignaux, 1995; Aitken and Taroni, 2004; Commission Appell, Darboux, Poincaré, 1904; Taroni et al., 1998; Taroni et al., 2006).

Figure 6.3.1 proposes a flowchart for the best development sequence to apply at a crime scene for various types of fingerprints (and bare footprints), with its attached formulations below. NIN, AB, and LeuR6G stand respectively for ninhydrin, Amido Black, and leuco-rhodamine 6G, whose syntheses were provided in previous chapters. The best way to identify a surface as being porous is to apply a drop of water and see if it penetrates the surface. Trace DNA collection on a porous surface will consist of cutting the area of contact for submission to the laboratory. It is up to the CSI to decide which forensic analysis comes first in terms of collection and preservation, DNA profiling, or fingerprint development. Ideally, if a fingerprint can be developed, the area around it could be swabbed for possible DNA.

In Figure 6.3.1, a green box means that DNA analysis is still possible after this treatment. A brown box jeopardizes such an analysis, and a red box dismisses any further DNA profiling. Of course, a green box at the end of a decision chain does not mean that DNA is automatically preserved if the process crossed a brown or red box. The various formulations are written in Table 6.3.1, with some superglue luminescent stains.

The DAB development in Table 6.3.2 should be applied after denaturation of fresh blood (spraying a solution of 5-sulfosalicylic in distilled water (22 g/L) for about two minutes, then washing with distilled water).

Superglue consists of fuming cyanoacrylate in optimal relative humidity conditions (Watkin et al., 1994; McLaren et al., 2010), which may be better

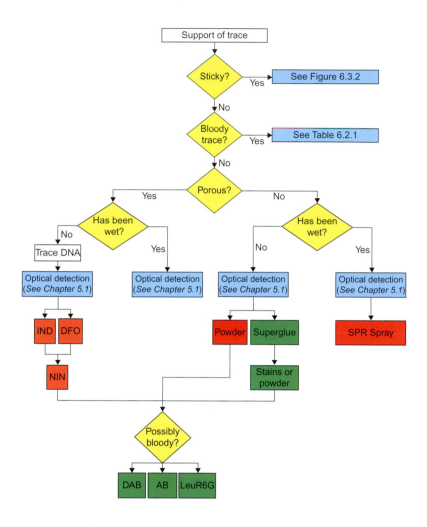

FIGURE 6.3.1 Fingerprint development flowchart for use at a crime scene. SPR, IND, DFO, and DAB stand respectively for small particles reagent, indanedione, 1,8-diazafluoren-9-one, and diaminobenzidine DFO-NIN-DAB.

done under a fumehood in the laboratory (Figure 6.3.2). Nevertheless, superglue pouches or cyanoacrylate fuming tubes (also called pens) exist for application in the field. Traditional powders may then be used (Figure 6.3.3).

Should a sticky or adhesive surface need to be processed for fingerprint development, the flowchart in Figure 6.3.4 could be applied; the formulations appear in Table 6.3.3.

Fingerprints on brass or some steel cartridge cases, but not lacquered materials, could be developed with commercial gun blueing. The reagent solution should be prepared with gun blue mixed with distilled water (1:40). Cartridges (or steel materials) could be slightly fumed with superglue before immersing the case in the reagent solution. The development should be monitored closely by gently stirring and rolling the cartridge in the solution. The development is stopped by dipping the casing in distilled water for two minutes (Cantu et al., 1998; Migron et al., 1998).

TABLE 6.3.1 Recommended Fingerprints Development Sequence on Crime Scenes

	Synthesis	Application	Observation
SPR (Margot and Lennard, 1988; Lee et al., 2001; Jasuja et al., 2008)	Black SPR: Concentrated solution: ROCOL AS® powder (10 g) mixed with 0.8 ml Tergitol® 7 in 100 ml water. Spray: Concentrated solution with 600 ml water. Gray SPR: 30 g molybdenum disulfide, 1 L distilled water, 3 drops Photo Flo 2000®. White SPR: 7.5 g zinc carbonate (ZnCO₃) in 50 ml of 1 ml Labolene® previously mixed with 125 ml distilled water. Fluorescent SPR: Available dyes: Rhodamine B, Rhodamine 6G, Acridine Orange, Anthracene, Cyano Blue, Basic Yellow. Dye solution: 0.01 g solid dye (or 10 ml liquid dye when available) in 10 ml White SPR.	Spray	After letting dry the developed fingerprint (occasionally with a fan), it could be transferred onto a fingerprint adhesive tape. For fluorescent dyes: - Rhodamine B (λ < 543 nm) - Rhodamine 6 g (λ < 524 nm) - Acridine Orange (λ < 489 nm) - Anthracene (λ < 400 nm) - Cyano Blue (λ < 280 nm) - Basic Yellow (λ < 280 nm)
IND (Stoilovic et al., 2007)	Dissolve 1 g 1,2-indanedione in 90 ml ethyl acetate. Add 10 ml glacial acetic acid. Dissolve in 900 ml HFE7100®.	Rapid submersing, let dry in the air for a few seconds. Second submersing. Let the paper completely dry and place it in a 100°C oven with a 60% relative humidity for 20 minutes (except documents with plastic windows, like business envelopes: 1 hour at 60°C).	Luminescence: Excitation: 530 nm. Emission: cutoff at 549 nm (orange).
DFO (Didierjean et al., 1998)	Dissolve 0.25 g DFO in 40 ml methanol, add 20 ml acetic acid. Complete with 940 ml HFE7100®.	Rapid submersing, let dry in the air for a few seconds. Second submersing. Let the paper completely dry and place it in a 100°C oven for 20 minutes (except plastic windows documents: 1 hour at 60°C). Else a vaporless dry iron can be used. If luminescence disappears, another heating is sufficient.	Maximal absorption at 560 nm, for a purple color. Luminescence: Exc: 555–560 nm. Em: 575–580 nm.

TABLE 6.3.2 DAB and Superglue Stains Synthesis Available on Crime Scene

	Synthesis	Application	Observation
DAB (Champod et al., 2004)	Sol. A: 160 ml distilled water and 20 ml phosphate buffer 1 M of pH 7.4 (26.8 g sodium dihydrogeno-phosphate and 2.9 g sodium hydrogen-phosphatein in 1,000 ml distilled water). Sol. B: 0.2 g DAB 3,3′-diaminobenzidine tetrahydrochloride in 20 ml distilled water. Sol. C: 30% hydrogen peroxide. Working solution to be prepared at the last moment: Sol. B mixed with sol. A and 1 ml sol. C.	Submersing protocol: Support is drowned in fresh sol. A for about 4 minutes. Developed fingerprints are then washed with distilled water. By contact: Spray distilled water for 30 seconds to 1 minute on the surface. This support should remain wet for 3–5 minutes. Take a porous paper or a tissue, place it on the questioned surface. Spray sol. A on it and keep the surface wet up to 5 minutes.	Fingerprints appear brown on bright background.
Superglue luminescent stains or powders (Champod et al., 2004; Sodhi et al., 2004)	Ardrox: Stock solution: 1 ml concentrated Ardrox diluted with 8 ml 2-butanone, and complete to 100 ml with petrol ether. Working solution: Dilute 5 ml stock solution into 100 ml petrol ether. R6G or BY40 or BR28: Stock solution: 0.1 g R6G or BY40 or BR28, 40 ml acetonitrile, 60 ml 2-propanol. Working solution: 5 ml stock solution in 95 ml petrol ether. Phloxine B or fluorescene powder: 0.05 g phloxine B or fluorescene into 25 ml ethanol. Adjust the solution pH to 4.0–4.5 by adding a 0.06% acetic acid solution in water. Add 2.5 g meshed aluminum, 1 g boric acid, 1 g talc, and 0.45 g barium carbonate. Allow the mixture to dry at room temperature for 4–7 days, and ground the dried mass with a mortar and pestle. Finally store the powder in a stoppered vessel.	For Ardrox, R6G, BY40, BR28: Apply solution with a pipette or by submersing on superglue-developed fingerprints at least aged 24 hours. Wash the support with water (use a pipette). For powders (phloxine B and fluorescene): Brush on superglue-developed fingerprints aged at least 24 hours.	Ardrox: Exc: 380 nm; Em: 500 nm. R6G: Exc: 525 nm; Em: 555 nm. BY40: Exc: 440 nm; Em: 490 nm. BR28: Exc: 495 nm; Em: 585 nm. BR28 + BY40: Exc: 495 nm; Em: 585 nm. Powders (phloxine B and fluorescene) are fluorescent by nature. It could also be enhanced with long UV.

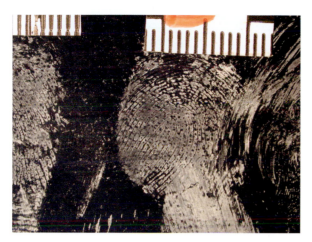

FIGURE 6.3.2 Superglue-fumed print. *With permission, courtesy Francis Hebrard, 2001.*

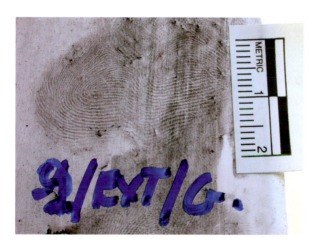

FIGURE 6.3.3 Powder development. *With permission, courtesy Francis Hebrard, 2003.*

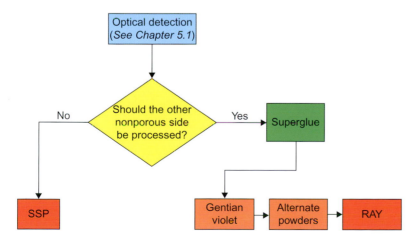

FIGURE 6.3.4 Flowchart for fingerprints development on sticky surfaces. SSP, BSP, and RAY stand respectively for sticky-side powder, black-side powder, and rhodamine-ardrox-yellow.

TABLE 6.3.3 Fingerprint Development Synthesis Available for Adhesive Surfaces

	Synthesis	Application	Observation
SSP (Champod et al., 2001)	Detergent solution: 10 ml Photo-Flo 200® mixed with 10 ml distilled water. Black or white fingerprint powder is mixed with detergent to have the consistency of paint.	Paint the adhesive surface with the powder suspension using a soft brush. Leave for 10 seconds to 1 minute. Rinse the tape under slowly running cold water. Repeat the process if necessary. Dry at room temperature.	Dark print. *See also alternate black/white powders later in the table.*
Gentian violet (Wilson, 2010)	1 g gentian violet in 1000 ml distilled water.	Gently brush the solution on the adhesive side of the tape with a soft brush. Leave for 1–2 minutes. Rinse with cold water.	Excitation: 505–570 nm. Emission: Red filter.
Alternate black/white powders (Wilson, 2010)	1 teaspoon of black or white powder, 20 drops water, 20 drops liqui-nox.	Gently brush the solution on the adhesive side of the tape with a soft brush. Leave for 30–60 seconds. Rinse with cold water.	Selective absorption. *SSP could also be applied.*
RAY (Wilson, 2010)	0.5 g BY40 + 10 ml glacial acetic acid + 0.05 g R6G + 4 ml Ardrox + 450 ml isopropanol or denaturated ethanol + 40 ml acetonitrile. Mix thoroughly with a magnetic stir.	Use wash bottle to apply. Rinse with cold water.	Excitation: 450–550 nm. Emission: Orange filter.

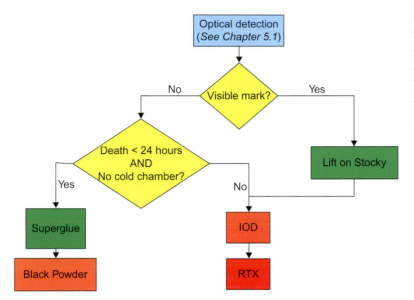

FIGURE 6.3.5 Flowchart of fingerprint development on dead skin. IOD and RTX stand for iodine and ruthenium tetroxide, respectively. Stocky stands for Stocky papers, which are positive fixed but unexposed photo paper.

Human Skin

As fingerprint development on human skin is typically conducted on the skin of deceased individuals (as mentioned before, perspiration confounds the collection of fingerprints on living individuals), this is more properly the province of the medical examiner and evidence collection in the morgue. Nevertheless, fingerprints can be positively retrieved with black powders for a short period of time after contact (Hebrard and Donche, 1994; Trapecar and Balazic, 2007). This period is typically too short for a successful intervention of the CSI, including obtaining the victim's consent, even if the process is trivial. A longer delay exists for a dead body, depending mainly on the time of death and the storage conditions. Figure 6.3.5 proposes a fingerprint development flowchart for skin on a dead body (Shin and Argue, 1976; Delmas, 1988; Hebrard and Donche, 1994; Fortunato and Walton, 1998; Wilgus, 2002; King, 2009); although highly toxic, RTX is mentioned and the protocol is in Table 6.3.5, for which iodine and RTX application appear, respectively, in Tables 6.3.4 and 6.3.5.

Integrating a Global Analytical Sequence

It is illusory to propose a universal list of chemical treatments from the crime scene to the final analysis in the laboratory for all evidence that could be subjected to chemical development. It depends on each laboratory's analytical resources, protocols, and regional jurisdictional requirements, not to mention the relationship between the laboratories and the CSIs, who may work for a different agency. Nevertheless, it is possible to propose such a homogeneous approach for fingerprint development, not only to inform the CSI about the available development to be done in laboratories, but also about possible disruption to other evidence, like DNA, in case a wrong choice

TABLE 6.3.4 Iodine Protocol. Caution: Heavy Skin, Eyes, and Lung Damages, if Unprotected.

	Synthesis	Application	Observation
IOD	1. To brush: Stock sol. A: 10 g 7,8-benzoflavone in 100 ml dichloromethane (10% w/v). Stock sol. B (to brush): 1 g iodine crystals in 1000 ml cyclohexane (0.1% w/v). Working solution (to be prepared just before use): 2 ml sol. A in 100 ml sol. B. Let quiet for 5 minutes before filtering and use. 2. To spray: Stock sol. A: 12 g 7,8-benzoflavone in 100 ml dichloromethane (12% w/v). Stock sol. B: 1 g iodine crystals in 1,000 ml Arklone® (0.1% w/v). Working solution (to be prepared just before use): 2 ml sol. A in 100 ml sol. B. Let quiet for 5 minutes before filtering and use. 3. Fuming process: Fuming solution (only to be used after iodine vapors fumigation): 0.3 g 7,8-benzoflavone in 10 ml dichloromethane. After dilution, dilute 90 ml petrol ether or cyclohexane.	Spray or swab sol. B (spray gives better results). Sol. A is used to fix the developed mark. For fuming: The sample is placed over iodine vapors (portable unit or dedicated container) until a bright brown fingerprint is visible. Do not overdevelop (less than 5 minutes). Immediately afterwards, apply 7,8-benzoflavone solution with a pipette or by submersing. A dark-blue staining of the iodine-developed fingerprint appears after solvent evaporation. The iodine-developed mark could be lifted on a silver plate by applying it on the mark.	An orange barrier filter can increase the contrast.

TABLE 6.3.5 RTX (Carcinogenic) Synthesis Available for Fingerprint Development on Dead Human Skin

RTX	Synthesis	Application	Observation
Sol. A: 1 g hydrated ruthenium (III) chloride in 1,000 ml bidistilled water. Sol. B: 113 g certium (IV) ammonium nitrate in 1,000 ml bidistilled water.	Sol. A: 1 g hydrated ruthenium (III) chloride in 1,000 ml bidistilled water. Sol. B: 113 g certium (IV) ammonium nitrate in 1,000 ml bidistilled water. Mix A and B solutions in equal quantities under activated fume hood (caution: toxic RTX vapors).	Spray the solution, or expose to vapors (in a close volume), or immerse the support in the working solution.	Fingerprints appear dark gray on bright gray background.

is made. Moreover, such a process ensures an analytical link between the scene and the laboratory, optimizing the odds to develop fingerprints.

The following approach described for fingerprint development could be extended to any other evidence type in close relationship with available forensic facilities and the advice of a forensic scientist. Since the relevant chemical protocols on crime scenes were already provided, they will not be repeated here. Nevertheless, bibliographical references of all protocols appearing on the charts below will be listed in the text.

Porous Surfaces

Many other treatments exist to develop or improve the contrast of fingerprints on porous surfaces. The blue parallelogram in Figure 6.3.6 relocates the ones proposed at the crime scene and described in Figure 6.3.1 (left part) within the known available development sequence (Crispino, 2003). Most of these treatments can only be performed in the laboratory for safety or heavy equipment reasons; others impede further DNA profiling, requiring the advice of fingerprint chemical experts. Blue words in the figure mean that DNA analysis can be performed after this treatment; green ones do not ensure a safe profiling. Red words totally prevent DNA identification. Bold arrows indicate a preferred development sequence. Alternative developments (fine arrows), depending on tests and forensic capacities, cannot be completed in the field. A short description of the treatment outside the blue area (addressed in Figure 6.3.1) is detailed next.

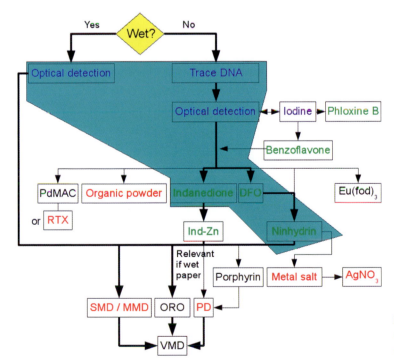

FIGURE 6.3.6 Complete development sequence on porous surfaces for fingerprints.

The figure also shows that the proposed development at the crime scene can be completed at various levels. First, not detecting a trace optically on a wet surface does not mean that no trace could be detected through chemical treatments, such as SMD/MMD, ORO, PD, or even porphyrin. Even for a dry surface, the optical detection step can be improved with iodine blowing, which lets fingerprints temporarily appear (Hammer et al., 1986; Siegel, 2007). Although the process is recursive, this technique is not routinely implemented due to the health hazards of working with iodine; commercial products exist, like Iodufol®, which improve these conditions. The transient appearance of brown iodine blown traces can be fixed with phloxine B or benzoflavone (Haque et al., 1983; Sodhi and Kaur, 2002; Flynn et al., 2004). The first one gives a red-colored complex and the second one gives a dark-blue staining. Iodine development and fixing is also of interest for thermal paper (like some cash register receipts) and, as such, do not allow development with organic solvents. Only benzoflavone fixation allows continuing fingerprint development on thermal paper surfaces.

Besides the prefered Indanedione/DFO–Ninhydrin sequence, PdMAC or RTX, organic powder, and Eu(fod)$_3$ are alternative, but ultimately dead-end, options. PdMAC (4-dimethylaminocinnamaldehyde) yields bright red and luminescent fingerprints at 610 nm for an optimal excitation at 505 nm (Brennan et al., 1995). RTX (ruthenium tetroxide), a highly hazardous compound, makes the fingerprints appear dark gray on a bright gray background (Mashiko et al., 1991; Mashiko and Miyamoto, 1998). The RTX protocol is convenient for polystyrene substrates; the RTX synthesis is listed in Table 6.3.5 for fingerprint development on a dead body and the reader is warned about its hazardous characteristics. RTX should be used by the CSI if no other alternative solution is available.

Organic powder can be brushed onto porous surfaces, the excess powder being brushed, blown, or tapped away. They are luminescent by nature and the emitted light can be enhanced by near UV. But magnetic-organic powder definitely inhibits DNA profiling (Sodhi et al., 2004).

Finally, Eu(fod)$_3$-Tris(6,6,7,7,8,8-heptafluoro-2,2-dimethyl-3,5-octanedionato) Europium (III) produces a luminescent signal at 614 nm for an optimal excitation at 350 nm (Allred and Menzel, 1997; Caldwell et al., 2001; Chongyang et al., 2004). Metal complexation of zinc with indanedione allows further development, which is not the case with metal salt complexation for ninhydrin under usual temperature conditions. Metal salt complexation induces a luminescence of indanedione (Hauze et al., 1998) or ninhydrin (Lennard et al., 1987; Menzel et al., 1990; Davies et al., 1995), but requires a dramatic cooling of the fingerprint under excitation light for ninhydrin; this is accomplished with liquid nitrogen flowing on the substrate. Liquid nitrogen can cause serious skin burns and the CSI should protect himself or herself during this protocol. As the last step of ninhydrin complexation is silver nitrate development for chloride-rich fingerprints on rough wood or paperboard, chemical developments available and applied beforehand on wet substrates could also prevent usual fingerprint detection on porous surfaces (Wallace-Kunkel et al., 2004; Stoilovic et al., 2007).

Optimizing this sequence could lead to the final complementary chemical treatments, which are difficult to conduct except in a laboratory, such as single metal deposition (SMD), multimetal deposition (MMD), oil red O (ORO), or physical developer, occasionally preceded by porphyrin (Murphy et al., 1999). SMD and MMD involve different chemical baths to develop dark-gray fingerprints with colloidal gold over a bright gray background. Both need siliconized dishes and immediate recording of developed fingerprints; currently, SMD looks more promising than MMD (Jones et al., 2003; Choi et al., 2006; Becue et al., 2007, 2008; Durussel et al., 2009).

ORO and PD are alternatives for wet porous surfaces. ORO currently appears more efficient than PD. Both of them reveal dark-gray fingerprints. This last chemical treatment should be applied directly without any prior treatments when faced with plywood supports (Beaudoin, 2004; Rawji and Beaudoin, 2006; Nicdaeid et al., 2009).

Vacuum metal deposition (VMD) is the very last technique to conclude the analytical sequence on porous surfaces, excepting radioactive development, which is practically abandoned today due to the needed detection material (Cuthbertson, 1969; Humm et al., 1990; Ramotowski and Cantu, 2001). VMD can also directly treat porous surfaces that cannot endure any liquid chemical treatment, such as tissue paper (Batey et al., 1998; Philipson and Bleay, 2007; Kusenthiran et al., 2010). The method consists of the deposition of a small amount of gold onto the trace support under high vacuum, followed by the deposition of a layer of zinc. Fingerprints should appear clear on a dark background; occasionally the reverse results may also occur.

Nonporous Surfaces

Using the same code of colors for texts and frames as Figure 6.3.6, Figure 6.3.7 shows the available fingerprint development sequence for nonporous surfaces. Once again, the crime scene sequence is shown in the blue frame, underlining that the iodine process (iodine/benzoflavone/phloxine B), the VMD, and the SMD/MMD are also available alternatives depending on the nature of the surface. VMD is, indeed, better carried out on nonporous surfaces than on porous ones (Misner, 1992; Masters and deHaan, 1996; Migron et al., 1998; Jones et al., 2001a, 2001b, 2001c, 2002; Suzuki et al., 2002). In contrast, iodine has a lower sensitivity on nonporous surfaces than on porous ones and SMD and MMD could also be relevant on nonporous surfaces (Donche and Musy, 1994; Roux et al., 1999).

Earprints

Listening on doors or windows before gaining entry to a premise or carrying a box or other object on the shoulder could transfer an earmark to the surface.

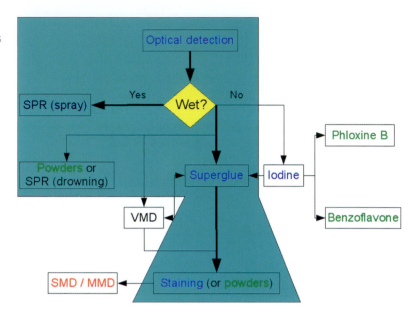

FIGURE 6.3.7 Complete development sequence for nonporous surfaces for fingerprints.

Ears have invariant proportions (Figure 6.3.8 shows the various imprints of an ear that could be observed on a mark), except for the lobe and the upper helix due to physical or sports-related changes (like boxers or rugby players) (Ianarelli, 1968; Crispino et al., 1998; Van der Lugt, 1998; Imhofer, 1906; Allison, 1969). As earmark individuality is still questionable (Champod et al., 2001), trace DNA could be collected, at least for intelligence purposes (Graham et al., 2007; Hammer and Neubert, 1989; Hunger and Hammer, 1989). Figure 6.3.9 shows the photography of the transfer of a developed earprint onto a gelatine. For example, the modus operandi of the perpetrator could be suggested, as when a burglar goes door to door, checking various apartments or flats for occupants. DNA notwithstanding, finding earprints could lead to finding other relevant traces in their vicinity.

Earprints are better developed on nonporous surfaces with powders. They should be lifted on gelatine or sticky transparent sheets and photographed 1:1 (or photocopied) with various contrasts. Comparison earprints can be collected with a rigid PET sheet, previously washed with alcohol and distilled water, and then dried. After each wash, three pressures on both of the suspect's ears should be applied successively (soft, medium, strong) to better capture any distortion. Powder should be immediately brushed to develop the print and a 1:1 photograph (or even a photocopy) of it made to store the information (Hammer, 1986).

Other Human Prints

Other human skin contacts can leave traces and potentially shed trace DNA, immersed in saliva, as with lip prints or bite marks, or in sweat, when a cheek

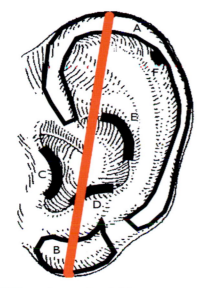

FIGURE 6.3.8 Contact surfaces of a left ear.

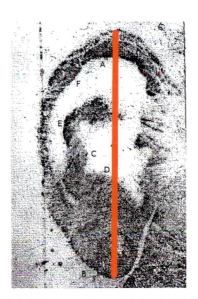

FIGURE 6.3.9 Description of a left earmark. A: the helix; B: the lobe; C: the tragus; D: the antitragus; E: the antihelix; F: the knob of Darwin. The length of the ear (red line here and on Figure 6.3.8) is defined as the greatest distance crossing the middle of the lobe reaching the upper part of the helix (Van der Lugt, 1997).

is pressed against a surface. Careful observations of the physical patterns of such marks can also provide relevant information for the case. For instance, lip prints can be classified into six patterns (Suzuki et al., 1970a) to possibly help with the exclusion of a suspect (Williams, 1991; Caldas et al., 2007) and even determine a pattern relevant to each person (Suzuki et al., 1970b; Tsuchihashi, 1974). The transfer of cosmetics can also limit the population of interest (Ehara et al., 1997; Webb et al., 2001, Kaur et al. 2009). Case reports also give examples of cheekprints or nose marks (Pertson, 1987; Girod et al., 1999).

Bite marks, human or animal, can also be detected and secured. Notwithstanding DNA collection, near UV or IR reflection photographs are means of helping with the visualization on bitten skin (Donnelly and Ciccone, 1987; Wright, 1998). Polymer casts can be taken from a freshly bitten object like fruit, cheese, a sandwich, and so on (Layton, 1966; Stoddart, 1973; Simon et al., 1974; Naru, 1997; Naru and Dykes, 1997; Clement, 2000; Pretty and Sweet, 2001; Pretty and Turnbull, 2001).

On victims, microtraces and DNA can be collected from under the nails to indicate cross-transfers (Stewart, 1990; Oz and Zamir, 2000; Cook and Dixon, 2007). Nails fragments, real or prosthetic, can also provide links with a victim or a perpetrator through their polish or enamels (Gupta et al., 2006).

Object Traces

With sufficient force, any object having contact with any matter has the potential to leave and/or collect a trace. With adequate detection methods, both transferred and received traces can be revealed and related, at least in theory. Such traces may only be vestiges or remnants, of possibly poor quality, of the contact between the items at the crime scene and their sources. The objects fall into classes of natural and manufactured items, sometimes poorly defined (Kwan, 1976), and implicitly depending on the population under question (Lukens and Bryan, 1974; Aitken et al., 2007).

Manufactured products tend to have markings either on them (as with stamped or engraved identifiers) or in them (as with taggants, objects or materials introduced into the production to covertly identify the item, or tracers). More overt than the lands and grooves in the barrel of firearms, fibers in textiles, glass compositional differences (say, between bottles and beakers), or even the tread patterns in shoe soles or tire treads (Biasotti, 1964; Cassidy, 1980; Bodziak, 1990; Vanderkolk, 1995; Miller, 2001a), these characteristics could classify the object under study as coming from a specific batch of similar items from the same production line (Houck, 2010).

On the other hand, use and "wear and tear" of objects leave traces of their "activity history," like breaks, scratches, and wear; cumulatively, these can lead a forensic expert to individual differentiation of similar objects though their respective lifetime use patterns, which are inferred through the impressions left at the crime scene. As both unique and class traits are detected, observed, and collected at once (all in the same impression), the first challenge is to distinguish which come from the production process (class characteristics) and which come from the specific-use history of the source. The former can be known only by studying the manufacturing processes of the product in question or the natural history of the plant, animal, or geologic sample under study. Indeed, many problems appear when addressing the lifetime of the production matrix itself, which could easily confuse class characteristics as individual ones, particularly if they are shared with products manufactured contemporaneously (Osterburg, 1969; Biasotti and Murdock, 1984; Houck, 2010; Vanderkolk, 1993; Schwartz, 2005; Brooks, 2006). Other difficulties occur when the same object does not necessarily produce two qualitatively or quantitatively similar responses when placed in contact with the same receptor, depending on the pressure, the time and dynamic of the contact, the strength or weakness of the object, and the retention capability and persistence of the transfer marks on the receptor, among many other materials constraints, notwithstanding potential background noise, as would be expected from similar observations of traces on randomly selected substrates (Pounds and Smalldon, 1975a, 1975b, 1975c; Walbridge, 2009).

Nevertheless, the crime scene examiner can still provide intelligence to investigators through the use of traces from tools, gloves, shoes, tires, bullets, and so on, to reconstruct the scene (Crispino, 2006) and even exclude a suspect object or to indicate that the population to focus on is restricted to a few statistical individuals (Smalldon and Moffat, 1973; Ribaux et al., 2003, 2010; Ribaux and Margot, 2003, 2007). Finally, as many manufactured objects are commercially traced by serial number or RFID (radio frequency identification devices), leads can be created through the determination of the owner's or manufacturer's identification (Parry, 1998; Lounsbury and Thompson, 2007; Medley, 2010).

Shoeprints and Tireprints

In Arthur Conan Doyle's first Sherlock Holmes novel, *A Study in Scarlet* (1887), the legendary detective explains to his accomplice Dr. Watson that, "there is no branch of detective science which is so important and so much neglected as the art of tracing footsteps." Progress in tracing shoes has been made since the end of the 19th century and general identification now focuses on manufacture and model identification; this is based on a thorough understanding of manufactured soles and shoes, their wear, and the significance of those marks (LeMay, 2010; Bodziak, 1986; Champod et al., 1999; Shor and Weisner, 1999). The forms and designs of the soles can be easily described, allowing classification systems (Girod, 1996), some computerized, that differentiate class and individual characteristics and require understanding the various modes of shoe/soles fabrication (Girod, 2002).

But shoeprints also provide relevant information for crime scene reconstruction and can indicate entry access, pathways, exits, and the number of persons involved; other possible information includes assessment of the gender, size and weight of the perpetrator (Cassidy, 1980; Jasuja et al., 1992), and the serial deposition of impressions (Girod, 1997, Napier, 2002). Figure 6.3.10 gives such an example. Quite similar comments could be made for tireprints (Figure 6.3.11), which allow crime scene reconstruction (Bodziak, 2008), vehicle model identification (Bessman and Schmeiser, 2001), narrowing if not individualizing a specific tire, and also linking cases or disjointed crime scenes to each other (Cook, 1981). Photography, as always, is required for both question and comparison materials (Segura, 1981; Thali et al., 2000; SWGTREAD, 2007a, 2007b, 2007c; Soule, 1961; Hueske, 1991; Hammer and Wolfe, 2003).

Contrast is central to the collection of a quality two-dimensional (2D) impression; relevant optical, physical, or chemical developments should be considered based on the substrate (porous/nonporous/shiny), the type of deposited materials (dust, blood, etc.), by analogy with fingerprint development (powders, superglue, protein staining, etc.), and appropriately adapting the method of collection (gelatin, adhesive lifter, dust lifter, etc.) (Shor et al., 1998, 2003, 2005). As 2D shoeprints and tireprints are made of particulate deposits, various developments can be applied depending on the suspected composition of the trace material (Table 6.3.6) (Martin, 2002; Croft et al., 2010). For instance, Figure 6.3.12 illustrates the development of a shoemark on ceramic with black powder.

FIGURE 6.3.10 Double homicide crime scene. The markers show partial or complete bloodied shoeprints indicating the perpetrator's activity at the scene. *With permission, courtesy Francis Hebrard, 2001.*

FIGURE 6.3.11 Various tireprints on a crime scene. *With permission, courtesy Francis Hebrard, 2002.*

TABLE 6.3.6 Possible Developments of Shoeprints on 2D Support

Target	Protocol	Synthesis	Preparation	Observation
Fe^{+++}	KCNS (potassium thiocyanate)	KSCN: 10 g. H_2O: 10 ml. Acetone: 80 ml. HCl: 10 ml.	Dissolve KSCN in water, then add acetone and HCl. The upper part of the solution is the reactant.	Spray on surface. Brown-reddish development of ferric ions.
Cl^-	$AgNO_3$	Solution: 5% AgNO3 in H_2O.		Spray on surface. Precipitate with any Cl^- to form AgCl, which becomes black under sunlight.

(Continued)

TABLE 6.3.6 (Continued)

Target	Protocol	Synthesis	Preparation	Observation
Metal ions	K4[Fe(CN)$_6$]	HCl: 10–12 ml. Ethanol: 90 ml. K4[Fe(CN)$_6$]: 5 g (potassium hexacyanoferrate(II) trihydrate). Distilled water: 95–100 ml.	Sol. 1: HCl and ethanol. Sol. 2: K4[Fe(CN)6] and water.	Spray sol. 1 on the trace. Wait for 10–20 seconds. Spray lightly with sol. 2. Prussian blue (deep blue) staining.
	Pyrrolidine	HCl: 10–20 ml. Ethanol: 80–90 ml. NH$_4$ (pyrrolidine dithiocarbamate): 1 g. Na citrate: 3 g.	Reactant 1: HCl + CH$_3$CH$_2$OH. Reactant 2: Dissolve other products together.	Spray. Dark black.
	α,α'-Dipyridyl	α,α'-dipyridy: 4 g. Ascorbic acid: 1 g. Methanol: 100 ml. HCl: 3 ml.	Dissolve α,α'-dipyridyl and ascorbic acid in methanol. Add HCl.	Spray. Red.
	o-phenanthroline	o-phenanthroline chloride: 0.05 g NaHSO$_3$ (sodium Hydrogen sulfite): 10 g. Distilled water: 100 ml.	Dissolve o-phenanthroline chloride and NaHSO$_3$ in water.	Spray. Red-orange.
	Sulfuric acid	Acetone: 120 ml. Distilled water: 15 ml. Dilute sulfuric acid (10% dilution from 97.5% sulfuric acid): 9 ml.	Mix acetone and water and slowly add dilute sulfuric acid. A white precipitate is formed and filtered off in the final step to produce a clear, colorless solution.	Spray. Maximum color development within 5–10 minutes.
	Bromophenol blue	Dissolve 1 g bromophenol blue powder in 5 ml methanol.	For any shoemark support (porous and nonporous).	Spray lightly onto the substrate. A blue coloration develops in basic conditions. A yellow coloration develops in acidic conditions.

Shoeprints on paper can be developed with an electrostatic detection apparatus (ESDA). Moreover, latent 2D traces on carpets or fabrics can be collected with an electrostatic lifter (ESL), a short-voltage high-intensity device transferring dust particles deposited by the trace source (shoe or tire) onto a charged foil (Milne, 1987; Majamaa, 1997).

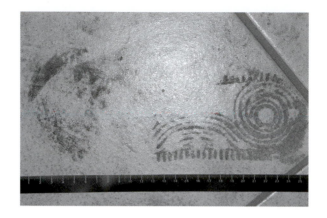

FIGURE 6.3.12 Shoemark development with black powder on ceramic. *With permission, courtesy Francis Hebrard, 2000.*

Three-dimensional (3D) casting can be performed with Duplicast (Vandiver and Wolcott, 1978), dental stone (Bodziak and Hammer, 2006), or polyurethane foam (Drexler, 1994; Wilson, 2004); a polymer cast would also be cost-effective, but special techniques for snow (or even slush) have to be understood (Adair and Shaw, 2007; Skreptak, 1988; Nause, 1992; Wolfe, 2008).

Casting 3D Impressions with Dental Stone

Making a Cast with Dental Stone, Using a Single Shoeprint as an Example
Materials Needed

- 1–1.5 kilograms of dental stone
- 4 liter sealable plastic bag
- A large disposable spoon
- 150–250 milliliters water per kilo dental stone
- Baby powder
- Scissors
- A form to support the cast

Making the Cast
Secure the form around the print; make sure the form is large enough to encompass the print. Do not disturb the print when placing the form. Put the dental stone in the plastic bag. Add the water a bit at a time until the mixture has a thickened but pourable texture (like cake batter). Seal the bag. Shake and squeeze the bag until the stone is completely mixed. Lightly sprinkle the baby powder in a single layer over the print (this helps fix the cast and to release it). Cut one corner of the bag at an angle with scissors to make a spout. Using the spoon as a guide, pour the mixture onto the spoon and guide it into the print and the form. **The mixture should not be poured directly into the print**; the force of the

---

mixture moving across the print could distort details. Using the tip of something sharp, scratch identifying information into the back of the cast before it dries. The cast will dry in 30 minutes. Using the spoon and being careful not to scratch the underside of the cast, pry the cast up out of the substrate. **Do not clean the cast**. Place the cast in secure, **breathable** packaging, label, and seal. The cast will need to dry 24–48 hours before it can be safely cleaned.

Making a Cast in Water

Materials Needed

- 1–1.5 kilograms of dental stone
- 4 liter sealable plastic bag
- A form to support the cast

Making the Cast

Secure the form around the print; make sure the form is large enough to encompass the print. Do not disturb the print when placing the form. Remove any debris or materials floating above the print. Slowly sprinkle dental stone over the impression and the form until the form is half filled with the dental stone. Prepare a mixture of dental stone as above but slightly thicker; **gently** spoon the mixture on top of the first layer of dental stone. The cast should be firm in 60 minutes; remove as above and allow to air dry for at least 48 hours.

Making a Cast in Snow

Materials Needed

- 1–1.5 kilograms of dental stone
- 4 liter sealable plastic bag
- A large disposable spoon
- 150–250 milliliters cold water per kilo dental stone
- Baby powder
- Scissors
- A can of Snow Print Wax
- Cardboard box large enough to cover the print
- A form to support the cast

Making the Cast

Secure the form around the print; make sure the form is large enough to encompass the print. Do not disturb the print when placing the form. Spray the Snow Print Wax over the impression; do not overspray. Wait 10 minutes. Mix the dental stone as above but use very cold water. **Carefully** pour the dental stone into the print. Cover the print with the box and allow the print to sit for at least 60 minutes. Remove the print and allow to dry for at least 48 hours.

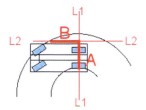

FIGURE 6.3.13 Measures A and B for inferring turning diameter.

All 3D plaster casts should employ the following general protocol:

- Prepare a frame or wall around the trace.
- When needed, prepare an appropriate amount of plaster (about 300 cl), avoiding bubbles by stirring lightly. Do not hesitate to add more liquid to the plaster (or equivalent) if it is too stiff.
- Pour half of the plaster onto the framed trace. Place a support, like a loop made from a wire clothes hanger, into the plaster as it is beginning to dry. Pour in the remaining plaster layer.
- Remove when completely dried.

Recognizing the sharp turn of a front wheel at a crime scene could discriminate vehicles of interest from suspected ones. As every vehicle has a minimal turning radius, measuring the outer margin of the track could be compared to vehicles of interest (Bodziak, 2000). To assess the minimum turning diameter:

- Study firstly the front wheel track traces, to support a sharp turning track.
- Identify the rear wheel track: rear wheels are always equidistant to each other and do not tilt on their vertical axis.
- Draw a perpendicular line between the shorter distance of the rear wheel traces (noted L1 in Figure 6.3.13).
- Identify the outer rim of the front wheel track, and draw a perpendicular line to L1 joining this track, noted L2.
- Measure the following distances:
    - A: the distance between the inner rear wheel track and the intersection between L1 and L2.
    - B: half the distance of L2.
- The turning diameter of the vehicle is given by $D = (B^2/A) + A$.

Further chemical analyses of tire compounds could also provide leads for investigation, requiring gum collection on the evidential support (Sarkissian, 2007).

Finally, remember that comparisons between the question and the comparison materials should be made under similar conditions, either both 2D or both 3D replicates, but there should never be a direct comparison between a trace and its potential source.

Gloveprints

Criminals may use gloves to avoid depositing fingerprints. Because of this, gloveprints should not be overlooked as either "nonevidence" or weak evidence. Gloves can be classified into four groups (Lambourne, 1987):

- Group 1: Leather or vinyl, including perforated leather
- Group 2: Fine fabric
- Group 3: Rough fabric
- Group 4: Rubber and latex

FIGURE 6.3.14 Safe key collected for analysis. *With permission, courtesy Francis Hebrard, 2004.*

As with other classifications, sewing, perforating, folding patterns, scratches, cuts, burns, and wear can lead to identification (Sirois, 1992; Martin, 2002). Methods of development are analogous to fingerprints and shoeprints; note also that gloves may have materials on them that are traces as well, like blood or explosive residues. DNA may be collected from inside the glove, as well, from skin cells, saliva, or hairs.

Toolmarks

Toolmark analysis can provide information regarding the type of tool used, its color (through paint or metal transfers), and its defects (Rathman, 1992; Van Dijk, 2000). Toolmarks, beyond comparisons, can also provide forensic intelligence, giving, for instance, useful information for linking burglaries to each other (Crispino, 2006; Crispino et al., 2010).

Collecting toolmark traces should begin with photographs taken (with a scale) under different lighting, including low angle, followed by polymer casting. Traces in the toolmark itself should be collected before casting. Additionally, collect blanks of the substrate for later comparison. If possible, collect the entire substrate and the toolmark as one entity (Feldman et al., 1980; Locke, 2006). Carefully protect the portion of the tool suspected to have been used to make the mark at the scene and never try to insert the tool back into the toolmark. Finally, keys (Figure 6.3.14) and locks should be collected in the case of break-ins or robberies (Cassidy, 1980; Kummer et al., 1997).

References and Bibliography

Adair, T.W., Shaw, R.L., 2007. The dry-casting method: A reintroduction to a simple method for casting snow impressions. J. Forensic Ident. 57 (6): 823–831.

Aitken, C.G.G., Taroni, F., 2004. Statistics and the Evaluation of Evidence for Forensic Scientists, second ed. Statistics in Practice. John Wiley and Sons, New York.

Aitken, C.G.G., Zadora, G., Lucy, D., 2007. A two-level model for evidence evaluation. J. Forensic Sci. 52 (2): 412–419.

Akulova, V., Vasiliauskiene, D., Talaliene, D., 2002. Further insights into the persistence of transferred fibres on outdoor clothes. Sci. Justice 42 (3): 165–171.

Alberink, I., Ruifrok, A., 2008. Repeatability and reproducibility of earprint acquisition. J. Forensic Sci. 53 (2): 325–330.

Allison, H.C., 1969. Ear identification. Pers. Ident. 99–109.

Allred, C.E., Menzel, E.R.A, 1997. Novel europium-biconjugate method for latent fingerprint detection. Forensic Sci. Int. 85 (2): 83–94.

Almirall, J.R., Cole, M.D., Gettinby, G., Furton, K.G., 1998. Discrimination of glass sources using elemental composition and refractive index: Development of predictive models. Sci. Justice 38 (2): 93–100.

Asbaugh, D.R., 1992. Defined pattern, overall pattern, and unique pattern. J. Forensic Ident. 42 (6): 503–512.

Asbaugh, D.R., 1999. Quantitative-Qualitative Friction Ridge Analysis: An Introduction to Basic and Advanced Ridgeology. CRC Press, Boca Raton, FL.

Barnum, C.A., Klasey, D.R., 1997. Factors affecting the recovery of latent prints on firearms. J. Forensic Ident. 47 (2): 141–149.

Batey, G.W., Copeland, J., Donnelly, D.L., Hill, C.L., Laturnus, P.L., 1998. Metal deposition for latent print development. J. Forensic Ident. 48 (2): 165–175.

Baudoin, P., Lavabre, R., Vayne, F., 2002. An unusual oxidation type on bulb filament after a car crash dive. J. Forensic Sci. 47 (2): 377–380.

Beaudoin, A., 2004. New technique for revealing latent fingerprints on wet porous surfaces: Oil red. O. J. Forensic Ident. 54 (4): 413–420.

Becue, A., Champod, C., Margot, P., 2007. Use of gold nanoparticles as molecular intermediates for the detection of fingerprints. Forensic Sci. Int. 168 (2–3): 169–176.

Becue, A., Scoundrianos, A., Champod, C., Margot, P., 2008. Fingerprint detection based on the in situ growth of luminescent nanoparticles—Towards a new generation of multimetal deposition. Forensic Sci. Int. 179 (1): 39–43.

Bennett, R.L., Kim, N.D., Curran, J.M., Coulson, S.A., Newton, A.W.N., 2003. Spatial variation of refractive index in a pane of float glass. Sci. Justice 43 (2): 71–76.

Bentsen, R.K., Brown, J.K., Dinsmore, A., Harvey, K.K., Kee, T.G., 1996. Post firing visualisation of fingerprints on spent cartridge cases. Sci. Justice 36 (1): 3–8.

Berry, J., 1991. The history and development of fingerprinting. In: Lee, H.C., Gaensslen, R.E. (Eds.), Advances in Fingerprint Technology. Elsevier, New York.

Bessman, C.W., Schmeiser, A., 2001. Survey of tire tread design and tire size as mounted on vehicles in central iowa. J. Forensic Ident. 51 (6): 587–596.

Biasotti, A., 1964. The principles of evidence evaluation as applied to firearms and tool mark identification. J. Forensic Sci. 9 (4): 428–433.

Biasotti, A., Murdock, J., 1984. "Criteria for identification" or "state of the art" of firearm and toolmark identification. Assoc. Firearms Toolmarks Examiners J., AFTE 16 (4): 16–22.

Biermann, T., Grieve, M.C., 1996. A computerized data base of mail order garments: A contribution toward estimating the frequency of fibre found in clothing. Part 2: The content of the data bank and its statistical evaluation. Forensic Sci. Int. 77: 75–91.

Bodziak, W.J., 1986. Manufacturing processes for athletic shoe outsoles and their significance in the examination of footwear impression evidence. J. Forensic Sci. Soc. 31 (1): 153–176.

Bodziak, W., 1990. Footwear Impression Evidence. Elsevier, New York.

Bodziak, W.J., 2000. Vehicle tire marks and tire track measurement. In: Siegel, J., Knupfer, G., Saukko, P. (Eds.), Encyclopedia of Forensic Sciences, in three volumes, pp. 1228–1235.

Bodziak, W.J., 2008. Tire Tread and Tire Track Evidence, Recovery and Forensic Examinations. Taylor & Francis/CRC Press, Boca Raton, FL.

Bodziak, W.J., Hammer, L.C., 2006. An evaluation of dental stone, traxtone, and crime-cast. J. Forensic Ident. 56 (5): 769–787.

Bommarito, C.R., Sturdevant, A.B., Szymanski, D.W., 2007. Analysis of forensic soil samples via high-performance liquid chromatography and ion chromatography. J. Forensic Sci. 52 (1): 24–30.

Bonfanti, M.S., De Kinder, J., 1999. The influence of manufacturing processes on the identification of bullets and cartridge cases—A review of the literature. Sci. Justice 39 (1): 3–10.

Brennan, J., Bramble, S., Gabtree, S., Wright, G., 1995. Fuming of latent fingerprints using dimethylaminocinnamaldehyde. J. Forensic Ident. 45 (4): 373–380.

Brinck, T.B., 2008. Comparing the performance of IBIS and BulletTRAX-3D technology using bullets fired through 10 consecutively rifled barrels. J. Forensic Sci. 53 (3): 677–682.

Brooks Jr., J.M., 2006. Identifying and sharing class characteristics of outsole impressions. J. Forensic Ident. 56 (5): 737–743.

Buckleton, J., Triggs, C., Taroni, F., Champod, C., Wevers, G. Experimental design for acquiring relevant data to address the issue of comparing consecutively manufactured tools and firearms. Sci. Justice 48 (3): 178–181.

Bull, P.A., Morgan, R.M., Sagovsky, A., Hughes, G.J.A., 2006. The transfer and persistence of trace particulates: Experimental studies using clothing fabrics. Sci. Justice 46 (3): 185–195.

Bunch, S.G., 2000. Consecutive matching striation criteria: A general critique. J. Forensic Sci. 45 (4): 955–962.

Caldas, I.M., Magalhaes, T., Afonso, A., 2007. Establishing identity using cheiloscopy and palatoscopy. Forensic Sci. Int. 165 (1): 1–9.

Caldwell, J.P., Henderson, W., Kim, N.D., 2001. Luminescent visualization of latent fingerprints by direct reaction with a lanthanide shift reagent. J. Forensic Sci. 46 (6): 1332–1341.

Caldwell, J.P., Kim, N.D., 2002. Extension of color suite available for chemical enhancement of fingerprints in blood. J. Forensic Sci. 47 (2): 332–340.

Campbell, G.P., Curran, J.M., 2009. The interpretation of elemental composition measurements from forensic glass evidence: III. Sci. Justice 49 (1): 1–7.

Cantu, A.A., Leben, D.A., Ramotowski, R., Kopera, J., Simms, J.R., 1998. Use of acidified hydrogen peroxide to remove excess gun blue treated cartridge cases and to develop latent prints on untreated cartridge cases. J. Forensic Sci. 43 (2): 294–298.

Cartier, J., Roux, C., Grieve, M.A, 1997. Study to investigate the feasibility of using X-ray fluorescence microanalysis to improve discrimination between colourless synthetic fibres. J. Forensic Sci. 42 (6): 1019–1026.

Cassidy, F.H., 1980. Examination of toolmarks from sequentially manufactured tongue-and-groove pliers. J. Forensic Sci. 25 (4): 796–809.

Cassidy, M.J., 1980. Identification des empreintes de chaussures. Service central des relations publiques de la gendarmerie royale du Canada. 118.

Champod, C., 1992. La valeur statistique des empreintes digitales partielles. Mémoire de thèse. Institut de police scientifique et de criminologie de l'Université de Lausanne, Switzerland.

Champod, C., Evett, I.W.A., 2001. Probabilistic approach to fingerprint evidence. J. Forensic Ident. 51 (2): 101–122.

Champod, C., Evett, I.W., Kuchler, B., 2001. Earmarks as evidence: A critical review. J. Forensic Sci., JFSCA 46 (6): 1275–1284.

Champod, C., Lennard, C., Aargot, P., Stoilovic, M., 2004. Fingerpriuts and Other Ridge Skin Impressions. CRC Press, Boca Raton, FL.

Champod, C., Voisard, R., Girod, A.A, 1999. Statistical study of air bubbles on athletic shoesoles. Information Bulletin foe Shoeprint/Toolmark Examiners. Proceedings European Meeting for Shoeprint/Toolmark Examiners 6 (1), pp. 105–121.

Chisum, W.J., 2001. The past, present, and future of criminalistics. Sci. Justice 41 (1): 55–61.

Choi, M., McBean, K., Wuhrer, R., McDonagh, A., Maynard, P., Lennard, C., et al., 2006. Investigation into binding of gold nanoparticles to fingerprints using scanning electron microcospy. J. Forensic Ident. 56 (1): 24–32.

Chongyang, L., Boyang, L., Shiyuan, Y., Jinzhang, G., Peizhen, Y., 2004. Study on the direct developing of latent fingerprint using a new fluorescent developer. J. Forensic Ident. 54 (6): 653–659.

Clement, J.G., 2000. Odontology. In: Siegel, J., Knupfer, G., Saukko, P. (Eds.), Encyclopedia of Forensic Sciences, in three volumes, pp. 1129–1137.

Cole, S.A., January 2006. Is fingerprint identification valid? Rhetorics of reliability in fingerprint proponents' discourse. Law Policy 28 (1): 109–135.

Commission Appell, 1904. Darboux, Poincaré. 2ème révision du procès Dreyfus. Rapport du 20 août 1904. Paris.

Cook, C.W., 1981. Footprints and tire tracks (class or individual characteristics?). Ident. News, 7–10.

Cook, O., Dixon, L., 2007. The prevalence of mixed DNA profiles in fingernail samples taken from individuals in the general population. Forensic Sci. Int. Genet. 1 (1): 62–68.

Coulson, S.A., Buckleton, J.S., Gummer, A.B., Triggs, C.M., 2001. Glass on clothing and shoes of members of the general population and people suspected of breaking crimes. Sci. Justice 41 (1): 39–48.

Crispino, F., 2001. Comments on JFI 51(3). J. Forensic Ident. 51 (5): 449–456.

Crispino, F., 2003. Computerized forensic assistance software (FAS 1.0) for training and standardized investigation in distributed and disconnected services. Forensic Sci. Int. 132 (2): 125–129.

Crispino, F., 2006. La trace matérielle: Un catalyseur d'information judiciaire. Revue de la gendarmerie nationale 221: 5–15.

Crispino, F., Brault, J., Burgueyre, P., 2009. Le coordonnateur en criminalistique. Un nouvel acteur du renseignement criminel. Revue de la gendarmerie 233: 6–15.

Crispino, F., Volckeryck, G., Kennerley, G., 1998. First international ear identification course. Inform. Bull. Shoeprint/Toolmark Examiners 4 (4): 13–17.

Croft, D.J., Pye, K., 2004. Multi-technique comparison of source and primary transfer soil samples: An experimental investigation. Sci. Justice 44 (1): 21–28.

Croft, S., NicDaeid, N., Savage, K.A., Vallance, R., Ramage, R., 2010. The enhancement and recovery of footwear marks contaminated in soil: A feasibility study. J. Forensic Ident. 60 (6): 718–737.

Curran, J.M., Triggs, C.M., Almirall, J.R., Buckleton, J.S., Walsh, K.A.J., 1997. The interpretation of elemental composition measurements from forensic glass evidence: I, II. Sci. Justice 37 (4): 241–249.

Cuthbertson, F., 1969. The chemistry of fingerprints. Atomic Weapons Research Establishment Report, 13.

Davies, P.J., Kobus, H.J., Taylor, M.R., Wainwright, K.P., 1995. Synthesis and structure of the zinc (II) and cadmium (II) complexes produced in the photoluminescent enhancement of ninhydrin developed fingerprints using group 12 metal salts. J. Forensic Sci. 40 (4): 565–569.

Delmas, B.J., 1988. Postmortem latent print recovery from skin surface. J. Forensic Ident. 38 (2): 49–56.

Demmelmeyer, H., Adam, J., 1995. Forensic investigation of soil and vegetal materials. Forensic Sci. Rev. 7: 119–142.

Didierjean, C., Debart, M.-H., Crispino, F., 1998. New formulation of DFO in HFE7100. Fingerprint Whorld 24 (94): 163–167.

Di Maio, V.J.M., 1999. Gunshot Wounds. Practical Aspects of Firearms, Ballistics, and Forensic Techniques, second ed. CRC Press, Boca Raton, FL.

Donche, A., 1995. Fingerprint developments on cartridge casings. J. Forensic Ident. 4.

Donche, A., Musy, C., 1994. Development of latent fingerprints on cartridge casings. Fingerprint Whorld 20 (75): 13–25.

Donnelly, W.J., Ciccone, R., 1997. Excluding a suspect using bite-mark evidence. J. Forensic Ident. 47 (3): 264–273.

Drexler, S.G., 1994. Test impressions of footwear outsoles using biofoam. J. Forensic Ident. 44 (1): 57–70.

Durussel, P., Stauffer, E., Becue, A., Champod, C., Margot, P., 2009. Single-metal deposition: Optimization of this fingerprint enhancement technique. J. Forensic Ident. 59 (1): 80–96.

Egli, N.M., 2009. Interpretation of partial fingerprints using an automated fingerprint identification system. Thèse de doctorat. Université de Lausanne. Faculté de droit et des sciences criminelles, Institut de police scientifique.

Ehara, Y., Oguri, N., Saito, S., Marumo, Y., 1997. Purge and trap G/C for the forensic analysis of lipstick. Bunseki Kagaku 46 (9): 733–736.

Evett, I.W., Williams, R.L., 1995. A review of the 16 points fingerprints standard in england and wales. Fingerprint Whorld 21 (82): 125–143.

Feldman, M.A., Meloan, C.E., Frizell, C., 1980. Connecting a knife or ice pick to a tire in a tire slashing. J. Forensic Sci. 25 (3).

Fields, C., Falls, H.C., Warren, C.P., Zimberof, M., 1960. The ear of the newborn as an identification constant. Obstret. Gyneol. 16 (1): 98–102.

Flynn, K., Maynard, P., Du Pasquier, E., Lennard, C., Stoilovic, M., Roux, C., 2004. Evaluation of iodine-benzoflavone and ruthenium tetroxide spray reagents for the detection of latent fingerprints at the crime scene. J. Forensic Sci. 49 (4): 707.

Fortunato, S.L., Walton, G., 1998. Development of latent fingerprints from skin. J. Forensic Ident. 48 (6): 704–717.

Gallusser, A., Christinat, G., 1997. Le sort d'une expertise criminalistique et des autres indices dans une affaire de crime d'assassinat manqué. Revue Internationale de Criminologie et de Police Technique 1.

Giang, Y.-S., Wang, S.-M., Cho, L.-L., Yang, C.-K., Lu, C.-C., 2002. Identification of tiny and thin smears of automotive paint following a traffic accident. J. Forensic Sci. 47 (3): 625–629.

Girod, A., 1996. Computerized classification of the shoeprints of burglars' shoes. Forensic Sci. Int. 82 (1): 59–65.

Girod, A., 2002. Exploitation et gestion systématiques des traces de souliers: Une approche complémentaire pour l'investigation des cambriolages. Thèse de doctorat. Institut de police scientifique et de criminologie de Lausanne.

Girod, A., Rochaix, P.-L., Sumi, P.-A., Melia, E., 1999. Case report of identifications using cheek skin patterns. Inform. Bull. Shoeprint/Toolmark Examiners 5 (1): 21–23.

Girod, A., 1997. Technical report—Shoeprints, coherent exploitation and management. Inform. Bull. Shoeprint/Toolmark Examiners 4 (1): 121–128.

Graham, E.A.M., Bowyer, V.L., Martin, V.J., Rutty, G.N., 2007. Investigation into the usefulness of DNA profiling of earprints. Sci. Justice 47 (4): 155–159.

Grieve, M.C., Biermann, T., 1997. The population of coloured textile fibres on outdoor surfaces. Sci. Justice 37 (4): 231–239.

Grieve, M.C., Biermann, T.W., Schaub, K., 2005. The individuality of fibres used to provide forensic evidence—Not all blue polyesters are the same. Sci. Justice 45 (1): 13–28.

Grieve, M.C., Wiggins, K.G., 2001. Fibers under fire: Suggestions for improving their use to provide forensic evidence. J. Forensic Sci. 46 (4): 835–843.

Grzybowski, R.A., Murdock, J.E., 1998. Firearms and toolmark identification: Meeting the daubert challenge. Assoc. Firearms Toolmark Examiners J. 30 (1): 3–14.

Gupta, N., Saroa, J.S., Sharma, R.S., 2006. Thin-layer chromatography of nail enamels. J. Forensic Ident. 56 (2): 198–209.

Hale, A.R., 1952. Morphogenesis of volar skin in the human fetus. Am. J. Anat. 91 (1): 147–181.

Hall, D., 2004. Quality matters: Science, advocacy, investigation. Sci. Justice 44 (2): 107–110.

Hammer, H.J, Neubert, C.J., 1989. Experimentelle Untersuchungen zur Auswertung von Ohrabdrücken. Kriminalistik und forensische Wissenschaften. Heft 73–74, 136–139.

Hammer, H.J., 1986. The identification of ear prints secured at the scene of the crime. Fingerprint World 12 (46): 49–51.

Hammer, H.J., Howorka, H., Jordan, H., Lindner, R., 1986. Identification of latent fingerprints on difficult surfaces using the iodine steam process. Fingerprint Whorld 11 (43): 56–61.

Hammer, L., Wolfe, J., 2003. Shoe and tire impressions in snow: Photography and casting. J. Forensic Ident. 53 (6): 647–655.

Haque, F., Westland, A., Kerr, F.M., 1983. An improved non-destructive method for detection of latent fingerprints on documents with iodine-7,8-benzoflavone. Forensic Sci. Int. 21: 79–83.

Hauze, D.B., Petrovskaia, O., Taylor, B., Joullie, M.M., Ramotowski, R., Cantu, A.A., 1998. 1,2-indanediones: New reagents for visualizing the amino acid components of latent prints. J. Forensic Sci. 43 (4): 744–747.

Hebrard, J., Donche, A., 1994. Fingerprint detection methods on skin: Experimental study on 16 live subjects and 23 cadavers. J. Forensic Ident. 44 (6): 623–631.

Houck, M.M., 2010. An investigation into the foundational principles of forensic science. PhD Thesis. Curtin University of Technology.

Howitt, D., Tulleners, F., Cebra, K., Chen, S., 2008. A calculation of the theoretical significance of matched bullets. J. Forensic Sci. 53 (4): 868–875.

Hueske, E.E., 1991. Photographing and casting footwear/tiretrack impressions. J. Forensic Ident. 41 (3): 92–95.

Humm, I., Coquoz, R., Lennard, C., Margot, P., 1990. L'utilisation des techniques radioactives pour la visualisation des empreintes digitales. Revue Internationale de Criminologie et de Police Scientifique 1/90, 101–107.

Hunger, H., Hammer, H.J., 1989. Zu Fragen der Identifikation durch Ohrmerkmale. Kriminalistik und forensische Wissenschaften. Heft 65–66, 75–79.

Ianarelli, A., 1968. L'identification par les oreilles. Revue Internationale de Police Criminelle, 227–229.

Imhofer, R., 1906. Die Bedeutung der Ohrmüschel für die Feststellung der Identität. Archiv für Kriminologie 26: 150–163.

Inman, K., Rudin, N., 2001. Principles and Practice of Criminalistics—The Profession of Forensic Science. CRC Press, Boca Raton, FL.

Jasuja, O.P., Jasvir, S., Manjari, J., 1992. Estimation of stature from foot and shoe measurements by multiplication factors: A revised attempt. Forensic Sci. Int. 50: 203–215.

Jasuja, O.P., Singh, G.P., Sodhi, G.S., 2008. Small particle reagents: Development of fluorescent variants. Sci. Justice 48 (3): 141–145.

Jochem, G., Lehnert, R.J., 2003. On the potential of Raman microscopy for the forensic analysis of coloured textile fibres. Sci. Justice 42 (4): 215–222.

Jones, N., Kelly, M., Stoilovic, M., Lennard, C., Roux, C., 2002. The development of latent fingerprints on polymer banknotes. J. Forensic Ident. 53 (1): 50–77.

Jones, N., Lennard, C., Stoilovic, M., Roux, C., 2003. An evaluation of multimetal deposition II. J. Forensic Ident. 53 (4): 444–488.

Jones, N., Mansour, D., Stoilovic, M., Lennard, C., Roux, C., 2001a. The influence of polymer type, print donor and age on the quality of fingerprints developed on plastic substrates using vacuum metal deposition. Forensic Sci. Int. 124: 167–177.

Jones, N., Stoilovic, M., Lennard, C., Roux, C., 2001b. Vacuum metal deposition: Developing latent fingerprints on polyethylene substrates after the deposition of excess gold. Forensic Sci. Int. 123: 5–12.

Jones, N., Stoilovic, M., Lennard, C., Roux, C., 2001c. Vacuum metal deposition: Factors affecting normal and reverse development of latent fingerprints on polyethylene substrates. Forensic Sci. Int. 115: 73–88.

Kaur, S., Singh, J., Garg, R.K., 2009. An examination of lip glosses by thin-layer chromatography. J. Forensic Ident. 59 (5): 525–536.

Kaye, D., 2009. Identification, individualization, uniqueness: What's the difference. Law Probab. Risk 8: 85–94.

Kempton, J.B., Sirignano, A., DeGaetano, D.H., Yates, P.J., Rowe, W.F., 1992. Comparison of fingernail striation patterns in identical twins. J. Forensic Sci. 37 (6): 1534–1540.

King, W.R., 2009. The effects of differential cyanoacrylate fuming times on the development of fingerprints on skin. J. Forensic Ident. 59 (5): 537–544.

Kummer, S., Bonfanti, M., Gallusser, A., 1997. Le processus de reproduction des clés et son intérêt en sciences forensiques (partie 1). Revue internationale de police technique 4/97: 479–492.

Kuppuswamy, R., Ponnuswamy, P.K., 2000. Note on fabric marks in motor vehicle collisions. Sci. Justice 40 (1): 45–47.

Kwan, Q.Y., 1976. Inference of Identity of Source. Dissertation thesis for the Doctorat in Criminology. Berkeley University.

Lambourne, G., 1987. Glove print identification. Criminologist 11 (1): 2–17.

Lavabre, R., Baudoin, P., 2001. Examination of lightbulb filaments after a car crash: Difficulties in interpreting the results. J. Forensic Sci. 46 (1): 141–155.

Layton, J.J., 1966. Identification from a bitemark in cheese. J. Forensic Sci. Soc. 6: 76–80.

Lee, H.C., Palmbach, T., Miller, M.T., 2001. Henry Lee's Crime Scene Handbook. Academic Press, New York.

LeMay, J., 2010. If the shoe fits: An illustration of the relevance of footwear impression evidence and comparisons. J. Forensic Ident. 60 (3): 352–356.

LeMay, J., 2010. The documentation of a large outdoor crime scene with a large number of footwear impressions: Their analysis and comparison. J. Forensic Ident. 60 (6): 738–747.

Lennard, C.J., Margot, P., Sterns, M., Warrener, R.N., 1987. Photoluminescent enhancement of ninhydrine developed fingerprints by metal complexation: Structural studies of complexes formed between ruhemann's purple and group IIb metal salts. J. Forensic Sci. 32 (3): 597–605.

Locke, R.L., 2006. Characteristics of knife cuts in tires. Assoc. Firearm Tool Mark Examiners J. 38 (1): 56–65.

Lounsbury, D.A., Thompson, L.F., 2007. J. Forensic Ident. 57 (2): 223–229.

Lukens, H.R., Bryan, D.E., 1974. The DS method for evidence characterization. J. Forensic Sci. 19 (4): 855–863.

Maccrehan, W.A., Reardon, M.R., Duewer, D.L., 2002. Associating gunpowder and residues from commercial ammunition using compositional analysis. J. Forensic Sci. 47 (2): 260–266.

Majamaa, H., 1997. Pathfinder: A new electrostatic dustprint lifter. Inform. Bull. SP/TM Examiners 3 (3): 15–18.

Margot, P., Lennard, C., 1988. Méthodes physico-chimiques récentes et séquences de détection des empreintes digitales. Revue Internationale de Criminologie et de Police Technique 2/88: 214–250.

Martin, J.-C., 2002. Investigation de scène de crime. Fixation de l'état des lieux et traitement des traces d'objets. Presses polytechniques et universitaires romandes. Lausanne.

Mashiko, K., German, E.R., Motojima, K., Colman, C.D., 1991. RTX: A new ruthenium tetroxide fuming procedure. J. Forensic Ident. 41 (6): 429–445.

Mashiko, K., Miyamoto, T., 1998. Latent fingerprint processing by the ruthenium tetroxyde method. J. Forensic Ident. 48 (3): 279–290.

Masters, N.E., DeHaan, J.D., 1996. Vacuum metal deposition (VMD) and cyanoacrylate detection of older latent prints. J. Forensic Ident. 46 (1): 32–48.

McDermott, S.D., Willis, S.M., 1997. A survey of the evidential value of paint transfer evidence. J. Forensic Sci. 42 (6): 1012–1018.

McLaren, C., Lennard, C., Stoilovic, M., 2010. Methylamine pretreatment of dry latent fingerprints on polyethylene for enhanced detection by cyanoacrylate fuming. J. Forensic Ident. 60 (2): 199–222.

Medley, L., 2010. The distribution of anti-felon identification tags. J. Forensic Ident. 60 (5): 501–509.

Menzel, E.R., Bartsch, R.A., Hallman, J.L., 1990. Fluorescent metal-ruhemann's purple coordination compounds: Applications to latent fingerprint detection. J. Forensic Sci. 35 (1): 25–34.

Merrill, R.A., Bartick, E.G., 2000. Analysis of pressure sensitive adhesive tape: I. evaluation of infrared ATR accessory advances. J. Forensic Sci. 45 (1): 93–98.

Migron, Y., Hocherman, G., Spinger, E., Almog, J., Mandler, D., 1998. Visualisation of sebaceous fingerprints on fired cartridge cases: A laboratory study. J. Forensic Sci. 43 (3): 543–548.

Miller, J., 2001a. An examination of the application of the conservative criteria for identification of striated toolmarks using bullets fired from ten consecutively rifled barrels. Assoc. Firearms Toolmarks Examiners 33 (2): 125–132.

Miller, J., 2001b. An introduction to the forensic examination of toolmarks. Assoc. Firearms Tollmarks Examiners 33 (3): 233–248.

Milne, R., 1987. The "pathfinder" wireless electrostatic mark lifing machine and the electrostatic lifting of shoe, tyre, and finger marks at crime scenes. Fingerprint Whorld 23 (88): 53–62.

Misner, A., 1992. Latent fingerprint detection on low density polyethylene comparing vacuum metal deposition to cyanoacrylate fuming and fluorescence. J. Forensic Ident. 42 (1): 26–33.

Moran, B., 2001. The application of numerical criteria for identification in casework involving magazine marks and land impressions. Assoc. Firearms Toolmarks Examiners 33 (1): 41–46.

Morgan, R.M., Bull, P.A., 2007. The use of grain size distribution analysis of sediments and soils in forensic enquiry. Sci. Justice 47 (3): 125–135.

Murphy, K.A., Cartner, A.M., Henderson, W., Kim, N.D., 1999. Appraisal of the porphyrin compound, (TPP)Sn(OH)2, as a latent fingerprint reagent. J. Forensic Ident. 49 (3): 269–282.

Napier, T.J., 2002. Scene linking using footwear mark databases. Sci. Justice 42 (1): 39–43.

Naru, A.S., 1997. Methods for the analysis of human bite marks. Forensic Sci. Rev. 9 (2): 123–139.

Naru, A.S., Dykes, E., 1997. Digital image cross-correlation technique for bite mark investigations. Sci. Justice 37 (4): 251–258.

Nause, L.A., 1992. Casting footwear impressions in snow: Snowprint-wax vs. pril sulphur. RCMP Gazette 54 (12): 1–7.

Neumann, C., Champod, C., Puch-Solis, R., Egli, N., Anthonioz, A., Bromage-Griffiths, A., 2007. Computation of likelihood ratios in fingerprint identification for configurations of any number of minutiæ. J. Forensic Sci. 52 (1): 54–64.

Nicdaeid, N., Buchanan, H.A.S., Laing, K., 2009. Evaluation of available techniques for the recovery of latent fingerprints from untreated plywood surfaces. J. Forensic Ident. 59 (4): 441–465.

Nichols, R.G., 1997. Firearm and toolmark identification criteria: A review of the literature. J. Forensic Sci. 42 (3): 466–474.

Nichols, R.G., 2007. Defending the scientific foundations of the firearms and tool mark identification discipline: Responding to recent challenges. J. Forensic Sci. 52 (3): 586–594.

Onstwedder III, J., Gamboe, T.E., 1989. Small particle reagent: Developing latent prints on water-soaked firearms and effect on firearms analysis. J. Forensic Sci. 34 (2): 321–327.

Osterburg, J.W., 1969. The evaluation of physical evidence in criminalistics: Subjective or objective process? J. Crim. Law Criminol. Police Sci. 50 (1).

Oz, C., Zamir, A., 2000. An evaluation of the relevance of routine DNA typing of fingernail clippings for forensic casework. J. Forensic Sci. 45 (1): 158–160.

Parry, D., 1998. Beating the burglars with 'smart ware' products. J. Forensic Sci. Serv. 26: 57–59.

Pepper, I., Pepper, H., 2005. Assessing the competency of crime scene investigators in the United Kingdom. J. Forensic Ident. 55 (4): 442–447.

Pertson, W.J., 1987. Ear, lip and nose prints: Another means of identification. RCMP Gazette 49 (9): 12–15.

Philipson, D., Bleay, S., 2007. Alternative metal processes for vacuum metal deposition. J. Forensic Ident. 57 (2): 252–273.

Poorman, J.K., Spring, T.F., 2004. Impact marks from ejected cartridge casings. J. Forensic Ident. 54 (5): 525–529.

Pounds, C.A., Smalldon, K.W., 1975a. The transfer of fibres between clothing materials during simulated contacts and their persistence during wear. Part I—Fibre transference. J. Forensic Sci. Soc. 15: 17–28.

Pounds, C.A., Smalldon, K.W., 1975b. The transfer of fibres between clothing materials during simulated contacts and their persistence during wear. Part II—Fibre persistence. J. Forensic Sci. Soc. 15: 29–38.

Pounds, C.A., Smalldon, K.W., 1975c. The transfer of fibres between clothing materials during simulated contacts and their persistence during wear. Part III—A preliminary investigation of the mechanisms involved. J. Forensic Sci. Soc. 15: 197–207.

Pretty, I..A., Turnbull, M.D., 2001. Lack of dental uniqueness between two bite mark suspects. J. Forensic Sci. 46 (6): 1487–1491.

Pretty, I.A., Sweet, D., 2001. The scientific basis for human bitemark analyses—A critical review. Sci. Justice 41 (2): 85–92.

Quinche, N., Margot, P., 2010. Coulier Paul-Jean (1824-1890): A precursor in the history of fingerprint detection and their potential use for identifying their source (1863). J. Forensic Ident. 60 (2): 129–134.

Ramotowski, R.S., 2001. Composition of latent print residue. In: Lee, H.C., Gaensslen, R.E. (Eds.), Advances in Fingerprint Technology. CRC Press, Boca Raton, FL, pp. 63–104.

Ramotowski, R., Cantu, A.A., 2001. Recent latent print visualisation research at the US secret service. Fingerprint Whorld 27 (104): 59–65.

Rathman, G.A., 1992. Tires and toolmarks. Assoc. Firearms Tool Mark Examiners 24 (2): 146–159.

Ravikumar, R., Rajan, P., Thirunavukkarasu, G., 2006. Bullets without striations—Fired or unfired? J. Forensic Ident. 56 (5): 730–736.

Rawji, A., Beaudoin, A., 2006. Oil red O versus physical developer on wet papers: A comparative study. J. Forensic Ident. 56 (1): 33–54.

Raymond, J.J., Roux, C., Du Pasquier, E., Sutton, J., Lennard, C., 2004. The effect of common fingerprint detection techniques on the DNA typing of fingerprints deposited on different surfaces. J. Forensic Ident. 54 (1): 22–44.

Reinholz, A.D., 2008. Albumin development method to visualize friction ridge detail on porous surfaces. J. Forensic Ident. 58 (5): 524–539.

Ribaux, O., Margot, P., 2007. Chapitre 21: La trace matérielle, vecteur d'information au service du renseignement. in Traité de sécurité intérieure. Presses polytechniques et universitaires romandes, Lausanne, sous la direction de Maurice Cusson, pp. 300–321.

Ribaux, O., Baylon, A., Lock, E., Delemont, O., Roux, C., Zingg, C., et al., 2010. Intelligence-led crime scene processing. Part II: Intelligence and crime scene examination. Forensic Sci. Int. 199: 63–71.

Ribaux, O., Girod, A., Walsh, S.J., Margot, P., Mizrahi, S., Clivaz, V., 2003. Forensic intelligence and crime analysis. Law, Probab. Risk 2: 47–60.

Ribaux, O., Margot, P., 2003. Case based reasoning in criminal intelligence using forensic case data. Sci. Justice 43 (3): 135–144.

Robertson, B., Vignaux, G.A., 1995. Interpreting Evidence—Evaluating Forensic Science in the Courtroom. John Wiley and Sons, New York.

Robson, D., 1994. Fibre surface imaging. J. Forensic Sci. Soc. 34 (3): 187–191.

Roux, C., Gill, K., Sutton, J., Lennard, C., 1999. A further study to investigate the effect of fingerprint enhancement techniques on the DNA analysis of bloodstains. J. Forensic Ident. 49 (4): 357–376.

Roux, C., Margot, P., 1997. An attempt to assess the relevance of textile fibres recovered from car seats. Sci. Justice 37 (4): 225–230.

Roux, C., Margot, P., 1994. L'estimation de la valeur indiciale des fibres textiles découvertes en relation avec une affaire criminelle—Utopie ou réalité? Revue internationale de police technique 2/94: 229–241.

Salama, J., Aumeer-Donovan, S., Lennard, C., Roux, C., 2008. Evaluation of the fingerprint reagent oil red O as a possible replacement for physical developer. J. Forensic Ident. 58 (2): 203–237.

Sarkissian, G., 2007. The analysis of tire rubber traces collected after braking incidents using pyrolysis-gas chromatography/mass spectrometry. J. Forensic Sci. 52 (5): 1050–1056.

Schwartz, A., 2005. A systematic challenge to the reliability and admissibility of firearms and toolmark identification. Columbia Sci. Technol. Law Rev. VI: 1–42.

Segura, M.A., 2001. Footprints and tire marks. Forensic Sci. Dig. 7 (1): 1–17.

Shin, S.H., Argue, D.G., 1976. Identification of fingerprints left on human skin. Can. Soc. Forensic Sci. J. 9 (2): 81–84.

Shor, Y., Tsach, T., Vinokurov, A., Glattstein, B., Landau, E., Levin, N., 2003. Lifting shoeprints using gelatin lifters and a hydraulic press. J. Forensic Sci. 48 (2): 368–372.

Shor, Y., Tsach, T., Wiesner, S., Meir, G., 2005. Removing interfering contaminations from gelatin lifters. J. Forensic Sci. 50 (6): 1386–1393.

Shor, Y., Vinokurov, A., Glattstein, B., 1998. The use of an adhesive lifter and ph indicator for the removal and enhancement of shoeprints in dust. J. Forensic Sci. 43 (1): 182–184.

Shor, Y., Wiesner, S., 1999. A survey on the conclusions drawn on the same footwear marks obtained in actual cases by several experts throughout the world. J. Forensic Sci. 44 (2): 380–384.

Siegel, J.A., 1997. Evidential value of textile fibre—Transfer and persistence of fibres. Forensic Sci. Rev. 9 (2): 81–96.

Siegel, S.D., 2007. A modified iodine-fuming method. J. Forensic Ident. JFI 57 (3): 378–382.

Simon, A., Jordan, H., Pforte, K., 1974. Successful identification of a bitemark in a sandwich. Int. J. Forensic Dent. 2: 17.

Sirois, J.B., 1992. Glove dots digits finger suspects. R. Can. Mounted Police Gazette 54 (2): 12–17.

Skreptak, M.G., 1988. Preservation of impressions in slush prior to casting. Ident. Can. 11 (2): 4–5.

Smalldon, K.W., Moffat, A.C., 1973. The calculation of discriminating power for a series of correlated attributes. J. Forensic Sci. Soc. 13: 291–295.

Sodhi, G.S., Kaur, J., 2002. Fingerprint detection using phloxine B dye. J. Forensic Ident. 53 (1): 8–13.

Sodhi, G.S., Kaur, J., Garg, R.K., 2004. Fingerprint powder formulations based on organic, fluorescent dyes. J. Forensic Ident. 54 (1): 4–8.

Soule, R.L., 1961. Reproduction of foot and tire tracks by plaster of paris casting. Ident. News, 8–12.

Spencer, R., 1994. Significant fiber evidence recovered from the clothing of a homicide victim after exposure to the elements for twenty-nine days. J. Forensic Sci. 39: 854–859.

Stauffer, E., 2007. Interpretation of automotive light bulb examination results: An intriguing case. J. Forensic Sci. 52 (1): 119–124.

Stewart, G.D., 1990. Sexual assault evidence collection procedures. J. Forensic Ident. 40 (2): 69–74.

Stoddart, T.J., 1973. Bitemarks in perishable substances. Br. Dent. J. 135 (6): 285–287.

Stoilovic, M., Lennard, C., Wallace-Kunkel, C., Roux, C., 2007. Evaluation of a 1,2-indanedione formulation containing zinc chloride for improved fingerprint detection on paper. J. Forensic Ident. 57 (1): 4–18.

Stoney, D.A., Thornton, J.I., 1986. A critical analysis of quantitative fingerprint individuality models. J. Forensic Sci. 31 (4): 1187–1216.

Suzuki, S., Suzuki, Y., Ohta, H., 2002. Detection of latent fingerprints on newly developed substances using the vacuum metal deposition. J. Forensic Ident. 52 (5): 573–578.

SWGTREAD, 2007a. Guide for the forensic documentation and photography of footwear and tire impressions at the crime scene. J. Forensic Ident. 57 (6): 912–917.

SWGTREAD, 2007b. Guide for casting footwear and tire impression evidence. J. Forensic Ident. 57 (6): 918–924.

SWGTREAD, 2007c. Guide for lifting footwear and tire impression evidence. J. Forensic Ident. 57 (6): 925–929.

Taroni, F., Aitken, C.G.G., Biedermann, A., Garbolino, P., 2006. Bayesian networks and probabilistic inference in forensic science. John Wiley and Sons, New York.

Taroni, F., Champod, C., Margot, P., 1998. Forerunners of bayesianism in early forensic science. Jurimetrics J. 38: 183–200.

Taroni, F., Margot, P., 2000. Fingerprint evidence—Correspondence. Sci. Justice 40 (4): 277–278.

Thali, M.J., Braun, M., Brüschweiler, W., Dirnhofer, R., 2000. Matching tire tracks on the head using forensic photogrammetry. Forensic Sci. Int. 113 (1–3): 281–287.

Trapecar, M., Balazic, J., 2007. Fingerprint recovery from human skin surfaces. Sci. Justice 47 (3): 136–140.

Tsuchihashi, Y., 1974. Studies on personal identification by means of lip print. Forensic Sci. Int. 3: 233–248.

Van der Lugt, C., 1997. Determining a person's height based upon the vertical distance of a located earprint. J. Forensic Ident. 47 (4): 406–419.

Van der Lugt, C., 1998. Ear identification-state of the art. Inform. Bull. Shoeprint/Toolmark Examiners 4 (1): 69–81.

Van Dijk, T.M., 2000. Tools. In: Siegel, J., Knupfer, G., Saukko, P. (Eds.), Encyclopedia of forensic sciences, in three volumes, pp. 1216–1228.

Vanderkolk, J.R., 1993. Class characteristics and could be results. J. Forensic Ident. 43: 119–125.

Vanderkolk, J.R., 1995. Identifying consecutively made garbage bags through manufactured characteristics. J. Forensic Ident. 45 (1): 38–50.

Walbridge, S., 2009. Determining the sheddability of various fiber types. MS Thesis, Michigan State University.

Wallace, J.S., 1990. Criminal aspects of firearms ammunition. Assoc. Firearms Toolmarks Examiners 22 (4).

Wallace-Kunkel, C., Roux, C., Lennard, C, Stoilovic, M., 2004. The detection and enhancement of latent fingerprints on porous surfaces—A survey. J. Forensic Ident. 54 (6): 687–705.

Watkin, J.E., Wilkinson, D.A., Misner, A.H., Yamashito, A.B., 1994. Cyanoacrylate fuming of latent prints: Vacuum versus heat/humidity. J. Forensic Ident. 44 (5): 545–556.

Webb, L.G., Egan, S.E., Turbett, G.R., 2001. Recovery of DNA for forensic analysis from lip cosmetics. J. Forensic Sci. 46 (6): 1474–1479.

Wertheim, K., Maceo, A.V., 2002. Friction ridge and pattern formation during the critical stage. J. Forensic Ident. 52 (1): 35–85.

Wiggins, K., Drummond, P., Hicks Champod, T., 2004. A study in relation to the random distribution of four fibre types on clothing (incorporating a review of previous target fibre studies). Sci. Justice 44 (3): 141–148.

Wilgus, G., 2002. Latent print recovery from human skin. J. Forensic Ident. 52 (2): 133–136.

Williams, T.R., 1991. Lip prints—Another means of identification. J. Forensic Ident. 41 (3): 190–194.

Wilson, H.D., 2010. RAY dye stain versus gentian violet and alternate powder for development of latent prints on the adhesive side of tape. J. Forensic Ident. 60 (5): 510–523.

Wilson, J.D., 2004. Casting tires with expandable polyurethane foam and other materials. J. Forensic Ident. 54 (2): 158–169.

Wolfe, J.R., 2008. Sulfur cement: A new material for casting snow impression evidence. J. Forensic Ident. 58 (4): 485–498.

Wright, F.D., 1998. Photography in bite mark and patterned injury documentation— Parts I & II. J. Forensic Sci. 43 (4): 877–887.

Other Types of Evidence

Because anything can be evidence, sometimes it is difficult to characterize or classify an individual item or a piece of evidence. Some evidence is both the substrate and the trace, for example, like a questioned document, and other types are means to a criminal act, like a cellphone. Evidence can be both biological and physical (like diatoms), or even be living (as with insects) or the by-products of life (like odors). This chapter will address a variety of evidence to be encountered by CSIs that may not fit into traditional crime scene categories.

Key Terms

Questioned documents
Digital evidence
Pollen
Forensic anthropology
Forensic entomology
Diatoms

Questioned Documents

Questioned documents analysis[1] covers a wide range of skills in forensic science from forgery and counterfeiting (Pfefferli, 2000) to handwriting analysis (Vos et al., 2000) or printed materials identification (from a printer,

---

[1] This is not to be confused with graphology, the pseudo-scientific study of handwriting of which the claims have not been verified.

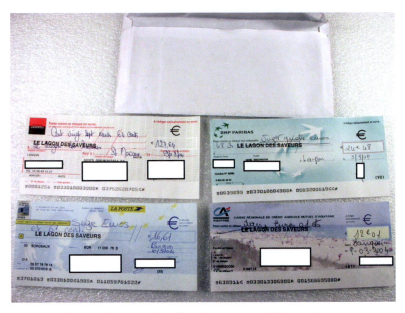

FIGURE 6.4.1 Questioned documents collected for writing comparisons. *With permission, courtesy Francis Hebrard, 2004.*

a typewriter, a photocopier, or a pen) through document dating (Purdy, 2000) or document security (Dalrymple, 2004). It uses pattern recognition methodologies, optical methods, including microscopy, and chemical analyses for ink, paint, or paper identification. Modern documents can be complicated and questioned document examination (QDE) may include identification of credit cards, driver licenses, passports, etc. (Gaudreau et al., 1997; Michaud and Estabrooks, 1998) (Figure 6.4.1). Interestingly, as computer technology has progressed, the number of documents has also increased (Giles, 2000; Greenfield, 2004). While some aspects of QDE—writing or signature comparison—have their detractors (Risinger and Saks, 1996; Evett, 2000; Zlotnick and Lin, 2001; Asicioglu and Turan, 2003; Found and Rogers, 2005; Taroni and Biedermann, 2005), they can provide some forensic information or, at the very least, investigative leads.

It should be no surprise that documents can be both the means of a crime and the substrate on which other evidence is found, like DNA or fingerprints, but also shoeprints or toolmarks (Bullock et al., 1994; Scarborough, 2001; Chaudhry and Pant, 2004; Scarborough and Dziemieszko, 2004; Mazella and Taroni, 2005; Lin et al., 2007; Mahajan and Arya, 2007), as they can even be traced when produced by computer facilities (Hill, 1999). Because even a single document can be exposed to numerous types of analysis or examination, including determining the integrity, falsity, identity, or origin (of both the materials used and the user) of documents, CSIs should not only focus on the document material itself, but also on all the materials constituting the evidence, like staples, tape, or clips, along with associated

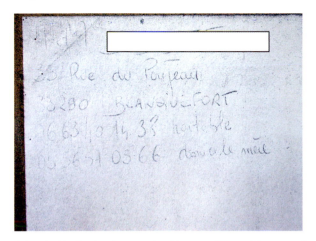

FIGURE 6.4.2 Indented writing developed on a questioned document. *With permission, courtesy Francis Hebrard, 2004.*

putative sources collected at the scene, like a ream of paper, printer or copier samples, pens, inks, etc. (Moryan, 2002; Spence et al., 2002).

The often fragile nature of documents means that great attention should be paid to protect such items of evidence. Paper bags or envelopes are the preferred means of storage and preservation; single-use plastic cases may allow access without touching the document. Sealed plastic bags, however, may also damage biological evidence, so care must be used. The CSI can help the QD examiner by noting the following (Levinson, 2001):

- Regarding a writing comparison: physical condition, surface of writing, and position of the writer.
- Fax machines, copiers, printers, typewriters, checkwriters, etc. leave marks on papers, from scratches present on the glass plate or repeated grip or trash marks.
- Other pieces of office equipment may also be relevant, such as paper cutters, staples, stamps, seals, paper clips, adhesive tapes, and so on, which may link a group of documents processed in the same way.

Indented handwriting examination can be carried out on documents without disturbing other evidence, like fingerprints (Barr et al., 1996) (Figure 6.4.2).

Computers, Cellphones, and Other Mass Storages

The range of electronic objects that may appear at a crime scene and their exploitation as evidence is vast (Marshall and Tompsett, 2002; Casey, 2004, 2009) and well beyond the scope of this book. CSIs should, nevertheless, be aware of potential objects that would keep digital "traces," how to collect the item, and occasionally, before switching it off, how to record a copy of volatile data (RAM data) without any loss of integrity of the original data using tools like Microsoft COFEE (Computer Online Forensic Evidence Extractor), which is specially dedicated to law enforcement investigations.

Classical devices containing digital data are computers, external disk drives (HDDs), compact discs (CD/DVD/Blu-ray), universal serial bus (USB) flash drives, memory cards, and DAT bands, but digital data are also stored on mobile phones, smart phones, and subscriber identity module (SIM) cards. Other media include smart cards (bank and credit cards, identification cards, season tickets, national insurance cards, discount cards, etc.), global positioning service (GPS) units (which records trips, addresses, and also the serial number of the vehicle, if it is integrated), and portable media players/computers (iPods, iPads, and the like) that can store any files, not just music. The list becomes more extensive when digital voice recorders, digital picture frame devices, and industrial photocopiers or industrial tracking systems, like radio-frequency identification (RFID) readers, are included.

A digital crime scene, much like the devices that comprise it, is composed of software and hardware. The digital crime scene collection process is better divided into two phases: system preservation and evidence collection (Carrier, 2005). The system preservation step aims to preserve the state of the digital crime scene, to reduce the amount of evidence that may be lost (volatile or overwritten). For a live analysis, the computer should be first disconnected physically from any network to avoid log messages, preventing connection from a remote system to modify or delete data. Any open files should be recorded on a temporal buffer directory to dismiss overwriting the originals. Software, like COFEE, can be of some use to collect volatile data on a USB drive immediately. Once the live data are secured, the system can be turned off for a dead analysis: simply switch off the computer without using the software prompts or menus. Duplicate copies of mass storage devices facilitate further analyses (Olivier and Shenoi, 2006).

When data are saved during a live or dead analysis, a cryptographic hash (such as MD5 or SHA-1) should be calculated to be later compared with hashes from copies. An identical hash deciphering would mean that data did not change even by one bit.

Likewise, a CSI could be requested to rapidly identify a connected device on the network (Marshall, 2003), in case of embezzlement, blackmail, or Internet frauds, for instance. Three important pieces of connection data should then be collected: an Internet Protocol (IP) address, the date and time of the connection, and the time zone of the device. Websites, such as http://ip-address.com, allow the CSI to collect the relevant IP address data to identify the user. Finally, data damaged through neglect or accident may be at least partly, if not fully, retrieved (Ross and Gow, 1999).

Pollen

Palynology is the study of the reproductive grains and spores of plants, called pollen. Pollen is specific to each type of plant and the grains themselves are very resistant to damage. The mixture of various pollens and spores characterizes a pollen batch, which has the ability to infer an environmental area (Taylor and Skene, 2003; Walsh and Horrocks, 2008). For instance, pollen found on the clothing of a suspect who brushed against flowers could support his presence in this area (Horrocks and Walsh, 2001; Brown et al., 2002; MacKay, 2009). Palynology can also be used with success to link illicit plant material specimens or samples, like cannabis, to a similar batch or determine the type of culture it was raised in (indoor or outdoor) (Coyle, 2005).

Pollen are easily identified by a specialist through microscopy; DNA analysis of pollen, as well as spores or fungi, can also be carried out by specialists (Weising et al., 1994). Rough or porous surfaces easily trap pollen grains and these materials should be collected and packaged in a paper bag for later analysis. Pollen may also be collected by swabbing objects with distilled water and retaining the swab as well as the item (Bull et al., 2006). Control samples should also be collected, with flowers coming first, leaves second, and branches last.

Bones

Decomposed bodies, skeletons, or single bones are another kind of evidence the CSI may have to deal with. Skeletal material on the surface should be flagged and collected systematically; buried remains should be excavated using basic archaeological techniques (Duhig, 2003). As with archaeological excavations of human remains, the body should be carefully and fully uncovered, one layer at a time, before any individual bone is removed (unless there is a danger of damage or loss). The ground should be cleared of all vegetation, the grave delineated, and the "work zone" kept clear of all personnel except those excavating. A trench may be dug alongside the grave to minimize damage during excavation. The soil is then removed in shallow layers, about 2–4 cm at a time. Photographs should document all of the steps and the whole uncovered body. All recovered soil should be sieved during excavation to help collect small pieces of bones or artifacts, such as bullets (Stout and Ross, 1991; Wood and Elmhurst, 1999; Warren and Schultz, 2002).

Bones can provide species identification, anatomical information, sex, age at death, and stature. Skeletal evidence can also infer disease, illness, or physical abnormalities, and assist with determining a postmortem interval and other taphonomic phenomena like scavenging, plant activity, thermal alteration or deterioration (Micozzi, 1991; Haglund and Reay, 1993; Adair, 1998; Pickering, 2001), and perimortem or healed trauma like fractures, blunt-force trauma, or sharp-force trauma (Bartelink et al., 2001; Ubelaker and Scammel, 1997; Reichs, 1998). Prosthetic devices should also be recognized and carefully

FIGURE 6.4.3 Femur articular prosthesis in a badly burnt and scavenged body. *With permission, courtesy Thierry Lezeau, 2005.*

collected, as they may provide relevant identification data regarding their manufacturer, model, or "owner" (Warren and Schultz, 2002) (Figure 6.4.3). The skull can also provide investigative leads through facial restoration or reconstruction (Owsley et al., 1992; Taylor and Gatliff, 1998; Coy and Ohlson, 2000; Rogers, 2005; Rogers and Goodheart, 2008; Stephan, 2002).

DNA analysis is available either on soft tissue samples on the bone marrow, as long as they are not putrefied, or the hard tissue of the bone itself (Lee et al., 1991; Al-Enizi et al., 2008; Coticone et al., 2010). Tooth pulp (dentin) is also a possible site of DNA recovery, either nuclear or mtDNA (Holland et al., 1995).

Insects and Time Since Death

Various methods are available to estimate time since death (the postmortem interval, or PMI), which are more or less accurate depending on the premise of the method and the relevant environmental conditions. Internal or external temperature, vitreous humor, development of livor mortis and adipocere, and chemical analysis are some methods that have been used. Environmental (temperature, humidity) and physiological (size, weight, and health of the victim) conditions can bias these methods, however; advanced decomposition often introduces an unacceptable error rate for them as well. Flies and necrophagous insects are less affected by such factors and can produce quite accurate PMIs. Minutes after death, blow flies arrive to lay eggs or live young (larvae; singular larva) in the dead flesh that will nurture them. Waves of insect activity assist and accelerate the decomposition process, depending on the state of decomposition of the corpse and the geographic area where it is located. Necrophagous insects are followed by insect predators and opportunistic species, some of them carnivorous, but all of them having their own predictable life spans. It is these life spans that allow forensic entomologists to determine how long a body has been exposed to insects present.

Collecting both maggots (juvenile insects) from and around the body and the remnants of their development (small, hard cases called pupae) allow the entomologists to infer the sequence of insects up to the first arrival. Other available information an entomologist might be able to provide would include the time of year a species is more active, if the body has been moved, or species that are notably absent, which might indicate attempts to obscure a crime. Collection of such evidence should follow the following protocol (Erzinçlioglu, 1990, 1991; Schoenly et al., 1991; Merritt et al., 2000; Adams and Hall, 2003; Huntington et al., 2007):

- Eggs and larvae are to be collected on and under the body with plastic tweezers or a scoop, placing them in glass or plastic containers. Place the larvae and insects collected on the body in a jar containing ethanol.
- Some species move away from a body to finish their life cycle underground. Therefore, half a dozen drill holes should be made randomly at a distance of 2–3 meters away around the body at a depth of 30–50 cm, depending on the nature of soil, to collect pupae and even larvae. Those maggots and pupae should also be preserved in alcohol.
- On and around the body, live specimens should be collected to be reared to adulthood. Live maggots should be placed in a cardboard container on fresh meat (place aluminum foil underneath) and kept at room temperature.
- All the specimens should be transported as soon as possible to the laboratory.
- An aerial sweep with a net above the body could be of some use to collect flying adult insects.

Water insects could also be analyzed for partially or fully immersed corpses (Hobischak and Anderson, 2002; Wallace et al., 2008). Further analyses on maggots are possible, including drugs in larvae from having fed on drugged tissues, DNA identification of insects, or even extracting human DNA from insects' guts.

Diatoms

Diatoms are microscopic unicellular algae that have a silica shell resistant to acids, heat, or body decomposition. They live in colonies, grow in abundance in fresh and salt waters, and their "skeletons" are widespread in soils. They belong to a class of more than 300 kinds and 1000 species (Peabody, 1977) (Figure 6.4.4).

Diatoms can be used to determine a lethal drowning: A massive inhalation of water introduces the diatoms into the lungs and they break through the

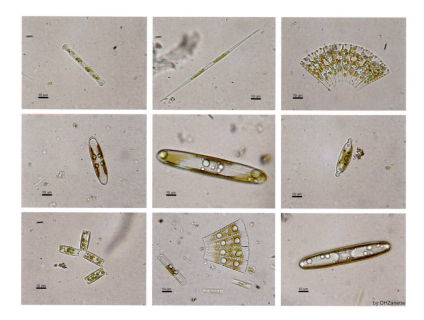

thin walls of the lungs and move to deeper organs through the bloodstream (Antonenko and Ferris, 1987). Because of the various environmental and nutritional requirements specific to each species, no two identical diatoms flora will be found within the same river or between two distant points of a few kilometers, or even at the same spot at two different times of the year. A qualitative and quantitative comparative analysis between diatoms found in the body and those from various potential drowning sites could help to locate the place of death (Ludes et al., 1996; Pollanen et al., 1997a; Horton et al., 2006; Zimmerman and Wallace, 2008).

The diatoms' exoskeleton is sensitive to basic compounds, so glass containers of questioned and known samples should be washed with molar sodium hydroxide (32 g NaOK in 1 liter distilled water) beforehand. At the crime scene, samples of 0.5 l glass containers of surface water and water down to the river bed (if possible; if not, then 50 cm deep in the water) should be taken as references. At autopsy, lung, liver, kidney, brain, and bone marrow biopsies (about 10 g each) will be collected and analyzed by the laboratory (Pollanen et al., 1997b; Ludes et al., 1999). False negatives should be considered, as urban water systems are generally low in diatoms; drowning in a bathtub, for example, might not register any diatoms in the samples.

Odors

Specially trained dogs have been routinely used to search for both live and deceased victims for years, as an efficient and cost-effective means to cover large areas. The quality of canine searches is dependent not only on the animal but also on its handler and environmental conditions; temperature, wind, sunlight, humidity, and barometric pressure are all factors affecting the results (Harvey and Harvey, 2003; Gaine et al., 2008). Canine searches can be useful for unexploded explosives, drugs, paper currency, or accelerant detection (Gialamas, 1996; Mesloh et al., 2002a, 2002b; Nowlan et al., 2007). They are not without their problems, however (Kurz et al., 1996; Tranthim-Fryer and De Haan, 1997; Katz and Midkiff, 1998). Research is ongoing in using dogs for lineup identification, but this use of canines for identification of interviewed suspects should be regarded with caution.

Conclusion

Evidence comes in many forms, including those beyond the standard types expected. Some types of evidence are complicated and not easily categorized. Nevertheless, whether physical, chemical, or biological, all evidence needs to be recognized and recovered to make the most of any useful investigative information.

References and Bibliography

Adair, T.W., 1998. Survival of physical evidence from a scavenged grave: A look at a case study and research from Colorado. J. Forensic Ident. 48 (4): 459–465.

Adair, T.W., Kondratieff, B.C., 2006. Three species of insects collected from an adult human corpse above 3300 m in elevation: A review of a case from Colorado. J. Forensic Sci. 51 (5): 1164–1165.

Adams, Z.J.O., Hall, M.J.R., 2003. Methods used for the killing and preservation of blowfly larvae, and their effect on post-mortem larval length. Forensic Sci. Int. 138 (1–3): 50–61.

Adlam, R.E., Simmons, T.I., 2007. The effect of repeated physical disturbance on soft tissue decomposition—Are taphonomic studies an accurate reflection of decomposition? J. Forensic Sci. 52 (5): 1007–1014.

Aginsky, V., 2000. Analytical methods. In: Siegel, J., Knupfer, G., Saukko, P. (Eds.), Encyclopedia of Forensic Sciences, in three volumes, pp. 566–570.

Al-Enizi, M., Hadi, S., Goodwin, W., 2008. The development of visual and chemical methods for predicting the likelihood of obtaining a DNA profile from degraded bone samples. Forensic Sci. Int. Genet. Suppl. Ser. 1, 2–3.

Anderson, G.S., 1997. The use of insects to determine time of decapitation: A case study from British Columbia. J. Forensic Sci. 42 (5): 947–950.

Anderson, G.S., 2000. Minimum and maximum development rates of some forensically important Calliphoridae (Diptera). J. Forensic Sci. 45 (4): 824–832.

Andrasko, J., 2002. Changes in composition of ballpoint pen inks on aging in darkness. J. Forensic Sci. 47 (2): 324–327.

Antonenko, N.E., Ferris, J.E., 1987. Diatom analysis in the determination of death by drowning. J. Can. Soc. Forensic Sci. 20: 1–11.

Arany, S., Ohtany, S., Yoshioka, N., Gonmori, K., 2004. Age estimation from aspartic acid racemization of root dentin by internal standard method. Forensic Sci. Int. 141: 127–130.

Archer, M.S., Bassed, R.B., Briggs, C.A., Lynch, M.J., 2005. Social isolation and delayed discovery of bodies in houses: The value of forensic pathology, anthropology, odontology and entomology in the medico-legal investigation. Forensic Sci. Int. 151: 259–265.

Asicioglu, F.A., Turan, N., 2003. Handwriting changes under the effect of alcohol. Forensic Sci. Int. 132: 201–210.

Baccino, E., De Saint Martin, L., Schuliar, Y., 1996. Outer ear temperature and time of death. Forensic Sci. Int. 83: 133–146.

Barr, K.J., Pearse, M.L., Welch, J.R., 1996. Secondary impressions of writing and ESDA-detectable paper-paper friction. Sci. Justice 36: 97–100.

Bartelink, E.J., Wiersema, J.S., Demaree, R.S., 2001. Quantitative analysis of sharp trauma: An application of scanning electron microscopy in forensic anthropology. J. Forensic Sci. 46(6): 1288–1293.

Benecke, M., 1998. Random amplified polymorphic DNA (RAPD) typing of necrophageous insects (diptera, coleoptera) in criminal forensic studies: Validation and use in practice. Forensic Sci. Int. 98: 157–168.

Benecke, M., 2001. A brief history of forensic entomology. Forensic Sci. Int. 120 (1–2): 2–14.

Benecke, M., Lessig, R., 2001. Child neglect and forensic entomology. Forensic Sci. Int. 120 (1–2): 155–159.

Bennett, M.J., Ragni, M.C, Hood, I., Hale, D.E., 1996. Comparison of post-mortem urinary and vitreous humour organic acids. Annu. Clin. Biochem. 29 (5): 541–545.

Beyer, J.C., Enos, W.F., Stajic, M., 1980. Drug identification through analysis of maggots. J. Forensic Sci. 25 (2): 411–412.

Bocaz-Beneventi, G., Tagliaro, F., Bortolotti, F., Manetto, G., Havel, J. Capillary zone electrophoresis and artificial neural networks for estimation of the post-mortem interval (PMI) using electrolytes measurements in human vitreous humour. Int. J. Legal Med. 116(1): 5–11.

Bourel, B., Hedouin, V., Martin-Bouyer, L., Becart, A., Tournel, G., Deveaux, M., et al., 1999. Effects of morphine in decomposing bodies on the development of Lucilia sericata (Diptera: calliphoridae). J. Forensic Sci. 44 (2): 354–358.

Bourel, B., Tournel, G., Hedouin, V., Gogg, M.L., Gosset, D., 2001a. Determination of drug levels in two species of necrophagous coleoptera reared on substrates containing morphine. J. Forensic Sci. 46 (2): 600–603.

Bourel, B., Tournel, G., Hedouin, V., Deveaux, M., Goff, M.L., Gosset, D., 2001b. Morphine extraction in necrophagous insects remains for determining ante-mortem opiate intoxication. Forensic Sci. Int. 120 (1–2): 127–131.

Brown, A., Marshall, T.K., 1974. Body temperature as a means of estimating the time of death. Forensic Sci. Int. 4: 125–133.

Brown, A.G., Smith, A., Elmhurst, O., 2002. The combined use of pollen and soil analyses in a search and subsequent murder investigation. J. Forensic Sci. 47 (3): 614–618.

Brunelle, R.L., 2000. Ink analysis. In: Siegel, J., Knupfer, G., Saukko, P. (Eds.), Encyclopedia of Forensic Sciences, in three volumes, pp. 591–597.

Bull, P.A., Morgan, M., Sagovsky, A., Hughes, G.J.A., 2006. The transfer and persistence of trace particulates: Experimental studies using clothing fabrics. Sci. Justice 46 (3): 185–195.

Bullock, K.M., Harris, J.S., Laturnus, P.L., 1994. Use of a simple coaxial lighting system to enhance fingerprint and handwriting evidence. Can. Soc. Forensic Sci. J. 27 (2): 69–80.

Byrd, J.H., Allen, C., 2001. The development of the black blow fly, Phormia regina (Meigen). Forensic Sci. Int. 120 (1–2): 79–88.

Cabirol, N., Pommier, M.T., Gueux, M., Payen, G., 1998. Comparison of lipid composition in two types of human putrefactive liquid. Forensic Sci. Int. 94: 47–54.

Campobasso, C.P., DiVella, G., Introna, F., 2001. Factors affecting decomposition and diptera colonization. Forensic Sci. Int. 120 (1–2): 18–27.

Canavelis, A., 2010. Par le bout de la truffe. Liaisons 99. Le magazine de la préfecture de police, p. 15.

Carrier, B., 2005. File System Forensic Analysis. Addison-Wesley, Reading, MA.

Casey, E., 2004. Digital Evidence and Computer Crime: Forensic Science, Computers, and the Internet. Academic Press, San Diego.

Casey, E., 2009. Handbook of Digital Forensics and Investigation. Academic Press, San Diego.

Chaudhry, R., Pant, S.K., 2004. Identification of authorship using lateral palm print—A new concept. Forensic Sci. Int. 141: 49–57.

Cho, H., Stout, S.D., Madsen, R.W., Streeter, M.A., 2002. Population-specific histological age-estimating method: A model for known African-American and European-American skeletal remains. J. Forensic Sci. 47 (1): 12–18.

Clery, J.M., 2001. Stability of prostate specific antigen (PSA) and subsequent Y-STR typing of Lucilia (Phaenicia) sericata (Meigen) (Diptera: calliphoridae) maggots reared from a simulated postmortem sexual assault. Forensic Sci. Int. 120 (1–2): 72–76.

Coticone, S., Barna, L., Teets, M., 2010. Optimization of a DNA extraction method for nonhuman and human bone. J. Forensic Ident. 60 (4): 430–438.

Coy, A., Ohlson, J.W., 2000. Special case in three-dimensional bone reconstruction of the human skull. J. Forensic Ident. 50 (6): 549–562.

Coyle, H.M. (Ed.), 2005. Forensic Botany: Principles and Applications to Criminal Casework. CRC Press, Boca Raton, FL.

Crane, A.C.J., Crane, S.L., 1997. A frequency study of cheque-writing styles. J. Can. Soc. Forensic Sci. 30 (3): 113–136.

Crosby, T.K., Watt, J.C., Kistemaker, A.C., Nelson, P.E., 1986. Entomological identification of the origin of imported cannabis. J. Forensic Sci. Soc. 26: 35–44.

Curran, A., Rabin, S., Furton, K. Analysis of the uniqueness and persistence of human scent. Forensic Sci. Commun. 7(2): 1–21.

Dalrymple, B., 2004. Background subtraction through exhibit substitution. J. Forensic Ident. 54 (2): 150–157.

Dawson, G.A., 1998. An evaluation of line quality in photocopied signatures. Sci. Justice 38 (3): 189–194.

DeHaan, J.D., Brien, D.J., Large, R., 2004. Volatile organic compounds from the combustion of human and animal tissue. Sci. Justice 44 (4): 223–236.

Dorriety, J.K., 2007. Cadaver dogs as a forensic tool: An analysis of prior studies. J. Forensic Ident. 57 (5): 217–225.

Duhig, C., 2003. Non-forensic remains: The use of forensic archaeology, anthropology and burial taphonomy. Sci. Justice 43 (4): 211–214.

Edston, E., Druid, H., Homgren, P., Öström, M., 2001. Postmortem measurements of thyroid hormones in blood and vitreous humor combined with histology. Am. J. Forensic Med. Pathol. 22 (1): 92–95.

Erzinçlioglu, Y.Z., 1990. Protocol for collecting entomological evidence. Forensic Sci. Int. 45: 191–192.

Erzinçlioglu, Y.Z, 1991. Forensic entomology and criminal investigations. Police J. 64 (1): 5–8.

Evett, I.W., 2000. Verbal conventions for handwriting opinions. J. Forensic Sci. 45 (2): 508–509.

Fiedler, S., Graw, M., 2003. Decomposition of buried corpses, with special reference to the formation of adipocere. Naturwissenschaften 90: 291–300.

Forbes, S.L., Stuart, B.H., Dadour, I.R., Dent, B.B., 2004. A preliminary investigation of the stages of adipocere formation. J. Forensic Sci. 49 (3): 566–574.

Forbes, S.L., Dent, B.B., Stuart, B.H., 2005. The effect of soil type on adipocere formation. Forensic Sci. Int. 154: 35–43.

Found, B., Rogers, D.K., 2005. Investigating forensic document examiners' skill relating to opinions on photocopied signatures. Sci. Justice 45 (4): 199–206.

Gaine, S.A., Rooney, N.J., Bradshaw, J.W.S., 2008. The effect of feeding enrichment upon reporting working ability and behavior of kenneled working dogs. J. Forensic Sci. 53 (6): 1400–1404.

Gaudreau, M.O., Purdy, D.C., Harris, J.S., 1997. Where document imaging and scientific image analysis meet. document forensics. Int. J. Forensic Doc. Examiners 3 (3): 261–264.

Gaudry, E., Blais, C., Maria, A., Dauphin-Villemant, C., 2006. Study of steroidogenesis in pupae of the forensically important blow fly Protophormia terraenovae (Robineau-Desvoidy) (Diptera: calliphoridae). Forensic Sci. Int. 160: 27–34.

Gialamas, D.M., 1996. Enhancement of fire scene investigation using accelerant detection canines. Sci. Justice 36 (1): 51–54.

Giles, A., 2000. Towards the paperless society. Sci. Justice 40 (2): 109–112.

Goff, M.L., 1993. Estimation of postmortem interval using arthropod development and successional patterns. Forensic Sci. Rev. 5 (2): 81–94.

Goff, M.L., Win, B.H., 1997. Estimation of postmortem interval based on colony development time for Anoplolepsis longipes (Hymenoptera; Formicidae). J. Forensic Sci. 42 (6): 1176–1179.

Goff, M.L., Miller, M.L., Paulson, J.D., Lord, W.D., Richards, E., Omori, A.I., 1997. Effects of 3,4-methylenedioxymethamphetamine in decomposing tissues on the development of Parasarcophaga ruficornis (Diptera: sarcophagidae) and detection of the drug in postmortem blood, liver tissue, larvae, and puparia. J. Forensic Sci. 42 (2): 276–280.

Grassberger, M., Reiter, C., 2002a. Effect of temperature on development of the forensically important holarctic blow fly Protophormia terraenovae (Robineau-Desvoidy) (Diptera: calliphoridae). Forensic Sci. Int. 128 (3): 177–182.

Grassberger, M., Reiter, C., 2002b. Effect of temperature on development of Liopygia (=Sarcophaga) argyrostoma (Robineau-Desvoidy) (Diptera: sarcophagidae) and its forensic implications. J. Forensic Sci. 47: 1332–1336.

Greenfield, C., 2004. Write into the future. J. Forensic Ident. 54 (6): 633–636.

Grim, D.L., Siegel, J., Allison, J., 2001. Evaluation of desorption/ionization mass spectrometric methods in the forensic applications of the analysis of inks on paper. J. Forensic Sci. 46 (6): 1411–1420.

Gunatilake, K., Goff, M.L., 1989. Detection of organophosphate poisoning in a putrefying body by analyzing arthropod larvae. J. Forensic Sci. 34 (3): 714–718.

Haglund, W.D., Reay, D.T., 1993. Problems of recovering partial human remains at different times: Concerns for death investigators. J. Forensic Sci. 38 (1): 69–80.

Hamilton, D.J., 1996. Adding a new dimension to validation with dynamic signature verification. Sci. Justice 36: 183–190.

Harvey, L.M., 2005. An alternative for the extraction and storage of DNA from insects in forensic entomology. J. Forensic Sci. 50 (3): 627–629.

Harvey, L.M., Harvey, J.W., 2003. Reliability of bloodhounds in criminal investigations. J. Forensic Sci. 48 (4): 811–816.

Harvey, L.M., Harvey, S.J., Hom, M., Perna, A., Salib, J., 2006. The use of bloodhounds in determining the impact of genetics and the environment on the expression of human odortype. J. Forensic Sci. 51 (5): 1109–1114.

Henssge, C., 1992. Rectal temperature time of death nomogram: Dependence of corrective factors on the body weight under stronger thermic insolation conditions. Forensic Sci. Int. 54: 51–56.

Hill, R.M., 1999. Document dating via the Internet. J. Forensic Ident. 49 (2): 114–116.

Hobischak, N.R., Anderson, G.S., 2002. Time of submergence using aquatic invertebrate succession and decompositional changes. J. Forensic Sci. 47 (1): 142–151.

Holland, M.M., Fischer, D.L., Roby, R.K., Ruderman, J., Bryson, J., Weedn, V.W., 1995. Mitochondrial DNA sequence analysis of human remains. Crime Lab. Digest 22/4: 109–115.

Horrocks, M., Walsh, A.J., 2001. Pollen on grass clippings: Putting the suspect at the scene of crime. J. Forensic Sci. 46 (4): 947–949.

Horton, B.P., Boreham, S., Hillier, C., 2006. The development and application of a diatom-based quantitative reconstruction technique in forensic science. J. Forensic Sci. 51 (3): 643–650.

Huntington, T.E., Higley, L.G., Baxendale, F.P., 2007. Maggot development during morgue storage and its effect on estimating the post-mortem interval. J. Forensic Sci. 52 (2): 453–458.

Introna Jr., F., Campobasso, C.P., Goff, M.L., 2001. Entomotoxicology. Forensic Sci. Int. 120 (1–2): 42–47.

Ionescu, L., 1990. Authenticity judgement with the help of paint-brush traces. Forensic Sci. Int.: 33–35.

James, R.A., Hoadley, P.A., Sampson, B.G., 1997. Determination of postmortem interval by sampling vitreous humour. Am. J. Forensic. Med. Pathol. 18 (2): 158–162.

Jayaprakash, P.T., 2006. Postmortem skin erosions caused by ants and their significance in crime reconstruction. J. Forensic Ident. 56 (6): 972–999.

Kaatsch, H.J., Schmidtke, E., Nietsch, W., 1994. Photometric measurement of pressure-induced blanching of livor mortis as an aid to estimating time of death: Application of a new system for quantifying pressure-induced blanching of lividity. Int. J. Legal Pathol. 106 (4): 209–214.

Kahana, T., Goldstein, S., Kugel, C., Hiss, J., 2002. Identification of human remains through comparison of computerized tomography and radiographic plates. J. Forensic Ident. 52 (2): 151–158.

Katz, S.R., Midkiff, C.D., 1998. Unconfirmed canine accelerant detection: A reliability issue in court. J. Forensic Sci. 43 (2): 329–333.

Keiper, J.B., Chapman, E.G., Foote, B.A., 1997. Midge larvae (Diptera; Chironomidae) as indicators of postmortem submersion interval carcasses in a woodland stream: A preliminary report. J. Forensic Sci. 42 (6): 1074–1079.

Kintz, P., Godelar, B., Tracqui, A., Mangin, P., Lugnier, A., Chaumont, A.J., 1990. Fly larvae: A new toxicological method of investigation in forensic medicine. J. Forensic Sci. 35 (1): 204–207.

Kintz, P., Tracqui, A., Mangin, P., 1994. Analysis of opiates in fly larvae sampled on a putrefied cadaver. J. Forensic Sci. Soc. 34 (2): 95–99.

Kirk, N.J., Wood, R.E., Goldstein, M., 2002. Skeletal identification using the frontal sinus region: A retrospective study of 39 cases. J. Forensic Sci. 47 (2): 318–323.

Komar, D., Beattie, O., 1998. Postmortem insect activity may mimic perimortem sexual assault clothing patterns. J. Forensic Sci. 43 (4): 792–796.

Komar, D., 1999. The use of cadaver dogs in locating scattered, scavenged human remains: Preliminary field test results. J. Forensic Sci. 44 (2): 405–408.

Kumagai, A., Nakahashiki, N., Aoki, Y., 2007. Analysis of age-related carbonylation of human vitreous humor proteins as a tool for forensic diagnosis. Legal Med. 9: 175–180.

Kurz, M.E., Schultz, S., Griffith, J., Broadus, K., Sparks, J., Dabdoub, G., 1996. Effect of background interference on accelerant detection by canines. J. Forensic Sci. 41 (5): 868–873.

Lee, H.C., Gaesslen, R.E., Bigbee, P.D., Kearney, J.J., 1991. Guidelines for the collection and preservation of DNA evidence. J. Forensic Ident. 41 (5): 344–356.

Lefebvre, F., Pasquerault, T., 2004. Temperature-dependent development of Ophyra aenescens (Wiedemann, 1830) and Ophyra capensis (Wiedemann, 1918) (Diptera, Muscidae). Forensic Sci. Int. 139 (1): 75–79.

Levinson, J., 2001. Questioned Documents: A Lawyer's Handbook. Academic Press, San Diego.

Lin, A.C.-Y., Hsieh, H.-M., Tsai, L.-C., Linacre, A., Lee, J.C.-I., 2007. Forensic applications of infrared imaging for the detection and recording of latent evidence. J. Forensic Sci. 52 (5): 1148–1150.

Lopes de Carvalho, L.M., Linhares, A.X., 2001a. Seasonality of insect succession and pig carcass decomposition in a natural forest area in southeastern Brazil. J. Forensic Sci. 46 (3): 604–608.

Lopes de Carvalho, M.L., Linhares, A.X., Trigo, J.R., 2001b. Determination of drug levels and the effect of diasepam on the growth of necrophagous flies of forensic importance in southeastern Brazil. Forensic Sci. Int. 120 (1–2): 140–144.

Lord, W.D., Dizinno, J.A., Wilson, M.R., Budowle, B., Taplin, D., Meinking, T.L., 1998. Isolation, amplification, and sequencing of human mitochondrial DNA obtained from human crab louse, Pthirus pubis (L.) blood meals. J. Forensic Sci. 43 (5): 1097–1100.

Lord, W.D., Goff, M.L., Adkins, T.R., Haskell, N.H., 1994. The black soldier fly Hermetia illucens (Diptera: stratiomyidae) as a potential measure of human postmortem interval: Observations and case histories. J. Forensic Sci. 39 (1): 215–222.

Ludes, B., Coste, M., Tracqui, A., Mangin, P., 1996. Continuous river monitoring of the diatoms in the diagnosis of drowning. J. Forensic Sci. 41 (3): 425–428.

Ludes, B., Coste, M., North, N., Doray, S., Tracqui, A., Kintz, P., 1999. Diatom analysis in victim's tissues as an indicator of the site of drowning. Int. J. Legal Med. 112 (3): 163–166.

MacKay, J., 2009. Forensic Biology. Gale Cengage Learning, Detroit, pp. 11–24.

Mahajan, M., Arya, S.P., 2007. Examination of writings concealed by black pressure sensitive adhesive tape. J. Forensic Sci. 52 (5): 1212–1213.

Maind, S.D., Chattopadhyay, N., Gandhi, C., Kumar, S.C., Sudersanan, M., 2008. Quantitative evaluation of europium in blue ballpoint pen inks/offset printing inks tagged with europium thenoyltrifluoroacetonate by spectrofluorometry and ICP-AES. Sci. Justice 48 (2): 61–66.

Malgorn, Y., Coquoz, R., 1999. DNA typing for identification of some species of Calliphoridae. An interest in forensic entomology. Forensic Sci. Int. 102 (2–3): 111–119.

Marineo, E.A., 1997. A pilot study using the first cervical vertebra as an indicator of race. J. Forensic Sci. 42 (6): 1114–1118.

Marquis, R., Schmittbull, M., Mazella, W.D., Taroni, F., 2005. Quantification of the shape of handwritten characters: a step to objective discrimination between writers based on the study of the capital character O. Forensic Sci. Int. 150: 23–32.

Marshall, A.M., 2003. An improved protocol for the examination of rogue WWW sites. Sci. Justice 43 (4): 237–248.

Marshall, A.M., Tompsett, B.C., 2002. Spam 'n' chips: A discussion of Internet crime. Sci. Justice 42 (2): 117–122.

Mazella, W.D., Buzzini, P., 2005. Raman spectroscopy of blue gel pen inks. Forensic Sci. Int. 152: 41–247.

Mazzella, W.D., Taroni, F., 2005. A simple logical approach to questioned envelopes examination. Sci. Justice 45 (1): 35–38.

Megyesi, M.S., Nawrocki, S.P., Haskell, N.H., 2005. Using accumulated degree-days to estimate the postmortem interval from decomposed human remains. J. Forensic Sci. 50 (3): 618–626.

Merritt, R.W., Higgins, M.J., Wallace, J.R., 2000. Entomology. In: Siegel, J., Knupfer, G., Saukko, P. (Eds.), Encyclopedia of Forensic Sciences, in three volumes, pp. 699–704.

Mesloh, C., Henych, M., Wolf, R., 2002a. Sniff test: Utilization of the law enforcement canine in the seizure of paper currency. J. Forensic Ident. 52 (6): 704–724.

Mesloh, C., Wolf, R., Henych, M., 2002b. Scent as forensic evidence and its relationship to the law enforcement canine. J. Forensic Ident. 52 (2): 169–182.

Mesloh, C., James-Mesloh, J., 2006. Trained dogs in the crime scene search. J. Forensic Ident. 56 (4): 534–539.

Michaud, S., Estabrooks, C., 1998. The development of a database for payment card embossing machines. Sci. Justice 38 (3): 143–150.

Micozzi, M.S., 1991. Postmortem Changes in Human and Animal Remains: A Systematic Approach. Charles C. Thomas.

Moryan, D., 2002. An unusual rubber stamp case. J. Forensic Sci. 47 (2): 399–401.

Mulhern, D.M., Ubelaker, D.H., 2001. Differences in osteon banding between human and nonhuman bone. J. Forensic Sci. 46 (2): 220–222.

Munoz, J.I., Suarez-Penaranda, J.M., Otera, X.L., Rodriguez-Calvo, M.S., Costas, E., Miguens, X., et al., 2001. A new perspective in the estimation of postmortem interval (PMI) based on vitreous [K+]. J. Forensic Sci. 46 (2): 209–214.

Naccataro, S., Petersen, S., John, G.L., 2008. Skull features as clues to age, sex, race, and lifestyle. J. Forensic Ident. 58 (2): 172–181.

Nolte, K.B., Pinder, R.D., Lord, W.D., 1992. Insect larvae used to detect cocaine poisoning in a decomposed body. J. Forensic Sci. 37 (4): 1179–1185.

Nowlan, M., Stuart, A.W., Basara, G.J., Sanderock, P.M.L., 2007. Use of a solid absorbent and a accelerant detection canine for the detection of ignitable liquids burned in a structure fire. J. Forensic Sci. 52 (3): 643–648.

Olivier, M., Shenoi, S., 2006. Advances in Digital Forensics II. Springer, New York.

Owsley, D., Mann, R., Ubelaker, D., DiZinno, J., 1992. Unknown to positive ID: A forensic anthropological investigation. J. Forensic Ident. 42: 6.

Owsley, D.W., Pelot, S.B., 1995. Three grams of bone and three dental fragments aid identification of a homicide victim. J. Forensic Ident. 45 (5): 519–529.

Page, D., 2008. Is forensic science going to the dogs? Forensic Mag. 5 (5): 33–40.

Peabody, A.J., 1977. Diatoms in forensic science. J. Forensic Sci. Soc. 17: 81–87.

Pfefferli, P.W., 2000. Forgery/Counterfeits. In: Siegel, J., Knupfer, G., Saukko, P. (Eds.), Encyclopedia of Forensic Sciences, in three volumes, pp. 580–584.

Pickering, T.R, 2001. Carnivore voiding: A taphonomic process with the potential for the deposition of forensic evidence. J. Forensic Sci. 46 (2): 406–411.

Pollanen, M., Cheung, C., Chiasson, D., 1997a. The diagnostic value of the diatom test for drowning, I. Utility: A retrospective analysis of 771 cases of drowning in Ontario. Canada. J. Forensic Sci. 42: 281–285.

Pollanen, M., Cheung, C., Chiasson, D., 1997b. The diagnostic value of the diatom test for drowning, II. Validity: Analysis of diatoms in bone marrow and drowning medium. J. Forensic Sci. 42: 286–290.

Poon, N.L, Ho, S.S.H., Li, C.K., 2005. Differentiation of colored inks of inkjet printer cartridges by thin layer chromatography and high performance liquid chromatography. Sci. Justice 45 (4): 187–194.

Powers, R., 2005. Remains to be seen!. J. Forensic Ident. 55 (6): 687–696.

Pretty, I.A., Addy, L.D., 2002. Associated postmortem dental findings as an aid to personal identification. Sci. Jus. 42 (2): 65–74.

Prince, D.A., Ubelaker, D.H., 2002. Application of Lamendin's adult dental aging technique to a diverse skeletal sample. J. Forensic Sci. 47 (1): 107–116.

Purdy, D.C., 2000. Document dating. In: Siegel, J., Knupfer, G., Saukko, P. (Eds.), Encyclopedia of Forensic Sciences, in three volumes, pp. 570–580.

Purkait, R., 2001. Measurements of ulna—A new method for determination of sex. J. Forensic Sci. 46 (4): 924–927.

Reichs, K.J. (Ed.), 1998. Forensic Osteology: Advances in the Identification of Human Remains, second ed. Charles C. Thomas.

Rhode, E., McManus, A.C., Vogt, C., Heineman, W.R., 1997. Separation and comparison of fountain pen inks by capillary zone electrophoresis. J. Forensic Sci. 42 (6): 1004–1011.

Risinger, D.M., Saks, M.J., 1996. Science and nonscience in the courts: Daubert meets handwriting identification expertise. Iowa Law Rev. 82: 21–74.

Robling, A.G., Ubelaker, D.H., 1997. Sex estimation from the metatarsals. J. Forensic Sci. 42 (6): 1062–1069.

Roeterdink, E.M., Dadour, I.R., Warling, R.J., 2004. Extraction of gunshot residues from the larvae of the forensically important blowfly Calliphora dubia. Int. J. Legal Med. 118 (2): 63–70.

Rogers, N.L., 2005. The first use of a composite image in forensic facial superimposition: The case of John Paul Jones, 1907. J. Forensic Ident. 55 (3): 312–325.

Rogers, N.L., Goodheart, A., 2008. Historic superimposed image of John Paul Jones was the brainchild of American diplomat Horace Porter: Update to Rogers, 2005. J. Forensic Ident. 58 (6): 712–722.

Ross, S., Gow, A., 1999. Digital Archeology: Rescuing Neglected and Damaged Data Resources. Humanities Advanced Technology and Information Institute (HATII), University of Glasgow.

Sadler, D.W., Robertson, L., Brown, G., Fuke, C., Pounder, D.J., 1997. Barbiturates and analgesics in Calliphora vicina larvae. J. Forensic Sci. 42 (3): 481–485.

Saini, K., Kaur, R., Sood, N.C., 2009. Determining the sequence of intersecting gel pen and laser printed strokes—A comparative study. Sci. Justice 49 (4): 286–291.

Saini, K., Saroa, J.S., 2008. Thin-layer chromatography of refilled photocopy toners. J. Forensic Ident. 58 (3): 315–326.

Scarborough, S., 2001. Success of hexane-based ninhydrin amino acid reagent processing on various inks and ages of porous evidence. J. Forensic Ident. 51 (6): 581–586.

Scarborough, S., Dziemieszko, A., 2004. Techniques for digital enhancement of latent prints obscured by disruptive backgrounds. J. Forensic Ident. 54 (2): 141–149.

Schaefer, M., Young, D., Restrepo, D., 2001. Olfactory fingerprints for major histocompatibility complex-determined by body odors. J. Neurosci. 21 (7): 2481–2487.

Schoenly, K., Griest, K., Rhine, S., 1991. An experimental field protocol for investigating the postmortem interval using multidisciplinary indicators. J. Forensic Sci. 36 (5): 1395–1415.

Schoon, G.A.A., 1998. A first assessment of the reliability of an improved scent identification line-up. J. Forensic Sci. 43 (1): 70–75.

Schoon, G.A.A., De Bruin, J.C., 1994. The ability of dogs to recognize and cross-match human odours. Forensic Sci. Int. 69 (2): 111–118.

Schroeder, H., Klotzbach, H., Elias, S., Augustin, C., Pueschel, K., 2003. Use of PCR-RFLP for differentiation of Calliphorid larvae (Dipter, Calliphoridae) on human corpses. Forensic Sci. Int. 132 (1): 76–81.

Simpson, G., Strongman, D.B., 2002. Carrion insects on pig carcasses at a rural and an urban site in Nova Scotia. J. Can. Soc. Forensic Sci. 35 (3): 123–144.

Singla, A.K., Thakar, M.K., 2006. Establishing the sequence of intersecting ballpoint pen and felt-tipped marker strokes. J. Forensic Ident. 56 (3): 382–387.

Spence, L.D., Francis, R.B., Tinggi, U., 2002. Comparison of the elemental composition of office document paper: evidence in a homicide case. J. Forensic Sci. 47 (3): 648–651.

Statheropoulous, M., Spiliopouou, C., Agapiou, A., 2005. A study of volatile organic compounds evolved from the decaying human body. Forensic Sci. Int. 153: 147–155.

Stephan, C.N., 2002. Do resemblance ratings measure the accuracy of facial approximations? J. Forensic Sci. 47 (2): 239–243.

Stout, S.D., Ross Jr., L.M., 1991. Bone fragments a body can make. J. Forensic Sci. 36 (3): 953–959.

Szinak, J., 1985. Identification of odours. Int. Criminol. Police Rev.: 58–63.

Takatori, T., 1996. Investigation on the mechanism of adipocere formation and its relation to other biochemical reactions. J. Forensic Sci. Int. 80: 49–61.

Taroni, F., Biedermann, A., 2005. Inadequacies of posterior probabilities for the assessment of scientific evidence. Law, Probability and Risk 4 (1–2): 89–114.

Taslitz, A.E., 1990. Does the cold nose know? The unscientific myth of the dog scent lineup. Hastings Law J. 42 (1): 15–134.

Taylor, B., Skene, K., 2003. Forensic palynology: Spatial and temporal considerations of spora deposition in forensic investigations. Aust. J. Forensic Sci. 35 (2): 193–204.

Taylor, K., Gatliff, B.P., 1998. Forensic art case study: Daisy Jane Doe. J. Forensic Ident. 48 (3): 273–278.

Thanasoulias, N.C., Parisis, N.A., Evmidiris, N.P., 2003. Multivariate chemometrics for the forensic discrimination of blue ball-point pen inks based on their Vis spectra. Forensic Sci. Int. 138: 75–84.

Tomberlin, J.K., Tertuliano, M., Rains, G., Lewis, W.J., 2005. Conditioned Microplitis croceipes cresson (Hymenoptera: braconidae) detect and respond to 2, 4-DNT: Development of a biological Sensor. J. Forensic Sci. 50 (5): 1187–1190.

Tranthim-Fryer, D.J., De Haan, J., 1997. Canine accelerant detectors and problem with carpet pyrolysis. Sci. Justice 37: 39–46.

Ubelaker, D.H., Scammell, H., 1997. Bones, chapter 7: Sex, size, race, age at death. J. Forensic Ident. 47 (3): 332–347.

Van Es, A., De Koeijer, J., Ven der Peijl, G., 2009. Discrimination of document paper by XRF, LA-ICP-MS and IRMS using multivariate statistical techniques. Sci. Justice 49 (2): 120–126.

Vass, A., Barshick, S.-A., Sega, G., Canton, J., Skeen, J.T., Love, J.C., et al., 2002. Decomposition chemistry of human remains: a new methodology for determining the postmortem interval. J. Forensic Sci. 47 (3): 542–553.

Vass, A., Smith, R.B., Thompson, C.V., Burnett, M.N., Wolf, D.A., Synstelien, J.A., et al., 2004. Decompositional odor analysis database. J. Forensic Sci. 49 (4): 1–10.

Vass, A., Smith, R.B., Thompson, C.V., Burnett, N.M., Dulgerian, N., Eckenrode, B.A., 2008. Odor analysis of decomposing buried human remains. J. Forensic Sci. 53 (2): 384–391.

Vos, M., Strach, S., Westwood, P., 2000. Handwriting. In: Siegel, J., Knupfer, G., Saukko, P. (Eds.), Encyclopedia of Forensic Sciences, in three volumes, pp. 584–590.

Wallace, J.R., Merritt, R.W., Kimbirauskas, R., Benbow, E., McIntosh, M., 2008. Caddisflies assist with homicide case: determining a postmortem submersion interval using aquatic insects. J. Forensic Sci. 53 (1): 219–221.

Walsh, K.A.J., Horrocks, M., 2008. Palynology: Its position in the field of forensic science. J. Forensic Sci. 53 (5): 1053–1060.

Warren, M.W., Schultz, J.J., 2002. Post-cremation taphonomy and artifact preservation. J. Forensic Sci. 47 (3): 656–659.

Weising, K., Nybom, H., Wolff, K., Mayer, W., 1994. DNA Fingerprinting in Plants and Fungi. CRC Press, Boca Raton, FL.

Wells, J.D., Introna Jr, F., Di Vella, G., Campobasso, C.P., Hayes, J., Sperling, F.A.H., 2001b. Human and insect mitochondrial DNA analysis from maggots. J. Forensic Sci. 46 (3): 685–687.

Wells, J.D., Pape, T., Sperling, F.A.H., 2001a. DNA-based identification and molecular systematics of forensically important Sarcophagidae (Diptera). J. Forensic Sci. 46 (5): 1098–1102.

Wood, W.K., Elmhurst, O., 1999. In that rich earth a richer dust concealed. Fingerprint World 25 (96): 233–238.

Yan, F., McNally, R., Kontanis, E.J., Sadik, O.A., 2001. Preliminary quantitative investigation of postmortem adipocere formation. J. Forensic Sci. 46 (3): 609–614.

Yoder, C., Ubelaker, D.H., Powell, J.F., 2001. Examination of variation in sternal rib end morphology relevant to age assessment. J. Forensic Sci. 46 (2): 223–227.

Zehner, R., Amendt, J., Krettek, R., 2004. STR typing of human DNA from fly larvae fed on decomposing bodies. J. Forensic Sci. 49 (2): 337–340.

Zimmerman, K.A., Wallace, J.R., 2008. The potential to determine a postmortem submersion interval based on algal/diatom diversity on decomposing mammalian carcasses in brackish ponds in Delaware. J. Forensic Sci. 53 (4): 935–941.

Zlotnick, J., Lin, J.R., 2001. Handwriting evidence in federal courts—From Frye to Kumho. Forensic Sci. Rev. 13: 87–98.

Crime Scene Reconstruction

In the strictest sense, all forensic work strives to reconstruct the events at a crime scene—who was involved, where did the crime occur, what was used to commit the crime, and so on—in an effort to retell a tale that no one other than the perpetrator or victim knew. Technically speaking, however, the phrase "crime scene reconstruction" is used to describe the process of applying science, the analysis of evidence, and reasoning to clarify and detail the most probable sequence of events related to a criminal act. It is technically applied to three particular events: accidents (mostly transportation), shootings, and homicides. All reconstructions involve some elements of human behavior (humans, after all, committed the acts in question), not only of the criminals but also of what had happened prior to the criminal event that set the "baseline" for "normal" activity. Sometimes the greatest challenge in crime scene reconstruction is determining what is signal (remnants of the crime) and what is noise (background material that was in place before the crime

Key Term
Crime scene reconstruction

occurred). Reconstruction may seem to be similar to criminal profiling or behavioral analysis. The two are linked but work from very different premises: Reconstruction asks, "What happened? How did it happen?" while profiling asks, "Why did this happen? Who did this and what kind of person is he or she?"

It has been argued that crime scene reconstruction is nothing more than police work, the investigative piecing together of the past (O'Hara and O'Hara 1973; Osterburg and Ward, 2010). As a CSI, do not confuse police work for crime scene reconstructions: reconstructions are solidly based on the scientific method, use physical evidence, and require both inductive and deductive reasoning. Police investigations may utilize some of these methods but not in the same coherent, systematic way that CSIs do. Also, crime scene reconstruction is explicitly **not** "recreating" or "reenacting" the crime scene—that is best left to fictional television shows and tabloid news programs.

Reconstructions can be classified as:

- Item-level reconstructions, where a particular object is the focus of the analysis, say, a firearm that malfunctions under certain conditions.
- Single incident–level reconstructions, where one specific occurrence subordinate to other events is examined; for example, a broken window or a gunshot is fired.
- Event-level reconstructions, where a series of incidents are correlated with a criminal act, like a homicide.
- Large-scale reconstructions, which are mass events requiring analysis, such as an airplane crash.

Multiple methods may be used in any given reconstruction, according to what is needed to answer the questions; other times, only one method is needed, say, in a shooting reconstruction. Some events are easier to work with than others; traffic accidents are often a matter of detail, measurement, and physics (Figures 7.0.1 and 7.0.2), allowing for high levels of certainty in conclusions. Others may be more complicated and may require specialists, like engineers or blood stain pattern analysts, to be in attendance or consulted.

Shooting reconstruction scenes become more complicated because of the mobility of the firearms, the actions and movements of the people, and the ballistics involved (ricochets, for example). Movement through a scene may be difficult to pin down, although sequencing through the oriented physical remnants of activity (shoeprints, for example, can indicate direction) and other placemarkers, like bullet holes or spent casings can identify the movement path. The motion is not constant, the acceleration is not linear, and the positioning is not always upright. Thus, the complexity of the shooting scene requires detailed measurements and sketches (Figure 7.0.3); these lend themselves to sophisticated computer-aided reconstructions for analysis and presentation (Figure 7.0.4).

Homicide reconstructions become complicated, as can be seen from the figures, but also offer more evidence due to the interactions of the criminal

FIGURE 7.0.1 A head-on collision of two automobiles. *Source: Wikimedia Commons.*

FIGURE 7.0.2 A 2005 Chevrolet Malibu involved in a crash. The car was hit head on by another car when the other car crossed the center line; the Malibu subsequently rolled over. The driver's seatbelt was buckled, which police say likely contributed to her survival. *Source: Creative Commons.*

(a)

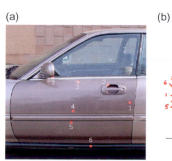

(b)

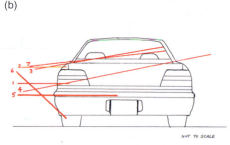

FIGURE 7.0.3 Shooting reconstruction involving a car using dowels as indicators (a) and a scene sketch of the incident (b). *Courtesy Alliance Forensics Laboratory.*

FIGURE 7.0.4 A computer-aided reconstruction of a shooting. *Courtesy Alliance Forensics Laboratory.*

and the victim. This is especially true of scenes where bloodstain patterns help determine the sequence of activities, location of individuals, and other reconstructive information.

Conclusion

Forensic investigations provide information upon which events at crime scenes are reconstructed. The crime scene represents the potential for learning who was involved, where the crime occured, what was used to commit the crime, and other questions relevant to the investigation. All evidence collection and analysis at the scene is documented to realize that potential in any later reconstructions, either informally through the normal forensic analyses or formally, as in accidents, shootings, and homicides.

References and Bibiliography

Bevel, T., Gardner, R., 2008. Bloodstain Pattern Analysis. CRC Press, Boca Raton, FL.

Chisum, W., Turvey, B., 2011. Crime Reconstruction, second ed. Academic Press, San Diego.

Gardner, M., Bevel, T., 2009. Practical Crime Scene Analysis and Reconstruction. CRC Press, Boca Raton, FL.

Garrison, D.H., 2003. Practical Shooting Scene Investigation. Universal Publishers, Macquarie Park, Australia.

Osterberg, J., Ward, R., 2010. Criminal Investigation, sixth ed. Anderson Publishing, New York.

O'Hara, C., O'Hara, G, 2003. Fundamentals of Criminal Investigation. C.C. Thomas, Springfield, IL.

An Archaeological Approach

Of Artifacts and Evidence

The goal of an archaeological excavation is to carefully collect and record all the available information about a prehistoric or historic site of human activity. The goal of processing a crime scene is to collect and preserve evidence for later analysis and reporting. Both of these processes involve "careful destruction": They are one-way approaches that deconstruct a contextual location for its later reconstruction. Once an artifact is unearthed or a piece of evidence collected, it cannot be "reburied" or replaced. Crime scenes and archaeological sites are both made up of the physical remains of past human activity and, in a sense, are snapshots of the "leftovers" of a completed process. The scene or site will never exist in exactly the same way as it did before the excavation or crime scene processing started. All the information, the relationships, and the context of the items must be documented as they

Key Terms
Taphonomy
C-transform
N-transform
Datum
Artifact
Feature
Organic or environmental remains

are "destroyed" to allow for some level of reconstruction in the laboratory or museum.

Archaeology, as a discipline, has existed for decades and has become increasingly theory- and science-based. The noted archaeologist Irving Rouse expressed the strategy of archaeology in four questions (Rouse, 1966):

1. What is the nature of the archaeological remains under study?
2. Who produced them?
3. When and where were they produced?
4. How did they change?

Questions 1 and 4 are traditionally in the province of forensic science, in that they address what kinds of evidence are encountered and how were they used in the crime being investigated. Questions 2 and 3, however, pertain just as much to the forensic profession, although they have rarely been addressed regularly and are left to manufacturer enquiries about specific products, like trash bags (Ryland and Houck, 2001). The answers to Questions 2 and 3 form much of the basis for evidentiary significance (Houck, 2010) and this kind of information should become integrated into forensic education and training to help create awareness of the range of possible materials and products to be encountered and their potential significance. Likewise, the concept of taphonomy, the study of an item from the time it is deposited until it is analyzed (borrowed from paleoanthropology), has gained traction in forensic science through anthropological applications and research (Haglund and Sorg, 2003). Taphonomy directly helps to answer Question 4, that is, what has happened to the item in a forensic context since it was produced. Using Rouse's questions as a basis, CSIs and forensic scientists would benefit from learning more about the "pre-evidence" they will encounter and how it is made, as well as the natural and human activities that brought it to its current evidentiary condition.

Another set of concepts from archaeology could help delineate items at a crime scene. A whole series of formation processes will have affected the way in which objects became evidence and change them after they became evidence; in essence, taphonomy. Archaeologist Michael Schiffer has made the useful distinction between taphonomic processes (what he calls "formation processes"): cultural formation processes, or C-transforms, for those instigated by humans and noncultural or natural formation processes; and N-transforms for those that occur in nature. For example, finding a bloody baseball bat that has been used as a weapon:

- N-transforms (those that occur naturally)
  - Drying and decomposition of the blood on the bat
  - Insect activity, drawn by the blood on the bat
- C-transforms (those that occur through human activity)
  - Criminal use
    - Fractures in the victim's skull

- Production
  - Lacquer on the surface of the bat
  - Shape of the bat
- Normal use
  - Fingerprints on the bat's handle (although this could be from criminal use as well)

The distinction between C- and N-transforms may help the CSI sort out the baseline, precrime context from the criminal one, providing better evidence detection and collection.

Terminology

Several archaeological terms may be of use in crime scene processing. The first is a *datum*, a fixed reference point for all three-dimensional measurements. At an archaeological site, a datum is chosen as the reference point and all measurements taken at the site can be related back to this reference point. For most archaeological sites in the United States, for example, this will be a U.S. Coast and Geodetic Survey marker (Figure 7.1.1), part of a system of tightly measured markers. At a crime scene, the datum should be something permanent, or nearly so, like the corner of a room, a tree, or a post. If no datum easily suggests itself, an artificial one, such as a post, nail, or mark, can be made. Ultimately, all measurements must be able to be referenced to the datum.

FIGURE 7.1.1 This is the U.S. Coast and Geodetic Survey mark for a station located at the peak of Prospect Hill in Wompatuck State Park, Hingham, MA. The marker is a brass disk, about 3.5 inches in diameter. The triangle indicates that this is a station mark (a regional reference point), and the small dot at its center indicates the precise location of the station. The disk has been recessed into a depression chiseled into a rock ledge. The station marker could be used as a datum for an archaeological site.

Other terms that can be borrowed from archaeology suggest the nature of what is found. An *artifact* is a humanmade or modified portable object. A *feature* is a nonportable artifact, such as a firepit, a house, or a garden. *Organic or environmental remains* (nonartifactual) are natural remnants that nonetheless indicate human activity, such as animal bones or plant remains but also soils and sediments. An archaeological site, then, can be thought of as a place where artifacts, features, and organic remains are found together in the context of the past activities; their location in relation to each other sets the internal context of the site.

To reconstruct this context once the site or scene has been processed, it is necessary to locate the position of each item. Thus, the provenience is the origin and derivation of an item in three-dimensional space, in relation to a datum and other items. When an artifact is uncovered at a site, it is measured to the reference points for that excavation unit including its depth. A similar process occurs at a crime scene when evidence is located. As the noted archaeologists Colin Renfrew and Paul Bahn (2000) put it,

> In order to reconstruct past human activity at a site it is crucially important to understand the context of a find, whether artifact, feature, structure or organic remain. A find's context consists of its immediate **matrix** (the material surrounding it), its provenience (horizontal and vertical position within the matrix), and its association with other finds (occurrence together with other archaeological remains, usually in the same matrix). (page 50)

The similarities between archaeology and crime scene processing are numerous and deep. Serious crime scene students would do well to study archaeological methods to enhance their forensic skills.

Time and Space

Like other historical science, forensic science employs one of the basic laws of history, which was developed by geologists, that of superimposition. Contemporary activities take place *horizontally* in space; changes in activities occur *vertically* through time. Broadly, the law of superimposition states that newer vertical layers lay on top of the older, lower ones. Geologists use the term *stratigraphy* to describe the analysis of superimposed layers of earth (Figure 7.1.2); archaeologists use this same law as they excavate: As they go down into the earth, they are going backwards through time. Stratigraphy relates to the idea of provenience, where the exact position, vertically *and* horizontally, of each and every found item is recorded.

Conclusion

Crime scenes and archaeological sites have much in common, both practically and conceptually. The basic principles are the same: establish the context of

FIGURE 7.1.2 Sidling Hill in Maryland. The stratigraphy of the hill, the layers of geological formations, can be seen in the cut side.

the scene, recognize objects and features that were involved in the activities of interest and distinguish them from "background" items, and document their recovery for later reconstruction. Although crime scenes have much shorter timeframes for their activities (hours or days, not hundreds or thousands of years), the approach of recognizing, recovering, and recording is the same for homicides as for ancient ruins.

References and Bibliography

Haglund, W., Sorg, M., 1996. Forensic Taphonomy. CRC Press, Boca Raton, FL.

Haglund, W., Sorg, M., 2003. Advances in Forensic Taphonomy. CRC Press, Boca Raton, FL.

Renfrew, C., Bahn, P., 2000. Archaeology: Theories, Methods, and Practice. Thames and Hudson, London.

Rouse, I., 1966. The strategy of archaeology. Bull. East. States Archaeol. Fed. 25: 12–13.

Ryland, S, Houck, MM, 2001. Only circumstantial evidence. In: Houck, MM (Ed.), Mute Witnesses: Trace Evidence Analysis. Academic Press, San Diego.

Bloodstain Pattern Analysis

Several well-researched textbooks on the subject of bloodstain pattern analysis (BPA) have been published in the last few years.[1] These and other similar works provide comprehensive guides to the terminology, the dynamics of blood droplets in flight and in motion, determining directionality (direction the blood droplet was traveling when it struck a target), characteristic bloodstain patterns, latent bloodstain enhancement techniques, bloodstain documentation schemes, and crime scene reconstruction. These guides should be studied thoroughly. However, it must be stressed that BPA also requires practical study. When many of the bloodstains being analyzed are as a result of blood that has been projected through the air and striking a surface, it

Key Terms
Passive stains
Impact spatter
Wipe
Swipe
Contact pattern

---

[1] Bevel, T., Gardner, R.M., 2008. *Bloodstain Pattern Analysis: With an Introduction to Crime Scene Reconstruction*, 3rd ed. CRC Press: Boca Raton, FL.; James, S.H., Kish, P.E., Sutton, T. P., 2005. *Principles of Bloodstain Pattern Analysis*, 3rd ed., illustrated, revised ed. Taylor and Francis/CRC Press: Boca Raton, FL.

behooves the CSI to take some blood and experiment, to try and recreate the stains. To this end it is highly recommended that crime scene investigators take basic, and if possible advanced, BPA classes from reputable sources; most of these courses use human blood that has been rendered safe, such as expired blood from a blood bank (it has been tested extensively but cannot be used for its original purpose). As with many branches of forensic science, it requires extensive training and practice to learn all the nuances of the techniques used in BPA. Investigators need to acquire experience in all of these techniques before they apply them with knowledge and confidence at crime scenes.

Based on the appearance, size, and location of the bloodstains, BPA can answer many questions about what happened at the crime scene and, sometimes, what did not happen. Because of this, BPA is often a gateway into crime scene reconstruction. Once they have mastered the skills and abilities needed to become an expert in BPA, investigators can apply their knowledge to the wider field of crime scene reconstruction. This section will deal with the practical aspects of what investigators do when they come upon a scene where there are patent bloodstains.

A panicked call from an officer at a bloody crime scene will seem like hyperbole when he claims the scene is covered in "buckets of blood." "Bucket" is not only an unscientific term, it is inaccurate. In reality, at a crime scene the amount of blood is never known until the scene is examined. A human male typically has five to six liters of blood in his system; a female of the same weight will have four to five liters. Forensic science students in the United States, who are not as familiar with the metric system as their European counterparts, often struggle with the concept of how much blood that is. When the volumes are expressed as eight bottles of red wine and six bottles of red wine, they grasp the concept immediately. Pouring eight wine bottles of water into a bucket then pouring it onto the floor will provide a great visual to communicate to anyone the large volume of blood that can be potentially encountered at a crime scene.

For example, Figure 7.2.1 shows the bedroom door of a crime scene in Seattle in 2002. Although it may look like dark brown carpet that doesn't match anything in the apartment, it is in fact so much blood that the carpet appears dark brown. In the hallway the following presented itself to the investigators (Figure 7.2.2). Perhaps the claim of "buckets" may not seem out of place—this is a great deal of blood. Until the CSI has enough experience to overcome it, there is a basic, visceral response to seeing this much blood. Even this scene, where the victim had his right hand severed and died of 234 sharp-force injuries of the head, neck, trunk, and extremities, needs to be dealt with in the same way as all crime scenes: freeze the scene; recognize, recover, and record physical evidence; utilize photography, videotaping, sketching, and note-taking.

Given the circumstances of the crime scene it is unlikely that too many of the stains are not blood. What about barely visible or latent bloodstains? For

FIGURE 7.2.1 Bloodstain pattern at crime scene.

FIGURE 7.2.2 Next bloodstain at the crime scene.

stains that are visible you can use Hemastix® or phenolphthalin reagent. These are presumptive color tests; if they give a positive result the samples tested are presumably blood, a swab is usually taken and the presence of blood is confirmed at the crime laboratory. For latent stains where blood is suspected, leuco crystal violet or amido black are often used in the form of sprays. These reagents react with the hemoglobin in blood to give violet or very dark blue colors, respectively. The colored reaction products are fixed so that they become permanent. Figure 7.2.3 shows a latent shoeprint that before being

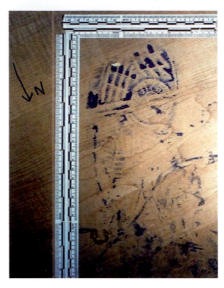

FIGURE 7.2.3 Bloody shoeprint at a crime scene.

sprayed with leuco crystal violet was barely visible on the kitchen floor of this same crime scene.

It should be remembered that crime scene investigations that require science-based screening tools are most reliable if someone is involved who understands the physics and chemistry of those tools. Some reagents used to test/enhance blood can give false positives if other materials are present (the older reagent luminol often gave false positives in the presence of rust deposits). Forensic scientists are best equipped to deal with any such results if they arise.

When working in such bloody crime scenes, it is imperative that everyone is aware of the risks of dealing with potential bloodborne pathogens. HIV and hepatitis are the two most common exposure risks. Of these, hepatitis is the more likely to be contracted. It is the responsibility of the investigator in charge to ensure that all investigators use personal protective equipment that includes at a minimum, eye protection, a face mask, a hooded Tyvek® suit, rubber gloves, and bootees.

The information you are likely to discover through an examination of the bloodstains includes (Bevel and Gardner, 2002):

- The direction a given droplet was traveling at the time of impact
- The angle of impact
- The probable distance from the target from which the droplet originated
- The nature of the force involved in the bloodshed and the direction from which that force was applied
- The nature of any object used in applying the force
- The approximate number of blows struck during an incident

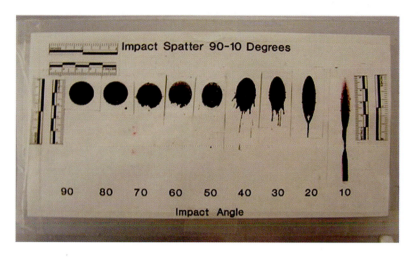

FIGURE 7.2.4 A photocopy taped to the inside of an investigator's notebook as an aid to bloodstains.

- The relative position in the scene of the suspect, victim, or other related objects during the incident
- Sequencing of multiple events associated with an incident
- In some instances, which hand delivered the blows from a beating

So how are the answers to all these questions determined? It is fortunate that only a few general rules govern most of the behavior of blood at crime scenes.

Directionality

The investigators can learn a lot of information about the bloodstains by determining their directionality, that is, the direction the bloodstains were traveling when they struck the target. It has been shown by high-speed photography that blood droplets in flight are in the form of spheres. The behavior of traveling blood can be compared to a ball of thin pancake batter. If the batter ball drops from vertically above onto a pan, the ball will flatten out to give a round pancake shape. If the batter ball is projected onto the pan, say at a 45° angle, the resulting pancake will be elongated in shape and a smaller ball may be projected in the direction of the original travel. For bloodstains, the motion in the 45° example gives rise to a "tail," which when inspected can tell which direction the bloodstain was traveling when it hit the target. During training, investigators typically produce similar stains by dropping blood onto cards that are set at angles ranging from 10° to 90° impact angle. When dried these can be photocopied and conveniently carried by the investigator as an aide memoire (Figure 7.2.4).

Grouping Bloodstains

Bloodstains can be group acccording to location, size, and shape. Consider the three oval stains on a white painted wall just right of center in Figure 7.2.5.

FIGURE 7.2.5 *Three oval stains at a crime scene.*

The tails indicate that the blood droplets were traveling in an eight o'clock to two o'clock direction. The directionality of the stains shows an impact angle of approximately 40° (compare to Figure 7.2.4). It is likely that this group of similar-shaped, similar-sized bloodstains in the same location have been generated by the same event.

Droplet Size and Force

The greater the force involved in their production, the smaller the size of the predominant blood droplet.

- Gunshot, with the high energies involved in production, produces blood droplets that are 1 millimeter (mm) and smaller in diameter. This is often termed high-velocity or high-energy spatter.
- Medium-velocity impact spatter, caused by a medium force event (such as a stabbing or a beating), give rise to stains that are from 1 mm to 4 mm in diameter.
- Low-velocity spatter, caused by a low-force event such as blood drops from a nose bleed, generates stains that are large, from 4 mm and up.

The phrases "high velocity," "medium velocity," and "low velocity" refer to the *mechanism that created the blood spatter* and not necessarily the speed at which the blood hits the surface it is deposited on.

Types of Bloodstains

There are five main categories of bloodstains: passive, impact spatter, transfer stains, other, and latent.

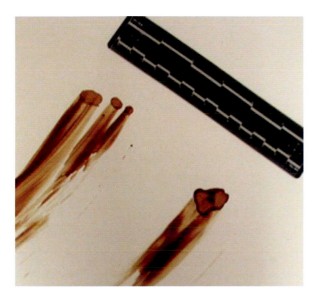

FIGURE 7.2.6 Transfer stains.

- Passive stains are mostly produced by the force of gravity and include drips, splashes, flows, and pools.
- Impact spatter stains are the result of an impact with an object to a blood source. They can produce both forward and backward spatter.
- Transfer stains consist of wipes, swipes, and contact/pattern transfer stains. Wipes are a result of an object moving through a preexisting bloodstain (see Figure 7.2.6).
- Swipes occur when a bloodied object moves across and transfers blood to a target.
- Contact/pattern transfer stains occur when a wet bloody object contacts another surface (see Figure 7.2.7).
- Other stains consist of projected, cast-off, and expired. Projected blood is from arterial spurts or gushes. Cast-off blood patterns occur when blood is released from or projected onto a surface from a bloody object that is in motion. Bloodied baseball bats and knives when swung give rise to these stains, which are typically very narrow or occur as "tramlines" when blood is projected from both sides of the weapon in motion (see Figure 7.2.8).
- Latent stains are by their definition not visible and need chemical enhancements to be seen, as in Figure 7.2.3.

Conclusion

Bloodstain crime scenes should be worked using the same systematic general crime scene procedures as with other crime scenes, using standard search patterns. One of the more quantitative approaches used at crime scenes,

FIGURE 7.2.7 Contact pattern.

FIGURE 7.2.8 Blood projected from both sides of a weapon in motion.

bloodstain pattern analysis can greatly assist in reconstructing criminal events. The potential biological hazards posed by human blood stains necessitate the use of personal protective gear and healthy caution.

Reference

Bevel, T., Gardner, R.M., 2002. Bloodstain Pattern Analysis: With an Introduction to Crime Scene Reconstruction, 2nd ed. CRC Press, Boca Raton, FL.

Photogrammetry and 3D Reconstruction[1]

As sketches and photographs are mandatory recording means for crime scene management requiring precision and reliability (Badger, 1989; Berg, 1995), the first crime scene maps based on pictures taken with calibrated cameras date back to the early 20th century. A calibration room was then used to correct the distances and angles recorded on crime scenes. Photogrammetry was born (Mathyer, 1986; O'Brien, 1989).

Documentation and analysis of crime or crash scenes are critical tasks within forensic work and must be instituted at the beginning of any forensic investigation (Graveson, 1999; Kanable, 2004). This chapter presents photogrammetry and the growing application of three-dimensional (3D)

Key Terms
Photogrammetry
LIDAR

---

[1] The authors are very indebted to Commander Laurent Chartier, Head of the Signal Image Voice Department of the Forensic Research Institute of the Gendarmerie Nationale (IRCGN – France) for having helped with this section.

laser scanning at crime or crash scenes. Both techniques yield 3D images of the crime scene; software then produces reconstructions using 3D models with realistic textures. Although it is based on images collected at the scene, rendering them as 3D reconstructions can be very influential to a jury; there is additional reason to make sure the models are accurate as possible. Animated reconstructions are even more susceptible to "interpretative" bias, as the CSI has provided the data to a third party that codes the software for the presentation. As with any new technology, the CSI must be sure of her methods and mindful of the impact it may have in court.

Photogrammetry

Photogrammetry is a process for determining geometric properties and distances from two-dimensional (2D) photographic images. The simplest version is determining the distance between two points in a photograph, given the scale of the image (which is why it is important to always provide a scale in images taken at crime scenes where measurements may be needed). Stereophotogrammetry (referred to as just "photogrammetry" herein for brevity) involves estimating the 3D coordinates of points on an object. This technique requires knowing the location of the camera in space, its orientation, and parameters (such as focal length and lens distortions). It can be used for topographic mapping, surveying, collision engineering, and crime scene recording (Saunders, 1988; Galvin, 2005a).

Points in 3D space are determined by measurements taken from two or more photographs taken from different positions (much like stereroscopy) and common target points are chosen in each photograph. Photogrammetry

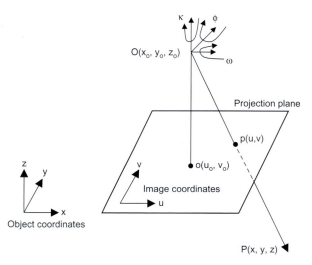

FIGURE 7.3.1 Projection plane, image coordinates, and object coordinates used in photogrammetry. The colinearity equation is complicated matrix algebra and is best left to software to calculate.

techniques rely on the collinearity equation[2] to deduce object coordinates (3D) from various sensor planes (2D) containing at least six common target points to solve the equations.[3] The camera location acts as the third point between common target points one and two, thus triangulating the points and deriving the location in 3D space (Figure 7.3.1). Many software programs, even freeware or shareware, exist for providing photogrammetry from overlapping images; the present section will refer to Photomodeler® but the general processes are the same regardless of the software used.

Calibration of the camera is the first step of the process, using eight photographs of a reference picture. This stage assesses the lens distortions (Figure 7.3.2). The crime scene examiner can then take various photographs of the scene, making sure there is enough overlap between any two successive photographs (Figure 7.3.3).

FIGURE 7.3.2 Lens calibration. *Courtesy Laurent Chartier, 2011.*

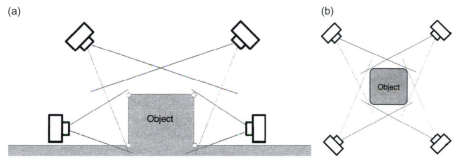

FIGURE 7.3.3 Overlap examples. *Courtesy Laurent Chartier, 2011.*

[2] The collinearity equation gives the geometry of a collection of rays connecting the center of a sensor (the camera), the first image point, and the second image point.
[3] Four points are sufficient for aerial photogrammetry, a technique called homography, as the ground is treated as an approximate plane.

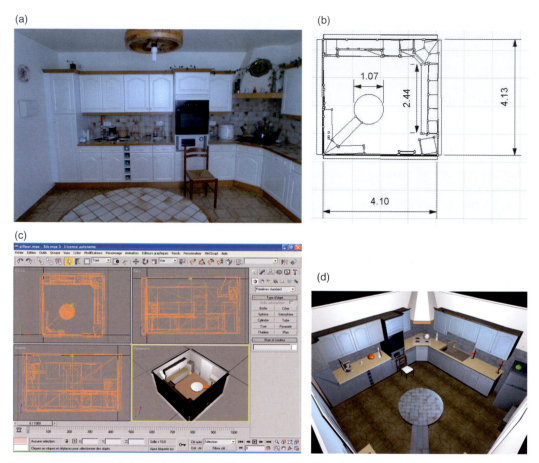

(a) (b) (c) (d)

FIGURE 7.3.4 (a) One of the original overlapping photographs; (b) exploitation in PhotoModeler®; (c) integration in 3ds Max®; (d) 3D reconstruction.
Illustrations and photographs courtesy Laurent Chartier, 2011.

The photographs are then registered in Photomodeler® and their overlapping points are marked in different views. After integrating the distortion parameters using the first photographs, the set of photographs is scaled with one measurement. Photomodeler® then draws the map of the scene and takes measurements. Finally, the results of Photomodeler® can be exported to animation software, such as Rhinoceros3D® and 3ds Max®, to create 3D animations, basing them on the various hypothesis of the investigation; a rendered example is given in Figure 7.3.4.

It should be noted that photogrammetric data are more accurate in the planar dimension (x, y) than in depth (z). Nevertheless, these data are comparable to the data generated by laser scanners. For example, a digital space scanned by a laser scanner can be orthorectified by photogrammetry through light detection and comparison to known figures (such as a LIDAR[4] grid), to assess distances and angles. For further information on the use of photogrammetry, see Brueschweiler et al. (2003) and Thali et al. (2003a, 2003b).

3D Laser Scanners

Modern tools such as the 3D scanner are able to collect, organize, and provide analytical tools for forensic investigations with sufficient quality and methodology to organize and analyze evidence, easing the usually heavy burden of taking photographs from general establishing shots to numerous details. It is a *complimentary* method to the traditional crime scene photographer, not a *replacement*; it allows recording the entire crime scene, locating all potential pieces of evidence at once, at the very beginning of the investigation. "Freezing" the images of the scene in this way establishes the crime scene—literally, the crime "seen"—and provides a baseline to check against in the case of adulteration or modification (Kanable, 2003; Hochrein, 2006; Joice, 2008). It not only secures the documented record of processing, but also provides data for later analysis for auditing or reconstruction purposes (Carey et al., 1996; Borghese et al., 1998; Galvin, 2007).

A scanner exhaustively covers all three dimensions of the crime scene in a quick and detailed manner, collecting a huge quantity of data within a precision of roughly 2–5 mm at 25 meters distance (Buck et al., 2007). Note that this precision is not the *accuracy* of the device, but its *resolution*. The accuracy of any single point should take into account not only the resolution, but also the background noise and any registration errors. This points out one other drawback: the scan only records what is visible and does so only via a normal photographic approach. Nevertheless, given its ease of use, its completeness of recording, and its ability to allow detailed analysis at a later date, 3D scanners will become an inescapable tool at crime scenes.

The device in Figure 7.3.5 scans everything in its line of sight by swiveling in 360 degrees, creating a several-million-point data set. These data will be then computed to perform measurements and precise analyses. To employ the scan for photogrammetry, overlapping scans are necessary, but the calibration and repositioning of the different scans are automatically made either through triangulation, as with regular photogrammetry, or using indicators (see the white ball on Figure 7.3.5) positioned by the CSI and identified as such in the data software.

Different technologies exist depending on an agency's needs and the size of the crime scene. For shorter ranges or smaller crime scenes, small 3D scanners

---

[4] LIDAR (Light Detection and Ranging) uses the same principles as radar. The LIDAR sends a signal to the ground from an airplane; some of the signal bounces back to the plane. The time for the light to travel back is used to determine the height of the object (the path from a treetop is shorter than the path to the ground, for example).

FIGURE 7.3.5 Laser/scan FARO LS420® used by the IRCGN. Notice the white ball at the bottom right that will serve to reposition the different scan shots. *Courtesy Laurent Chartier, 2011.*

FIGURE 7.3.6 Lower mandible scanned with Nextengine®. *Courtesy Laurent Chartier, 2011.*

(such as the MVC 3D® camera from Mantis Vision® or the 3D Scanner from NextEngine®) use photogrammetry or stereo-matching to collect images of objects. These 3D scanners record the laser ray of a source with a camera, varying the angles to assess point coordinates by triangulation. These devices can be very accurate to collect an image of an object in a short range; this kind of a 3D scanner is used in forensic odontology and anthropology to compare a 3D model of a suspect's jaw and bite mark evidence on a victim (Figure 7.3.6) (Schoenhofer, 1998; Myers et al., 1999).

For middle- and longer-range scans, 3D scanners emit a beam of light (visible or not) and measure the distance of a point by the part of the beam reflected to the instrument; this is essentially the same as LIDAR (see footnote 4) but without the airplane. The shape of the object is assessed by the time of flight of the incident and reflected beams; this technology allows very long range, up to 2 km for some devices like Leica® or Optec® LIDARs. Another technology for middle- and long-range scanning is phase-based scanning, where a continuous laser beam is used, signaling a phase change when striking an object. The difference in phases between the incident and the reflected light beams is proportional to the distance from the device to the object. But, as the beam transmission is continuous, it also needs more energy than other 3D scanners mentioned. As a consequence, the phase-based scanners can operate only from very short range to about 100 meters. Therefore, time-flight scanners (like the Trimble®) are more convenient for car crash reconstruction and phase-based scanners (like the FARO® shown in Figure 7.3.5 or the FARO® Photon®, Zoller + Fröhlich®, or Leica® models) are better dedicated to crime scene recording.

The accuracy of the scanner can be set by the user based on the scene and any further digital processing that may be planned. The speed, resolution, and later processing need to be balanced given the time available, resources, and nature of the crime.

Background noise depends both on the system and the surface struck by the laser beam. Glossy and dark surfaces create the noisiest data; a glossy surface is highly reflective, and the laser beam can be totally reflected, in many directions, then transmitted back to the receiver after many ricochets, giving a ghostly picture of "point clouds." Similarly, inclined surfaces decrease the energy sent back to the device. A dark surface, however, absorbs the light and does not reflect enough energy back to the receiver. In this case, dusting an object with a light-colored powder can improve the signal clarity and response.

Finally, accuracy of a 3D scan also depends on errors in recording. To decrease these errors, the CSI has to use well-placed references around the scene; recording between two point clouds needs at least three references. The most common reference is the sphere, because its center can always be determined very accurately from any viewpoint. Another way to decrease record errors is to place the scanner in the center of the location to be scanned, with spheres at the outskirts of the main area to reposition the various shots.

Once the various errors have been minimized, the CSI can conduct the 3D scanning. The CSI running the scan should confer with all the different forensic scientists at the scene to assess the needs of each, such as ballistics, blood pattern analysis, and crime scene reconstruction; for absent colleagues with whom to confer, the CSI must evaluate as best as possible what *apparent* and *potential* analyses are needed and allocate resources appropriately. Based on these decisions, the range and the various locations for the scanner on the scene are chosen. A short range is better for ballistics, blood pattern analysis, or height determination (from security or surveillance CCTV); medium or long range are better for larger crime or crash scenes. The different locations of the device are determined by the crime scene configuration. At any position, the scanner should have the largest field of view to detect the maximum number of references (this increases accuracy). For this reason, the scanner is better placed in front of each room in a corridor, or close to a window or a door to link the inside and the outside in the 3D model. According to the positioning of the scanner, different sphere references will be positioned throughout the area, aiming at meshing the various point-cloud shots by triangulation. Spheres should be positioned at different elevations; moreover, spheres should be placed in the middle range between any two positions of the scanner and not too close to one position or very far from another one. This placement helps with registration and accuracy later on.

The first scan taken will be used to calibrate the measurement at the scene. As manufacturers annually certify the scanning device, a specific calibration is needed for each mission between two such controls; the scanners, unlike cameras, are precision measuring instruments and must be treated as such. To calibrate, CSIs can use a reference layout or a known distance at the crime scene to calibrate patterns (for example, the scanner's container used to transport it between scenes, because its dimensions are known). Any scans after this first one are to record the scene. The scanner need not be recalibrated between scans at a crime scene but should be recalibrated between individual scenes.

Case Examples of 3D Laser Scanner

Three-dimensional models can help explain hypotheses and present easily intelligible reconstructions using either 3D animation or 2D views for the trier-of-fact. Data can then be computed to perform measurements and precise analyses; the application of the scanner is limited only by the resolution of the instrument and the ingenuity of the CSI. A few examples will be presented here to demonstrate its utility.

Road, Train, Ship Accidents

Large-scale scenes pose particular problems for the CSI, if only because of the scale of the evidence to be examined or the size of the scene itself. Three-dimensional models allow reliable analysis of large-scale scenarios, like large vehicle accidents such as train, bus, or ship accidents. The acquisition time can be short (six minutes for each position of the scanner). After the acquisition stage, the CSI can take measurements or analyze damage in postprocessing with very good accuracy at any point in the 3D model (Figures 7.3.7).

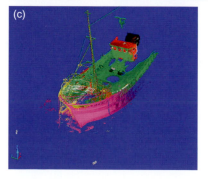

FIGURE 7.3.7 (a) Air photograph from a bus-train collision; (b) 3D reconstruction from the previous scene; (c) 3D reconstruction of ship wreckage. *All illustrations and photographs courtesy Laurent Chartier, 2011.*

Bloodstain Pattern Analysis

Bloodstain pattern analysis can be assisted by 3D scanning to record the crime scene, examine it, and reconstruct the event. Phase-based scanners allow work to be conducted inside a very small area and some of these scanners come with software that includes forensic tools for bloodstain pattern analysis. For instance, FARO Scene® software from FARO® provides the analyst 3D evaluations of area of origin. Interactions between 3D modeling and bloodstain pattern analysis should occur in five steps:

1. Appraisal of the bloody scene to define to 3D model priorities.
2. Positioning of reference spheres and scales at the crime scene; for each blood stain set, each square (about 50 × 50 cm) needs four targets or matching points for the registration phase.
3. Scanning of the crime scene with a 2–3 mm precision at 5 m (about seven minutes for each position of the scanner).
4. Afterward, the crime scene examiner should take high-definition photographs for each bloodstain area, for which the four previously marked matching points recorded should not be too close to the edges of the pictures to prevent repositioning on the 3D scan. This technique is called 3D/2D mapping (see Figure 7.3.8 as a reconstruction result) (Galvin, 2005b; Schiff, 2007).
5. The bloodstain pattern analyst can then use a forensic package to assess the area of origin (Figure 7.3.9).

Like with photography, 3D scanners do not replace the traditional measurements for bloodstain pattern analysis and these data need to be collected, photographed, and analyzed *in addition to* any 3D scanning that is employed.

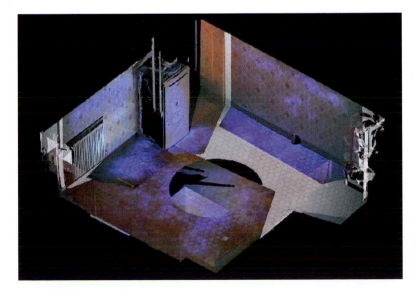

FIGURE 7.3.8 3D/2D mapping after bloodstain detection. *Courtesy Laurent Chartier, 2011.*

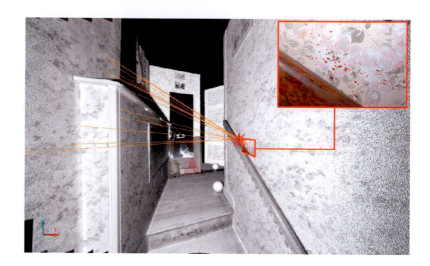

FIGURE 7.3.9 Bloodstain pattern analysis in 3D modeling. *Courtesy Laurent Chartier, 2011.*

Shooting Reconstructions

Shooting scene reconstructions and hypotheses analysis can also be supported by photogrammetry and 3D scanning, to establish trajectories, corroborate witness accounts, or to help determine sequence of firings. The partnership between the CSI and the firearms specialist follows the same methodology as the one previously described for bloodstain pattern analysis: appraisal of the scene priorities, positioning of references, scanning, photography, and analysis. These references could opportunistically be ballistic sticks of a trajectory reconstruction kit belonging to the ballistic expert. The 3D technician can thus select two sticks on the 3D model to draw the trajectory line. The ballistic expert is then able to use the 3D model to export different views (front view, top view, side view, etc.) to be inserted in his final report (Figure 7.3.10).

The 3D model can also be used for presentations in court and layouts (such as for positioning a human body) and can be inserted into the model to study various scenarios.

Height Determination

A 3D scanner typically comes with software tools to assess the height of a suspect from CCTV or survey photographs. The questioned picture is imported in the 3D model through the 3D/2D mapping technique. The contact between the foot of the questioned person and the ground or floor is marked, with the projection on the ground or floor along the optical line of the camera; the camera is then located on the 3D capture. The height can then be assessed (Figure 7.3.11).

Object Comparison

Individual objects can be scanned in three dimensions, such as antiquities, with a good accuracy allowing measurements (Figures 7.3.12(a) and (b)) and even 3D superimposition using differently colored layers to show differences

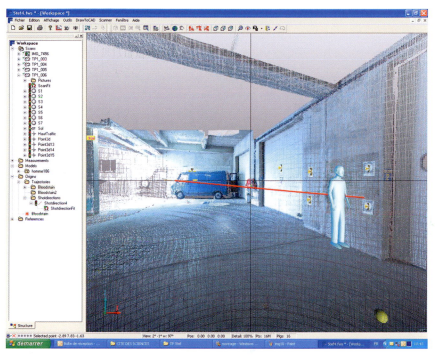

FIGURE 7.3.10 Shooting incident reconstruction. *Courtesy Laurent Chartier, 2011.*

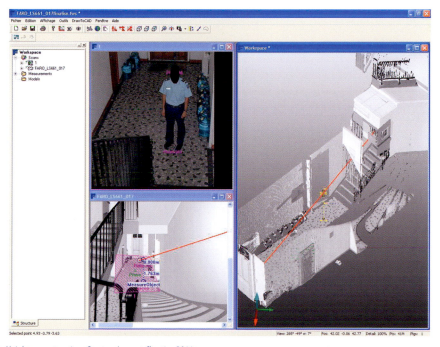

FIGURE 7.3.11 Height reconstruction. *Courtesy Laurent Chartier, 2011.*

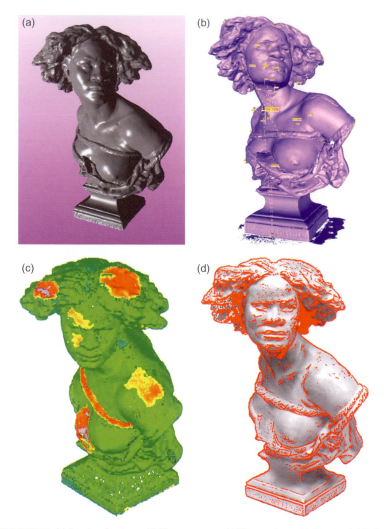

FIGURE 7.3.12 (a) Questioned sculpture; (b) 3D measurements; (c) 3D comparisons with the original; (d) edge extraction from catalog. *All illustrations and photographs courtesy Laurent Chartier, 2011.*

(Figure 7.3.12(c)). Comparison with photographs in a catalog is possible, using edge extraction (Figure 7.3.12(d)) between the photographed reference and the sculpture at hand to highlight any differences. If the photographs are not scaled, however, the measurements must be interpreted with caution.

Bombing Scenes

Bombing scenes can be studied through 3D reconstruction, recording and comparing damaged areas. Moreover, the scanner raw data and software such as Matlab® allows various hypotheses of crime scene reconstruction to be quantitatively evaluated; for instance, coloring different damaged

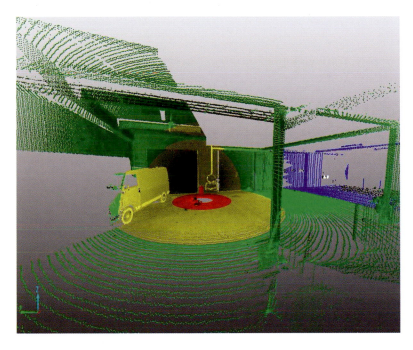

FIGURE 7.3.13 Explosion reconstruction. *Courtesy Laurent Chartier, 2011.*

areas around the explosion center, relating to varying levels of exposure to the explosion, to be compared with the actual damaged areas to look for correlation or confirmation (Figure 7.3.13).

Potentially Contaminated Scenes Such as a Terrorist Attack

When the crime scene itself is contaminated, as would be the case in a chemical, biological, radiological, or nuclear (CBRN) attack, 3D scanning and modeling offers the CSI field team an efficient tool to assess the scene safely with less initial exposure to hazardous conditions. The contaminated area can be defined, and missions allocated to the various teams (explosive ordinance disposal, CBRN specialists, or forensic, for example) for evidence collection (Figures 7.3.14(a) and (b)). Preparation for each mission can be done on the 3D scanned model collected by a single team with easily carried equipment (Figure 7.3.14(c)).

Conclusion

From the start of work at the crime scene, documentation and analysis are critical tasks. Technology to aid in these tasks is reaching the crime scene in the form of photogrammetry and 3D laser scanning. These methods can make collecting images and measurements easier and more precise. But, as with any new technology, CSIs must be sure of their methods and mindful of the impact they may have in court before they apply them.

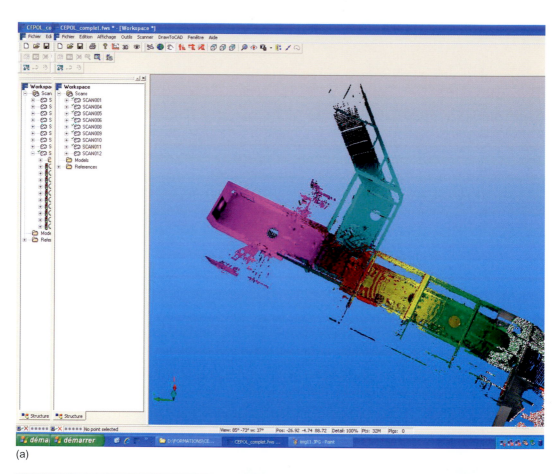

(a)

(b) (c)

FIGURE 7.3.14 (a) Large view of the CBRN crime scene; (b) closest view; (c) 3D scanners are easily packed and carried into contaminated scenes. *Courtesy Laurent Chartier, 2011.*

References and Bibliography

Badger, J., 1989. Precise diagrams possible with computer drawing. Law and Order 37 (10): 16–18.

Berg, E., 1995. The evolution of the crime scene diagram. J. Forensic Ident. 45 (1): 25–29.

Borghese, N.A., Ferrigno, G., Baroni, G., Pedotti, A., Ferrari, S., Savare, R., 1998. Autoscan: A flexible and portable 3D scanner. IEE Com. Graphics Appl., 38–41.

Brueschweiler, W., Braun, M., Dirnhofer, R., Thali, M.J., 2003. Analysis of patterned injuries and injury-causing instruments with forensic 3D/CAD supported photogrammetry (FPHG): An instruction manual for the documentation process. Forensic Sci. Int. 132: 130–138.

Buck, U., Albertini, N., Naether, S., Thali, M.J., 2007. 3D Documentation of footwear impressions and tire tracks in snow with high resolution optical surface scanning. Forensic Sci. Int. 171: 157–164.

Galvin, B., 2005a. Photogrammetry mapping for crime scenes. Law and Order 53 (3): 36–41.

Galvin, B., 2005b. Portable solutions at the crash scene. Law Enforc. Technol. 32 (11): 73–82.

Galvin, B., 2007. Complex crime scene becomes clearer. Evid. Technol. Mag. 4 (6): 12–17.

Graveson, G.W., 1999. Crime scene mapping. Law and Order 47 (11): 45.

Hochrein, M.J., 2006. The different levels of crime-scene mapping offer some unique opportunities. Evid. Technol. Mag. 4 (6): 24–40.

Joice, B., 2008. Forensic mapping: The use of total stations and mapping software to produce scale diagrams. J. Forensic Ident. 58 (1): 15–26.

Kanable, R., 2003. Crime scene digitization: A dream made reality. Law Enforc. Technol. 30 (2): 90–93.

Kanable, R., 2004. 2D today & tomorrow: 2D technology has its place in accident and crime scene reporting. Law Enforc. Technol. 31 (7): 106–115.

Mathyer, J., 1986. Photographie et police. Rev. Int. Police Tech. 2: 223–252.

Myers, J.C., Okoye, M.I., Kiple, D., Kimmerle, E.H., Reinhard, K.J., 1999. Three-dimensional (3-D) imaging in post-mortem examinations: Elucidation and identification of cranial and facial fractures in victims of homicide utilizing 3-D computerized imaging reconstruction techniques. Int. J. Legal Med. 113 (1): 33–37.

O'Brien, M.W., 1989. Scale model use in criminal trials. J. Forensic Ident. 39: 359–366.

Robinson, E., 2007. Crime Scene Photography. Academic Press, Amsterdam.

Saunders, G., 1988. Photogrammetric revolution. RCMP Gaz. 50 (9): 1–9.

Schiff, D., 2007. Crime scene 3D viewpoints: Illustrating what was seen at the scene. Forensic Mag. 4 (3): 42–46.

Schoenhofer, T., 1998. Portable non-contact 3D scanner. CRM 21 (5): 25.

Thali, M.J., Braun, M., Markwalder, T.H., Brueschweiler, W., Zollinger, U., Malik, N.J., Yen, K., Dirnhofer, R., 2003a. Bite mark documentation and analysis: The forensic 3D/CAD supported photogrammetry approach. Forensic Sci. Int. 135: 115–121.

Thali, M.J., Braun, M., Brueschweiler, W., Dirnhofer, R., 2003b. 'Morphological imprint': Determination of the injury-causing weapon from the wound morphology using forensic 3D/CAD-supported photogrammetry. Forensic Sci. Int. 132: 177–181.

Special Crime Scenes

Special Crime Scenes

At some point in each CSI's career, he or she will be presented with a special crime scene, one for which they are ill-prepared, either technically or emotionally. Scenes of mass fatalities, hazardous materials, difficult situations, or terrorist activities require a highly trained, specific forensic approach (Figure 8.0.1). They require extensive cooperation, communication, logistics, and very often the combined efforts of multiple agencies bringing to bear their combined resources to tackle the issues of scene management, disaster victim identification (DVI), and possible criminal investigation. Scenes like the attacks on the World Trade Center (both the 1993 bombing and the attack on September 11, 2001), the Oklahoma City Bombing, Flight 93 that went down in Pennsylvania (also on September 11, 2001), the Madrid train bombings, the 2005 London subway attacks, and many, many other natural and human scenes push the limits of forensic capabilities and the CSI's abilities.

Key Term
Disaster victim identification (DVI)

FIGURE 8.0.1 Special crime scenes, involving mass fatalities, hazardous conditions, toxic materials, or difficult locations present particular challenges and hazards to the CSI: (a) Oklahoma City Bombing; (b) Hurricane Katrina; (c) TWA Flight 800; (d) American Airlines Flight 587. *Sources: (a–c) Wikimedia Commons; (d) NOAA via Wikimedia Commons.*

Every crime scene is unique and requires an adaptive, specific, and comprehensive approach. This is even truer for special environments, such as being underwater and underground; these locations are hazardous both for CSI's and the evidence. Specialized training, both in the classroom and in simulations, is central to being prepared for the unthinkable.

Disaster and Mass Fatalities

A disaster involving mass fatalities creates a specific problem that only forensic science can solve: Who died? These situations are more than massive crime scenes, they are situations requiring extensive cooperation, communication, logistics, and dedication. Hurricanes, floods, airplane crashes, bombings, spree killings, and other tragedies like these all require the combined efforts and resources of multiple agencies to tackle the issues of scene management, disaster victim identification (DVI), and possible criminal investigation.

A mass fatality incident is defined as an event where the number of deceased individuals who must be located, identified, and released for final disposition exceeds the local or regional resources. This may seem like a vague definition but there is no standard threshold for what constitutes a "mass fatality." The response to a mass fatality inevitably requires multiple agencies and

Key Term
Mass fatality

organizations becoming involved, whether local, state, federal, military, or a combination. No one agency can manage a mass fatality without assistance from other agencies. All agencies involved need to work together to see that the recovery and processing of remains is as comprehensive and complete as possible, the victims' families are identified and notified, and the agencies' normal daily operations are maintained as best as possible.

Some events that cross jurisdictions, like pandemics or coordinated but unconnected attacks, may be managed as separate incidents or multiple individual incidents; a centralized command may be created, however, to coordinate responses once the incidents are connected. The incident command will vary depending on the type of disaster or mass fatality and could be the region's chief medical examiner, the Department of Public Health, the state police or equivalent, a federal agency (like the Federal Emergency Management Agency, FEMA, or the Centers for Disease Control, CDC), or a federal law enforcement agency, such as the FBI.

As was stated previously, one of the most important tools at a crime scene is communication: at a disaster, it is critical. Ironically and sadly, communicating across agencies can be the most difficult thing to accomplish, as was revealed in the responses to the September 11, 2001 attacks in New York City and Arlington, Virginia. Each of the public emergency services and the military may have entirely independent, and in many cases noncompatible, radio communication systems. Therefore, coordination of the following activities is required for effective disaster event response:

- Information management with status updates and analysis
- Identification, allocation, and provision of required personnel and material resources
- Implementation of operational plans for victim management
- Provision of accurate information regarding the identification of previously missing victims to families and local authorities

Electronic media, like text messaging or email, can be good for *information* but tend to lack the necessary context and emotion for *communication*. Do not ignore the power of a face-to-face conversation. Chaos can be delayed or even avoided by having a clearly defined command structure and delineated communication channels.

Emergency Communications Remain a Challenge 10 Years after 9/11

Although some improvements have been made in emergency management communications, there is still a great deal of work left to do in this area. Chris Russo, a 25-year firefighting veteran, a 9/11 first responder, and founder of ELERTS Corporation, recently told *Homeland Security News Wire*,

> *Interoperability between public safety agencies was inadequate, and in many cases nonexistent. The first responders on the scene at Ground Zero arrived from many different agencies and geographical jurisdictions. We were severely hampered by not being able to communicate with each other, as radio systems did not allow for interagency communications….There were some redundant communications systems, but in some cases, they were located alongside the primary systems and subsequently lost in the collapse. Many communications systems are designed with a redundancy, but it is based on routine loss, not catastrophic loss of infrastructure….9/11 was a massive wake-up call that our public safety communications were grossly inadequate for managing catastrophic events, with multiple agencies responding to the crisis.*

The accelerating pace and diversity of communication technologies and how the public uses them continue to be one of the greatest challenges to emergency communications. For example, the use of Twitter, a social networking application, in the 2011 east coast earthquake exceeded its use when Osama bin Laden was killed, hitting about 5,500 Tweets (messages) per second. Planning, funding (particularly funding beyond an uncertain annual grant cycle), and innovation will be required to improve these badly needed services.

Sources: Emergency communication remains a challenge ten years after 9/11, *Homeland Security News Wire*, September 9, 2011; US East Coast earthquake generated more Tweets than Osama bin Laden death, *The Telegraph*, August 25, 2011.

The Disaster Scene

Perimeter security is even more important in large-scale events simply due to their size. A two-zone perimeter may be required. The inner perimeter would include all areas in which victims, evidence, or property would be contained. Entry into the inner perimeter must be strictly controlled and documented, limited to authorized personnel. An outer perimeter will be established by law enforcement at the maximum distance from the event that can be secured. No one other than assigned emergency workers should be allowed within the outer perimeter. If the incident involves hazardous materials, hot, warm, and cold zones (in increasing ranking of safety) will be established. A data management system must be established to log, track, and update evidence, remains, contacts, personal effects, and disposition; the number of individuals or items of evidence may number in the thousands. A death scene initially should be treated as a crime scene, protected to minimize disturbance until all survivors can be removed.

The transition from search-and-rescue to CSI functions—searching for and recovering evidence and bodies—is a major shift in operations; transitions are always difficult, particularly in intense situations where command may shift from one agency to another. The incident command in conjunction with the leaders of the CSI and forensic teams should consider various factors as part of the situation assessment in the operations transition. A completely or partially new team of professionals may be needed in the evidence search phases. A coherent, consistent, and expandable numbering system must be implemented for tagging and tracking evidence, human remains, and personal effects. Determine what recovery and evidence processing methods are relevant to the event, and select and document them. Establish staging areas, *separate* from those used for survivor recovery, to facilitate evidence processing. Rotating shift schedules may be required, depending on available staff and resources; plan time for regular breaks and meals, debriefings, communications, and counseling.

Once the transition has been established, the primary functions for personnel responding to a mass fatality event are:

1. *Body recovery*, including bodies and body parts, marking and documenting the location of remains, and transporting them to the next stage of processing, either decontamination or the morgue
2. *Evidence recovery*, as per normal CSI protocols
3. *Decontamination,* removing chemical or biological contaminants, if necessary, to render remains or evidence safe for further handling and examination
4. *Examination*
   a. Remains: triage for identification methods (fingerprints, odontology, anthropology, etc.) and autopsy in the morgue
   b. Evidence: documentation, collection, packaging, preservation
5. *Identification and death certification*
6. *Processing for final disposition*

Given the nature of the event, the focus is typically on the identification of all individuals who died as a result of the incident.

Human Remains

Each unit of human remains is tagged, numbered, and removed from the site by authorized personnel (law enforcement or the office of chief medical examiner, OCME). Remains are transported to the morgue by a transportation team. All personal effects found on a body or in association with human remains are not removed and stay with the body when it is placed into the body bag. Each human remain is placed into a separate body bag and given a separate number. Depending on the size and nature of the event, the chief medical examiner (CME) will determine where to establish an event morgue. The site may be at the OCME or another location closer to the incident. The

CME lays out the morgue giving consideration to the physical condition of the decedents, the number of decedents, and the number of personnel needed to perform morgue functions. The operational areas may include areas for decontamination, admitting, forensic pathology, forensic photography, personal effects, fingerprinting, odontology, radiology, anthropology, DNA, and release of remains. The event morgue may be a portable facility purchased and prepared prior to the incident or it may be one set up in a preexisting but nonforensic facility, such as a National Guard armory, unused warehouse, or even a parking lot with tents. Regardless, the facility should have the following to support morgue operations:

- Secure perimeter
- Hot and cold running water
- Electricity
- Drainage
- Biohazardous waste disposal capacity
- Parking
- Restrooms
- Communications
- Refrigerated space for storage of remains (could be coordinated through FEMA)

The morgue should have a workflow defined (Figure 8.1.1) to facilitate a systematic operation and promote consistency of operations.

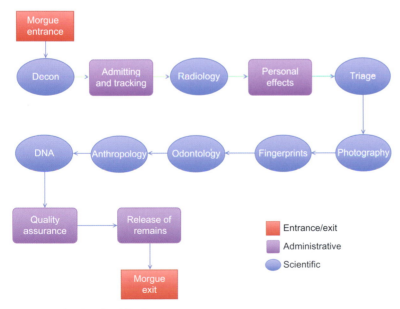

FIGURE 8.1.1 A suggested workflow for a temporary morgue.

Along with the rest of forensic science, forensic DNA typing has revolutionized disaster victim identification, which allows for identification of any biological sample and the association of body parts, as long as sufficient DNA can be recovered from the samples. The methodology has even progressed to the point where tissue samples can be quite degraded and still render useful identifications. Other methods, including anthropology, dental records, fingerprints, and even tattoos, should be used in a hierarchical process in the mass fatality identification effort. Although DNA samples may be taken from each individual for later exclusionary or linking analysis, these other methods of identification can reduce or even eliminate the need for DNA analysis, which requires more labor, resources, and time.

Conclusion

Crime scenes with mass fatalities presents particular—and sometimes extreme—challenges to the CSI. Approaching them as merely massive scenes is a mistake: They are some of the most difficult scenes to work, organizationally, technically, and personally. The scale of damage is only one aspect, however, and the issues of mass identification must be approached with structure, forethought, and consideration for the living and the dead.

Bibliography

Capstone Document: Mass Fatality Management for Incidents Involving Weapons of Mass Destruction, 2005. U.S. Army Research Development & Engineering Command and Department of Justice, Office of Justice Programs, Office for Domestic Preparedness.

Disaster Victim Identification Guide, 2009. Interpol, Lyon, France.

Lessons Learned from 9/11: DNA Identification in Mass Fatality Incidents, 2006. National Institute of Justice, Office of Justice Programs, U.S. Department of Justice, Washington, DC.

Mass Fatality Incidents: A Guide for Human Forensic Identification, 2005. National Institute of Justice, Office of Justice Programs, U.S. Department of Justice, Washington, DC.

Mass Fatality Plan, 2005. National Association of Medical Examiners.

Terrorist Crime Scenes

There was a time when crime scenes caused by terrorist activity were confined to "other" countries on the nightly news. It is unfortunate but terror crime scenes have become a fact of life in most countries, even western democracies.

These scenes are typically caused by two groups of terrorists: external and domestic. The external terrorists we have become familiar with in the United States since February 1993, when they bombed the World Trade Center, followed with the airliner attacks at the Pentagon, the World Trade Center, and Flight 93 that went down in Pennsylvania on September 11, 2001. In March 2004, a series of bombings of trains took place in Madrid, Spain, causing widespread damage and death, and in 2005 in London, England, similar destructive attacks took place on the transport system. Many of these bombings and attacks have been carried out by al-Qaeda or al-Qaeda-inspired terrorist cells.

Key Terms

Improvised explosive device (IED)
VBIED

We have also endured bombings and other terrorist attacks that were caused by domestic terrorists. In the United States, the most devastating attack was by Timothy McVeigh, who set off a deadly explosion with a moving van packed with ammonium nitrate and fuel oil at the Alfred P. Murrah Building in Oklahoma City on April 19, 1995. Investigation uncovered that he was motivated by his hatred of the federal government and angered by what he perceived as its mishandling of the Waco Siege (1993) and the Ruby Ridge incident (1992); McVeigh timed his attack to coincide with the second anniversary of the deadly fire that ended the siege at Waco. Other incidents have been caused by various groups with interests that were as diverse as animal rights, anti-abortion, anti-Semitism, and white supremacy.

European governments have sustained domestic attacks from separatist groups for over 50 years, the most famous groups being the Provisional IRA (PIRA) from Northern Ireland and the ETA in Spain.

Governments, police agencies, and emergency management agencies have been forced to prepare for terrorist threats, no matter what the motivation of the group likely to perform the destructive act. Terrorists have also killed other than by bombings or shootings. Domestic terrorists in Japan, in 1994, released clouds of sarin gas, a chemical weapon, in the Tokyo subway, killing 12 and injuring thousands. The types of terrorist threats are usually confined to chemical, biological, radiological, and nuclear (CBRN). The section that follows will focus on incendiary/explosive terror incidents.

Terrorists sometimes use conventional military weapons suck as rockets, rocket-propelled grenades, or mortars, but often they use improvised explosive devices (IEDs).

No matter what the incident, when a crime scene investigator arrives at the scene of an explosion, he has the same objective as at any other investigation: to gather physical evidence that will assist the trier of fact, who will successfully prosecute the suspect if he or she is responsible for the explosion. The forensic scientist at the scene will make observations and collect evidence that will attempt to later do the following (Vermette, 2012):

- Determine the explosive used
- Determine sources of IED components
- Compare physical evidence from the crime scene
- Corroborate statements
- Link criminal cases

Before we proceed to look at how these tasks will be accomplished, let us look at the construction and components of IEDs. An IED has five components: a power source (battery), a switch (trigger), an initiator (detonator or fuse), a charge (explosive), and a container (body). How these come together to cause an explosion is limited only by the ingenuity of the bomb maker. The IED can vary in size from a small black powder pipe bomb to a large truck filled with ammonium nitrate and fuel oil.

The power source is usually a battery. Its function is to supply enough energy to the detonator; the power source is often alkaline flashlight batteries or car batteries for larger devices.

The switch or trigger is either a direct or indirect means of setting the device off. In booby traps this can be mechanisms such as a trip wire or a pressure switch; simple timers or alarms; radio signals generated by a cell phone; or a timer or firing button that someone presses. The PIRA in their early campaigns, before they became much more sophisticated, used white plastic–coated electrical wire up to hundreds of feet in length as command wire to connect the watching terrorist with the firing button to the detonator. The white command wire was painted green to make it blend in with the green Irish countryside and less visible from overhead surveillance.

The detonator or blasting cap is a small explosive charge that sets off the main charge. Detonators are usually electrical. The main charge is the primary explosive; this can be a military explosive such as C-4, or various types of improvised explosives that may be fertilizer-based, pyrotechnic-based, or peroxide-based. The container houses the device and it may be filled with metal shrapnel, such as nails or nuts and bolts, for antipersonnel uses. The container may be designed to form a shaped charge to force the blast in a specific direction.

It is not difficult to find information on how to construct an IED. The phrase "how to make and IED bomb" generates over 5.5 million hits on Google. Terrorist organizations have learned to share information, and in Iraq and Afghanistan where military explosives are easily accessible, the use of IEDs in the form of roadside bombs has been the cause of most of the deaths and injuries to U.S. forces.

Bombers typically use one of three methods for delivering their weapon. They may conceal the device in a package that may be in plain sight, hidden or buried, and detonate it remotely. This can happen domestically too. An Army veteran with extensive ties to white supremacists was sentenced to 32 years in Spokane, Washington, in December 2011 after being found guilty in a plot to bomb a Martin Luther King Jr. Day parade earlier in the year. The pipe bomb was in a backpack discovered and disabled before it could explode. It was loaded with lead fishing weights coated in rat poison.

Bombers may also place the IED in a vehicle's trunk (vehicle-borne IED, or VBIED) and park the vehicle alongside, for example, a convoy route in the Middle East.

The last delivery method is by a suicide bomber. The suicide bomber may strap an IED to his body (most suicide bombers are young males) and either walk to, or drive a VBIED to, a target area and explode it.

What happens when an IED explodes? A crater will form, and with most such explosions the device and shrapnel will be blown out in a radial pattern over a large area. Pieces of the device are often later found, and if the crime scene team knows what to look for, valuable information can be obtained about the design of the device. Due to this need for device recognition, the searching of explosive evidence does not lend itself to the large volunteer group that is often used in outdoor searches. It is best carried out by a team of trained bomb technicians and forensic scientists.

As noted previously, smaller local police agencies often have neither the expertise nor the logistical support to handle large explosion incidents. In the United States, the ATF and FBI may be able to provide scene response, investigative assistance, and laboratory services in cooperation with local agencies and the state crime laboratories.

How large an area should be searched? In a typical post-blast crime scene, such as the detonation of a small pipe bomb, according to Sachtleben (2012), "the outer perimeter is determined by measuring the distance from the point of detonation to the furthest item of evidence, then adding an additional 50% to that distance." For VBIEDs this perimeter could be up to 1.5 miles in all directions from the blast site.

Before any searching can begin the safety of the search team has to be considered. There may still be other devices that have not detonated. Terrorists have been known to set off an IED to draw security forces and investigators to the scene before they detonate a much larger IED. The area must be thoroughly cleared of any devices. Another issue for terrorist attacks on urban areas is the structural integrity of the buildings after the blast. As 9/11 showed, explosions followed by fire can severely weaken the building supports, rendering them unsafe to be entered. If there is any fear that this is the case, then structural engineers should be consulted.

The system that is used to initiate the charge in an explosive device consists of a power source, a switch, and a blasting cap. In the post-blast search investigators will be looking for fragments of batteries, timers, switches, circuits, wire, and the blasting cap. The recognition of how these look, and hence their ability to be found post-blast, stems from observing these items after test explosions, during training exercises by the bomb investigation team. Depending on the construction of the device the team may be looking for container fragments, duct tape or electrical tape, chemical residues, and unburned explosives. All of these initiating systems post-blast should still be considered a possible source of DNA and fingerprint evidence.

Due to the volatile nature of explosive vapors, investigators and surfaces can be easily contaminated. Personnel should wear disposable Tyvek-like clothing and head and feet protection. Gloves should be changed often. The outer packaging and containers for collection of such explosives evidence must be checked for contamination before being used. Explosive samples and soil samples should be collected in nylon, vapor-resistant bags, or in clean metal cans.

The strip, grid, and zone search patterns discussed previously can be equally as effective when use for explosion crime scenes. The best chance of finding residue from the explosion is at the point of detonation or objects close to it. Porous materials or objects with cracks and ridges tend to collect a large amount of useful residues. Materials from near the blast site, such as foam, pipe threads, cardboard, or any rough-surfaced items, should be collected. Do not forget to submit control samples; when soil from a blast site is collected, also collect a sample of similar soil from an area away from the seat of the blast. Explosion scenes like burial scenes may involve the sifting of large amounts of debris. Ergonomic sifting racks with different size screens should be made ready before going to the scene.

Conclusion

Even though an explosion scene is different from other crime scenes, the same general crime scene procedures of freezing the scene; recognizing, recovering, and recording physical evidence; and photographing, videotaping, sketching, and note-taking still apply.

When all the samples collected at the scene have been analyzed, the construction of the device and the explosives used may be determined. DNA and fingerprints may link items to a suspect. If that suspect's home is subsequently searched (after it has been cleared of any explosive devices), bomb-making materials may link to other bombing incidents.

References and Bibliography

Bolz, F., Dudonis, K., Schulz, D., 2011. The Counterterrorism Handbook. CRC Press, Boca Raton, FL.

Marshall, M., Oxley, J., 2008. Aspects of Explosives Detection. Elsevier, Amsterdam.

Sachtleben, D.J., 2012. Vehicle-borne improvised explosive devices. In: Beveridge, A. (Ed.), Forensic Investigation of Explosions. Taylor & Francis, New York.

Thurman, J., 2011. Practical Bomb Scene Investigation, second ed. CRC Press, Boca Raton, FL.

Vermette, J.-Y., 2012. General protocols at the scene of an explosion. In: Beveridge, A. (Ed.), Forensic Investigation of Explosions. Taylor & Francis, New York.

CBRN Crime Scenes

Modern technology, warfare, and terrorism highlight the dangers of chemical, bacteriological, radiological,[1] and nuclear (CBRN) incidents or crimes.[2] Just as all of these methods can be easily labeled weapons of mass destruction (WMD), each of them can also be thought of as weapons of mass *disruption*, creating chaos, interrupting needed services, and inciting panic in a populace; nuclear, of course, has overwhelmingly the greatest lethal capacity of all the others. History shows that chemical or bacteriological warfare or criminal use are not an invention of the 20th century (Wieviorka, 1988; Falkenrath et al., 1998; Carus, 2001;

Key Terms
CBRN
weapons of mass destruction (WMD)

---

[1] "Radiological" is distinguished from "nuclear" due to the potential use of a so-called "dirty bomb," which would explode, but only to disperse radiological material, not detonate a nuclear bomb.
[2] The U.S. Department of Defense also uses the acronym CBRNE to include high-yield explosive incidents.

FIGURE 8.3.1 Wear protection contingency for CBRN crime scene management. *With permission, courtesy Thierry Lezeau, 2010.*

Chaliand and Blin, 2004); chemical warfare started with poisoned arrow tips and various noxious or blinding agents, such as calcium oxide, mustard, or bitumen. Toxins or microorganisms may be invisible, colorless, or even odorless, but can be very efficient if dispersed in fine droplets or applied to common surfaces. A public area could be contaminated for hours or days, continually affecting or infecting people until the cases are linked through death investigations, toxicology, and autopsies. Thus, what constitutes a CBRN crime scene may be obvious, as in an explosion, or hidden, as with microorganisms. While examples are thankfully rare, the forensic community should certainly question itself about this inescapable challenge (Raymond, 2006).

In the forensic mission awaiting the CSI at a CBRN site, the first concern would certainly be personal safety and security; if the CSI is hurt or succumbs, no evidence will be collected, no analysis of the scene will be conducted, and further work might be hampered. Indeed, a CBRN crime scene can hardly be managed by a single, even if brilliant, crime scene examiner or forensic scientist; the very nature of these scenes demands a highly trained team effort, not only well informed about their techniques but also recognizing the importance of a priori intelligence gathering before intervening. Operational contingencies also impact the strategy of intervention. Trace collection can be difficult wearing CBRN protective equipment (Brown et al., 2010) (Figure 8.3.1), and the decontamination process could damage collected evidence.

But the focus on the CBRN threat on site should not be systematically translated as an immediate and exclusive focus on the CBRN evidence (Drielak, 2004). Indeed, collecting "typical" evidence at such crime scenes could inform the investigators of the true nature of the threat, the modus operandi, and perhaps lead to the identity of the perpetrators (Reutter et al., 2010). As CBR forensic analysis can be expected to take a long time (Rahni, 2002; Horita and Vass, 2003), traditional trace evidence could speed the implementation of countermeasures (Figure 8.3.2). Nevertheless, the

FIGURE 8.3.2 Searching for and collecting traditional evidence in a contaminated area. *With permission, courtesy Thierry Lezeau, 2010.*

CSI should also be aware that the CBRN environment can damage DNA or even fingerprints (Wilkinson et al., 2005, 2007, 2009; Socratous and Graham, 2008; Colella et al., 2009) and that priority is given to the decontamination procedure (Muller Vogt and Sorensen, 2002) even if it might damage evidence. A complete coverage of identifying CBRN materials is beyond the scope of this book and, properly, is the province of CBRN scientists. Rather, an operative framework for the CSI to share with the relevant officers and scientists involved on the case is offered. The following steps are adapted mainly from Drielak (2004).

The First Four Things to Do in a CBRN Incident

Information Gathering, Assessment, and Dissemination
Recognizing that a CBRN has or may occur is critical. Information may be received and disseminated via a number of routes, including intelligence agencies, the public, emergency service control rooms, predetermined risk information contained in operational response plans, labeling of hazardous substances and transportation containers, and first responder observations of signs and symptoms (victims, animals, plants, the surrounding environment).

Scene Management
The scene should be isolated to mitigate consequences. Effective scene management ("hot-zone" management) is required to control access to and from the incident scene, control movement of contaminated victims, provide safe working methods for responders, and contain the release of any substances.

Saving and Protecting Lives

Saving lives is the top priority of all responding agencies. Contamination of victims/casualties must be considered as part of the initial assessment and effective methods for rescue, decontamination, and medical treatment must be provided. The provision of timely warnings and/or evacuation of the public where appropriate may also contribute to saving lives by reducing the risk of exposure.

Additional/Specialist Support

Following the immediate operational response, specialist advice should be sought to assist with consequence management. This may include hazard identification or confirmation and establishing levels of contamination, medical support, transport and treatment of casualties, and supplementing emergency service resources. Where necessary, regional, national, and international resources can also be used to maintain or provide a sufficient level of emergency provision and response. Specialist advice and resources may also be required as part of the recovery management phase, including the provision of long-term health monitoring, psychological support, building and environmental decontamination, reestablishing public confidence, and supporting a return to normality.

Source: NATO Civilian Emergency Planning Civil Protection Committee.

Preparing for Forensic Collection

Prior to engaging a CBRN scene, any reusable tools for collecting evidence first need to be sterilized. Table 8.3.1 summarizes the minimum necessary washing process, before sealing the tools in a vacuum pack before use.

Collecting Relevant Evidence

Relevant evidence may be available outside the area of greatest contamination and threat to human life (the "hot zone"), as management of the crime scene will have already started after an incident or an attack. The rescue, Explosive Ordinance Disposal (EOD), or SWAT teams should be rapidly identified, questioned, and screened for possible evidence, as well as any other first responders. Because they could interfere with later chemical analysis, samples of used materials to counter the threat and secure the crime scene should be collected, such as tear gas canisters, fire extinguisher powder, and others.

For hot crime scenes, preparation aims at assessing the threat to define the protection level and the decontamination needs, taking weather conditions into account and any information already collected, whether forensic or

TABLE 8.3.1 Sterilization Procedures for CBRN Collection

Evidence Type	Sterilization Procedure
Chemical	1. Wash glass vessels in an ultrasonic bath of hot water and nonphosphate agent. 2. Rinse with tap water, followed with three rinses of HPLC grade water. 3. Complete drying in a 300°C oven. 4. Treat the inside surface with Regisli (N,O-bis, (trimethylsily)trifluoroacetamide) in toluene. 5. Rinse with toluene, then with methanol, then with dichloro-methane. 6. Dry in a 300°C oven for 4 hours. 7. Soak in HPLC grade water for 48 hours. 8. Rinse three times with dichloro-methane. 9. Dry at room temperature. 10. Store with sealed caps and stoppers in a clean environment.
Bacteriological	1. If no DNA analysis is required: pressurized steam in autoclave (121°C) for 15 minutes for both tools and sampling media. 2. If DNA will be requested: 8 hours baking at 180°C.
Radiological	Distilled water on stainless-steel tools and containers.

eyewitnesses. Finally, accepted standard protocols will be proposed to the members of the forensic team(s) under control of the command structure to ensure each member is clear on what is being done. This stage should particularly decide:

- What kind of materials should be sampled (bulk, solid, liquid, gas)
- Which containers will be used
- Which types of evidence will be collected
- What kind of controls or blanks would be required for further analysis
- Where the specialized working area will be located
- How to manage the refuse within the crime scene (waste area) and outside of it
- If collection materials will be allowed to be reused by washing and, if so, by what method they will be cleaned
- If the decontamination process should be upgraded

If the incident happens in an industrial facility, material safety data sheets (MSDSs) should be readily available. It should, nevertheless, be remembered that some regulations could require such information only for compounds with a concentration over 1%, and many industrial chemicals are deadly below this limit.

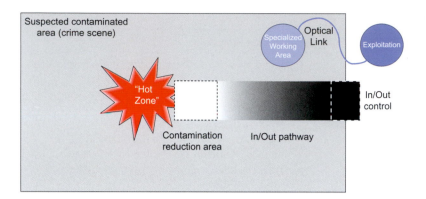

FIGURE 8.3.3 Hot crime scene schematic.

CBRN specialists, if not the rescue teams, will have defined a hot zone area with an entry point (Figure 8.3.3). The area surrounding the hot zone can be symbolized with a number of safety zones. First, there is a clear delineation of the crime scene and the area potentially contaminated. No entry should be then allowed without authorization of the command structure, which should be composed of at least the following:

- The *crime scene coordinator*, in charge of defining the evidence collection strategy and the evidence sampling sequence.
- The *scientific officer*, analyzing the data collected prior to and during the entry team work, to define the relevant evidence and appropriate containers.
- The *safety officer*, identified as the decision point person, who is in charge of checking individual safety (time of exposure, required protection) and assessing the contamination and hazards.

The hot zone(s) within the crime scene area must have a defined and clearly marked corridor for entry and exit. The hot zone(s) may not be physically connected to the crime scene and may be identified first through witness accounts (rescue, SWAT, intelligence teams, victims), and later after the intervention of the entry team. The entry and exit control zones need to be delineated and this is where the decontamination point will be located. Other areas would be later defined within the crime scene delineation, such as the contamination reduction area facing each hot zone to limit CBRN dispersal around the scene, and perhaps a specialized working area to secure and seal evidence away from the hot zone. One or more of these areas could be viewed by outside personnel via camera links. Multidisciplinary teams (Figure 8.3.4) could even be engaged in hot zone areas, so long as each specialist is aware of their individual assignments.

When CBRN evidence needs to be collected, Table 8.3.2 details this kind of sampling.

FIGURE 8.3.4 Multidisciplinary team engaging the crime scene with a 3D laser. *With permission, courtesy Thierry Lezeau, 2010.*

TABLE 8.3.2 CBR Collection

Type	Air/ Aerospray	Solid/ Bulk	Liquid/ Surface	Skin
C	Sorbent tubes with calibrated pump, and stainless-steel evacuation canisters with certified flow restrictors.	Stainless-steel sterilized materials.	Sterilized synthetic gauze.	1. Check for dermal cuts and abrasion areas to avoid. 2. Dabbing and lifting motion on the skin only once on one area. 3. Chemical handbag wash. 4. NO BRUSHING, NO SOAP. 5. AVOID WATER IF VX AGENT SUSPECTED.
B	Nonviable materials: membrane filters (cellulose ester, PVC, and polycarbonate). Viable materials: nutrient media needed (Malt Extract Agar (MEA), Tryptic Soil Agar (TSA), Rose Bengal, Peptone) by impaction onto plates or liquid impingement.			1. Check for skin cuts and abrasion areas to avoid. 2. Dabbing and lifting motion on the skin only once on one area. 3. Chemical handbag wash.
R				

Outside the immediate crime scene, a clearly marked, safe gathering area should be identified, to regroup the various people and material resources to be used in the field; this should include a parking area for "clean" transportation vehicles. The location of these areas must be upwind of the defined hot scene area.

FIGURE 8.3.5 Heavily equipped "entry team" officer ready to enter the hot zone. *With permission, courtesy Thierry Lezeau, 2010.*

Entering the Hot Crime Scene

With defined plans, an "entry team" of at least two CBRN-educated CSIs will enter the scene to assess it (Figure 8.3.5). One of the CSIs will record the crime scene (photographs, videotape, drawings, scanning, etc.), while the areas of interest will be identified. Environmental samples, such as air, water, or radiological, should also be taken, if needed; air flow may be an important determinant of the scene delimitation and tools as simple as a child's balloon may assist in this. Patterns of residue, stains, chemical stratification, and other patterns or gatherings should be noted and recorded. Be aware that the contaminated conditions may decrease humidity and this may interfere or confound hygroscopic devices or methods, like spot tests, some detectors, carbon adsorption tubes, etc.

An Operative Flowchart

CBRN crime scene management is neither in the unique province of the CSI nor of CBRN scientists or experts; it may have been the ultimate cause but the goal of such management is not purely to focus on the CBRN agents. Global assessment, partnership, and a common understanding of roles will improve the outcomes of the investigation. Figure 8.3.6 aims at synthesizing this approach.

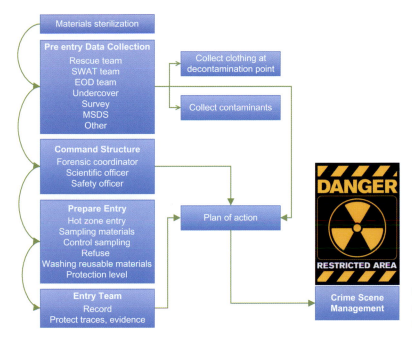

FIGURE 8.3.6 CBRN-contaminated crime scene general flowchart management.

Conclusion

Although it has been stated elsewhere in this book, it is absolutely true in CBRN incidents: *Communication is everything at a crime scene.* People, even professionals, will be scared, information may be scarce or even false, and needed services may be disrupted. At no other time will it be more important for CSIs to be clear on what is asked of them, what they have done, and what is to be completed. Many lives may depend on what happens next at the scene and CSIs must be ready for that responsibility.

References and Bibliography

Brown, P.I., McLellan, T.M., Linnane, D.M., Wilkinson, D.M., Richmond, V.L., Horner, F.E., et al., 2010. Influence of hydration volume and ambient temperature on physiological response while wearing CBRN protective clothing. Ergonomics 53 (12): 1484–1499.

Carus, W.S., 2001. Working Paper. Bioterrorism and Biocrimes. The Illicit Use of Biological Agents Since 1900. Center for Counterproliferation Research. National Defense University, Washington D.C.

Chaliand, G., Blin, A. (Eds.), 2004. Histoire du Terrorisme. Bayard.

Colella, M., Parkinson, A., Evans, T., Lennard, C., Roux, C., 2009. The recovery of latent fingermarks from evidence exposed to ionizing radiation. J. Forensic Sci. 54 (3): 583–590.

Drielak, S.C., 2004. Hot Zone Forensics.

Falkenrath, R.A., Newman, R.D., Thayer, B.A., 1998. America's Achilles' Heel: Nuclear, Biological and Chemical Terrorism and Covert Attack. The MIT Press, Cambridge, MA.

Horita, J., Vass, A.A., 2003. Stable-isotope fingerprints of biological agents as forensic tools. J.Forensic Sci. 48 (1): 1–5.

Marret, J.-L., 2000. Techniques du Terrorisme. Presses universitaires de France.

Muller Vogt, B., Sorensen, J.H., 2002. How Clean Is Safe? Improving the Effectiveness of Decontamination of Structures and People Following Chemical and Biological Incidents. U.S. Department of Energy Chemical and Biological National Security Program.

Rahni, D., 2002. Anthrax insights. J. Forensic Ident 52 (1): 86–97.

Raymond, T., 2006. The future of forensic scientists. Aust. J. Forensic Sci. 38 (1): 3–21.

Reutter, D., Shutzer, S.E., Craft, C.M., Fletcher, J., Fricke, F.L., Holowachuk, S.A., et al., 2010. Planning for exercises of chemical, biological, radiological, and nuclear (CBRN) forensic capabilities. Biosecur Bioterror 8 (4): 343–355.

Socratous, E., Graham, E.A.M., 2008. DNA reviews: DNA identification following CBRN incidents. Forensic Sci. Med. Pathol. 4 (4): 255–258.

Wieviorka, M., 1988. Sociétés et terrorisme. Fayard.

Wilkinson, D.A., Hancock, J., Lecavalier, P., McDiarmid, C., 2005. The recovery of fingerprint evidence from crime scenes contaminated with chemical warfare agents. J. Forensic Ident. 55 (3): 326–361.

Wilkinson, D.A., Sweet, D., Fairley, D., 2007. Recovery of DNA from exhibits contaminated with chemical warfare agents: A preliminary study of the effect of decontamination agents and chemical warfare agents on DNA. J. Can. Soc. Forensic Sci. 40 (1): 15–22.

Wilkinson, D.A., Larocque, S., Astle, C., Vogrinetz, J., 2009. The effects of aerosolized bacteria on fingerprint impression evidence. J. Forensic Ident. 58 (1): 65–79.

Underwater and Underground Crime Scenes[1]

If every crime scene is unique and requires an adaptive, specific, and comprehensive management, the requirements increase enormously for special environments, such as underwater and underground crime scenes, due to their uncommon, if not evidence-hostile, conditions and the related dangers for the investigators (Figure 8.4.1). Preplanning, organization, and specialist teams are mandatory to collect and secure evidence and to be able to analyze them at the scene. Because scenes like these are easily identified in advance and do not generally require immediate emergency response, preparations are relatively easy to do.

Underwater Scenes

Underwater scenes can be of various types and depth: swamp, river (with or without currents), quarry, lake, or even at sea (Figure 8.4.2). For decades,

---

[1] The authors are indebted to Lieutenant-Colonel Jean-François Voillot, former head of the Criminal Intervention National Unit of the Forensic Research Institute of the French Gendarmerie in Rosny sous Bois, France (IRCGN), and to Warrant Officer Denis Gagnier serving at the Forensic Cell of the Gendarmerie District Command of the Pyrénées-Atlantiques, for having contributed excellent content for this chapter.

FIGURE 8.4.1 Intervention in dangerous area to retrieve a dead body. *With permission, courtesy Denis Gagnier, 2009.*

FIGURE 8.4.2 Water-based crime scene in a swamp. *With permission, courtesy Denis Gagnier, 2010.*

before the advent of the classic "scaphander" diving suit and Cousteau and Gagnan's invention of the demand regulator breathing apparatus in 1943 (which allows normal breathing through decompression of 200 bars in a bottle of compressed air to the diving pressure, 2 bars at 10 m depth and 5 bars at 40 m (Teather, 1994)), such crime scenes were impossible to manage due to their location. Tides, droughts, or fishermen brought disparate pieces of evidence to the law enforcement agencies. Dangers still exist for investigators working these crime scenes as cold, current, tide, swell, waves, visibility, and even animals can present hazards, to say nothing of the water itself. Getting into the water can even be difficult because of impediments such as ice, flotsam, or pollutants on the surface (Figure 8.4.3). Just like

FIGURE 8.4.3 Obstacles to accessing a dead body. *With permission, courtesy Denis Gagnier, 2010.*

FIGURE 8.4.4 Protective materials may also be prone to disturb the scene. *With permission, courtesy Denis Gagnier, 2006.*

terrestrial scenes, each water crime scene will require a different approach to minimize the loss of evidence and to maximize information. Different search strategies and recovery operations will also be required because of the setting and access to the scene.

To protect against these unfriendly conditions, divers use materials and equipment such as a half or full waterproof suit, neoprene socks, and gloves to stay warm. This protective clothing can limit the CSI's movement and dexterity. Fins may be needed for movement underwater but whirlpools created by their movement could disturb the crime scene. These are some of the challenges faced by the underwater CSI (Figure 8.4.4).

Locating the Scene

The first, and sometimes greatest, challenge is to locate the area of interest or the evidence to collect. Witness statements, water flow rates at various depths, wind direction, and speed are good starting points to improve the search efficiency. If a body is suspected, cadaver scent dogs might help locate areas where the body was introduced to the water; the decomposition products may also be detected, depending on currents and weather. As a body decomposes, the gas generated by bacterial action fills the body cavity and will cause the remains to float for a period of time (Figure 8.4.3), favoring the action of currents and tides. If the body is punctured by an object or animal activity, the body will, of course, partially or completely submerge (Brooks and Brooks, 1997; Fernández-Jalvo, 2003). Criminals will weight bodies to keep them underwater; depending on the method of weighting, this can be excellent evidence to help source the materials or identify the criminals. Grappling hooks should be used with great care when trying to pull a floating body in, as they can severely damage evidence and create false wounds that can complicate an autopsy. Instead of immediately diving into the water and attempting to retrieve the remains, evidence detected on the surface should be located and marked either by a buoy or a GPS recording (Figure 8.4.5).

For bodies in a relatively shallow body of water where CSIs can walk, waterproof detectors can be used. In deeper water requiring a boat search, side-scan sonar can detect bodies at shallower levels and traditional sonar can profile various depths depending on their frequency: the longer the wavelength, the deeper the search, but also the lower the resolution (Ruffell, 2006).

FIGURE 8.4.5 Buoy marking evidence located from the surface. *With permission, courtesy Denis Gagnier, 2006.*

Working the Scene

Once the surrounding area is searched, the perimeter can be identified and marked; a search grid has to be defined to ensure a full search of the entire perimeter. This may be outlined by buoys on the surface or a physical grid can be placed underwater with precut PVC tubes of known length, filled with sand. Anchors and lines will mark the underwater area to match the surface grid. In case of low visibility, lines can be placed to help the divers move around the scene within each grid. Two divers can then drag a rope over the search area to snag any protruding object.

The best approach is to have CSIs qualified for underwater investigations, to help translate the traditional terrestrial investigation principles to the underwater scene (Figure 8.4.6). Specialized training courses are often available to certify CSIs in underwater crime scene work; previous diving certifications are necessary. If trained CSIs are not available, then the CSI on the surface should assist the divers with the preservation and packaging of evidence.

Besides the divers' equipment, specialized forensic equipment and technology are necessary to lift evidence from its position and properly collect it. Waterproof cameras and video cameras with special lighting have to be used, if the water clarity allows it. Advanced diving robots can also be used to view the crime scene remotely, providing for viewing on the surface. Complementary to these methods, or as a subsidiary to these in case of lack of water clarity, sketching and good notes should be taken as always. Despite the diving clothing and gloves, one-use gloves should still be used underwater when sampling biological evidence to minimize contamination (Dutelle, 2007).

FIGURE 8.4.6 Underwater photographs are taken to record the scene before lifting the evidence (here with a hydroplane). *With permission, courtesy Denis Gagnier, 2010.*

FIGURE 8.4.7 Crime scene examiners protecting the hands, feet, and the head of a decayed immersed body. *With permission, courtesy Denis Gagnier, 2009.*

Global positioning systems (GPSs) can be of some help to locate evidence. Once located, photographed, and sketched, evidence would be transported to the surface and then to the laboratory in proper containers to preserve the consistency of the evidence (Figure 8.4.7). Many items that have been submerged for some time tend to deteriorate rapidly once removed from the water due to oxidation or damage from salt. Water washes over and dilutes evidence, possibly damaging or destroying microtraces, drugs, or biological evidence. Aquatic microorganisms could digest part of the evidence; marine animals can also be damaging, especially to remains. The best preservation method would be to package the evidence in a bucket or a container with the water in which the object was located. This protocol is mandatory for ferrous evidence, such as tools or firearms. Indeed, an immersed weapon could appear to be in good condition in the water (Figure 8.4.8), but will start to rust as soon as it hits the air, inducing permanent changes to its characteristics. To avoid this, wash the weapon with clear water and a plastic brush, rinse it, immerse it in pure alcohol, and dry it with an air gun. When dry, submerge it in oil and maintain it in a dry place; a desiccator or placing the item in a nitrogenous container may also help. Before collecting the weapon, describe the position of the mechanism (hammer, safety mechanism, engaged ammunition, etc.) and determine if fingerprint development should be conducted before any conditioning, if there is any chance to find latent traces (Figure 8.4.9).

FIGURE 8.4.8 Rifle just extracted from water, to be rapidly preserved before transportation. *With permission, courtesy Denis Gagnier, 2009.*

FIGURE 8.4.9 Recording of the position of an immersed rifle before lifting. *With permission, courtesy Denis Gagnier, 2008.*

Photographing the evidence as it is found underwater is crucial for badly damaged evidence as it could unfortunately be the only and last record of such evidence. Evidence showing some deterioration should be immediately treated; electrolysis is one means of doing so, and encasing the item in plastic is preferred for badly damaged evidence. Quickly transporting the evidence to the laboratory will optimize the safe retrieval of the evidence. Evidence with little or no actual damage may be packaged and sent for analysis.

For items too large to carry to the surface, buoyant lift bags can be used to lift large objects, to minimize damage, and reduce danger for the divers both from straining and from any suction effects. A careful controlled inflation of the bags will slowly raise the object to the surface.

Preservation of Materials in Water

Despite its destructive aspects, water tends to preserve certain types of evidence. Water has a lower temperature than air, and acts as a natural light filter, which reduces the speed of bacterial activity. Sediment, such as sand or mud, also protects covered items (Stevens, 2007).

Bodies degrade more slowly in water than in the air and the stages of decomposition are somewhat different. Firstly, wrinkled or "pruned" skin appears at the hands and feet within 20 minutes (Camps et al., 1976). Secondly, a distinct pallor also appears on the skin, particularly at wound edges; nevertheless, postmortem lividity (livor mortis) is still affected by the movement of the body due to tides, animal activity, or other artifacts, such as propeller marks from passing boats. Thirdly, postmortem rigidity (rigor mortis) is similar in or out of the water, although the water's cooler temperature changes the timing of the rigor. Later phases of decomposition are affected by the body's properties, such as weight or wounds, but also by environmental parameters, such as water temperature, depth, fauna, and currents (Davis, 1986, 1992; Cotton et al., 1987; Haglund, 1993; Kahama et al., 1999; Gruspier and Pollanen, 2000).

Divers should notice the nature of the water's bottom (rocky, sandy, muddy, grassy, debris, etc.), the surface of the water, boating activity, temperatures at the bottom and the surface, and the various currents around the body (Figure 8.4.10). The position of the body should be described (face up or down, lying on the bottom or floating), any visible wounds, and the state and nature of clothing. Hands and feet (even if the victim is wearing shoes) should be

FIGURE 8.4.10 Currents can have a strong effect on evidence. *With permission, courtesy Denis Gagnier, 2009.*

protected with plastic bags to protect potential traces (soil, GSR, blood, etc.) that will be secured later.

Water samples should also be taken around the body, at a middle depth, at the surface, and upstream and downstream to collect and compare diatoms. The body should then be placed in a body bag that allows water to drain without losing debris (Figure 8.4.7). The lipids in fingerprint secretions are resistant to water because of their hydrophobic nature. Small-particle reagent (SPR) is the preferred technique to use and can be applied either in the laboratory or immediately after the evidence has been retrieved from the water, regardless of if the substrate is porous or not (Gamboe, 1989). For pieces of evidence to be treated in the laboratory, the substrate should be transported in a bucket of fresh water.

Water dilutes biological fluids if they did not dry on the evidence before being submerged (Rammer and Gerdin, 1976). Dried biological fluids trapped in fabric can be analyzed by biologists to extract enough DNA, such as dried fluids around bite marks (Soltyszewski, 1996; Sweet and Shutler, 1999). The evidence should be allowed to dry at room temperature and packaged in material that allows air to pass, such as craft paper. Bite marks should be immediately swabbed first with a moistened cotton swab, then with a dry one, after being removed from the water.

Case reports indicate that water is not necessarily an obstacle to retrieving fibers or hair (Deadman, 1984a, 1984b; Kupferschmid et al., 1994; Peacock, 1996). Let the item of evidence dry, taking care not to move the item; it can then be tape-lifted as normal.

Documents, surprisingly, can survive being submerged in water. Drying is mandatory before any analysis. Freezing the document appears to be the best technique to preserve it immediately after retrieving it from water. It has been suggested to dry any frozen pages through the help of freeze-drying (Taylor, 1986), allowing paper to recover its flexibility. Of course, water-based inks are very sensitive to water, but others, like ballpoint pen ink, resist the effects of water quite well. To improve the detection of traces, the document should be secured in a clean, unused plastic liner, any excess water should be removed, and then the entire package should be frozen.

Submerged vehicles should be described in detail, including the position of the windows, doors and locks, brake and gearshift levers, flywheel, switch key, airbags, seatbelts, damage, and so on. The location of any of the bodies and objects inside and around the vehicle should be described as they are found; winching the vehicle to the surface will profoundly disturb this crime scene (Figure 8.4.6). It is better to remove bodies from vehicles before removing the vehicles from the water. A slow winching allows water to drain from the vehicle; the CSI should be ready to secure more pieces of evidence that may bob to the surface during winching (Figure 8.4.11).

FIGURE 8.4.11 Slow winching of an immersed car. *With permission, courtesy Denis Gagnier, 2009.*

FIGURE 8.4.12 Underground areas can be difficult to enter when the CSI is properly equipped. *With permission, courtesy Brice Maestracci, 2009.*

Underground Scenes

Perhaps even more so than underwater scenes, underground scenes are difficult to enter and are not convenient for standard forensic investigations. Darkness, fear of heights (acrophobia) or being enclosed (claustrophobia), and the dangers of tight spaces do not ease forensic work (Figure 8.4.12).

FIGURE 8.4.13 Dangers to the CSI increase within confined areas, particularly toxic ones, such as this liquid manure silo. *With permission, courtesy Denis Gagnier, 2006.*

Other dangers include being trapped underground, toxic gases, and falling. Additional protective gear here includes a helmet, gloves, pads, and perhaps even an oxygen breather. The CSI's hands should be free to photograph or sketch the scene while hanging from a rope. Access to the scene may require climbing gear, such as rated climbing cords of 8–11 mm, descenders (devices that utilize mechanical means to grab rope in one direction while allowing free passage in the other), pitons, and other equipment.

Because of the difficulty to gain access to the crime scene, each CSI probably will be able to take only one crime scene kit each. The kits should be compact, practical, and not jeopardize either the movement or the safety of the examiner when wearing one. Checklists are good ideas, as it may be difficult to backtrack to retrieve forgotten items once the CSIs are down at the scene. Likewise, it may not be possible to retrieve all of the available evidence from an underground scene and so it is even more important to clearly select only the most relevant and important evidence to collect and carry back to the surface.

Speleological[2] techniques are also useful for investigations involving enclosed or difficult-to-access areas, such as drains, wells, mines, or any similar confined space (Figure 8.4.13). Underground underwater scenes are some of the most complex and dangerous of these special crime scenes and require superior attention under pressure, control, and self-knowledge from the CSI (Figure 8.4.14). Disasters, like the wreck of the *Costa Concordia* (Figure 8.4.15) off the coast of Tuscany in 2012, may need to have both underwater and climbing skills applied even though they are not technically "underground." Such crime scenes require a long and exhausting approach to the crime scene that necessarily will limit the ability to manage the underwater crime scene.

---

[2] Speleology is the scientific study of caves; spelunking is the recreational pastime of investigating caves.

FIGURE 8.4.14 Complexity increases with underground aquatic crime scenes. *With permission, courtesy Brice Maestracci, 2009.*

FIGURE 8.4.15 Disaster scenes, like the wreck of the *Costa Concordia* in 2012, may require a combination of underwater and climbing skills and equipment. *Photo credit: Roberto Vongher.*

Bringing equipment for both scenes creates logistical issues, not the least of which is getting all of the diving equipment to pass through tight squeezes and reloading the materials afterward to keep going.

Conclusion

Special crime scenes, like those underwater or underground, create particular complexities and hazards for the CSI. Planning, organization, and specialist teams are crucial for success at these difficult scenes. Special equipment is required as well, like scuba diving gear and rock climbing equipment. Scenes like these are easily identified in advance, they rarely necessitate emergency response, and, therefore, time is on the side of the investigators.

Reference and Bibliography

Becker, R.F., 1976. Myths of Underwater Recovery Operations. FBI Law Enforcement Bulletin, Chicago, IL.

Becker, R.F., 1995. The Underwater Crime Scene. Charles C. Thomas, Springfield, IL.

Brooks, S.T., Brooks, R.H., 1997. The taphonomic effects of flood waters on bone. In: Hagliund, W.D., Sord, M.H. (Eds.), Forensic Taphonomy: The Postmortem Fate of Human Remains CRC Press, Boca Raton, FL, pp. 553–558.

Cotton, G., Aufderheide, A., Goldschmidt, V., 1987. Preservation of human tissue immersed for five years in fresh water of known temperature. J. Forensic Sci. 32 (4): 1125–1130.

Davis, J.H., 1986. Bodies found in water: An investigative approach. Am. J. Forensic Med. Pathol. 7 (4): 291–297.

Davis, J.H., 1992. Bodies in water: Solving the puzzle. J. Fla. Med. Assoc. 79 (9): 630–632.

Deadman, H.A., 1984a. Fiber evidence and the Wayne Williams trial: Part I. FBI Law Enforcement Bull. 53 (3): 12–20.

Deadman, H.A, 1984b. Fiber evidence and the Wayne Williams trial: Part II. FBI Law Enforcement Bull. 53 (5): 10–19.

Dutelle, A., 2007. Underwater crime scene response, part 2 of 2: Investigation techniques. Evid. Mag. 5 (5): 24–32.

Fernández-Jalvo, Y., 2003. Experimental effects of water abrasion on bone fragments. J. Taphonomy 1 (3): 147–163.

Gagnier D., 2009. Le Cocrim et la police technique et scientifique en milieux subaquatique et souterrain, diplôme universitaire de coordinateur des opérations de criminalistique, Université René Descartes, Faculté de médecine, Laboratoire d'éthique médicale et de médecine légale, unpublished.

Gamboe, T.E., 1989. Small particle: Developing latent prints on water-soaked firearms and effect on firearms analysis. J. Forensic Sci. 34 (2): 312–320.

Gruspier, K.L., Pollanen, M.S., 2000. Limbs found in water: Investigation using anthropological analysis and the diatom test. Forensic Sci. Int. 112 (1): 1–9.

Haglund, W.D., 1993. Disappearance of soft tissue and the disarticulation of human remains from aqueous environments. J. Forensic Sci. 38 (4): 806–815.

Kahama, T., Almog, J., Levy, J., Shmeltzer, E., Spier, Y., Hiss, J., 1999. Marine taphonomy: Adipocere formation in a series of bodies recovered from a single shipwreck. J. Forensic Sci. 44 (5): 897–901.

Kupferschmid, T.D., Van Dyke, R., Rowe, W.F, 1994. Scanning electron microscope studies of the biodeterioration of human hair buried in soil and immersed in water. In: Llewellyn, G.C., Dashek, W.V., O'Rear, C.E. (Eds.), Biodeterioration Research 4 Plenum Press, New York, pp. 479–492.

Peacock, E.E., 1996. Characterization and simulation of water-degraded archaeological textiles: A review. Int. Biodeterior. Biodegradation 38 (1): 35–47.

Rammer, L., Gerdin, B., 1976. Dilution of blood in fresh water drowning. Postmortem determination of osmolarity and electrolytes in blood, cerebrospinal fluid and vitreous humor. Forensic Sci. 8: 229–234.

Ruffell, A., 2006. Underwater scene investigation using ground penetrating radar (GPR) in the search for a sunken jet-ski, Northern Ireland. Sci. Justice 46 (4): 221–230.

Siver, P.A., Lord, W.D., McCarthy, D.J., 1994. Forensic limnology: The use of freshwater algal community ecology to link suspects to an aquatic crime scene in southern New England. J. Forensic Sci. 39 (3): 847–853.

Soltyszewski, I., Moszczynski, J., Pepinski, W., Jastrzebowska, S., Makulec, W., Zbiec, R., et al., 2007. Fingerprint detection and DNA typing on objects recovered from water. J. Forensic Ident. 57 (5): 681–687.

Stevens, S., 2007. Investigating water deaths: Clearing the muddy waters of drowning investigations. Law Enforcement Technol. 34 (7): 110–119.

Sweet, D., Shutler, G.G., 1999. Analysis of salivary DNA evidence from a bite mark on a body submerged in water. J. Forensic Sci. 44 (5): 1069–1072.

Taylor, L.R., 1986. The restoration and identification of water-soaked documents: A case study. J. Forensic Sci. 31 (3): 1113–1118.

Teather, R.G., 1994. Encyclopedia of Underwater Investigations. Best Publishing Company, Flagstaff, AZ.

Voillot, J.-F., 2001. La scène de crime subaquatique: une étude. Mémoire de criminalistique chimique. Institut de police scientifique et de criminologie, Lausanne, unpublished.

Index

A

Absorene®, 219
Air-scenting dogs, 76
Alternate light sources (ALS), 144, 145f
Amido black, 261
Apocrine glands, 260
Archaeology
    archaeological terms, 319–320
    artifacts, 317–319
    set of concepts, 318–319
    strategy of, 318
Arson as chemical evidence, 213–224
    bloody traces or prints developments relevant to arson scenes, 223t
    fingerprint development protocols relevant to arson scenes, 221–222t
    fire scene examination, 213
    site of ignition, 213
    soot removal process and proposed fingerprint developments, 220t
Artifacts as evidence, 317–319

B

Bank robbery patterns, 22
Barrier filter, 141–144
Biological evidence, 189–191, 209
    bones, 254
    cadaver, 254
    DNA and trace DNA, 240–254, 247t
    exploitable semen, 251
    fast Blue B and MUP tests, 252t
    feces, 253
    hair, 253–254
    physiologically altered bloodstains (PABS), 250
    SAADD mnemonics, 246–250
    saliva, 252–253
    semen, 251–252
    spatter groups for quick interpretation of blood, 249t
    tests giving color reactions, 243, 244–245t
    urine, 253

Bloodstain pattern analysis (BPA)
    case example, 324, 325f
    categories of bloodstains, 328–329
    determining directionality, 327
    3D laser scanning, 339
    droplet size and force, 328
    grouping of bloodstains, 327–328
    information collected, 326–327
    practical aspects of, 324
    reagents used, 324–326
    risks of dealing with potential bloodborne pathogens, 326
    science-based screening tools, 326
    terminology, 323–324
Bloodstains, categories of, 328–329
Bomb-related crime scene, 224–225
Butterfly effect, 14

C

Camcorder®, 150–151
Canine searches, 302–303
Centers for Disease Control and Prevention (CDC), 181
Chain of custody
    complexity of, 111f
    definition, 105
    documentation for, 106–109
    example, 109–111
    forensic DNA analysis and, 105–106
    handwritten, example of a, 107f
    illustration of importance, 105–106
    problems with, 111–112
    report, 107f
Chemical, biological, radiological, and nuclear (CBRN) crime scenes
    collection of evidence, 366–369, 369t
    command structure, 368
    cordoning outside the hot scene area, 369
    CSI at, 364
    entering the hot scene area, 370
    first four things to do in, 365–366
    forensic collection, 366
    hot zone(s) within, 368
    material safety data sheets (MSDS), 367
    operating flowchart, 370

    sterilization procedures for CBRN collection, 367t
Chemical, biological, radiological, and nuclear (CBRN) evidence, 159
Chemical evidence
    arson, 213–224
    drugs, 211–213
    explosion scene, 224–228
    gunshot residue (GSR), 228–233
Chemical evidence enhancement, 208–209
Clue-based method, 5–6
Coaxial episcopy, 148–149
Collection of evidence. see also biological evidence; chemical evidence; impression evidence
    biological evidence, 159
    bones, 299–300
    casting, 167
    chemical, biological, radiological, and nuclear (CBRN) crime scenes, 366–369
    cigarette butts, 163
    coat from a suspect, example, 161–162
    computers, cellphones, and other mass storages, 297–298
    control materials, 158
    diatoms, 301–302
    digital crime scene, system preservation steps, 298
    eggs and larvae, 301
    estimate time since death, 300–301
    explosion scene, 225–227, 226f
    guidelines, 167, 167t, 168t, 169t, 170t, 171t, 172t, 173t, 174t, 175t, 176t
    insect activity, 300–301
    lifting, 166
    maggots and pupae, 301
    materials and containers, 160–162
    microtaping, 164–165
    packaging and sealing of materials, 159
    pipetting, 165
    plastic one-use tweezers, 163
    pollen, 299
    prosthetic devices, 299–300, 300f
    scraping, 167

Collection of evidence (*Continued*)
skeletal material, 299–300
soft tissue samples, 300
storage and preservation of
materials, 159
swabbing, 166
sweeping, 166
tamper evident tape, 160f
tapelifting, 164
techniques to, 162–176
terrorist attack scenes, 358
tooth pulp (dentin), 300
types, 158–159
use of canines for identifying
odors, 302–303
use of paper bindle or
"pharmacist's fold", 163
using tweezers, 162–163
vacuuming, 164
whole substrate collection, 162
The Commonwealth Native Title Act
1993, 68
Computer forensics, 76
Contamination of evidence, 178–179
Counterfeiting, 295–296
Crime scene, 11
access to, 12–13
Brown-Goldman murders, 15–16
chain of custody, 16–17
classification, 23
Clint Eastwood as Dirty Harry, 50
competing priorities, 56–57
complicated, 23–24
contamination issues, 49
defining and controlling
boundaries, 59–60
definition, 23–24
documentation of, 16
fruit of the poisonous tree, 17
glove protection protocols, 49
intelligence work and, 28–29, 28f
interaction of the normal and
criminal environments, 13–14
investigator-in-charge, role of,
51–52
legal authorization to, 12
logistical problems, 50
as a matrix of people and locations,
23, 24f
one person/one location, 23–24
preserving a, 62–63
resources of time, personnel, and
money, 48–49
safety and physical well-being of
officers and other individuals, 56

securing a, 59–61
sensitive dependence on initial
conditions, 13–15, 13f
staged, 25–26
steps to minimize loss of evidence,
49
submitting evidence for analysis,
17–18
team-oriented crime scene
philosophy, 50–51
teams as high performance work
organizations, 50–51
totality of information at a, 14–15
*Crime Scene Investigation: A Guide for
Law Enforcement*, 16
Crime scene investigators (CSIs), 4,
11, 95–96
challenges, 25
detection of traces at places of fire,
218–224
3D scanning, conducting of, 337
experienced, 24
forensic scientist becoming, 44–48
goal of, 13
goals of a crime scene search, 134
mental fatigue, 47–48
optimal excitations and emission
settings, 145–149
potential problems associated with
cumulative stress disorder, 46–47
reconstruction of crime scene, 314
role a evidence officer, 158
role in questioned documents
examination (QDE), 296–297
scene investigation guidelines, 16
training, 44
Crime scene photography, 114–118
calibration of the camera, 333, 333f,
334f
digital, 115
3ds Max®, 334
number of images taken, 117
photographs of the scene, 333
Photomodeler®, 334
problems in, 118
reconstruction based on
photographs, 115. *see also*
reconstruction of crime scene
Rhinoceros3D®, 334
traditional 35 mm camera *vs*
modern digital camera, 116
using 3D laser scanner, 335–343
Crime scene reconstruction analysis,
97–98
Criminal Investigation, 6–7

C-transforms, 318–319
Cuvier, Georges, 5
Cuvier's principle of correlation of
parts, 5

D

Dallas County, forensic services in, 18
Death, estimating time since,
300–301
Death investigation case, 96–97
blood-like stains, 96–97
case of an elderly woman found
dead by her son, 96–97
defense wounds, 96
visual inspection for the presence
of any wounds, 96
Detection, 135. *see also specific
headings*
human remains detection (HRD),
76–77
illumination of the target, 145
optical, 135
physical and chemical tests, 140
staging and, 25
tool at crime scene, 140
of traces, underwater, 381
Diatoms, 301–302
Digital crime scene, 298
identical hash deciphering, 298
Internet Protocol (IP) address, 298
Digital crime scene photography, 115
advantages, 116
megapixel (MP), 116
property of digital images, 116
3D laser scanner, 335–343
accuracy, 335–337
bloodstain pattern analysis, 339
bombing scenes, 342–343
calibrate the measurement at the
scene, 337–338
case examples, 338–343
CSI and, 337
"freezing" the images of the scene,
335
height determination, 340, 341f
middle and longer range scans,
336
object comparison, 340–342, 342f
for photogrammetry, 335
shooting scene reconstructions,
340, 341f
terrorist attack scenes, 343, 344f
train, bus, or ship accidents, 338
DNA typing, 189

Documentation of crime scene, 16, 113–114
Double-gloving, 184
Drucker, Peter, 3–4
Drugs as chemical evidence, 211–213
 commonly encountered drugs of abuse, 212t
 confirmatory testing, 213
 drug flowchart to identify active substances at crime scene, 214f
 presumptive spot test approach, 213, 215–217t

E

Earmark detection, 151
Earprints, 271–272
Eccrine glands, 260
Electromagnetic radiation, 140
 continuum of, 141
 spectrum, 142f
Emergency medical technicians (EMTs), 54, 57–58, 62
Emission filter, 141–144
Eu(fod)$_3$ – Tris(6,6,7,7,8,8-heptafl uoro-2,2-dimethyl-3,5-octanedionato) Europium (III), 270–271
Evidence, 7–8. *see also* recovering evidence; searching for evidence; submission of evidence
 classification and resolution, 32–34
 commonality of relationship, 33
 concept of physical remnants, 7–8
 in courtroom, 18–19
 digital, 76
 grouping of objects (class), 33
 identifying common source, 33, 34
 individualization of, 35
 known and questioned items, 38
 loss of physical, 58
 materials and containers, 160–162
 proxy data, 7–8
 recognizing, 100
 recording, 102–103
 recovering, 100–102
 relationships and context, 36–38, 36f
 residual, 7
 searching for, 100–102
 seizing of, 12–13
 six degrees of separation, 34–35
 in stranger-on-stranger crimes, 36
 study and analysis of, 37f

submitting for analysis, 17–18
techniques to collect, 162–176
transfer of, 29–31
types, 158–159
Exchange Principle, 29
Exigent circumstances doctrince, 12–13
Explosion scene, 224–228
 bomb-related crime scene, 224–225
 collection of evidence, 225–227
 explosives flowchart, 227f
 laboratory analyses, 228
 protection of, 225f
 spot tests approach, 227–231t
Explosive Ordinance Disposal (EOD) officers, 224–225
Explosives, 197–199

F

Federal Emergency Management Agency (FEMA), 352
Ferrotrace®, 233
Fingerprint detection, 151
Fingerprints development sequence
 on crime scenes, 260–271, 263t
 flowchart for, 265f, 267f
 on human skin, 267
 Iodine Protocol, 268t
 on nonporous surfaces, 271
 on porous surfaces, 269–271, 269f
 RTX (carcinogenic) synthesis available for, 268t
 synthesis available for adhesive surfaces, 266t
Firearms evidence, 200–203
Fire scene examination, 213
First aid responders, 56–57
First Amendment of the U. S. Constitution, 83
First officer, duties and importance of, 74
First responder at the scene of crime, 53
 documentation of actions and observations, 63
 dual responsibilities of, 56
 example, 54
 handing over the charge, 64
 initial response/receipt to an incident, 55
 possible threats to life, 56
 releasing the scene, 63
 temptations of, 61

training for, 61–62
The Five-Second Rule, 31
Fluorescence radiation, 141–144
Forensic anthropologists, 75
Forensic entomologist, 77–78
Forensic light source, 144–145
 coaxial episcopy, 148–149
 3D impressions, 154
 dried blood, 153
 dried semen, 153
 fiber, hair, glass, 153–154
 gunshot residue, 154
 photoluminescence of a trace, 149–151
 proposed illumination and wavelengths for various types of marks, 152t
 reflection of the incident beam, 147–148, 148f
 use of, 146t
 UV-A reflection techniques, 150–151
 white light and selective absorption, 146–147
Forensic nurses, 75–76
Forensic odontology, 75
Forensic science
 hunting for indicators or clues, 4–5
Forensic Science Education Programs Accreditation Commission (FEPAC), 43–44
Forensic scientist
 as crime scene investigators (CSIs), 44–48
 and guilty feeling, 46
Forensic teams
 air-scenting dogs, 76
 at car search crime scenes, 78
 communication, importance of, 72
 computer forensics, 76
 duties and importance of first officer, 74
 forensic anthropologists, 75
 forensic entomologist, 77–78
 forensic nurses, 75–76
 forensic odontology, 75
 group becoming teams, 77
 latent print expert, 75
 list of people included, 73–79
 medical examiner, 74
 photographer, 75
 prosecutor at the crime scene, 75
 scene detective, 74
 size and makeup of, 72–73
 trackers, 76

Forgery, 295–296
Fourier transform infrared (FTIR)
    spectroscopic imaging, 150–151
Fourth Amendment to the
    Constitution, 12
Freud, Sigmund, 78
Fruit of the poisonous tree, concept
    of, 17
Fung, Dennis, 15

G

Garbage truck forensics, 92–93
Gardner, Ross, 115–116
Gendarmerie, French, 162–176
General crime scene procedures
    case of a missing person, 90–92
    3 Rs, 90
    scientific crime scene procedures,
        90
Geographic information systems (GIS)
    and crime mapping, 124
    portable gear, 125f
GEOINT, 28
Gloveprints, 280–281
Gunshot residue (GSR), 228–233
    on cloths, 233
    collection kits for, 228
    detection, 232t
    muzzle-to-target distance, 228
    scanning electron microscopy
        (SEM) approach, 228
    shooter's hands detection, 233t
Gunshot residue (GSR) detection,
    208–209

H

Hairs, classification of, 33
Handwriting analysis, 295–296
Hemastix®, 324–326
High performance workplace
    organization, 51
Historical science and forensics, 320
Holmes, Sherlock (fictional detective),
    6–7
Homicide reconstruction, 314–316
Homicide scene, 78
HUMINT, 28

I

Impression evidence, 195–197. see
    also fingerprints development
    sequence on crime scenes

class characteristics, 195
clothing impressions, 196
DAB and superglue stains
    synthesis, 261, 264t
DNA analysis, 261
dust impression, 195–196
earprints, 271–272
of fabric, 195
fingerprints, palmprints, and bare
    footprints, 260–271, 263t
gloveprints, 280–281
human skin secretions, 260
human traces, 260–274
individualizing characteristics, 195
object traces, 274–281
other human prints, 272–273
packaging of, 196
photographing of impressions,
    195–196
powder development, 265f
shoeprints, 195, 275–280
in soil and snow, 196
test impressions (exemplar prints)
    of tires, 197
tireprints, 275–280
toolmarks, 281
wear characteristics, 195
Improvised explosive devices (IEDs),
    358–359
    agencies handling, 360
    detonator or blasting cap, 359
    impact of explosion, 360
    methods for delivering, 359
    personal protection equipment
        during search, 360–361
    post-blast search, 360
    power source, 359
    switch or trigger, 359
Improvised explosives devices (IEDs),
    224
Information, communication of
    communicating to superiors, 86–87
    media, 82–85
    at work, 86
Information profile of crimes, 14–15
Infrared region, 141
Initial responding officer(s)
    ensuring medical attention, 57–58
    procedure of, 55
    safety and physical well-being of
        officers and other individuals, 56
Insect activity, analysis of, 300–301
Intelligence community, 28
Intelligence cycle, 28
Interdependent teams, 73

Investigator-in-charge
    as an ambassador for the forensic
        services, 69
    concept of an, 66
    in the entertainment media, 65–66
    guidance on avoiding hazards or
        obstructions in approaching
        crime scene, 67
    investigating the discovery of
        buried human remains, 68
    leadership at the scene, 69
    location, a place, a set of
        coordinates, 67
    relationship with the PIO, 82–83
    security of crime scene, 68–69
    warrant to search, 67–68
Investigator-in-charge, role of, 51–52
    taking over the charge, 64

J

Japanese Navy Mitsubishi G4M
    bomber airplane, 79

K

Knowledge work, 3–4
Knowledge worker, 3–4
Known evidence, 38

L

Latent print expert, 75
Latent prints evidence, 205
Latex gloves, 184
Leuco-rhodamine 6G, 261
Locard's Exchange Principle, 129, 130,
    136–137
Luminescence, 141–144

M

MASINT, 28
Mass fatality incident
    commands, 352
    defined, 351–352
    disaster scene, 353–354
    effective disaster event response,
        352
    human remains, 354–356
    mode of communication, 352–353
    response to a, 351–352
    suggested workflow for a
        temporary morgue, 355f
Material Safety Data Sheet (MSDS), 183

McVeigh, Timothy, 358
Measuring a crime scene, 119–120
  distance and angle an object, 119–120
  rectangular technique, 119–120
  triangulation technique, 119–120
Media
  communication of information, 82–85
  PIO and, 85
  police and, 84
Medical examiner, 74
Microsoft COFEE, 297–298
Mikrosil®, 219
Morbidity and Mortality Weekly Report (MMWR) Series, 181
Morelli, Giovanni, 5–7
  metodo sperimentale, 6
  observation and method, 5–6
Multi-metal deposition (MMD), 271
Mundorff, Dr. Amy, 100

N

National Institute for Occupational Safety and Health (NIOSH), 181
Native American Graves Protection and Repatriation Act, 68
Necrophagous insects, 300–301
Neoprene gloves, 184
Ninhydrin, 261, 270
Nitrile gloves, 184
Nonforensic personnel
  communicating to superiors, 86–87
  media, 82–85
  public as reporters, 85–86
N-transforms, 318–319

O

Occupational Safety and Health Administration (OSHA), 181, 182–183
Odors, identifying, 302–303
Oil red O (ORO), 271
Operational intelligence, 27
OSINT, 28

P

Palynology, 299
Pathogens encountered at crime scenes, 180–181
Personal protection equipment, 184–185

during bloodstain pattern analysis (BPA), 326
double-gloving, 184
eye protection, 184
face shields, 184
foot protection, 184
hand protection, 184
IEDs explosion search, 360–361
respiratory protection, 184–185
Photogrammetry, 332–335
Photographer, 75
Photography, crime scene. see crime scene photography
Photoluminescence of a trace, 149–151
Physical match examinations, 199–200
Poe, Edgar Allen, 6–7
Polyvinyl chloride (PVC), 184
Polyvinyl chloride (PVC), 184
Post-traumatic stress, 46–47
Preliminary search, 97–99
  case example of missing middle-aged woman, 98–99
  obvious physical evidence, 97–98
  signs of drinking alcohol, 99
  signs of struggle, 99
  transient evidences, 99
Preserving a crime scene, 62–63
Project management in laboratory, 45
Prosecutor at the crime scene, 75
Prosthetic devices, 299–300, 300f
Psychological debriefing (PD), 46–47
Public information officer (PIO), 82–83, 85

Q

Questioned documents, 295–297
  counterfeiting, 295–296
  crime scene investigators (CSIs), role of, 297
  examination (QDE), 295–296
  forgery, 295–296
  handwriting analysis, 295–296, 297
  preferred means of storage and preservation, 297
  signature comparison, 295–296
Questioned evidence, 38

R

Recognizing evidence, 100
Reconstruction of crime scene
  challenges, 313–314

classification of, 314
computer-aided, 316f
CSI, role of, 314
homicide, 314–316
shooting scenes, 314, 315f, 316f
Recording evidence, 102–103
Recovering evidence, 100–102
  distinctions between specimens collected, comparisons, and controls to be collected, 131t
  goals of a crime scene search, 134
  traces, marks, prints, signs, clues and exhibits, 130–133
  useful evidence, 133–134
REDOX stock solutions, 220
Red region of visible light, 141
Rouse, Irving, 318
RTX (carcinogenic) synthesis, 268t, 270
Rule of law, 12–13
RUVIS®, 150–151

S

Sachtleben, Don, 60–61
Safety at scene, 180–185
  chemical, 183–185
  ingestion of a corrosive material, 182
  inhalants, 182
  injection of contaminants, 182
  pathogens encountered at crime scenes, 180–181
  personal protection equipment, 184–185
  preserving the evidence at the scene, 180
  skin contact as route of contaminant entry, 182
  sources and forms of dangerous materials, 182
  transporting hazardous materials, 185
  Universal Precautions, 182–183
  web-based, 181
Scene detective, 74
Schiffer, Michael, 318–319
Scientific crime scene procedures, 90
Scraping of biological materials, 190
Screening of crime scene, 145–149
  specific, 151–154
Searching for evidence, 100–102, 134–138
  controlling contamination, 137
  grid or checkerboard method, 101

Searching for evidence (*Continued*)
  nondestructive means of, 135
  optimizing, 136–137
  practical, 135–136
  trail search, 102
Search warrants, 12
Sebaceous glands, 260
Securing a crime scene, 59–61
  principle, policy, and procedure,
    60–61
Selective absorption, 146–147
Serial numbers, restoring, 233–235
  nitric acid test, 234t
  restoration chemicals to swab, 235t
Shoeprints, 275–280
  on paper, 277
  possible developments of, 2D
    support, 276–277t
SIGINT, 28
Single metal deposition (SMD), 271
Sketching a crime scene, 120–124,
  122f
  example of a homicide, 121–124
  rough sketch at the crime scene,
    121
  scale diagrams, 120–124
  three-dimensional diagrams,
    121–124
Specialized knowledge, 4
  in the context of forensic
    professionals, 4
Stelfox, Peter, 14–15
Stereophotogrammetry, 332
Strategic intelligence, 27
Styrofoam mailing container,
  190–191
Submission of evidence
  biological evidence, 189–191
  explosives, 197–199
  firearms evidence, 200–203
  general, 188–189
  impression evidence, 195–197
  latent prints evidence, 205
  physical match examinations,
    199–200
  toolmark evidence, 203–204
  trace evidence, 191–195

T

Tactical intelligence, 27
Taphonomy, 318
Teams, kinds of, 72–73
Teamwork and crime scene
  investigation, 66
Terrorist attack scenes, 349
  3D laser scanning, 344f
  domestic attacks from separatist
    groups, 358
  domestic terrorists, 358
  external terrorists, 357
  groups involved, 357, 358
  methods for delivering weapon,
    359
  observations and collection of
    evidence, 358
  types of weapons used, 358
Threats to evidence
  contamination, 178–179
  damage, 177–178
  decomposition, 179
  deterioration, 178
  infestation, 179
  losing a piece of evidence, 179–180
  tampering, 180
Three-dimensional casting, 278–279
  general protocol for, 280
Tireprints, 275–280
Title 49 of the U.S. Code of Federal
  Regulations, 185
Toolmark evidence, 203–204
Toolmarks, 281
Trace evidence, 191–195
  fragments of cloth and fibers,
    192–193
  fragments of protective coatings,
    193–195
  glass, 191–192
  hairs, 191
  human, 260–274
Traces as evidence, 130–133
Trackers, 76
Transfer process of evidence, 29–31
  direct, 29–30
  The Five-Second Rule, 31

human traces, 260
indirect, 29–30
planned collection order, 31
second part of, 31
Transporting hazardous materials,
  185
TV crime scene investigation shows,
  114

U

Ultraviolet-visible region, 141
Underground scenes, 382–384
Underwater scenes, 373–375
  locating the scene, 376
  photographing the evidence, 379
  preservation of materials in water,
    380–381
  protective clothing of CSI, 375, 377
  "scaphander" diving suit, 373–375
  working the scene, 377–380
Universal Precautions, 182–183
U.S. National Transportation Safety
  Board (NTSB), 66
UV-A reflection techniques, 150–151

V

Vacuum metal deposition (VMD), 271
Videotaping of crime scene, 118–119
  audio function of video camera,
    119
  camera movement, 118–119
  videographer's assessment of
    scene, 118
Volatile data, 76

W

Warrant, 12
Water Resources Department Act, 68
Weapons of mass destruction (WMD),
  363–364

Z

Zadig ou la Destinee, 4–5